The 55th North Carolina
in the Civil War

Also edited by Jeffrey M. Girvan

"Deliver Us from This Cruel War":
The Civil War Letters of Lieutenant Joseph J. Hoyle,
55th North Carolina Infantry (McFarland, 2010)

The 55th North Carolina in the Civil War

A History and Roster

Jeffrey M. Girvan

McFarland & Company, Inc., Publishers
Jefferson, North Carolina, and London

The present work is a reprint of the illustrated case bound edition of The 55th North Carolina in the Civil War: A History and Roster, *first published in 2006 by McFarland.*

LIBRARY OF CONGRESS CATALOGUING-IN-PUBLICATION DATA

Girvan, Jeffrey M., 1971–
The 55th North Carolina in the Civil War :
a history and roster / Jeffrey M. Girvan.
p.   cm.
Includes bibliographical references and index.

ISBN 978-0-7864-7503-2
softcover : acid free paper ∞

1. Confederate States of America. Army. North Carolina Infantry Regiment, 55th.
2. North Carolina — History — Civil War, 1861–1865 — Regimental histories.
3. United States — History — Civil War, 1861–1865 — Regimental histories.
4. North Carolina — History — Civil War, 1861–1865 — Registers.
5. United States — History — Civil War, 1861–1865 — Registers.
6. North Carolina — Genealogy.
7. Soldiers — North Carolina — Registers.
I. Title: Fifty-fifth North Carolina in the Civil War.   II. Title.
E524.555th.G56   2013   973.7'456 — dc22   2006001520

BRITISH LIBRARY CATALOGUING DATA ARE AVAILABLE

© 2006 Jeffrey M. Girvan. All rights reserved

No part of this book may be reproduced or transmitted in any form or by any means, electronic or mechanical, including photocopying or recording, or by any information storage and retrieval system, without permission in writing from the publisher.

On the cover: The 55th North Carolina battle flag (North Carolina Division of Archives and History); background: Battle of Gettysburg map (Library of Congress)

Manufactured in the United States of America

*McFarland & Company, Inc., Publishers
Box 611, Jefferson, North Carolina 28640
www.mcfarlandpub.com*

Table of Contents

Acknowledgments vi
Preface vii
Introduction 1

1. May–October 1862: Activities in North Carolina 5
2. October 1862–April 1863: For the Honor of the Regiment 17
3. June–July 1863: Forgotten Courage — the Regiment at Gettysburg 39
4. August 1863–March 1864: Politics, Winter, and God 76
5. April–June 1864: Preparing for the Death Angel 91
6. July 1864–April 1865: Fading into Legend 120

Epilogue 142
Appendix A. The 10 Companies of the Regiment 145
Appendix B. Regimental Roster 146
Appendix C. Officers and Enlisted Men Who Died from Disease While Serving with the Regiment 160
Appendix D. Officers and Enlisted Men Who were Killed in Action or Reported Missing in Action While Serving with the Regiment 164
Chapter Notes 169
Bibliography 183
Index 189

Acknowledgments

Historical studies are collaborative efforts. Historians formulate their own theses and know their subject, but locating and researching valuable sources, and editing manuscripts requires assistance from many people. I owe thanks to several individuals who gave me valuable advice and pointed me in the right direction. I would like to thank the archivists and Weymouth T. Jordan, Jr., and his colleagues who are currently working on the North Carolina Civil War Roster Project for the North Carolina Department of Archives and History in Raleigh, North Carolina, and the fine librarians and student assistants who work in the manuscript departments at the libraries of Duke University in Durham, North Carolina, East Carolina University in Greenville, North Carolina, Meredith College in Raleigh, North Carolina, and the University of North Carolina in Chapel Hill, North Carolina. Also, thanks go to the curators and research assistants at the Museum of the Confederacy in Richmond Virginia, and the historians at the Fredericksburg and Spotsylvania National Military Park in Fredericksburg, Virginia, the Gettysburg National Military Park, in Gettysburg, Pennsylvania, the Petersburg National Battlefield in Petersburg, Virginia, and at the Richmond National Battlefield in Richmond, Virginia.

I also would like to thank those individuals who offered me advice on editing my manuscript. Several professors at East Carolina University in Greenville, North Carolina, critiqued the manuscript including David E. Long, Michael A. Palmer, John A. Tilley, and Jack Karns. My brother Greg Girvan assisted me by proofreading several drafts of the manuscript and by making style and grammatical changes.

I spent many hours away from my wife Jodi and sons Jared and Joshua while researching and writing this book. Fortunately my wife is very understanding and gave me her full support. For this, and for all of my family who have supported me, I am deeply grateful.

Jeff Girvan, *March 2006*

Preface

The 55th Regiment North Carolina Troops currently remains a little-known fighting unit of the Army of Northern Virginia. The goal of this book is to illustrate how much this regiment impacted the war and to demonstrate why the soldiers involved deserve more attention from Civil War historians.

When the Old North State declared "First at Bethel, Farthest at Gettysburg and Chickamauga, Last at Appomattox"—a phrase designed to describe North Carolina's role in the Civil War—it referred in part to the 55th. "Farthest at Gettysburg" alluded to the 55th North Carolina's role in the July 3rd attack known as Pickett's charge. The intriguing fact is that the 55th is reputed to have penetrated Union ranks more deeply than any other at Gettysburg. Yet, even owning this distinction, little has been written about the unit's fighting at Gettysburg or at the many other battles it engaged in.

Because the regiment was a footnote in a larger story, most sources have overlooked its role in the Civil War. Fortunately, numerous members of the 55th North Carolina wrote memoirs and letters to loved ones, recounting in great detail the regiment's formation, camp life, battle history, and surrender. The manuscript departments at Duke and North Carolina universities have preserved several collections of letters written by members of the 55th North Carolina. Expressed in these letters are the soldiers' political views, religious beliefs, personal feelings on patriotism, sentiments toward fellow soldiers and officers, and how they were affected by combat.

The 55th North Carolina in the Civil War: A History and Roster records in chronological order, the history of the regiment from its formation in the spring of 1862, tracks the unit through its combat under the Army of Northern Virginia, and culminates with its dissolution in April 1865. Drawing on letters, memoirs, diaries, and recollections of the men who fought with the 55th, the book tells more than just a battlefield history of a Confederate regiment. These individual perspectives provide an insightful glimpse into the everyday life of the common soldier, meticulously conveying the influence of religion and politics, as well as the effects of disease and combat. Among the many interesting events contained in the book are a duel between two officers of the 55th and two officers of an Alabama regiment, and an analysis of the little-known Suffolk campaign.

This history of the 55th North Carolina is not the first to be published. The unit's historian, Charles M. Cooke, wrote a short detailed account in 1901 for Walter Clark's five-volume *Histories of the Several Regiments and Battalions From North Carolina in the Great War 1861–1865*, which was published by Nash Brothers in 1905. Although Cooke's chronicling of the events clearly amplifies the positive contributions of the regiment and endures as a great narrative written by someone who experienced the war firsthand, the intention of this book is to offer a more definitive account. Cooke, like most unit historians writing about their own regiments or companies, used the opportunity to honor his comrades and the regiment, and as a result omitted much. For instance, Cooke makes no mention of Private James T. Jennings of Company H, 56th Regiment Pennsylvania Volunteers, and his capture of the 55th North Carolina's battle flag on August 19, 1864, for which the young Federal soldier won the Congressional Medal of Honor. Also, according to Cooke, all of the men who served with the 55th were honorable and courageous individuals; however, he fails to cite desertions and neglects to write about those who chose to run from battle instead of into it. These oversights are commonly found in journals written by war unit historians. The point here is not to criticize Cooke's 25-page history of the 55th; in fact, Cooke's credible rendering of other aspects of the war proved very useful in establishing a timeline of events and afforded an opportunity to see how a member of the regiment remembered the unit's war experiences.

The historians working for the North Carolina Department of Archives and History have done a magnificent job of collecting information on the state's regiments in their Civil War Roster Project, which is one of the best compilations of primary material and unit histories in the United States. These historians have gathered an abundance of materials from enlistment papers to pension records, which they make readily available for study. Their work presents ample information on the number of men who served with the 55th North Carolina throughout the war, and biographical information on most of those who fought with the regiment. The state archives and library also contain a considerable amount of materials pertaining to the Civil War that grant additional understanding of the men who served with the 55th North Carolina.

For anyone interested in studying North Carolina's Civil War regiments, the best place to start is Louis H. Manarin and Weymouth T. Jordan Jr.'s informative multi-volume series *North Carolina Troops, A Roster*, published by North Carolina's Division of Archives and History. This revealing anthology of soldier biographies and regimental histories currently has 16 volumes and, once completed, will include every fighting unit from North Carolina that served during the Civil War, including Home Guard and Junior Reserve battalions. These volumes were published using the research completed by the Civil War Roster Project and offer solid overviews of regimental histories. Their work provided me with a better understanding of the organization and structure of the 55th North Carolina than Cooke's version, and the accompanying roster information was invaluable.

The 55th North Carolina joined General Lee's army after the celebrated victories at Second Manassas and Chancellorsville, and though it didn't clash in these earlier conflicts, it marched north with the Army of Northern Virginia during the fateful summer of 1863 and participated in many major battles throughout the end of the war. By the time the Confederacy surrendered at Appomattox, this once superlative fighting force had been reduced to nothing more than a skeleton of its former greatness. A comprehensive study of this regiment presents a microcosm of the Army of Northern Virginia in the twilight of its existence.

Introduction

On May 20, 1861, a body of delegates representing all of North Carolina's counties voted unanimously to secede from the Union. After South Carolina militia had fired on Fort Sumter, President Abraham Lincoln had called for 75,000 volunteers to be raised by the states to suppress the insurrection. Lincoln summoned North Carolina Governor John W. Ellis to provide two regiments of militia for immediate service. This call for men and several additional factors ended any doubts the majority of citizens in the Old North State had about seceding. As one citizen remarked, "North Carolina cannot remain much longer stationary; she must write her destiny either under the flag of Mr. Lincoln and aid to coerce the south or unite with the south to resist and defend their rights."[1]

On April 17, before the citizens had a chance to act, Governor Ellis issued a call for 30,000 troops to defend North Carolina against the United States. Before the legislature had established policies for organizing and financing North Carolina regiments, many eager recruits were signing up all across the state. On June 10 a small Confederate force defeated a much larger Federal contingent at Big Bethel, Virginia. Among the Rebel troops that fought there was the first North Carolina Volunteers. The war had begun and North Carolina stood solidly with the South.[2]

Once in the Confederacy, North Carolina made important contributions to the South's quest for independence. Approximately one-fifth of all the provisions and supplies used by all Rebel armies came from the Old North State. An estimated 125,000 men from North Carolina eventually served in Confederate regiments and state militia units. Though the total number of soldiers who served in the Confederate military is unknown, at least one-eighth of all the soldiers who fought for the South were from the Old North State. Only 19,000 of these fighting men were draftees. Over 23,000 North Carolinians deserted during the war, more than from any other state in the Confederacy. By the end of the war approximately 40,275 North Carolina soldiers had been killed in battle or had died from disease while serving in the army. One-fourth of all Confederate soldiers killed on the battlefield were from North Carolina.[3]

With the enthusiasm for the war at its peak in 1861, state officials had little difficulty filling the ranks of the 10 regiments of troops. Those who had enlisted before the secession convention, held in May 1861, had only agreed to fight for 12 months. However, after May all new recruits were enlisted for three years' service or the duration of the war, whichever came first. And instead of having the designation "volunteers" these new units would be known simply as "State Troops." The first 10 volunteer regiments were eventually required to change their numerical designation by adding a factor of "10" to their original number. Thus the first Volunteers became the 11th North Carolina State Troops Regiment. By the end of the war North Carolina organized 72 regiments, with an additional eight regiments of reserves and 4,000 home guard troops assigned to protect important and vulnerable areas of the state.[4]

One of those 72 fighting regiments was the 55th North Carolina. By the spring of 1862 Confederate officials in Richmond and state officials in Raleigh had realized their mistake in assuming that the war would be short and cost few lives. Countering Federal movements across the borders of the Confederacy required additional troops from every Southern state. In March the process of organizing local companies was undertaken again, soon to be aided by the enactment of the Confederate Conscription Act of 1862.[5]

The 55th North Carolina was probably one of the least homogeneous regiments from that state. The ranks of the unit were filled by men from every region in the state and represented over 20 counties. This regiment was a microcosm of the state. These counties varied in political ideology, social institutions, total population, slave count, and economic stability. The majority of counties represented in the regiment contained less than 4,500 slaves, but the unit had a company of men from Granville which according to the 1860 Federal Census had more slaves than any other county in North Carolina. Though several counties represented by the regiment were among the state's top cotton producers, a number of the unit's soldiers came from tobacco growing areas. In addition to differences in economic and social systems, the numbers of citizens living in these various counties varied in their support for secession.[6]

Most of the soldiers who fought with the 55th owned no slaves and worked as yeoman farmers or farm laborers. Although farmers constituted the majority of the regiment, there were also blacksmiths, teachers, merchants, lawyers, doctors, and mechanics. It is reasonable to assume, on the basis of the soldiers' letters and the 1860 Federal Census information, that most of the men who fought for the 55th were not strongly motivated by questions regarding slavery. However, they still felt motivated to resist when "outsiders" invaded their soil, and they were not about to let Yankees dictate how they should live their lives.[7]

The majority of the soldiers did not rush to the Confederate banner in 1861. When word of the conscription law reached North Carolina in April 1862, many men who had stayed home in 1861 felt obligated to join the fight. In addition to those who believed it was their responsibility to assist the South, many probably enlisted simply because they understood that it would only be a matter of time before they would be drafted. They wanted to at least join a company of their own choosing. Several of these reluctant warriors and conscripts supported the Confederate cause. In his work *For Cause and Comrades: Why Men Fought in the Civil War,* James M. McPherson asserts that only about 46 percent of all North Carolina soldiers avowed to patriotic convictions. This conclusion suggests that the average soldier from North Carolina did not fully support the causes giving rise to the war. In personal letters and messages sent to local newspapers by men fighting with the 55th, patriotic ideas were often expressed. Some of the remaining written accounts even condemned fellow soldiers for not being likewise devoted to the struggle. McPherson's claim may be accurate, but it should be noted that the majority of letters, articles, and papers left by the members of the 55th indicate a devotion to the Confederacy.[8]

The men who served in the 55th North Carolina understood their duty and strove to act honorably and courageously. Throughout the war individual soldiers became exhausted, fell sick, or were wounded in battle. But the 55th had a relatively small number of soldiers who deserted or went AWOL. An example of this behavior was expressed in a letter written by Private George W. Pearsall of Company G to his wife late in the war. The young private stated, "I have had the dierreor for 4 or 5 days very bad but have not stoped."[9]

The experiences shared by those who fought with the 55th were not significantly different from those of other regiments from North Carolina. However, the unit is unique in several aspects. Most of the officers and common soldiers who enlisted in the 55th entered the war late and had no prior military experience. Also, a number of these troops were drafted and would most likely never have enlisted. The regiment was not officially organized until May 1862, well after First Bull Run and on the eve of the Seven Days' Battles. The 55th did not march north with Lee's army in September 1862. It did not repulse Major General Ambrose Burnside's attack at Fredericksburg in December of that same year. The regiment was not present for what many historians have asserted was Lee's greatest victory at Chancellorsville. In fact, the 55th did not even join the Army of Northern Virginia until the end of May 1863. But starting with the Gettysburg campaign the unit experienced some of the war's most horrific fighting, and on several occasions would be in the very heart of the conflict's most dreadful carnage.

After the first year of the war only four Confederate brigades contained regiments that were not exclusively from one state.[10] Among these distinct units was the 55th North Carolina. In April 1862, before being placed into the Army of Northern Virginia, the 55th was temporarily assigned to Brigadier General Joseph R. Davis's Mississippi brigade. The regiment remained in Davis's command until January 1865 when it was placed in Brigadier General John Cooke's North Carolina brigade. Being placed with soldiers from Mississippi did not hinder the regiment's fighting spirit, and it went on to prove itself time and time again in some of the bloodiest battles of the Civil War starting at Gettysburg.

The 55th North Carolina was among those Confederate regiments first on the field at Gettysburg on July 1, 1863, and participated in Pickett's charge on the last day of the battle. Among those troops of Brigadier General James Johnston Pettigrew's command were more than 100 members of the 55th North Carolina. Even though three men from the regiment are thought to have made it farther than any other Confederate soldier, the role of the 55th and all of Joe Davis's brigade in the famous charge, and in the entire battle of Gettysburg, has been largely ignored or downplayed by historians.

In the horror that accompanied the battle of the Wilderness, the men in the 55th North Carolina once again found themselves in the midst of the some of the worst and bloodiest fighting of the war. The regiment, with the rest of Davis's brigade, stood firm for hours against repeated Federal attacks. Without support, and against a foe practically five times their number, Davis's men held out until darkness finally put an end to the day's carnage. Yet as with the battle of Gettysburg, very little is said about the regiment's actions on May 5, 1864.

Although the regiment was comprised of men who had not rushed to the call to arms when the war began, these fighting soldiers still gave all they had in some of the most dreadful days of the war. Historians have valued the units that fought hard every day from Bull

Run to Appomattox. However, the 1862 regiments made important contributions to the war effort and sacrificed just as much as those individuals who answered the call in 1861.

This history of the 55th North Carolina is a soldier's story. Whenever possible those who experienced the history for themselves are allowed to assert and describe their views. Their words, just as they were written, will appear throughout the text. Misspellings and mistakes in syntax and grammar appear just as they were written some 135 years ago. Their unique perspective enhances our understanding of what it was like to fight for the Confederate States of America.

1

May–October 1862: Activities in North Carolina

"Our boys are anxious to meet them in open field at almost any odds"

During the latter half of March through May 1862 able-bodied men throughout North Carolina began organizing companies of troops to assist the Confederate armies, which had realized that additional regiments would be needed to stop Federal forces from invading and occupying the young nation's territory. The company was the smallest structured unit in the Civil War armies and often consisted of men from the same community. The average infantry company contained anywhere from 64 to 83 privates and about 19 officers. The company was frequently divided into platoons, squads, patrols, or detachments. According to historian David J. Eicher, companies were an important part of the military structure because "they reflected the localism that dominated mid-nineteenth-century America."[1]

Cleveland County native Peter Mull and Howell G. Whitehead of Pitt County were two of the numerous men gathering recruits and forming companies throughout North Carolina. By the middle of May these units had arrived at Raleigh and were organizing into regiments. Mull's Cleveland County troops and Whitehead's Pitt County men joined eight other companies and created the 55th Regiment North Carolina Troops on or about May 16, 1862, at Camp Mangum, which was located several miles west of the state capital. In theory the regiment was to contain about 1,000 able-bodied men; however, keeping the ranks full proved a problem for both armies. The 10 companies that joined together to form the regiment consisted of men from every region in the state, but were predominately from the Piedmont.[2]

The average soldier who fought with the 55th North Carolina was in his early to mid-twenties, but several individuals as young as 16 joined the ranks in April and May and men as old as 50 fought with the unit throughout the war. The majority of men who enlisted with the 55th were farmers or farm laborers and were not members of the planter class. A number of those recruited to fight with the regiment, probably conscripted, had enough money to send substitutes in their place. Approximately 64 substitutes fought with the 55th, including Private Bryant Bass of Company A, who remained with the unit until it surrendered with the rest of Lee's Army of Northern Virginia at Appomattox. During the

Private John P. Elixson, Company K. Private Elixson was a farmer from Granville County when he enlisted on May 6, 1862, at the age of 20. Private Elixson does not seem to have handled the rigors of soldier life well, spending at least five or more months in Confederate hospitals with various illnesses. (Courtesy of the North Carolina Division of Archives and History, Raleigh, North Carolina.)

Colonel John Kerr Connally. A former cadet at the United States Naval Academy and a strict disciplinarian, Connally would serve as the regiment's colonel until being severely wounded at Gettysburg on July 1, 1863. Although he never returned to the 55th, Connally commanded a brigade of junior and senior reserves during the Wilmington campaign 1864–65. (Courtesy of the North Carolina Division of Archives and History, Raleigh, North Carolina.)

first few months of its existence the regiment had approximately 850 soldiers in its ranks, including officers and enlisted men, and would never have that many troops present and accounted for again.[3]

During May, while recruits were still being added to company rosters, the regiment began drilling and learning how to be part of a military unit. Lieutenant Sidney Smith Abernethy directed most of the 55th's training while it was at Camp Mangum. Abernethy had been an officer with the 30th North Carolina Regiment, but had resigned his commission to begin his duties as the 55th North Carolina's drillmaster. The newly formed regiment drilled four hours a day and participated in dress parades. The men also spent time performing guard duty.[4]

The field officers of the 55th included several men who had previously served with other regiments and had briefly seen action in 1861. John Kerr Connally, from Yadkin County, became colonel of the regiment in May. Connally had attended the United States Naval Academy before joining the 11th North Carolina Volunteers, which became the 21st North Carolina State Troops Regiment, at the age of 22. The 21st saw limited action at the

Battle of Bull Run. During his tenure with the 21st Connally had served as the captain of Company B, but regimental politics and infighting between the unit's officers had compelled him to resign. Connally wanted to command his own regiment, and after resigning went to Raleigh to offer his services to one of the newly forming regiments. After being appointed colonel of the 55th, Connally immediately brought discipline to the raw recruits and hoped to make his new command the best regiment in all of the Confederate armies.[5]

Alfred Horiatio Belo, who had also served as a captain with the 21st North Carolina, joined the 55th as assistant quartermaster on November 1, 1862. Belo, a resident of Forsyth County, had resigned his commission as captain of Company D, 21st North Carolina, primarily for the same reasons Connally had. Belo hoped to gain command of one of the new North Carolina regiments that began forming in March and April 1862. In May 1862 Belo had been assigned by North Carolina Governor Henry T. Clark to assist with the drilling and training of conscripts and recently enlisted soldiers. After spending several months in Raleigh supervising the training of new recruits Belo joined Brigadier General Robert F. Hoke's staff, which at that time was serving with Lieutenant General Thomas "Stonewall" Jackson's command in the Shenandoah Valley. After a brief stay with Hoke's command Belo was appointed assistant quartermaster with the 55th North Carolina. Shortly after joining the regiment Belo had been appointed major, and would continue moving up the chain of command until wounds received at Cold Harbor forced him to resign.[6]

Lieutenant Colonel Alfred H. Belo. The second commander of the regiment, Belo was wounded at Gettysburg but returned to service in January 1864. He was wounded again at Cold Harbor on June 3, 1864, and would never return to command. (Courtesy of the North Carolina Division of Archives and History, Raleigh, North Carolina.)

Belo's promotion to the rank of major occurred after the death of James S. Whitehead. Whitehead, a lawyer from Pitt County, had previously served as a private with the 10th North Carolina State Troops Regiment. Whitehead had seen action near Hatteras Inlet in 1861, and had been taken prisoner when the Federals captured forts Clark and Hatteras, which were located along the North Carolina coast protecting Hatteras Inlet. After a brief period of captivity Whitehead became the captain of Company E, 55th North Carolina. After briefly serving with Company E. Whitehead received a promotion to the rank of major on May 19, 1862. The lawyer turned soldier died in August 1862 of disease and never had the opportunity to prove his worth in combat with the 55th North Carolina.[7]

Abner S. Calloway, who had assisted in the organization of Company B, was elected lieutenant colonel on May 19, 1862. However, Calloway proved to be incompetent and in January 1863 Colonel Connally asked him to resign.

Maurice T. Smith, captain of Company K, replaced Calloway on March 10, 1863. Smith, a Granville County native and one of the few members of the regiment that belonged to the planter class, proved to be a courageous and resourceful officer.[8]

With the regiment's command structure established, the men began to form a cohesive bond. During their stay at Camp Mangum the North Carolinians' spirits were high. Food was plentiful and the soldiers spent their time singing and conversing. The unit's men were content to continue their stay at the camp and spent little time discussing the war. Their training caused most of the troops to feel confident about how they would perform on the battlefield.[9]

Around the end of May the soldiers of the 55th received shirts, shoes, and other clothing items, and at the beginning of June the men obtained canteens and knapsacks. Although the regiment had been organized for almost a full month by June 11, the men still had not been issued arms. Though the troops did not have their muskets they continued to drill, participate in dress parades and perform guard duty.[10]

Private Joseph J. Hoyle of Company F wrote his wife on May 23, 1862, that the men were eating well, being provided flour, cornmeal, bread, bacon, beef, peas, and rice. In spite of what appeared to be a good diet, disease and sickness ravaged the regiment during the first months of its existence. Hoyle informed the Raleigh news-paper *Spirit of the Age* that several deaths had occurred. Measles and fever forced many of the men of the 55th into the hospital in Raleigh, and also cost several soldiers their lives.[11] Rural farmers young and old were very prone to contract diseases early in their service as soldiers because their bodies' immune systems were not prepared to ward off diseases that were common in the cities. Also, the physical examinations required by the Confederate government for all new recruits were not administered until the fall of 1862, by which time practically all of the eligible white males of the South were already serving in the army. Thus men unfit to serve often contracted illnesses upon their first exposure, and being in such close contact with other men caused sickness to spread like an epidemic. But even these examinations, when finally administered, proved insufficient in stopping unfit men from joining the army.[12]

Private Alexander Adcock, Company K. Private Adcock was a farmer before he enlisted in the Confederate Army on March 1, 1862, at the age of 23. Like many young men not accustomed to the diseases that were found in camp he succumbed to illness in June 1862 and died at Goldsboro, North Carolina, in August of that year. (Courtesy of the North Carolina Division of Archives and History, Raleigh, North Carolina.)

Although the Confederate government did not implement a policy to weed out those individuals unfit for military training until the fall of 1862, several members of the 55th were discharged for being "physically unfit for military service." One of these soldiers was John D. Ruffin of Company A. Ruffin was discharged at Camp Campbell, near Kinston, North Carolina, on July 15, 1862.[13]

The monotony of camp life soon began to have an effect on the 55th North Carolina. Private James K. Wilkerson of Company K complained to his family that the strict rules were beginning to irritate him, especially when he was denied a few hours' leave to have himself photographed. The constant call to clean the camp and the long and tedious eight-hour guard details at night angered Wilkerson. He longed to go home and be with his family.[14]

Private Wilkerson was not the only soldier of the regiment to become depressed by the listlessness of camp life and begin praying to be rejoined with his loved ones. Private Hoyle did not like being away from his wife, Sarah. Writing her at the end of May, Hoyle wrote, "I think of you a great deal and often I feel the tears running fast down my cheeks."[15] The two privates were, however, able to focus their attention on other aspects of camp life to relieve their loneliness. Hoyle had his faith in God to keep him content, and Wilkerson enjoyed bargaining for food, clothing, and other items of "necessity." Wilkerson spent his time selling his boots, buying a set of buttons for sixty cents, and peddling a pound and a half of butter for sixty cents. Wilkerson, like many other members of the 55th, sold personal items to make extra money, but several soldiers in the regiment dishonored their comrades by stealing money from other men.[16]

Private James K. Wilkerson, Company K. Private Wilkerson saw action in some of the Civil War's bloodiest battles and somehow survived. (Courtesy of the North Carolina Division of Archives and History, Raleigh, North Carolina.)

On June 27, 1862, the 55th North Carolina received orders to move from Camp Mangum to a site near Kinston. The following morning a hundred members from the regiment were sent to Raleigh to obtain muskets. Although troops in the Federal armies would have Springfield rifled muskets, in the early years of the war many Confederate units were equipped with the United States Percussion Musket, Model 1842, which with its .69-caliber smoothbore barrel had inadequate accuracy. Memoirs and letters written by men who served with the 55th assert that during the Suffolk campaign in the spring of 1863, the regiment was armed with smoothbore muskets, which may indicate that the unit was indeed furnished with the 1842 musket. Most soldiers in the Southern armies didn't receive rifled muskets until after the Gettysburg campaign.[17]

On the evening of the 28th, possibly the morning of the 29th, the regiment climbed into railroad cars and traveled east to Kinston. The news of the transfer dampened the spirits of several men of the regiment. Wilkerson declared the area to be unhealthy and the water unfit to drink.[18]

The 55th North Carolina reached Camp Campbell, seven miles west of Kinston, by nightfall on June 29. Although Wilkerson had reservations about being stationed near Kinston, the regiment's campsite seemed acceptable to most of the men. Private Hoyle explained the unit's situation in a letter to the editor of the *Spirit of the Age*.

> We occupy a very pretty encampment on the Atlantic and N.C.T. Rail Road, among the long leaf Pines. We have as good water as we could expect for this country. Our rations have proven Sufficient thus far, and on the whole, this place seems to be better adapted to our well being than at Camp Mangum. The health of the Regt, is comparatively good. The South Mountain Rangers [Company F] are all on foot.[19]

Sergeant Ezra Mull of Company F reported that the health of the regiment was "quite good," stating "There is but little sickness." Sergeant Mull also reported that six of the regiment's men had died from colds and measles, but that most had died in the hospital in Raleigh.[20] Included among those who were sick in July was Wilkerson, who informed his parents that he too had the measles and was in the hospital.[21]

Through the remaining days of July and into August the men of the 55th North Carolina expected the Union army to attack, and many were very willing to meet the Yankees on the field of battle. Hoyle stated that the regiment was ready to show the Yankees some "North Carolina pluck."[22] It would not be long before the regiment was called upon to face the enemy on their own soil.

During the evening of July 25 the men of the 55th were ordered to prepare to march. The troops were told they would be moving out in 10 minutes, but the excitement soon ended and the soldiers were sent back to their tents. Early the following morning, however, the regiment marched out of their camp and prepared to meet a Federal force said to be advancing toward Kinston. The 55th marched through the sand and dust, finally reaching Kinston around 6:00 p.m. Although the distance was only about eight miles several of the men fell out of line from exhaustion, a clear sign of the regiment's inexperience. Later during the war the regiment would at times march 20 or more miles a day.[23]

The 55th spent the evening camped in a field outside of Kinston without blankets or tents for cover because they had been ordered to only bring arms and cartridge boxes. Later that night it began to rain, prompting the soldiers to search for shelter. Several of the men, including Joseph Hoyle and first Lieutenant William H. Hull of Company F, found shelter in nearby slave huts. Anticipation of a fight with the Federals and the discomfort of cramped quarters prevented many of the men from getting much sleep.[24]

The 55th North Carolina remained at Kinston until August 1. The Federals never attempted to attack Kinston while the 55th was stationed there. The regiment's pickets captured four Union soldiers, but the 55th would not face their enemy in battle as many had anticipated. With only bacon and hard bread to eat while at Kinston the men of the 55th were happy to return to Camp Campbell, but many were dismayed that they had not had the opportunity to prove themselves in battle. Those so eager to prove their worth in combat would not have to wait long.[25]

Early in the war Federal military leaders realized that if they could control the Albemarle, Pamlico, Core, and Bogue sounds they would be in a position to effectively control one-third of the state of North Carolina. These commanders also understood that if Union forces controlled North Carolina's east coast they could threaten the Wilmington and Weldon Railroad, the primary line running south from Richmond, Virginia.[26]

A series of barrier islands perforated by a half-dozen inlets run along the North

Carolina coast. Only one of these inlets, Hatteras Inlet, was navigable by large ships.[27] Once past this barrier the Federals would be in a position to control the Pamlico and Albemarle sounds. Control of these sounds would give the Federals the opportunity to utilize the rail and canal connections to the interior of the state.

Not long after North Carolina seceded from the Union, the state military leaders made preparations to defend their coast. These officials authorized the construction of several new forts including forts Hatteras and Clark to protect the state's numerous inlets. These two forts were extremely important to the protection of North Carolina's coast because they guarded the main inlet north of Beaufort. A small fleet of five armed steamers, referred to by many North Carolinians as the "mosquito fleet," was established as a second line of defense.[28]

During the last week of August 1861 Major General Benjamin Butler and a Union naval detachment under the command of Commodore Silas Stringham succeeded in capturing forts Clark and Hatteras. The Federal occupation of these two forts and the abandoning of forts Oregon and Ocracoke by the Confederates effectively gave the Union forces control of the inlets to the Pamlico Sound. In February 1862 an expedition under the command of Major General Ambrose E. Burnside and Commodore L. M. Goldsborough captured Rebel positions on Roanoke Island, and during the next several weeks Union forces gained control of North Carolina ports for 150 miles up and down the sounds.[29]

Burnside planned to continue his thrust into the heart of North Carolina with a move against the railroad hub in Goldsboro. Problems in Virginia, however, forced the United States War Department to order him to assist Major General McClellan, who was having problems near Richmond. Major General John G. Foster was left in command of the Department of North Carolina.[30]

Foster did not remain idle while the war raged in Virginia. He ordered the construction of fortifications in several areas and began sending detachments on reconnaissance missions to learn the topography of the surrounding area and to keep the Rebels at bay.[31] It was during one of these attempts to reconnoiter the surrounding area that the 55th North Carolina Regiment received its baptism of fire.

On August 7, 1862, three Federal boats, the armed steamer *Massasoit*, the *Pilot Boy*, a pilot boat, and the navy gunboat *Ellis*, traveled up the Neuse River to within seven miles of Kinston. A four-gun battery on the left bank of the river and several underwater obstructions prevented the Union boats from traveling up the Neuse any farther. Several Union officers landed on the bank of the river opposite from where the battery was stationed and successfully reconnoitered the area.[32] The 55th North Carolina Regiment was sent to prevent the Federals from landing troops.[33]

The Federals were unable to get ashore, but they did succeed in accomplishing their mission, which was to reconnoiter the area. While Union officers scouted the territory, their gunboats fired several shells into the battery. The Confederates were unable, or unprepared, to return fire. Once the officers completed their reconnaissance the small floating detachment returned to New Bern.[34]

The 55th North Carolina troops formed in a line of battle on the south side of the river and the Federal gunboat positioned itself directly across from them. The regimental chaplain, William B. Royall, would later write that although the unit was unable to return fire because it had been subject to direct fire from the Federal vessels for some period of time, the troops proved their courage and "stood this test of fortitude manfully."[35]

The Union barrage did little damage, wounding only one soldier of the 55th in the attack. The unlucky soldier had one of his eyebrows grazed by a shell fragment. Royall explained that the young soldier, probably Private Solomon Hoyle of Company F, suffered "no further damage than a temporary spoiling of his good looks." The regiment's baptism of fire was brief and had cost no lives, but to some in the command, the failure to do battle with the Federals left a bad taste in their mouths. The unit's encounter with the Federals near Kinston, although limited, was greatly enhanced by their training and the men were eager to encounter the Federals again. Royall commented, "Our boys are anxious to meet them in the open field at almost any odds."[36]

After the battle the regiment's morale was high, but sickness once again ravaged the troops. The health of the regiment diminished rapidly, as the weather became hotter. Fever and mumps wracked the 55th throughout the remaining days of August 1862.[37] Disease was not the only factor that plagued the unit during this time. Although the engagement near Kinston lifted the spirits of most of the men, a group of men from Company B deserted and returned to their homes. These dissatisfied soldiers were primarily from Wilkes County, North Carolina, and succeeded in resisting all attempts to compel them to return to their command.[38]

The months away from loved ones taught the soldiers of the 55th North Carolina to be self-sufficient. Without their wives or mothers and sisters there to assist them in the everyday necessities like washing and cooking, the men had to learn how to do things on their own. Private Hoyle informed his wife that he had been washing his clothes and was surprised that he ever learned how to it. He also complained that the cost to have someone do his washing for him was too much, and so he had to do it all by himself. The task of washing his own clothes was not as hard as he had expected he explained to his wife, but some of the other soldiers in his company would rather pay someone else to do their laundry, even to the point, Hoyle claimed, of spending the majority of their pay.[39]

Throughout March and April 1862 General Robert E. Lee continued to request that North Carolina send as many troops as possible to Virginia to help Confederate operations against McClellan. Major General Theophilus H. Holmes, who was given command of the Department of North Carolina at the end of March 1862, continued to refuse these requests until he had a better understanding of Burnside's operations in the state.[40] By April 22 Holmes felt confident enough to send Lee several regiments that were stationed in North Carolina. In a letter dated August 8, 1862, Governor Clark informed Lee that the troops sent by Holmes were the best-trained soldiers under his command and that the regiments left in the state were raw troops. Governor Clark also stated that the regiments left were chosen because it was deemed that they would "stand the usual camp diseases better at home than if removed."[41] One of these "raw" regiments was the 55th North Carolina, whose men did not handle the camp diseases in their home state very well. During June and July approximately 130 men from the regiment were on sick furlough or in local hospitals.[42]

The Union activities in eastern North Carolina, although minor in scope, were becoming more and more vexing to the state officials in Raleigh. Governor Clark, who had in the past few months graciously allowed North Carolina troops to be sent to Virginia to help Lee halt McClellan's advance toward Richmond, now feared that Union forces would strike Goldsboro. This anxiety forced Clark to request Lee to send an expeditionary force to North Carolina to help stave off disaster. The general, believing that he needed even more troops than he had, explained to the governor that failure in Richmond would be even more devastating to the Confederacy than any Federal operations could be in eastern North Carolina.[43]

General Lee's opposition to North Carolina's request for more troops meant that any offensive operations designed to force the Federals to postpone offensive moves in the state would have to be implemented by the small commands already stationed in eastern North Carolina. The first of these offensive strikes against Union forces in eastern North Carolina occurred on September 6, 1862. Colonel Stephen. D. Pool of the first North Carolina Artillery led a force of troops consisting of soldiers from the 10th North Carolina Artillery, and the eighth, 17th, and 55th North Carolina Infantry regiments.[44]

On September 2, 1862, while at camp near La Grange, several miles northwest of Kinston, the soldiers of the 55th were informed by Colonel Connally that 200 men were needed to participate in a "daring" operation. Practically the entire regiment stepped forward after Colonel Connally asked for volunteers. Captain Peter Mull of Company F and Captain Maurice T. Smith of Company K commanded the detachment, which was organized into two commands of 100 men each. Another member of the regiment, Captain Wilson Williams, was so eager to join the expedition that he volunteered to accompany the men as a first lieutenant. Connally agreed and Williams joined his comrades.[45]

The special detachment of 200 men from the 55th North Carolina were given orders to cook three days rations and be prepared to depart camp early the following morning. On the morning of the 3rd the strike force left camp heading northeast. During the march the overall commander of the detachment, Captain Mull, informed the men that their objective was to attack Washington, North Carolina, which had been under Union control since March 21, 1862. During the march 200 soldiers from the 17th North Carolina joined the 55th North Carolina.[46]

On the evening of September 4, the detachments from the 55th and 17th North Carolina regiments passed through Greenville, North Carolina, and followed the Tar River toward Washington. During the morning of September 5 150 men from the eighth North Carolina joined the detachment. The expedition moved swiftly and by 4:00 p.m. was within seven miles of Washington. Here the men from the eighth, 17th, and 55th North Carolina regiments met a small 200-man cavalry unit under the command of Captain R. S. Tucker, and about 70 men of the 10th North Carolina Artillery acting as infantry.[47] The detachment, now under the command of Captain Stephen D. Pool, numbered around 820 men.

On September 5, at approximately 10:00 p.m., the Confederate strike force set out for Washington. The Confederates moved toward Washington in a roundabout way in order to surprise the Federals. The Confederate force, with the aid of heavy fog, surprised the Union's outer pickets and successfully pushed them back into the town. Private Hoyle, however, stated that the fire from the Union pickets momentarily caused disorganization among the majority of Rebels. Captain Pool then ordered the detachment to divide into two columns. The first column, containing the 55th North Carolina, exuberantly letting out the "rebel yell," advanced into the center of town, while the second group, with the help of one six-pound brass gun and a three-pound rifle, attempted to turn the Union's left flank.[48]

While the Rebel cavalrymen reorganized near the outskirts of Washington and tried to force the Union troops out of the town by making wild charges, all of which failed to achieve the desired objective, the 55th regrouped in the center of town. The fight, Private Hoyle wrote, "now commenced in earnest." The Union troops hid in lots and cellars and shot at the advancing Confederates. The Union commander, Lieutenant Colonel Edward E. Potter, placed a 12-pounder in open streets and opened up on the Rebels. Hoyle stated that the Federal artillery had little effect on the men of the 55th North Carolina, claiming that the shots were too high to do much damage. Lieutenant Colonel Potter reported that his gunners were all hit by enemy fire, forcing him to remove his artillery from the town.[49]

While the 55th North Carolina fought in the center of town the second column of Confederates tried to turn the Union flank. Woken by the sound of gunfire, the Union sailors on the gunboats *Picket* and *Louisiana* attempted to aid their comrades. Around five o'clock the Rebels fired several volleys across the decks of the *Louisiana*. A few moments later the *Picket* exploded, killing the ship's commander, Captain Sylvester D. Nicoll, and 19 of his men. The official Federal report states that a mistake while opening the magazine caused the explosion aboard the *Picket*, but both Federal gunboats had come under fire and the possibility that a Confederate shot caused the destruction cannot be overlooked.[50]

It soon became apparent to Potter that the Confederate force meant to dig in and continue the fight until they had taken the town. After several hours of fierce street fighting the Confederates, with the help of four brass guns they had captured near the town hospital and quickly turned against their former owners, the Federals retreated to the safety of their gunboats. At approximately 6:30 a.m. the Union forces had withdrawn from the town and the *Louisiana* began shelling the Rebels. The gunboat opened with accurate precision, firing over 150 projectiles at the Rebels including shell, grape and solid shot. The 55th North Carolina and the remaining Confederates were forced to retreat, but they were able to take the four brass guns they had captured with them. By 8:00 a.m. the Confederates had completely withdrawn from Washington.[51] Private Hoyle described the assault in a letter to the *Spirit of the Age*.

> The yankees were concealed in lots and cellars, from which they shot at our men. Their batteries, which were so planted as to sweep the streets, now opened upon us, but with little effect, as the shot generally passed entirely over our heads. But prior to this, our cavalry had made a charge into town, and drove the yankee cavalry (500) entirely out. Capt. Tucker's company was most conspicuous in this dash. Finally we succeeded in driving the enemy to his gunboats, except at one battery. We have taken five pieces of his artillery which were turned upon him with effect. The gunboats had commenced their old trade of shelling and as our men were in no condition to do further execution we retreated, carrying with us the cannon we had taken.[52]

After the battle Hoyle wrote that the Confederates killed 150 Union troops and captured 12. He also stated that the Rebel losses did not exceed 35, declaring "over two-thirds of whom are wounded and missing." The young private also claimed that the Confederate assault would have been a success if the men had not panicked as they advanced into Washington. The rapid return of four Federal cavalry companies and one artillery battery caused confusion and panic throughout the Rebel ranks. These Federal troops had just begun a march out of Washington and were heading for Plymouth to assist the navy in an attack on Hamilton. The force consisted of about 263 men and was able to return to Washington swiftly to help prevent a Confederate victory.[53]

The report provided by Major General James G. Martin, serving as North Carolina's adjutant general and the Confederate officer who had conceived the attack on Washington, informed Major General Samuel G. French, commander of the Department of North Carolina and Southern Virginia, that Confederate losses were heavy during the attack on Washington. The Union reported that its losses at Washington were eight killed, 36 wounded, and 12 men missing.⁵⁴ Major General J. G. Foster put the Confederate casualties at 33 killed and about 100 wounded. The Union commander at Washington, Lieutenant Colonel Potter, added that the Federals captured 20 Rebels and that his cavalry reported that the Confederates had carried off "many dead and wounded."⁵⁵

Among the Confederate wounded was Captain Peter Mull, who had been seriously injured while leading his men against a Federal battery. The members of the 55th who saw Mull believed his wounds to be mortal. Report of his imminent death soon swept through the entire regiment.⁵⁶ The 55th suffered seven men killed, eight wounded, and 11 captured during the raid on Washington. The men of the unit fought bravely, but were outgunned by the Federals, who possessed rifled arms while the 55th was armed with old smoothbore muskets, and who were well protected during the arduous street fighting.⁵⁷

The Confederate detachments made their way back to their camps, but several wounded were captured when Federal cavalry overtook two ambulances on the Greenville road. For the remaining days of September 1862 the 55th North Carolina moved their campsite several times. On September 17 the regiment moved to Wyse's Fork, about five miles southeast of Kinston. The days at Wyse's Fork were not happy ones for the men of the regiment, according to Private Wilkerson. The soldiers were forced to sleep on the ground, which remained wet after several days of constant rain, without tents. Also, to keep the men fit, the regiment drilled twice a day and several men were sent to gather fodder for the horses. All of these uncomfortable situations must have been taxing on Wilkerson who, in addition to sleeping on the wet ground, sore feet from marching, and drilling every day, had to endure the pain of having a tooth pulled.⁵⁸

On September 23 the regiment set up camp at Trenton, North Carolina, and prepared to meet an anticipated Federal attack at any moment. The men of the 55th "lay under arms all night" and the regiment's pickets located the Union troops near New Bern. On the evening of September 26 the regiment loaded their guns and marched to the Trent River Bridge. At the bridge the command prepared for an attack by the Federals, but no assault came. The men lay down in ranks to sleep and after spending the night on the cold wet ground they returned to camp.⁵⁹

The nights spent sleeping in the cold and rain began to take a toll on the regiment. By the end of September disease once again plagued the men of the 55th. Many sick soldiers were affected so badly that they were sent to nearby hospitals. Private Hoyle informed the readers of the *Spirit of the Age* of the plight of the men in the regiment, with particular attention to his own company, and asked for those at home to pray for the regiment.

> The health of our regiment is not good. All our sick (nearly) have been sent to the hospital at Goldsboro and Raleigh. As a specimen of our condition, I will state that our Co. (F) numbers 76, and only 32 report for duty. We hope our friends will not forget us in their supplications at the throne of mercy, Remember our beloved, yet bleeding country, also, God will hear faithful prayer.⁶⁰

The health of the regiment did not deter its leaders from performing their duties. On September 27, Colonel Connally and his staff made a small reconnaissance. They got within six miles of New Bern and their presence forced the Federal pickets to retreat behind a wall built to obstruct any further intrusion. Private Hoyle thought that the act was courageous and that it had an uplifting effect on the men, as he informed the readers of the *Spirit of the Age* of Connally's mission.

Col. Connally and staff made a reconnoisance in the direction of Newbern yesterday. When within about six miles of Newbern, they came in contact with the yankee pickets, charged them and drove them some distance, when a well constructed fence, built for the purpose, arrested their further progress. The enemy took several deliberate fires from behind this obstruction at our heroes, but without effect. Part of the pickets were said to be negroes. This was a daring exploit and will teach the wretches what they may expect, should they come beyond their fortifications.[61]

The 55th North Carolina made no more movements until October 1, when the regiment learned that it would soon be attacked by a Union detachment. Colonel Connally immediately ordered the regiment to travel back to Kinston. The regiment left Trenton and made a hard 25-mile forced march to Wyse's Fork. After a day's rest the men of the regiment formed a marching column and prepared to forge ahead to Kinston.[62]

The regiment awoke at 1:00 a.m. and was extremely tired and at least 125 men refused to continue marching and decided to rest on the road. Company K had the responsibility of guarding the rear as the regiment moved toward Kinston. The captain of Company K, Maurice T. Smith, ordered his men to fix bayonets and charge several of the stragglers who had refused to march. Captain Smith informed his company that Colonel Connally had ordered that the stragglers be forced to keep up with the regiment.[63]

One member of the regiment received the punishment of "bucking and gagging," which was at times inflicted on soldiers who were stragglers, shirkers, or drunkards. The soldier was placed on the ground and his hands and feet were bound in a seated position. The offending soldier's knees were pulled up between his arms and a stick was inserted running under his knees and over his arms. The soldier was then gagged by having a stick shoved sideways into his mouth and tied to his head to keep it secure. Private Wilkerson, a member of Captain Smith's company, participated in the bayonet charge to move the stragglers and witnessed the unfortunate soldier being punished. The two men left to watch the bound soldier were given orders to kill him if the Federals appeared. This punishment seems to have been effective in motivating this straggler to move, according to Wilkerson, who wrote that the soldier could "Walk very well after While, after he got over his Stiffness from being Buck so long." The regiment continued on to Kinston without rest, food or water, and many of the men made the march in shoes that were falling apart as they walked. Private Wilkerson wrote, "we suffered a great deal for Water and something to Eate on those marches, we wont allowed to fall out of ranks to get any water."[64]

Though anticipated, a Federal attack failed to materialize. During the evening of October 3, 1862, the regiment moved by rail to Petersburg, Virginia. The 55th's time in North Carolina had ended, and it would soon join Robert E. Lee's Army of Northern Virginia.

2

October 1862–April 1863: For the Honor of the Regiment

"Every man, with some few individual exceptions did his duty"

During the first week of October 1862, the 55th North Carolina reached Petersburg, Virginia. The regiment bivouacked four miles from the city and spent the next few weeks building breastworks, drilling, and repairing roads to ease the movement of artillery. The regiment called its new bivouac Camp French after its departmental commander, Major General Samuel French. The new campsite did not go unnoticed by the Federals, and occasionally the men of the 55th were forced to cease laboring and take shelter from Union gunboats that shelled the camp.[1]

Upon arriving in Virginia the 55th North Carolina remained an orphaned regiment. The regiment was not assigned to any brigade. Instead it was placed under the direct command of French, who commanded the Department of North Carolina and Southern Virginia. After they settled in at their new location French ordered the recently arrived North Carolinians to perform provost duty in Petersburg. On October 29 the unit moved from Camp French to an area near the Model Farm, west of Petersburg.[2]

While stationed near the Model Farm the troops of the 55th actually had the opportunity to sleep indoors, in houses. The men were very pleased and the accommodations were luxurious compared to the many nights they had spent sleeping on the cold hard ground. Most of the houses selected had kitchens and were kept warm by brick chimneys. Private Wilkerson informed his father that the room he was staying in "will hold 96 men, only two men to a bunk."[3]

Although their accommodations were pleasant enough to please most of the men, the war continued to dampen spirits and kept many soldiers depressed. Months away from home and the monotony of camp life depressed the men as did sad news from the fields of battle. Countless numbers of the men had friends and family serving in other regiments in both theaters of war, and occasionally word would reach one of them that a friend or loved one had died. Private Hoyle had friends and family serving in several different regiments currently serving in the Army of Northern Virginia. His best friend, Sergeant Roderick M. Sherrill of Company D, first North Carolina State Troops Regiment, had died of typhoid fever in Richmond on September 8, 1862. How much his death affected Private Hoyle can be inferred from the words he wrote to his wife upon learning of the death of his friend.

> You know he was my dearest friend, and well he deserved my most worthy affections, for he was among the chosen noble young men. I feel that his place cannot easily be filled. Sarah, I loved him as a brother, and I hope to meet him on the shores of eternal bliss. I trust his soul is gone to rest.[4]

Sarah Hoyle, Joseph Hoyle's wife, would know the agony of loss several times before the end of the war. Not only would she lose two of her brothers, but her husband would be one of the thousands killed in combat during the Civil War.

November brought snow and colder days to the Petersburg area, and although Private Wilkerson was elated that the house he stayed in had a brick chimney, many soldiers had to do without. Private Hoyle wrote to his wife that several of the houses chosen for the regiment had no chimneys. As the men had to make small fires to keep warm, the rooms lacking chimneys quickly filled up with smoke and the soldiers' eyes burned with pain. Many of the soldiers found relief from these smoke-filled rooms while performing guard duty, a responsibility the men of the regiment performed at least every third day. Occasionally some individuals had guard duty every day.[5]

On November 14 the regiment moved to a new campsite for the third time since arriving in Virginia. The 55th North Carolina encamped at an area around Dunn's Hill and took up residence in the houses there, which were located near several local powder mills. The new homes were second-rate compared to the ones back at the Model Farm. These new quarters were smaller and had no well-constructed bunks for the men. The officers, however, occupied "comfortable quarters" and had a "delightful time" while stationed near Petersburg.[6] Signs of eminent battle also trickled through Petersburg as Confederate troops continued to march through the city on their way to the front, and rumors of Federal advance upon the vital railroads located near Petersburg continued to circulate through the camps. Private Hoyle received some information through an acquaintance serving in Lieutenant General James Longstreet's command that proved to be more than just hearsay.

> I met up with a friend P. J. Johnson this morning. He belongs to Longstreet's Corps and they have fallen back on this side of Culpeper Court house. He says Lee's entire army will fall back in order to obtain supplies. Reports say yankees still keep advancing on Weldon. They seem determined to try it, and no doubt with a large force as this would be one of the most important places they could take. Our men are preparing to defend it. Troops are passing through Petersburg every day. We may look for an important battle in this vicinity before long, if the yankees come on.[7]

It would not be long before two divisions under Longstreet would move into southeastern Virginia to gather supplies for Lee's army, and the 55th North Carolina would be caught up in this campaign.

The tediousness of provost guard duty soon had an effect on the spirits of the regiment. The men of the 55th North Carolina spent practically every other day on provost duty, which meant a 24-hour shift of patrolling the streets of Petersburg. Those on duty had to carry their daily provisions with them, or spend what little money they had to buy them in the city. The four-month wage of $44 that many of the men received in October was quickly spent in the city. Provost duty may have been monotonous, but in a letter to his mother Wilkerson admitted that there was also "a good deal of fune" in the city.⁸ Along with the boredom and the lure of city shops, those on provost duty had to be on guard against possible violent reactions from the people they arrested. Drunks posed the greatest threat and the young private feared that some of the regiment's men would be killed before Christmas.⁹

While the men of 55th North Carolina performed provost guard duty at Petersburg, disease once again swept through the camp. From November through February mumps, pneumonia, typhoid, smallpox and several other ailments forced many soldiers into hospitals or an early grave. The decline in the regiment's health did not go unnoticed by the men in the ranks. Joseph J. Hoyle, who had been promoted to the rank of sergeant on November 25, 1862, blamed the decline in the regiment's overall health on exposure.

> The health of our Regiment seems on the decline for the few last weeks, which is no doubt attributably to the exposure we have had to endure. For while we have comfortable quarters, it will be remembered that we are on duty at least half our time.¹⁰

Diseases of pleasure also debilitated several of the soldiers in the 55th North Carolina. The degenerative effects the soldier life has on the moral standards of an individual are infamous, and the men who wore the gray and butternut uniforms of the Confederacy did not escape the vices brought about during months of inactivity. Sergeant Hoyle openly stated in a letter to the *Spirit of the Age* that the 55th North Carolina Regiment was "not exempt from the prevailing wickedness of the Army."¹¹ Petersburg became a well-known haven for prostitutes, and the sexually transmitted diseases spread by these women infected several members of the 55th. The regimental sick reports listed 13 new cases of gonorrhea in October alone. Numerous cases of the disease were also reported throughout November and December.¹²

At least a few of the members of the 55th North Carolina had the opportunity to return to their home state and leave the monotony of provost duty and camp life behind them. Private Joseph Hoyle and several men from the regiment were ordered to escort Federal prisoners to Fort Caswell, which was located along the North Carolina coast on Oak Island. Hoyle and his fellow soldiers traveled by steamboat and spent several days admiring the local sights and enjoying the view of the Atlantic Ocean. Hoyle spent time collecting seashells that he then had sent to his wife in Knob Creek, North Carolina. By November 19 they were back in Virginia.¹³

The 55th North Carolina remained near Petersburg throughout the winter of 1862–63. Although the men of the regiment did not share in the glories of battle that Confederate regiments experienced at Fredericksburg that December, they still experienced the same cold winter wind and were in constant want of provisions. The battle reports from Fredericksburg poured into the company campsites and the men of the 55th were elated to hear that General Lee's army had defeated the Federals in a victory that was "disastrous in the highest degree" for the Union.¹⁴ Victory may have raised morale, but the hardships of soldiering during the winter sapped some of the high-spiritedness. The men of the regiment spent the long winter without receiving new clothing. Many of the soldiers had no shoes and were "nearly naked for the want of clothes."¹⁵

In mid–December Adjutant Henry T. Jordan wrote a letter to the *North Carolina Standard* describing the hardships his fellow soldiers were enduring.

> I ask a little room in your paper to inform the friends of the soldiers of the 55th N.C. Regiment of the condition in which their sons, brothers, fathers and husbands are painfully enduring the rigors of the present severe weather, and to support the means by which their necessities may

be relieved. Many of the men are without a change of clothing, many are thinly clad, many are barefoot, and many are without bed-clothing of any kind, using tente and flies in place of blankets. Ther suffering is great and painful to witness. I will say for them officers, non-commissioned officers, and privates, that no body of men ever yielded a more cheerful performance of duty than do the members of this regiment. No one ever shirks a duty — no one ever asks to be excused, unless he is really unable to do duty.[16]

Jordan also informed the readers of the *Standard* that the men of his regiment needed their assistance and that soon men from each of the unit's companies would be sent home to collect provisions. The young adjutant asked that the people of North Carolina be ready to give by appealing to their patriotism.

In a few days, probably, one man from each company will be detailed to go home to collect supplies of clothing and bed-clothing. Now be you ready to meet them with warm hearts, and open hands, and unstrung purses. Give of your abundance — spare some of your luxuries — remember that if they are not shortly supplied with shoes, among other things, they will dye the frozen ground red with the blood of torn feet, as they walk the sentinels' weary beat by night and day. Remember, it is for you, and for North Carolina, and for their whole country, that they are suffering thus. Remember, and let the rememberance warm your hearts within you, and show by your acts that ye are indeed the mothers, and fathers, the sisters, the wives and the daughters of such men.[17]

The harsh winter weather continued to plague the regiment and effect the unit's fighting ability. The numbers of men present and fit for duty in the 55th North Carolina fluctuated from day to day. Illness was the main cause for this constant variation, but other factors accounted for some of the change. In November the unit had 26 officers and 466 men present for duty with an aggregated total present of 684. The totals aggregate present and absent, however, were 814. During the first few months of the regiment's existence desertion had been a small problem. Numerous privates, including Braswell Renfrow, a substitute in Company A, and William T. Foster of Company B deserted prior to July 2, 1862, and several others left the regiment without leave during the winter months. The causes of desertion in the Confederate armies varied. Many deserters did not fully believe in the Southern "cause," some were afraid to fight, or simply homesick and hungry, and others were conscripts who waited for the perfect moment to escape the rigors of war.[18] Why those who deserted the 55th North Carolina did so is not known, but the regiment had its share of conscripts and men from counties that were generally not sympathetic to the Confederacy.

Incarceration, the death penalty, and appeals to patriotism were all ways the Confederacy tried to prevent desertion. The death penalty seemed fit for a deserter from the 55th North Carolina in December. Wilkerson informed his father that a member of the regiment was to be shot on December 17 for desertion. The youthful private and several other members of the regiment hoped that the doomed man would be pardoned. Those chosen to serve as the firing squad, Wilkerson reported to his father, had to practice shooting in unison. This soldier may have been Private John Hinchey of Company B, who had deserted in June but was apprehended sometime during the winter. Hinchey's sentence was commuted to hard labor, and he was sent to Fort Caswell to begin his punishment on February 9, 1863.[19]

Illness and desertion were not the only factors limiting the number of men serving in the 55th North Carolina. From the time the regiment came into being, Colonel Connally pushed his men hard and expected his officers to do the same. Several officers did not quite meet the standards expected by the young colonel and resigned their commissions. Connally wanted several officers to resign because he believed they were simply "incompetent" and "unfit" to lead troops. Captain Samuel J. Forester of Company B, and Third Lieutenants William Quinn of Company C and Alexander T. Grady of Company G were among the 10 officers Connally removed from command between June 1862 and March 1863. Several of these officers, including Captains William J. Bullock of Company A and Jesse P. Williams of Company G, were asked to resign primarily because they were leaders of discontented factions and were "striving to prejudice both officers & men against their commanding officers, thereby injuring the efficiency of the Regt by weakening its discipline."[20]

The number of able-bodied soldiers in the 55th North Carolina was not drastically reduced by desertion, and though men did leave the ranks without leave more recruits continued to join the regiment. One of these newcomers was Henry C. Davis, who enlisted on December 19, 1862. Another man to join the ranks of the regiment during the second winter of the war was Bryant Bass, a 50-old substitute from Wayne County who served for the duration of the war and surrendered at Appomattox.[21]

The dreariness of provost duty dragged on throughout the winter. Several companies from the 55th North Carolina were detached to the Model Farm in December to watch paroled prisoners. Colonel Connally commanded the troops stationed in and around Petersburg while General French was absent.[22] The regiment began drilling for one hour every evening after those on provost duty returned from their shifts, indicating a change in the hours spent on provost duty.[23]

By the beginning of February 1863 most of the men of the 55th North Carolina had received winter clothing. Most of the soldiers now had blankets and shoes, which helped keep the men warmer as the weather worsened. Many of the men were probably happy that they were finally receiving winter attire. Sergeant Hoyle, however, could not help wondering how the Confederate government had the audacity to charge the men $9 for a pair of pants, $6 for shoes, and $1 for a pair of socks when the patriotic women of North Carolina had donated most of the materials.[24]

Having to purchase needed clothing from the government was made even more irksome because the men had not been paid since October, and realized that their pay would be substantially reduced. Some of the soldiers were able to raise money by selling the very items of clothing they so desperately needed. Several of the men sold their pants and coats for $15. For some the new supplies simply provided a means to make money or trade for things they needed or wanted.[25]

Snowstorms wracked southern Virginia in the early part of February and the cold wind made the men huddle together by their fires. The regiment returned to Camp French, located four miles east of Petersburg, during the last weeks of January. Sergeant Hoyle described their new quarters as being "very comfortable" and "made of pine poles and earth." Hoyle went on to describe, somewhat unflatteringly, how the soldiers of the 55th North Carolina spent their time in camp.

> Although the soldier endures many hardships and privations, yet he enjoys many agreeable hours, which none but the soldier can appreciate. Human nature covets enjoyment; in fact man cannot live without it. Place him in any condition, whatever, and he will invent some mode to gratify this craving principle of his nature. Sociality forms the great principle of enjoyment in camp, and as this is a rich medium of information, you would naturally conclude

that soldiers ought to become wise men; but unfortunately conversation is generally conducted to excite the ludicrous propensites, rather than to any instructive end. But I would be doing injustice, were I not to tell you that some of our men apply their unoccupied time in reading and other useful pursuits.[26]

March did not bring an end to the cold and snow, but the furloughs many of the men of the 55th received in February helped raise morale. The regiment's spirits were high and they were glad to finally be relieved of provost duty. The unit moved to Camp Green, near Franklin Depot, and set up temporary quarters. The men had no tents, but were able to construct "shanties." The regiment had been assigned to this location to guard a pass on the Blackwater River.[27]

It was also during the first week of March that the 55th North Carolina was temporarily assigned to the brigade of Brigadier General Joseph R. Davis. When the regiment had arrived in Virginia it remained under the command of Major General French and was not placed in a brigade until sometime after mid–December, at which time it was placed under the command of Brigadier General Raleigh E. Colston. The 55th North Carolina only remained in Colston's brigade for a short time.[28] On March 5, 1863, the regiment joined Brigadier General Davis's brigade; the move became official on April 7, 1863. The transfer, at first perceived to be temporary, lasted until January 1865. Accompanying the 55th in Davis's brigade were the second, 11th, and 42nd Mississippi Infantry regiments.[29] The 26th Mississippi Infantry Regiment and the first Confederate Battalion joined the brigade in April 1864.

Brigadier General Joseph R. Davis was President Jefferson Davis's nephew, and the son of Isaac Davis. Joseph Davis was a successful Mississippi lawyer and farmer, and served as a secessionist Democrat in the Mississippi state Senate in 1860, before joining the Confederate Army in April 1861. He first served as a lieutenant colonel of the 10th Mississippi Infantry Regiment, and then became aide-de-camp to President Davis in August 1861. He was promoted to brigadier general on September 15, 1862. Joseph R. Davis served in the Army of Northern Virginia until surrender at Appomattox on April 9, 1865.[30]

On March 9 the regiment traveled 12 miles down the Blackwater River and pitched tents. The men spent their time in this new location drilling and performing picket duty. After five days the men of the 55th struck their tents and marched through Camp Green to Camp Holmes, near Ivor Station. After spending the rest of March at Camp Holmes drilling and performing picket duty the regiment once again moved to Camp Green. The regiment bivouacked a few hundred yards from Camp Green near the 11th Mississippi. The continuous marching from place to place along the Blackwater River had Wilkerson complaining that the regiment was constantly on the move and that the men would "all get killed marching so much." However, the terrain reminded some of the soldiers of eastern North Carolina. Sergeant Hoyle claimed that one need only dig two or three feet into the ground to get water.[31]

The fatigue of constant marching was doubled by the fact that at the time when the men were expending more energy and in need of extra nourishment their rations were reduced. The daily ration for a soldier in the 55th North Carolina during this period was one pound of flour, and one-fourth of a pound of meat, which was primarily fat. Private Wilkerson informed his mother that the men were not eating much and that all he had eaten in days was cold bread.[32] The food shortage was felt by most of the regiments serving in the Confederate armies and was not unique to the 55th. The Confederate armies were in dire need of supplies and the subsistence department possessed a scarce amount of fresh meat. Large supplies of small cattle, bacon, corn, and other supplies were thought to be located in southern Virginia and eastern North Carolina. General Lee decided to send Lieutenant General James Longstreet and two of his strongest divisions to Suffolk and the Nansemond River area in southern Virginia to gather these abundant supplies.[33]

By the spring of 1862 the Confederate government had to declare a general reduction of the daily ration authorized to be given to soldiers since the war began. In January 1863 Commissary General L. B. Northrop called for a curtailment of the daily meat ration. Lee, who had argued against the 1862 reduction, informed Confederate Secretary of War James A. Seddon that his army had been living on a daily issuance of four ounces of bacon, eighteen ounces of flour and occasionally small portions of rice, molasses, or sugar.[34] The lack of supplies did not mean that the Confederacy as a whole was starving. At the same time Lee's men were receiving a few ounces of bacon a day, troops in North Carolina were being issued half a pound. The deficient rail system in the south caused this disparity. The supplies were there, but without a proper transportation system thousands of pounds of foodstuffs spoiled at depots.[35]

After Burnside's disastrous attempt to crush the Army of Northern Virginia at Fredericksburg and his failed attempt to cross the Rappahannock River in January 1863, which literally got the Army of the Potomac stuck in the mud, he asked President Lincoln to sack several officers for insubordinate behavior. Instead of removing or demoting other officers, Lincoln replaced Burnside and on January 25 placed Major General Joseph Hooker in command of the Army of the Potomac.[36] Burnside's transfer ultimately led to General Lee's decision to move Longstreet and approximately 15,000 troops to retake Suffolk if possible and gather needed supplies for the army from eastern North Carolina and southern Virginia.[37]

Major General Hooker's rise to command meant that Burnside's service with the Army of the Potomac was over. Burnside had asked President Lincoln to relieve Hooker of command, so any working relationship that had existed beforehand had vanished. To protect the army's morale the War Department decided to send Burnside and the IX Corps, which he had commanded before being appointed commander of the Army of the Potomac, to Camp Butler, located on the James River at Newport News. The 15,000-man army corps would simply have to remain in southern Virginia until the War Department could decide where it could do the most good.[38]

On February 7 the IX Corps began its move to Newport News, and the daily arrival of Federal troops sent shock waves of panic through the corridors of power in Richmond. The fear of another major move on the Confederate capital similar to McClellan's Peninsula campaign chiseled into the thoughts of those working in the Confederate War Department. The Army of Northern Virginia could not prevent a move on Richmond that came from south of the James River. The Confederates only had about 6,000 troops in and around Petersburg, including the 55th North Carolina, and another 5,000 in Richmond. The Union forces in Suffolk numbered over 11,000 and at Fort Monroe, Yorktown, and Norfolk there were some 10,000 men ready for action.[39] These numbers did not include the newly arriving IX Corps, which would place the total number of Federal troops stationed in southeastern Virginia at over 36,000. With Confederate forces being outnumbered three to one, the panic that spread through the Rebel leadership is understandable. With a large force stationed in lower Virginia the Federals could effectively attack Richmond, capture Petersburg, or even invade North Carolina.

The Confederates, of course, had no idea of the personnel conflicts raging in the Army of the Potomac, and therefore had to assume that the transfer of the IX Corps to Newport News indicated imminent offensive action by the Federals. Fearing a move on either Richmond or the Petersburg and Weldon Railroad, which was the Army of Northern Virginia's only rail supply line east of the Blue Ridge Mountains, Lee made plans for possible countermeasures. He ordered Major General George Pickett's division to move to Richmond and Major General John Bell Hood's division to be prepared to advance if called upon. Brigadier General Joseph Davis's brigade was also recalled from North Carolina and ordered to reinforce the troops guarding the Blackwater River.[40] The 55th was placed under Davis's command shortly after his brigade's return to Virginia, and the anxious temperament in Richmond explained the reasons the regiment spent most of March traversing up and down the Blackwater.

James Longstreet had hoped that Lee would send him and his First Corps to Tennessee to reinforce General Braxton Bragg and the Army of Tennessee after their disastrous defeat at the Battle of Murfreesboro. Longstreet saw the potential for a strategic concentration of troops in Tennessee, but Lee felt his "Old War-Horse" would be more useful in southeastern Virginia. So on February 18 the commanding general of the Army of Northern Virginia sent Longstreet to speak with Secretary Seddon in Richmond. After reassuring the secretary that he would provide adequate protection for the capital, Longstreet left for Petersburg and established his new headquarters. The snow continued to fall in Virginia throughout February, and Longstreet settled in to his new post as commander of the Department of Virginia and North Carolina.[41] The seeds of the Suffolk campaign, although still several months away, had been planted.

By mid–March Lee informed Longstreet that he should focus all of his attention on gathering supplies from North Carolina and lower Virginia. Secretary Seddon also wanted the lieutenant general to concentrate on obtaining provisions and thus requested that he begin scouting the area around Suffolk to ascertain if an attack on the city was plausible. Longstreet did not share the secretary's optimism and believed an attack on Suffolk would be futile, especially when the Federals had over 20,000 troops stationed at Newport News. The lieutenant general's mind quickly changed when he visited the Blackwater line, 20 miles west of Suffolk, and realized that a move against the city would achieve several objectives. Longstreet believed an offensive against Suffolk would divert pressure from his operations in North Carolina and at the same time open up a larger area for his foraging duties. The land around the Chowan and Blackwater rivers was rich with bacon, corn, and salt fish. The Federals would be bottled up in Suffolk, leaving Richmond and Petersburg safe.[42]

Lee and Longstreet agreed that a move on Suffolk would provide adequate assistance to the supply-gathering mission in southern Virginia and North Carolina. At his headquarters in Petersburg, Longstreet made preparations to cross the Blackwater on April 8 or 9. The U.S. naval attack on Fort Sumter, which began on April 7, prompted General Pierre G. T. Beauregard to ask Longstreet for assistance. The lieutenant general advised Secretary Seddon that perhaps he should send reinforcements to South Carolina and abort the planned attack on Suffolk. Seddon disagreed, and the offensive against Suffolk remained Longstreet's primary concern. Talk of a coming attack on Suffolk spread through the company camps of the 55th North Carolina.[43]

Longstreet's appointment to the command of the newly organized Department of Virginia and North Carolina, which encompassed the area from Richmond to Wilmington, caused some confusion in the minds of the men already in charge of departments in this quarter. One of these officers, Major General French, whose division included the 55th, believed the lieutenant general was maneuvering him out of command. As French saw, it Longstreet hastily decided to move toward Suffolk, taking with him one of the major general's divisions and a number of batteries without informing him of his intentions.[44] The confusion and rancor that existed between Longstreet and French would ultimately have a dramatic effect on the 55th North Carolina.

The hard marches and limited food may have damped the spirits of many of the men and had a detrimental effect on the overall health of some of the soldiers, but the regiment as a whole was in good condition, although smallpox had infected several of the troops.[45] One member of the 55th informed the readers of the *Biblical Recorder* of the general state of the regiment.

> Our regiment is in better trim now than it has been for some time. After being inspected by Gen. Longstreet's Inspector General two days ago, he remarked that he was glad to find the regiment in such good condition.[46]

Although some of the soldiers considered the regiment to be in good shape the commanding officer did not share this belief. As the winter months faded away Colonel Connally felt the days his men had spent in winter quarters had reduced the structure he had worked so hard at perfecting. Believing that an organized daily schedule had to be reinstituted he issued a general order on April 2. In this order the young colonel outlined the regiment's day-to-day timetable.

> The orderly hours hereafter will be as follows: Reveille 5 A.M, surgeon's call 6; guardmounting, 7; recitation of non commissioned officers from 8 to 9; company drill from 9 to 11; battalion drill 2:30 P.M. to 4:30; dress parade 5; tattoo 8; officers recitation 8 to 9; taps 9.[47]

Connally also detailed what type of cooking utensils mess groups, which were divided into units consisting of 15 men each, were allowed to carry and who was responsible for gathering the instruments used for food preparation when the regiment was on the march.

Colonel Connally had spent some time rearranging his unit into what he hoped would be a more effective fighting force. Connally's plan called for dividing the 55th North Carolina into two wings. He believed his two chief lieutenants, Lieutenant Colonel Maurice T. Smith and Major Horiatio A. Belo, could be placed in command of these wings, which, he anticipated, would make controlling the regiment more manageable. Smith and Belo would also be responsible for ensuring that every officer under their new command had a firm understanding of how to train and administrate a company of soldiers. The colonel described this new command structure in an order dated April 2, 1863.

> Lieut Col. Smith and Maj. Belo will take charge of the right and left wings of the Regt. respectively. They will instruct the officers on regulations as well as tactics, and be responsible for their efficency on drill, and their knowledge of military matters generally. They will be present at, and supervise company drill. To the purpose of equaling the strength of the two wings of the Regt. the position of the companies are arranged, and companies will be posted from right to left in the following order: companies "H," "A," "F," "E," "C," will constitute the right wing of the com, "B," "D," "I," "G," "K," will constitute the left wing. This arrangement will go into effect tomorrow evening at drill.[48]

It would not be long before Connally would be presented with the opportunity to test his new formation and the quality of his officers.

On April 11 the Confederate forces, including the 55th North Carolina, crossed the Blackwater on pontoons. Suffolk protected the approaches to Norfolk that were located across Hampton Roads from Portsmouth. The Union stationed troops in the city in May 1862 and by September these soldiers were under the command of Major General John J. Peck. By April 1863 the defenses built by Peck's men encircled the city in a 14-mile perimeter and included eight forts strategically located for optimal protection. These defenses were manned by a little more than 17,000 Union troops. Longstreet, who had requested naval assistance before the campaign had begun, understood that without the aid of the Confederate navy he had little chance of taking Suffolk by force. After being denied the necessary naval support the lieutenant general resorted to a siege.[49]

During the first few days of the siege the Confederate troops dug their own earthworks, while sporadic skirmishes and artillery exchanges occurred at different locations along the Rebel lines. Sixty men from the 55th North Carolina, which was said to be the largest regiment in Longstreet's command, had been detached to work on Smoot's Battery, located about three miles north of Suffolk along the Nansemond River. The battery commanded by Captain David L. Smoot contained two 30-pounder Parrott rifles. The battery was positioned on the extreme left of Major General Hood's line. Major General French, who joined the troops around Suffolk on April 13, ordered another battery to be positioned on Hill's Point. This battery, commanded by Captain Robert M. Stribling, was placed on Hill's Point itself in the old Battery Huger and contained two 24-pounder howitzers and three 12-pounder Napoleons.[50]

On April 17 Longstreet ordered French to send the 55th North Carolina Regiment to protect the batteries stationed on Hill's Point. Heavy skirmishing continued and would do so "every day for ten days." Connally ordered three of the regiment's companies, under the command of Captain William H. Williams of Company I, to move to Norfleet's house, on the Reed's Ferry Road, and to report to Major L. M. Shumaker, who assigned them to guard the batteries located in the vicinity. The three companies were posted about a mile to the rear of Hill's Point, and as previously stated, a detachment of 60 men from these companies was sent to complete the works.[51] The next day the remaining companies joined their comrades and began guarding the batteries. The 55th was positioned at various points along the Reed's Ferry Road. Shumaker advised Colonel Connally to set up picket posts at various locations. Each post was to consist of four men and a corporal. A detachment was posted at LeCompte's house directly behind Stribling's Battery; another was at the ferry on the Western Branch River; another was along the road between the ferry and LeCompte's house; another was directly behind Smoot's Battery; and a company was stationed at Moore's house, south of LeCompte's house. Although French had advised Connally to post the company at LeCompte's house instead of Moore's, the young colonel decided to follow the directions of Shumaker, who knew the area better.[52]

The Federals made several attempts to prevent the Rebels from crossing the Nansemond in a hope of getting into the rear of the forces at Suffolk. Gunboats had been ordered to divert the Confederates' attention and keep their forces divided. From April 12 through the 17 shells from Hill's Point hit several gunboats, including the *Mount Washington*, the *Teaser*, and the *Coeur de Lion*. The Federals, realizing that the Confederate guns stationed on Hill's Point, especially Battery Huger, were able to bombard their gunboats at will decided to capture the old fort.[53]

On the morning of April 19 the Federal flotilla under the command of Lieutenant

William B. Cushing took position 700 yards from Smoot's Battery. The Rebel guns opened on the Federals and the Union gunboats returned fire. The shelling lasted into the afternoon. Longstreet heard the cannonade while at his headquarters seven miles away. He quickly sent a dispatch to French, who had been sick in bed, asking if the regiment ordered to protect the guns had in fact been posted. The regiment (the 55th North Carolina) had, but French worried that the pickets from Hood's division that were posted with the artillerymen in Battery Huger would not be enough to repel a Union advance.[54]

French, whose concerns for the safety of the batteries grew more intense as the minutes passed, instructed Major Shumaker to show Longstreet's dispatch to Connally and ordered him to tell the young colonel to position his regiment to "repel any landing of infantry against the batteries." French also advised Connally to post his men near Stribling's Battery. Shumaker did not receive French's dispatch until 8 o'clock that evening. However, sometime between 4:00 and 6:00 p.m. Connally did receive French's orders from another member of the major general's staff, Lieutenant Colonel George A. Cunningham. This new intelligence, however, did not prompt the young colonel to act swiftly. Connally, taking the lieutenant colonel's calm tone as an indication that French's orders were not of grave importance, mistakenly did not move his troops closer to Stribling's Battery.[55]

Upon receiving French's orders Connally, who was unfamiliar with the topography of the area, sent Lieutenant Colonel Maurice T. Smith and Major Alfred H. Belo to reconnoiter the position of the batteries. The thought of scouting the surrounding area had apparently not come to the mind of the inexperienced Connally before this time. Smith and Belo were sent to determine how many men would be needed to support the batteries, and where to station these supporting troops. The two scouts had not been gone for more than an hour when Connally reported hearing loud cheering from the direction of the river.[56]

On April 19 around 6:00 p.m. the Federals assaulted Stribling's Battery. The assault began with an artillery barrage from the Union gunboats that were positioned within range of the battery. At the same time the Federals landed 270 troops from the eighth Connecticut and 89th New York regiments 400 yards above Stribling's Battery. The Union infantrymen carried 40 rounds of ammunition and were supported by four boat howitzers. The Federals advanced rapidly toward the fort and swiftly broke into the battery. After a short skirmish they captured the Rebel fort and forced the surrender of seven officers, 130 Confederate troops, and five guns.[57]

Moments after the fort's capture an officer rode to Connally's position and informed the colonel that Stribling's Battery had fallen into enemy hands. Connally immediately ordered his men to gather their weapons for an assault on the fort. The colonel posted one company at Moore's house to support those soldiers from the regiment who had been posted in various locations on picket duty. Before leaving his post Connally also stationed two companies to support Smoot's Battery, and then he and his remaining seven companies departed for Hill's Point.[58]

Minutes after the seven companies of the 55th North Carolina had began marching toward the captured battery they came upon Brigadier General Evander McIvor Law's assistant adjutant general, Captain Leigh R. Terrell. Two companies accompanied Terrell from the 48th Alabama Infantry Regiment. Captain Terrell had been sent by Law to relieve Captain David L. Boozeman's troops, which had been stationed in Stribling's Battery. Connally, having never seen the fort himself, asked Captain Terrell if a direct assault could succeed. Terrell advised Connally that a charge would be utterly futile: Not only would his men have to advance through a deep ravine, but also Connally's troops would be under direct fire from six Federal gunboats that now protected the battery. Taking the captain's information into consideration, Connally amended his decision and decided, correctly, not to attack the fort.[59]

Connally refused to give up on the captured battery altogether. In an attempt to ascertain if the Federals still occupied the battery the young colonel ordered his men to advance to within 500 or 600 yards of Stribling's Battery. Once his troops were in position Connally ordered his troops to form a battle line and lie down. In an effort to discover if Federal troops were still in the fort, Connally sent Lieutenant Colonel Maurice Smith and two companies to advance on the battery until fired upon. Smith and his detachment had not gone more than 60 yards when the Union troops opened fire. Smith quickly retreated, but several of the advanced troops returned fire. The Federals, seeing the discharging muskets, now knew where the advancing Rebels were located and opened on their location with everything they had. The captured guns, the howitzers, and the Union gunboats fired repeated shots at the area occupied by the 55th North Carolina. The "heavy cross-fire" was more than the regiment could bear and Connally quickly ordered his men to fall back out of the range of the grapeshot and shell.[60]

Fearing that the Federals were planning an assault on Smoot's Battery, Connally halted his men about a half a mile from Fort Huger and ordered them to form a second line of battle. Connally advanced skirmishers, under the command of Belo, to meet the supposed Union advance. The 55th held this line under intermittent fire from Federal gunboats until approximately 1:00 a.m. when Law ordered the regiment to fall back to the outskirts of nearby woods.[61]

The shelling that the 55th North Carolina experienced was "furious" even by the standards of those who had been under enemy fire in the past.[62] Joseph Hoyle, who had recently been promoted to lieutenant and had been suffering from dysentery during most of the siege, informed the readers of the *Spirit of the Age* about the loss of Stribling's Battery and the night the men of his regiment spent dodging Federal shells.

> One week ago an attack was made to secure the river below the town (Suffolk) from the passage of gunboats by planting batteries on the shore. But the enterprise proved a failure for the present, and after a day's engagement the guns were withdrawn. We lost one battery of five guns by the experiment—damage to the Yankees, if any, unknown. Our regiment (55th N.C.) was detailed to defend the batteries, but unfortunately for the one lost we were not ordered forward till it was taken. The enemy then poured shot and shell among us terribly, and our boys will long remember that memorable Sunday night; 8 or 10 were wounded in our regiment—only 2 badly—none killed.[63]

The Federals continued to rain shot and shell into the regiment's position even after Connally ordered his men to retreat to the outskirts of the nearby woods. One member of the regiment claimed that the 55th remained under fire "all night Sunday and nearly all day Monday," occasionally moving from place to place to avoid the Federal shells. Connally's men were only able to return fire when the Federals appeared a short distance from the river, which did not occur often.[64] Colonel Connally's official report on the loss of Stribling's Battery explains how the young officer perceived his orders and the day's events.

> I have the honor to state that in compliance with Special Orders, Numbers 3, Headquarters French's Command, dated April 17, three companies from my regiment marched on Friday night, the 17th, to Norfleet's house, on the Reed's Ferry road, and on Saturday morning, the

18th, reported to Major Shumaker for duty, as specified in the order. The fort intended for the reception of the two 32-pounder rifled pieces which my regiment was to support not having been completed, a detail of 60 men was, by order of Major Shumaker, made from the three companies to finish it. This having been done on Saturday evening, the 18th, the guns were placed in position during the night. On Saturday night, the 18th, I moved with the seven remaining companies of my regiment to Norfleet's house, and some time during the evening communicated with Major Shumaker, who advised me to place 4 men and a corporal at Le Compte's house, 4 men and a corporal at Reed's Ferry, 4 men and a corporal at a point nearly equi-distant between Le Compte's house and the ferry, and a company at Moore's house to support the three points mentioned. He also advised me to place a company near the gate at the entrance of the field in which the battery of 32-pounder pieces was situated to support it. In addition to this advice I received an order from General French in exact accordance with the major's advice, except that the company placed at Moore's should be placed at Le Compte's house. In posting my men I obeyed General French's orders to the letter except as to placing a company at Le Compte's house. This I did not do because Major Shumaker told me that he was thoroughly acquainted with the posts mentioned, and that it was better to place the company at Moore's, which I did. On Sunday evening, the 19th, Colonel Cunningham rode up to my quarters some time between 4 and 6 o'clock and told me in substance — I do not remember his language — that General French wished me to support the batteries. The order was general, and I immediately ordered Lieutenant-Colonel Smith and Major [A. H.] Belo to go and ascertain the position of the batteries, the number of men necessary for their support, the ground to be occupied by the support, and to report to me as early as possible. They had not been gone more than an hour or an hour and a half when I heard loud cheering in the direction of the river. A few moments afterwards an officer (I know not who) rode up and reported that Stribling's battery had been charged by the enemy and captured. I immediately ordered my regiment under arms, left one company at Moore's house to support the three posts mentioned above, two companies at the gate referred to support the battery of 32-pounder pieces, and with the seven other companies proceeded as rapidly as possible to the house nearest Stribling's battery, which was in the fort known as the Old Fort. There I came up with Captain [L. R.] Terrell, General Law's assistant adjutant-general, with two companies from the Forty-eighth Alabama Regiment. I inquired of the captain what he was doing there, and learned that he had been sent by General Law with the two companies mentioned to relieve the two companies which were in the fort when it was captured. He stated that he had arrived too late — that the fort had been taken before he could render assistance. I had never been to the fort, knew nothing of its position or the grounds around it, and asked Captain Terrell if he could give me any information concerning it, telling him that I intended to charge and retake the guns. He stated that he had been to the fort and knew all about its position; that it was situated on a point of land extending down to the river and that there was a deep ravine or marsh in its front over which my men could not possibly charge. In addition to this the fort was defended by six gunboats— three above and three below — and two land batteries across the river. I intended to charge and retake the fort, if possible, but upon learning its position and defense from Captain Terrell knew that it would be worse than folly to make the attempt. Wishing, however, to ascertain if it was still occupied by the enemy I moved up to within some 500 or 600 yards of the fort, formed line of battle, and ordered the men to lie down. I then ordered Lieutenant-Colonel Smith, with two companies deployed as skirmishers, to advance until fired upon, then to fall back upon the regiment. He had not advanced more than 50 or 60 yards before he was fired upon by the enemy's skirmishers, and, as ordered, fell back. The fire of my skirmishers discovered to the enemy the position of the regiment, when they opened upon me a heavy cross-fire from the six gunboats and two batteries. I immediately withdrew my regiment out of range of their grape-shot, and, thinking they would probably advance with the intention of capturing the battery of 32-pounder pieces in my rear, formed a second line of battle about half a mile from the Old Fort, threw forward skirmishers under command of Major Belo, and, although shelled from the gunboats, awaited patiently the enemy's advance until, I suppose, about 1 a.m., when General Law came up and told me that I was too far in advance and to fall back upon the skirt of woods some quarter of a mile in my rear; also to draw in my line of skirmishers. I obeyed General Law's orders. This, as stated above, was about 1 o'clock. At daylight, or very soon thereafter, General Hood came up and placed me under command of General Robertson, with whom I remained until near sundown, when I was ordered by General Hood, through General Robertson, to rejoin my brigade. General Law not attempting to retake the fort during the night of the 19th, and General Hood not attempting it on the 20th, establishes the fact that the attempt would have been injudicious, and that I was fortunate in meeting with Captain Terrell, whose statement relative to its position and defense alone prevented my making it. It will be seen, major, from this report that I did not have any men in or near the fort when it was captured; that it was attacked so soon after Colonel Cunningham left me that I could not possibly have placed men in position for its support; that when captured two companies from General Law's brigade were moving forward to relieve the two companies which were in it, and that I moved with all possible dispatch to recapture the fort, had it been possible. As I was the commanding officer on the field at the time, I deem it my duty to give Captain Terrell's statement concerning the action of the two companies under his command, which was that all the men in the two companies deserted him except nine. I do not know the names of the nine men who remained with the captain or I would give them, thinking they deserve favorable notice. The fire upon my regiment, as you may well imagine, was very heavy indeed, yet both officers and men received it unflinchingly and with veteran-like steadiness. Lieutenant-Colonel Smith, Major Belo, and Adjt. [H. T.] Jordan behaved with the utmost coolness and gallantry. I had 10 men wounded (1 mortally) and 1 man missing, supposed to have been killed.[65]

Connally, as inferred from his report, believed he had done all that was asked of him, and that his regiment had shown courage under fire.

The night of April 19 would prove to be a turning point for the men in the 55th North Carolina. The North Carolinians held together during a horrific night of shelling, and the loss of Stribling's Battery, however costly, would provide the backdrop that would inflame several officers to defend the honor of their regiment. The regiment's morale remained high and Lieutenant Hoyle remarked, "Our men are in good spirits and I believe will do their duty whenever called upon." Hoyle was not the only member of the 55th to boast of the regiment's performance. "I.G.C.," who was most likely Assistant Surgeon Isaac G. Cannady, claimed that the men, except for a few shirkers, "such as every regiment as large as ours is sure to have in it, men who are so constituted naturally, that they can not stand fire," did their duty. "I.G.C." went on to describe the pride the men of the 55th North Carolina felt after facing such immense enemy fire for the first time together as a regiment.

> Our own feelings, in regard to the conduct of the regiment, for that trying twenty hours without food, drink, or anything else but shells were a sense of pride thrilling our bosoms that out of over six hundred men there were so few who were so base as to lag behind when their comrades in arms were pressing forward, to drive the enemy from our sacred soil. These were the emotions which made us feel proud that we had been able to discharge our whole duty....[66]

The joyful mood that the men of the 55th North Carolina felt after bravely standing in the face of the enemy would not last long. The Confederate army, which could not stand to lose any artillery, had lost five pieces, and someone would have to account for the mishap. The Federals had captured Stribling's Battery and Longstreet was not in a celebratory mood. The loss of Fort Huger irritated the lieutenant general, who blamed the capture of the fort on a "lack of vigilance" on the part of the parties involved. The Confederate commander, however, did not single out any individual or regiment for the failure. French placed the blame on the garrison posted in Fort Huger, declaring, "It appears to me that if the garrison was surprised, they were negligent; if not surprised, they did not offer a sufficient resistance."[67]

The primary cause of the debacle was the relationship between Longstreet and French. French, fearing that Longstreet wanted a South Carolinian, Brigadier General Micah Jenkins, to take over his command, insisted upon joining his division, which included the 55th North Carolina, at the front. Longstreet offered French the command of the army's artillery, which the major general refused, but French agreed to offer his expertise in positioning the guns. After providing assistance and directing the placement of the artillery French, without informing Longstreet, reassigned command of the guns to the artillery chiefs of Pickett's and Hood's divisions.[68]

After the Federals captured Stribling's Battery, French informed Longstreet that the defense of the batteries was the responsibility of the respective divisions. French insisted that he had agreed only to assist in placing the guns and not to command or defend them. The major general also explained to Longstreet that the division commanders knew they were responsible for the batteries' defenses and offered as proof the fact that Hood's and Law's troops were stationed in Fort Huger when it was captured. Longstreet countered stating that he had placed French in command of all artillery "exclusively." Longstreet added that he had twice ordered the major general to send the 55th to defend the batteries. French denied that he had been so ordered and reaffirmed that the divisional commanders were to provide for the batteries' protection.[69]

The factors resulting in the loss of the battery are numerous, but neither Confederate general can completely escape responsibility. French, who should have remained in Petersburg, having no orders to join his men at Suffolk, should have informed his superior, Longstreet, of his decision to place the division commands in charge of the batteries. Longstreet failed to affirm his authority over French, and the "devious attempt to separate French from his command" created confusion in the chain of command.[70] Longstreet's final report on the capture of Stribling's Battery, although not relieving French of blame, does not excuse those involved, but does give the impression that the inexperience of some of the officers and men involved ultimately caused the debacle. Of those involved in the loss of the battery the lieutenant general stated, "I do not know that any of them deserve particular censure."[71]

Longstreet, who felt the 55th North Carolina could have retaken the fort with the minimal loss of 75 men, may not have officially blamed the regiment, but talk among the army besieging Suffolk indicated that at least some of the troops did. The nearly 300 entrenched Federals plus 700 troops sent to reinforce their position, and the nine pieces of artillery prepared to repulse any Rebel charge obviously were not considered when Longstreet made his report. The lieutenant general must not have known about the now nine Federal naval vessels that defend the fort from assault.[72] Had Longstreet seen the force arranged against the 55th first hand he most certainly would have agreed to suspend a counterattack.

Several experienced officers including French, Law, and Hood agreed that an attempt to retake the fort would be pure folly. Before the sun had risen on April 20 Hood had sent four companies of Texans and a detachment from the 55th under the command of Major Belo to scout the Federal position. Belo and his men advanced under cover of smoke that was emanating from a nearby barn and several farm houses that were left burning after the Union barrage. Belo was able to ascertain that the fort was held by a strong force of infantry and artillery, and covered by gunboats above and below the battery. Once Belo informed

Hood of the Federal force the major general agreed that an assault would still be foolish. After arriving at the front Longstreet still wanted an assault made, but after hearing Belo's intelligence the lieutenant general concurred with his fellow officers and suspended the attack.[73]

When one considers the scope of events that occurred during the Civil War, the loss of Stribling's Battery is inconsequential. However, for the officers and common soldiers of the 55th North Carolina it became a litmus test for courage and honor. A number of factors led to the capture of Stribling's Battery by Federal troops on April 19, and although the regiment cannot fully be excused from culpability, their role in the affair was minimal. The orders commanding Colonel Connally to move his troops closer to Fort Huger arrived just a little over an hour before the Federal assault. Connally still had ample time to move his men forward, but did not believe there was cause for alarm.

Colonel Connally stated in his official report that the order sent to him by French and delivered by Lieutenant Colonel Cunningham was "general" in nature and did not reflect any sense of urgency.[74] Connally's belief that the order was not imperative can be supported by the fact that French did not think his men were responsible for the fort's defense. If the major general was under the impression that the batteries were being defended by Hood's and Pickett's men he would not have felt it necessary to send an urgent message to Connally ordering him to do the same. French admitted in his report that he thought the protection of the batteries was the duty of Hood and Pickett.[75]

Colonel Connally, who had limited experience commanding troops in combat situations, was not fully aware of the need for tighter security around the batteries. Obviously, the young officer understood that the batteries were possible targets for Federal assaults, but he was not informed that Union troop transports had been spotted above Fort Huger. This vital intelligence, reported to Shumaker by Major Francis Boggs and Captain S. Taylor Martin earlier in the day on April 19, was never given to Connally.[76] It is quite possible that had Connally, as green as he was, known Federal troops had been seen in transports moving above Fort Huger he would have understood the gravity of the situation.

One may assume that Colonel Connally's lack of vigilance can be credited to his inexperience and to the fact that he was not properly informed of the seriousness of the situation. The colonel's failure to scout the terrain around Hill's Point properly, however, proved costly and may have been one factor leading to the loss of the battery. In his excellent study of the Suffolk campaign, Steven A. Cormier asserts that had Connally known the terrain he could have easily moved troops close enough to Stribling's Battery to repel the Federal assault.[77]

The generals may have disagreed on who was responsible for the Union success and refused to place any direct blame on one person or regiment, but the junior officers were not so forgiving. Several officers serving on Law's staff openly stated that they believed the 55th North Carolina had been responsible for the loss of Stribling's Battery. Their accusations would ultimately lead to a duel between officers.

The duel may have originated as an evolutionary progression from the traditional revenge fights that were prevalent in early Germanic and Celtic tribes in Europe. Family feuds were also known to have occurred among American hill-country yeomen in the South. Individuals dueled over an assortment of reasons, but mainly because another person had affronted their manliness or character. Fighting for one's honor became, for many men living in the South, a necessary device to bolster the cult of chivalry that was so evident in the Old South.[78]

2. October 1862–April 1863: For the Honor of the Regiment

Throughout the day of April 20, Colonel Connally received word that two of Brigadier General Law's staff officers had reported that the loss of Stribling's Battery was the fault of the 55th North Carolina. Connally, after verbally degrading the two officers he heard were responsible for the accusation, immediately went to Law's headquarters and asked the general if the report had been made. Law responded that two members of his staff had written the report. Connally, his anger rapidly intensifying, declared the report to be a lie and informed Law that he would speak to the two officers.[79]

The two officers, Captains Terrell and John Cussons were in their tent when Connally confronted them. Terrell admitted he had written the report and declared that he would stand by it. Cussons, however, informed Connally that he had nothing to do with the report, but stated that if the youthful colonel had ordered his men to retreat in the face of the enemy they had done so with extreme swiftness. Connally, not one to take an insult, told Cussons, "I hold you responsible sir, for that remark," Cussons bowed and declared he would be "most happy to accommodate" the young colonel.[80]

Connally mounted his horse and rode back to his headquarters to meet with his field officers, all of whom were under the age of 30. The young colonel informed his staff that they had to defend the honor of the regiment. He and Lieutenant Colonel Maurice Smith would challenge Terrell and Cussons to a duel. If the two senior officers were killed then every other member of the colonel's staff was expected to carry on until all were dead or unable to fight because of serious wounds. The officers agreed except for Smith, who, as a devout Christian, declared he did not believe in duels and would not participate. Smith's courage was widely known by the men, and the other officers respected his decision. Major Belo offered to take Smith's place and Connally agreed.[81]

Around 10:00 a.m. on the 21st the dueling parties prepared for their contest of honor. Connally and Belo arrived with their seconds (Captain E. Fletcher Satterfield of Company H and Lieutenant W. H. Townes of Company D) at the chosen location, an old field about a mile north of the 48th Alabama's camp. The two Alabama officers, having been challenged, had the privilege of choosing the weapons. Terrell chose double-barreled shotguns and Cussons selected Mississippi rifles. Once the weapons had been selected the distance was then set at 40 paces.[82] One witness to this event was a private in the 11th Mississippi Infantry Regiment, Christopher Chambers of Company B. Dr. B. F. Ward, a friend of Chambers, asked the young private to allow Belo to use his Mississippi rifle. Chambers reluctantly allowed Belo to borrow his weapon, stating that he felt it was a shame for men of his brigade to get into deadly contest.[83]

A number of onlookers arrived in time to witness the first duel between Belo and Cussons. Cussons, who had been an adventurer in California before the war, was referred to as "Law's wild man" by the men in his regiment and was reputedly a crack shot. At the given signal the two men fired their rifles but both bullets missed their mark, although Belo's shot went through Cussons' hat. Cussons asked Belo if he was satisfied; the major responded "No." The rifles were reloaded by the seconds and once again the men prepared to fire. Moments later the word was given and the two officers fired their rifles again. Once again Belo's shot missed, but the Alabama captain's aim had improved. Cussons' shot passed through Belo's coat and had grazed his neck. Upon completion of his second shot Cussons declared, "Major this is d—d poor shooting we are doing today. If we don't do better than this we will never kill any Yankees."[84]

About 150 yards across the field from Belo and Cussons, the seconds of Connally and

Terrell had come to an agreement. The truth of this agreement may never be known as both sides disagree on the final outcome. The North Carolinians claimed that the Alabamians offered to retract their report, but the men from Alabama stated that Captain Satterfield unconditionally withdrew the challenge.[85] As Belo and Cussons prepared to fire their rifles for a third time, Captain Satterfield suddenly arrived and informed the two officers that an agreement had been reached. Belo and Cussons met and shook hands, each thankful no serious injuries had occurred.[86]

Whether Longstreet or any of his immediate subordinates knew about the duel is unknown. A number of lower-ranking officers and enlisted men were fully aware of the incident and had witnessed the duel. Members of the 55th North Carolina understood what had happened and gleefully shared their feelings with friends. Those who had participated felt obligated to defend the honor of their regiment. Captain Satterfield told his father that it was his duty to support Colonel Connally, and Major Belo stated that he "had to challenge Cousins."[87] Duty and honor meant something to the men of the 55th and they were not about to let anyone say that they hadn't done everything that was asked of them.

Letters to North Carolina newspapers informed the state's citizens that the honor of the 55th North Carolina must be preserved. "I.G.C." wrote to the *Biblical Recorder* that someone had to be responsible for the loss of Stribling's Battery and sarcastically stated "if any thing goes wrong in a fight where there are any North Carolinians, they must bear the blame." He went on to declare that if something had not been done to correct the false belief that the 55th had acted in a cowardly fashion, the character of the men and officers of the regiment would be forever damaged. "I.G.C." wondered how the men of the regiment could face their loved ones, stating that such an incident would "make our friends and relatives at home blush with shame when our names are mentioned."[88]

Satisfied that the regiment's honor was intact, the officers and enlisted men of the 55th North Carolina continued their duty near Suffolk. On the evening of April 20 the regiment received orders to rejoin Davis's brigade, which was stationed south of Stribling's Battery. The Federals continued to shell the Confederate lines periodically, but with little effect. Lieutenant Hoyle wrote: "Our picket lines extend within rifle range of the enemy's fortifications, and picket firing is a daily business, but little damage is done."[89] One company from the 55th was hurriedly sent to perform picket duty near Hill's Point during the night on April 21. This company was sent without rations and must have been a concern of Major General French who sent Longstreet's adjutant general, Major G. Moxley Sorrel, a dispatch requesting that these men be relieved. When not skirmishing with the Federals, the men of the 55th constructed breastworks and rifle pits, and set up abatis around their positions. Occasionally soldiers were commandeered to tear up the tracks of two railroads near their position and then ordered to drag the iron away.[90]

The constant fighting around Suffolk dampened the spirits of many of the men of the 55th North Carolina. Private R. F. Smith told his wife that he was very "tarid of this war" and warned his brother to "stay away from the army if you can." Smith reported that he had been through hard times, but he knew that worse was yet to come. The lack of food also depressed the men, as they could not find much to eat.[91] Apparently the supplies being gathered by Longstreet's men were not being shared with the troops besieging Suffolk. Smith informed his wife, "Wee have not got any thing to eat half of our time." Dysentery, probably from polluted drinking water, spread throughout the regimental camps, adding to the depressing conditions.[92] Private Wilkerson wrote home on May 10 and informed his mother that she would hardly recognize him. Besides being sunburned the young private had lost weight and was "not well in the bowles in a long time." Wilkerson was quick to add, however, that he continued to do his duty even though he had been sick for some time.[93]

On the night of April 29 and into the morning of the 30th severe thunder and lightning storms hammered the men around Suffolk. The 11th Mississippi reported several men killed by the violent weather, as those on picket duty were hit hardest. Heavy skirmishing continued during the rest of April and on May 1 the Federals attacked the Rebels near the South Quay Road. The 99th New York Volunteers had been ordered to reconnoiter the Rebel rifle pits by Brigadier General Alfred Terry. Major General Peck had ordered the probing assault to solidify his belief that Longstreet's forces were still besieging Suffolk in large numbers. Hooker believed he could defeat Lee's army if he could prevent Longstreet from reinforcing the general's troops stationed in northern Virginia. The Confederate works in front of Terry's position had become unusually quiet and Peck, wanting to be sure his recommendations to Hooker were accurate, sent the New Yorkers forward. Peck's questions were answered after the Federals were forced to retreat after encountering a strong contingent of Confederates. The detachment reportedly had 13 men killed and 31 wounded.[94]

The strong force of Confederates that pushed the Union troops back belonged to Joseph Davis's brigade. The Union attack began with a 30-minute artillery barrage aimed at weakening the forward Rebel pickets and causing confusion in their rear. Around 4:30 p.m. on May 1, 210 soldiers from the 99th New York Volunteers, under the command of Lieutenant Colonel Richard Nixon, advanced against the Confederate earthworks.[95] One member of the 99th New York Volunteers recalled years later the terrific battle and stated, "before us we saw the smoke and fire as it issued from the enemy's rifles; beyond, emerging from the woods, regiments to reinforce them marched steadily; at a glance we saw a shell explode in the midst of one of their battalions [Belo's men]; they scarcely heeded it, and closing their ranks, on they came."[96]

When the attack began, Colonel Connally ordered Captain Peter Mull and Company F to reinforce the Rebel troops already in the forward rifle pits. Mull and his men advanced rapidly through a severe artillery barrage, and although several of the company's best soldiers were killed, their ranks continued to move forward. Connally, judging that more troops were needed, sent Major Belo and four of the regiment's companies to support the embattled Confederates. Determined to prove that they were not cowards and were willing to fight to the death, the invigorated troops of the 55th marched on through shell and ball.[97]

Private Wilkerson wrote to his father several days later and described the engagement that he participated in on May 1. Just as veterans of World War II, Korea, Vietnam, and other armed conflicts that occurred in the twentieth century rarely expressed the horrors of battle in their letters home, Private Wilkerson abruptly ended his battlefield descriptions before revealing too much.

> I tell you we saw pretty rough times that evening, the Balls an Shells falling an bursting all around us. We were under heavy shelling for better than 2 hours from the yankees breast works and batteries, I can't begin to tell nothing about it so I will change the subject.[98]

The 55th North Carolina was the only regiment on the battle line that was armed with smoothbore muskets, which limited its effective firing range to about 100 yards. In his history of the regiment Charles M. Cooke stated that he believed the Federals knew the troops from the 55th were armed with inferior weapons and thus chose their line to attack. This statement may have been accurate, but Major Belo's strategy of ordering his men to hold their fire until the Yankees were well within range of their muskets may have drawn the Union troops into their position. Years after the war ended Belo gave his account of how the soldiers in the regiment proved their courage under fire.

> I double-quicked my men to the pits without much loss in spite of the heavy firing. On arriving I instructed the captains to order the men not to fire until I gave the command. The two regiments came in good order within easy range of our muskets, and I paid no attention to the firing on our right or left. They came in easy range and I gave the command to fire and broke them up in great disorder. They retired in confusion, but were rallied by their officers and re-formed and made a second charge. This time I let them come a little closer and ordered my men to take good aim and shoot low. At the command a deadly volley was poured into them and continued so that theywere routed back inside their breastworks. Just about this time Colonel [Maurice T.]Smith came and presented Colonel Connally's compliments and desired to know if I wanted additional reinforcements. I returned my compliments to Colonel Connally and said, "No, I think the battle is over and won."[99]

Belo had allowed the Federals to advance so near the regiment's line that the troops in the pits were able to see distinguishing facial features. Cooke wrote, "Every one of the men in the rifle pits had his musket in position and his finger on the trigger, and at the word "fire" the sound of Major Belo's command, seemed to expand into one grand roll of musketry."[100] Just as Israel Putnam at Bunker Hill bellowed "Don't fire until you see the whites of their eyes! Then, fire low," Major Belo had successfully maneuvered the Federals into a deadly vortex and proved that the men of the 55th North Carolina could stand firm in the face of their enemy. Wilkerson wrote that the 55th had killed or wounded several hundred Federal troops, most of whom were lying within 100 yards of the Confederate rifle pits. As the rest of regiment moved forward to support their embattled comrades, the Union soldiers had had enough and began falling back.[101]

During the assault two Federal color-bearers had been shot down and a third waved his regiment on as he crawled forward. A member of the 55th North Carolina informed the readers of the *Biblical Recorder* of the incident. His words, while seemingly praising the young man's courage, declared his utter contempt for the Union.

> The stars and stripes are now trailing in the dust, having twice fallen and the bearer has humbled himself by crawling on his knees, dragging his rag behind him, and thus may it ever be when that once proud flag waves over a band of robbers and thieves, trying to devastate and pillage our homes, and may they ever meet with the same reception, and always return in the same confusion with their flag trailing in the dust, whenever they advance on our courageous boys.[102]

Content that they had proven their worth, the men of the 55th North Carolina gloated over their small victory. Encouraged by the Mississippi regiments that were part of their brigade, the North Carolina troops deservingly felt a sense of pride and were ready to move on to their next engagement. Prophetically, Private Smith had written home near the end of April telling his loved ones that times were only going to get worse. Private Smith could not have known how accurate his words would be. As the summer of 1863 dragged on, the men of the 55th would meet the Federals again in a little corner of Pennsylvania.

On the evening of May 3, Longstreet sent orders to his division commanders that they must withdraw their troops from Suffolk. During the final days of April, Lee had finally become aware of Hooker's intentions and wired the War Department requesting reinforcements. By April 30 Longstreet had received General Samuel Cooper's message ordering him to return to Lee's army. Longstreet began preparing for a withdrawal of his troops on May 1 by ordering his chief quartermaster, Major S. P. Mitchell, to move the supply trains back across the Blackwater River. With a sense of urgency Longstreet informed Major Mitchell to make this move as quickly as possible. After recalling his foraging troops the lieutenant general was ready to return to Lee.[103]

Longstreet's troops never arrived in time to support Lee, but even without the additional troops the Confederates defeated Hooker at the battle of Chancellorsville. The battle, however, was costly for the Confederacy, especially with the death of Thomas "Stonewall" Jackson on May 10. But once again Lee proved to be too much for the Federals. Longstreet ordered his divisions to withdraw simultaneously using the same roads they had used when they had advanced toward Suffolk. French's division was ordered to take up a defensive position near Holland Corners until Pickett's division had completely withdrawn. Davis's brigade was in the lead of French's division as it marched along the South Quay Road to Holland's Corner where they took up defensive positions to support the withdrawal.[104]

During the first week of May, French issued General Order No. 4, informing his two division commanders, Davis and Jenkins, to be prepared to move toward Franklin Depot on May 3. The brigade marched away from Suffolk, resting periodically, and finally reached its old camp near Franklin on the morning of May 5.[105]

Around 6:00 a.m. the 55th North Carolina, with the rest of Davis's brigade, began marching toward Ivor Station. After a five-mile march over deep muddy roads, which were made harder to travel on because of the ruts left by the wagons and artillery, the regiment cut short its advance. After a short evening march the 55th halted and bivouacked for the night. A heavy rain continued throughout the night making rest difficult and the roads even worse than they had been the day before. The next day the regiment continued its march toward Ivor Station, but orders soon arrived informing the unit to turn around and return to Franklin Depot. By the 7th of May, Longstreet had received word from General Lee that Major General Joseph Hooker and his Army of the Potomac had been defeated and were retreating back across the Rappahannock River. Lee informed Longstreet that the crisis that had made his advance to the Rappahannock line imperative had passed and there was no need to "distress" the troops with a forced march.[106]

On the night of May 7 the 55th North Carolina arrived at Camp Hoke, their new position located about 12 miles from Franklin. This new camp was located about four miles from the Blackwater River. Davis's brigade was again ordered to protect the line along the Blackwater, and the men spent the much-needed repose from fighting Federals washing their clothes and nurturing their sore and blistered feet.[107]

Steven A. Cormier contends in his scholarly study of the Suffolk campaign that Longstreet's foraging efforts in North Carolina and southeastern Virginia were "most impressive." Although the Confederate Subsistence Department's files were destroyed in the Richmond fire of April 1865, one can reason that Lee received more than enough bacon and other supplies to sustain Lee's Gettysburg campaign. Cormier asserts that even if the conservative estimate of 1,300,000 pounds of pork was gathered by Longstreet's foraging parties during the Suffolk campaign, and the Army of Northern Virginia consumed 37,500 pounds of pork per day, the amount gathered during Old Pete's operations would have sustained Lee's men for more than a month, making possible the invasion of the North.[108]

Although the men of the Army of Northern Virginia were also able to acquire supplies along their march north, the additional supplies provided by Longstreet's campaign would allow Lee more latitude in forming his strategy for the invasion knowing he had adequate provisions for his troops.

Some historians contend that the Suffolk campaign was a failure primarily because Longstreet did not capture the Federal garrison at Suffolk and did not position his troops in a way more easily accessible to assist General Lee if the need arose, which of course it did. This argument, though true in many respects, ignores the fact that it was Lee's duty, as the overall commander, to decide how long Longstreet's forces remained south of the James River where they were too far away to be recalled if the Federals began advancing and threatening the Army of Northern Virginia's position along the Rappahannock. Lee, in what is possibly his greatest military feat, shattered Hooker's command and forced the Federals back across the Rappahannock without Longstreet, which makes the argument academic. However, had the Army of the Potomac succeeded in driving the Confederates back toward Richmond the burden of defeat would have rested solely on General Lee's shoulders.

During the siege of Suffolk, Federal casualties were 41 killed, 223 wounded, and two missing. Confederate casualties amounted to about 900, of whom 400 were reported missing or captured. Although Longstreet's adjutant, Major Sorrell, claimed that nothing had been gained from the siege of Suffolk, the men of the 55th North Carolina gained some valuable experience.[109] Not only did the common soldiers learn that their officers would defend the honor of the regiment, but they also fought together as a cohesive unit and prevailed against their enemy. One member of the regiment exalted the men of the 55th North Carolina in a letter to the *Biblical Recorder*.

> The standing of the 55th regiment is yet high; and she gained a reputation on yesterday of which veterans might well be proud. Individual instances of bravery might be mentioned, but where every one did his duty, we might do injustice by mentioning any.[110]

It is not known how many soldiers serving in the 55th North Carolina were killed or wounded during the Suffolk campaign, because no official casualty list has been found. For the May 1 engagement "J.G.C." reported to the *Biblical Recorder* that the regiment had 11 men wounded, four of whom were seriously injured.[111] Among the wounded were Noah W. Cook, whose wounded right leg was later amputated, and G. W. Randall, who was injured in the arm. The heavy skirmishing that encompassed the regiment's time in Suffolk also motivated several individual acts of gallantry. Corporal Westly A. Williams of Company F was "publicly commended" by Colonel Connally for his courage under fire. Williams's bravery earned him a promotion to sergeant in May.[112] Encouraged by their performance on May 1 the men of the 55th were eager to meet the enemy once again on the field of battle.

3

June–July 1863: Forgotten Courage — the Regiment at Gettysburg

"Don't let the Mississippians get ahead of you"

On May 4, 1863, several members of the 117th New York Volunteers crept into the Confederate trenches and rifle pits that surrounded the city of Suffolk and found them abandoned. These troops quickly returned to Suffolk and reported their discovery to their commanding officer, Major General Peck. Peck sent a small detachment of cavalry to follow the Confederates.[1]

Davis assigned his men the task of guarding the fords and crossings of the Blackwater River. By May 10 the 55th North Carolina was posted on the road between Ivor Station and Franklin Depot. The regiment's campsite was about 12 miles above Franklin and, according to Lieutenant Hoyle, the men spent little time in camp because the majority of their time was spent "marching up and down the [Blackwater] river, conforming to the expected movements of the enemy." The regiment spent several days near Joiner's Church waiting for further orders and anticipating a fight with the Federals. Although no major engagements occurred near the Blackwater the 55th participated in several skirmishes "nearly every day."[2]

The 55th North Carolina spent much of May performing picket duty and building earthworks. This was tedious duty and letters from soldiers indicated that this period of time tended to lower the morale of the regiment. During this time Private Wilkerson and several other soldiers from the 55th spent time erecting posts for stringing telegraph line. This 12-man work detail set up posts from Ivor Station to Franklin, Virginia. They enjoyed the rare pleasure of eating eggs and freshly made bread during these days. Wilkerson enjoyed these luxuries, especially considering that the tasty treats sent to him from home had arrived spoiled. The work detail wasn't easy, but Wilkerson wrote his parents that he enjoyed it more than being in camp. When the men were not working they spent their time fishing and swimming in the Blackwater River. Foraging also became a favorite diversion for the men. Apple brandy was one of the most sought-after items in addition to food stuffs they desired to supplement their meager diet.[3] It was also during May that the 55th North Carolina officially became part of the Army of Northern Virginia, paving the way for their participation in the battle of Gettysburg.

The battle of Chancellorsville had lifted the spirits of the fighting men of the army, but the loss of Stonewall Jackson detracted from the joy they should have felt about winning such a stunning victory. The war continued to grind on with no immediate end in sight and Lee had no time to celebrate or to mourn. On May 7, General Lee wrote to President Davis requesting that his army be strengthened by reinforcements. After the battle of Chancellorsville, Lee began to focus on taking the offensive and knew he would need more troops considering that his next battle would be on northern soil, and the Confederates would not enjoy the advantages of knowing the terrain and being able to fight on the defensive. Before Chancellorsville there had been several attempts to transfer part of Lee's army to the west, where Vicksburg, Mississippi, was in jeopardy. The defeat of the Army of the Potomac would cause the Confederate armies fighting in the western theater to renew their demands for reinforcements. To supply the west with troops, President Jefferson Davis would have to strip them from Lee's army.[4]

On May 16 Lee met with President Davis and his cabinet to discuss the possibilities of an offensive campaign in the East. Although the Confederate high command most likely discussed Lee's strategy, the decision had apparently already been made. On the morning of May 16, as Lee met with the Confederate cabinet, Major General Pickett's division and two regiments of North Carolina cavalry were moving north from the Suffolk area. In his study of Lee's northern offensives Michael A. Palmer asserts that Davis invited his cabinet to meet with Lee only as a formality and possibly in an attempt to spread the responsibility "for what he knew to be a high-stakes gamble."[5]

By May 18 Lee was back at his headquarters near Hamilton's Crossing and beginning to make preparations for an offensive campaign. The cabinet, with the exception of Postmaster General John Reagan, had endorsed another invasion of the North.[6] The proposed invasion was not the only concern on Lee's mind during May. With Stonewall Jackson gone the Army of Northern Virginia needed a new corps commander, and replacing the incomparable lieutenant general may have been more troublesome for Lee than planning the offensive. Unable to find an officer he felt would be competent to command Jackson's old corps, Lee decided to divide his army into three smaller corps, as opposed to the two-corps composition that had served him so well since leaving the peninsula. While Longstreet remained in charge of the First Corps, Lee placed Lieutenant General Richard "Dick" Ewell in command of Jackson's Second Corps and A. P. Hill in charge of the newly formed Third Corps. Both Ewell and Hill had served previously as division commanders.[7]

Hill was a Virginian and graduated from West Point in 1847. He saw limited action during the Mexican War, but fought well in the Seminole War in Texas and Florida. Hill resigned from the United States Army in March of 1861, and became the colonel of the 13th Virginia Volunteers. He moved swiftly up the ranks until being appointed lieutenant general in May 1863 after the death of Stonewall Jackson.[8]

On May 20 Lee forwarded his recommendation to President Davis and promptly received approval. The Army of Northern Virginia, which had previously consisted of eight divisions, was expanded to nine, each corps comprised of three divisions. Henry Heth, new to the Army of Northern Virginia, was placed in command of one of the divisions in A. P Hill's Third Corps.[9] Heth was a graduate of the West Point Class of 1842, and served in the

United States Army during the Mexican War. The major general's division was organized on May 30 and contained the brigades of Pettigrew, Archer, Brockenbrough, and Davis.[10] The 55th North Carolina had become part of the Army of Northern Virginia.

Davis's brigade spent the remaining days of May swimming and fishing and reading copies of the newly arrived *Les Miserables* by Victor Hugo. Concerns for their loved ones at home also remained heavy on the minds of the individual soldiers as a letter written to the *Biblical Recorder* shows. The letter also provides insight into the provisions the men were receiving during this time.

> The extravagant prices of all the necessaries of life demanded by those who had them stored away was a just cause of uneasiness to the soldiers in the field. Receiving only eleven dollars a month, and a fourth of a pound of bacon with a small quanity of flour per day, they could do but little to aid their families at home. The fear that they were suffering has done more to sink the spirits of the soldier and to discourage him than the hardships and dangers of the camp, or the superior numbers of the foe that confronted him. Danger he could have met without shrinking, hardships he would have endured without a murmur, could he have been assured that his wife and little ones were free from want.[11]

Several of the men in the 55th North Carolina spent their time guarding a bridge that crossed the Blackwater. As they relaxed, the Army of Northern Virginia prepared to advance north. On June 2 Davis ordered his men to cook three days' rations and to be prepared to march. That day, as a heavy rain fell, the soldiers in Davis's brigade struck their tents and gathered what items they could carry. The rain continued to fall, and Davis's troops were soaked as they tried to sleep without the benefit of their tents to ward off the weather, and as water pelted their unprotected bodies.[12]

On June 3 at 3:00 a.m. Davis's brigade prepared to march, and by 5:00 a.m. the troops were moving toward Ivor Station. After five hours of marching the formation reached Ivor Station and around 3:00 p.m., after several hours of rest, boarded railcars for Petersburg. The brigade arrived in Petersburg two hours later and then marched toward Richmond the following morning. After a 23-mile march the men of Davis's command rested for the night several miles south of Richmond. By June 6 most of Davis's brigade had reached Hanover Junction, having traveled by rail. The 55th North Carolina and one Mississippi company, however, marched from Richmond to Hanover Junction. Private Wilkerson informed his parents that his regiment had been ordered to protect the supply wagons and therefore had the misfortune of having to walk.[13]

By June 7 they finally arrived at Fredericksburg having spent four hard days riding railcars and marching. They relieved the remaining troops of Ewell's Second Corps who were still on picket duty around the town. Private Wilkerson described the marching as very difficult, and told his parents that many soldiers had become so tired of carrying their supplies that they tossed their extra clothes away. He also wrote that hundreds of pairs of shoes, which had either worn out or begun cutting into the men's feet, were left behind as the men marched on.[14]

Once at Fredericksburg, Davis's brigade began performing picket duty on a line about 42 miles long. The 55th North Carolina joined the rest of the Third Corps. A. P. Hill had been ordered to resist any attempt by the Federals to cross the Rappahannock in force. He had also been instructed by Lee to conceal the movement of the Confederate army and to fall back toward Richmond if attacked by a superior force.[15] On the other side of the river the Federals were present in force, which proved too tempting to Rebel scouts, who occasionally spoke to or taunted the blue-clad soldiers. The Confederate artillery occasionally shelled the Federal lines, but according to Private Wilkerson the Union artillery did not return fire during this time. Lee had ordered A. P. Hill to make periodic demonstrations to deceive the Federals into believing that the Army of Northern Virginia was still encamped around Fredericksburg.[16]

By the beginning of June the Army of Northern Virginia was better equipped than it ever had been previously, and the rank and file were in high spirits. The 55th North Carolina was, in the opinion of the regiment's historian, "both in respects to its discipline and its appearance one of the finest regiments in the army." As the men of the regiment moved into their positions along the Rappahannock they were well clothed and the company ranks were full.[17]

As the soldiers in the 55th North Carolina kept watch along the river they expected a Federal attack at any moment. The observations made by the men in the ranks were not completely without merit. Hooker had proposed to President Lincoln that the Army of the Potomac strike the rear of Lee's army at Fredericksburg and then withdraw and assault the rest of the Confederate troops who were moving north. Lincoln disagreed with Hooker, explaining to the general that such a move would entangle his army across the Rappahannock "like an ox jumped half over a fence and liable to be torn by dogs front and rear without a fair chance to gore one way or kick the other."[18] Hooker did make several demonstrations against the Confederate troops stationed near Fredericksburg, but made no serious attempts to engage the Rebels. Although the Federals made no major assaults against the Confederate works they began shelling the Rebel positions occasionally, and at times severely.[19]

The concerns and duties the men shared along the battle line seemed less onerous as their rations increased. Private R. F. Smith wrote a letter to his wife that the men in his company were "gitting more to eat then wee was when wee was down on black water." The increase in food, however, did not lift the young private's spirits. Praying for the bitter conflict to end he told his wife "I hope and trust the war will soon end and the balance of my time that I haf to live in this world I want to spend with you as long as wee both live."[20]

Although the men of the 55th North Carolina were eating more, the overall health of the regiment declined shortly after their arrival near Fredericksburg. Lieutenant Hoyle reported that the decline in health was most likely caused by the poor quality of the water the men were drinking. Hoyle also reported that during the night of June 14 the Federal forces in front of the 55th North Carolina had retreated back across the Rappahannock. During the night the men on picket duty distinctly heard the clatter of men and supplies moving across pontoon bridges. Believing the noise indicated an imminent attack the troops braced themselves for an assault they were sure would be coming in the morning. However, as the sun broke forth the Confederates were amazed to see that the Federals had withdrawn. Hoyle reported that the supplies, especially several guns left behind by the Yankees, indicated that they had made a hasty withdrawal.[21] The Union troops, part of Major General John Sedgwick's VI Corps, retreated back across the river and rejoined the rest of the Federal army that was moving northward. By June 13, 10 days after Lee's troops had begun marching northward and west, Hooker realized that the Army of Northern Virginia was on the move and immediately ordered his men to pull back from their positions near Fredericksburg.[22]

Davis's troops vacated their defensive positions in front of Fredericksburg on June 14 as A. P. Hill's corps followed the rest of Lee's army toward Pennsylvania. Hill's corps marched west along the south side of the Rappahannock. To prevent the Federals from moving against the Third Corps, Lee ordered Longstreet's First Corps to march northward along the east slope of the Blue Ridge Mountains to lure Hooker away from Hill's troops. Lee's plan succeeded and Hill's men continued their march unmolested.[23] The men were not sure exactly where they were headed, but believed they would soon be in a fight with the Federals. At least Lieutenant Joseph Hoyle believed as much as he confided in a letter to his wife.

> Our troops have already penetrated into the valey of Va., and a few days ago, General Ewell's corps captured Winchester including 12,000 prisoners. This may not be the correct number. We are going up in that direction and it may be you will hear of us going into Maryland before we stope. I do not know where Hooker's yankee army is but I expect we will have plenty fighting to do before we reach the Potomac River. It is very warm and hard marching, but we all stand it as well as could be expected thus far.[24]

A sense of patriotic euphoria accompanied many of the men marching north that summer. Hoyle asserted in the same correspondence that he was ready to give the last full measure of devotion in order that the Southern Confederacy would succeed.

> Dear Sarah, we are beginning to see hard times now, but I am very willing to endure them, for we are no better than poor soldiers who have to endure such hardships. I am willing to do my part for my country, and if it is God's will that my life should be sacrificed in the service of my country, I will die contented.[25]

The 55th North Carolina moved northward traveling about 15 miles a day. On June 16 the regiment passed through an area where the battle of Chancellorsville had been fought. Several of the regiment's officers described the carnage that still remained on the battlefield.

> Passed over the battle ground of Chancellorsville and although the battle had been fought about 30 days I had to stuff my nose full of cotton to prevent being knocked down by an odious scent arising from at least 1000 dead horses lying in close proximity to the road. I saw several dead Yankees lying on the roadside that had never been buried.[26]

Captain Edward D. Dixon of Company C recalled many years later the conditions on the battlefield where he and his men marched. Dixon stated that the trees and bushes were riddled with bullets from rifles and some were completely severed from artillery fire. The young captain declared that there "was no lack of evidence as to the slaughter of men" that had occurred on the field just one month earlier. Dixon ended his description prematurely, stating that to "fully describe the scene would be entirely too gruesome."[27]

Captains Howell G. Whitehead and Dixon were not the only ones moved by the dreadful battlefield. Assistant Surgeon LeGrand James Wilson of the 42nd Mississippi Infantry Regiment also commented on the scene in his memoirs written at the turn of the century.

> It had been about six weeks since that terrible battle was fought, and the stench was, in places,perfectly awful. The little hillocks, scattered here and there along the route for several miles, were silent witnesses of the savagery of man, and the horrors of war. These men had been buried hastily, and many of them hardly covered beneath the sod, and here and there an arm or a leg was sticking out, the flesh stripped from the bones by the beasts of the field and the vultures of the air that had congregated in countless numbers to satiate their hunger with human food.[28]

Unfortunately for the men serving in Davis's brigade, they would soon experience firsthand the type of carnage they observed while traveling through the Chancellorsville battlefield.

The dreadful sights witnessed by the soldiers as they marched through the Chancellorsville battlefield did not sap them of their patriotic feelings. Lieutenant Hoyle informed his wife that he and the men in his regiment were beginning to see some hard times, but were very willing to do their part for their country. As Hoyle had said, "if it is God's will that my life should be sacrificed in the service of my country, I will die contented."[29]

As Davis's brigade moved north the men observed the beautiful Virginia countryside and the majestic Blue Ridge Mountains. One evening the men watched a splendid lightning storm, which was "blinding to the eye, and beautiful and grand beyond description."[30] All of the towns and sights, however, were not equally pleasant as the rest. On June 17 and 18 the regiment passed through "a very dreary looking country" and several days later marched through a small town named Funktown. Captain Whitehead stated that the name suited the village because it was "the lowest looking place & the meanest people" he'd ever seen.[31]

On June 19 the brigade passed through Sperryville and marched up the eastern slopes of the Blue Ridge near Chester Gap. Davis's men marched 27 miles on that day, but were up at dawn the following day. The brigade spent the first half of June 20 struggling up to the summit of Chester Gap. By noon they had reached the top and were permitted to rest. From their elevated position the men were able to see the beauty of the Shenandoah Valley. Before the day ended the men were once again on the march and they moved down the western slopes of the Blue Ridge. After marching to within three miles of Front Royal the brigade received orders to bivouac for the evening.[32]

At 4:00 a.m. on June 21 the brigade started through Front Royal and traveled down the Winchester Turnpike. Several citizens of the town greeted the men and gave them water. After passing Front Royal the command moved east and began marching toward the Potomac River. While marching north the brigade crossed through the Shenandoah River. Captain Whitehead wrote in his diary that the men "shucked" their clothing and waded through the river. Unfortunately the bottom of the river was "covered with sharp rocks" and the crossing was a painful one. Davis's troops marched about 12 miles that day before camping in a splendid grove approximately three miles from Berryville. The following day the men rested and regained their strength.[33]

As the men of Davis's brigade closed the distance between themselves and the Potomac they began to experience a sense of enthusiasm, which spread through the ranks. LeGrand Wilson stated that the men were excited that they would soon be bringing the war to the North.[34] While marching toward Maryland the brigade passed through Charles Town and received a warm welcome. Captain Whitehead wrote in his diary that the "ladies were very enthusiastic & a Dixie flag waved over every house." The rabid abolitionist John Brown had been executed in the town in 1860 and the historical significance did not go unnoticed by Captain Whitehead, who wrote that the "Court house in which old Brown was condemned to the gallows had been converted into a horse stable."[35] Lieutenant Hoyle informed his wife of the tumultuous reception the men received as they marched through the town.

> We passed through Charlestown this morning, amid the cheering demonstration of a thousand hats and handkerchiefs. The ladies not only showed us sympathy by waving hats and handkerchiefs, but were very generous in giving us bread, milk, butter, honey, etc. I have never seen a more unanimous show of kindness. We passed in sight of Harper's Ferry, going above, and camped in a mile or two of the Potomac, near Shepperds Town.[36]

On June 25 the men of Davis's brigade waded across the Potomac River below Shepherdstown.[37] LeGrand Wilson witnessed the crossing and recalled the glorious sight many years later.

> The scene which presented itself was enough to arouse enthusiasm in every southern heart.Over the hills beyond the river as far as the eye could reach a line of gray soldiers were marching, cheering as they went, their bright arms glittering in the sunshine. Below at the river the men were marching across, holding their cartridge boxes up to keep them dry.[38]

After crossing the Potomac the 55th North Carolina marched through Sharpsburg, Maryland, and camped near Hagerstown, Maryland. On June 27 Davis's brigade marched through the town and bivouacked near Fayetteville, Pennsylvania. The following day was a Sunday and the 55th rested. Many of the weary troops washed their clothes for the first time in weeks and spent the day relaxing and eating good meals. The brigade was on the move again early the next morning and marched through the mountains near Cashtown, Pennsylvania. By the evening of June 30 they had reached Cashtown and were well into Pennsylvania. During the long trek north Lieutenant Hoyle was suffering from poor health, but the determined officer continued to march with his regiment.[39]

As Hill's corps marched into Pennsylvania, Longstreet's troops followed close behind near Chambersburg, and a part of Richard Ewell's corps, which had crossed into the Keystone State over a week before Hill, was at Carlisle preparing to move into Harrisburg. Another part of Ewell's corps, under the command of Major General Jubal Early, was entering York. Lee knew where all of his principal lieutenants were except for Major General J. E. B. Stuart.[40]

The flamboyant cavalry commander had dashed northward in mid–June after his troopers were surprised at the battle of Brandy Station. The question of whether Lee had authorized Stuart to lead his troopers around the Union army is still being debated by historians and is not the subject of this study. Unfortunately Stuart's movements had led him farther away from Lee and had left the Army of Northern Virginia blind in enemy territory. Without his cavalry to guide his movements, Lee did not know if he was "the hunter or the hunted."[41]

While Lee's army moved north, Hooker hesitated. When he finally decided to move his forces, Lee's troops had already crossed into Pennsylvania. Hooker had yielded to pressure from Washington and had finally sent Major General Alfred Pleasonton and his cavalry corps out to find Lee, but made no further moves. While Lee moved onto Union soil Hooker strengthened his position around the Bull Run Mountains. By June 24, after Lee had already succeeded in stealing a two-day march on Hooker, the befuddled Union officer finally realized that the Confederates were invading the North.[42]

On June 25, the same day the 55th North Carolina had crossed the Potomac, Hooker had finally ordered his army to move. He made several good decisions in a vain attempt to recapture the initiative, but he soon began bombarding Washington with pleas for more troops. Hooker's requests were denied. Possibly looking for an excuse to give up his command, the major general refused to yield and again requested that his army be reinforced with troops posted to protect the capital. Once again he was turned down. Then Hooker asked that the defense of Harper's Ferry be abandoned and the troops there be transferred to his command. When Major General Henry Halleck, the general in chief of the Union armies, refused this request as well, Hooker offered to resign. President Lincoln accepted

Hooker's resignation and on June 28 placed Major General George Gordon Meade in command of the Army of the Potomac.[43]

Although the tired Confederates were now in the land of plenty many of the soldiers, including those in the 55th North Carolina, behaved reasonably well. There were of course those who stole whatever they could get their hands on and destroyed property in a vain attempt to show the northern populous what the South had been enduring for the past two years, but many of the troops respected the wishes of their commander. General Lee had issued a proclamation, General Orders No. 72, prohibiting the destruction or damaging of private property and only allowed certain officers to seize needed materials.[44] A soldier serving in Davis's brigade stated that while on provost duty in Hagerstown he had been ordered to keep Rebel troops out of the town. He claimed that only a few arrests were made because "General Lee had issued very stringent orders about molesting private property and committing depredations, and his men well understood him."[45]

As the 55th North Carolina marched into Pennsylvania many of the homes they passed had been abandoned. Several individuals had left in such haste that they had forgotten to shut their doors, but as tempting as it was the men stayed in their ranks. Although it is unknown if the fighting men of the regiment plundered the homes they passed they did acquire food and other necessary provisions from the local inhabitants. Most of the items that were seized were paid for in Confederate currency or bartered for.[46]

During the early hours of June 29 Davis's brigade was sent out to protect Confederate engineers who were ordered to map the topography of the Pennsylvania countryside for General Lee. The brigade marched approximately six miles away from Cashtown and set up camp for the night. By the following evening the engineers had finished their work and Davis's troops marched back to Cashtown before nightfall.[47]

On June 30 Heth ordered Brigadier General James Johnston Pettigrew to march his brigade into Gettysburg to reconnoiter the area and to seize any provisions, especially any shoes that he found. Pettigrew's men traveled the eight miles between Cashtown and Gettysburg following the Chambersburg Pike, but were met by a strong Federal picket line. The Federal troopers were members of Brigadier General John Buford's cavalry brigade, and had been ordered to prohibit Confederate forces from scouting the Union position. Pettigrew, who was unaware of the size of the Federal force in front of him, and who had been ordered not to encourage an engagement, decided to withdraw his troops without attempting to push forward.[48]

After returning to Cashtown, Pettigrew immediately went to inform Heth that Federal forces were in Gettysburg. As Pettigrew was relating his information to Heth, A. P. Hill appeared at the major general's headquarters. Believing, as Lee did, that the Federals were moving west, and not north, Hill concluded that the Union cavalrymen seen near Gettysburg were merely a scouting party. Dismissing any cause for alarm, Heth asked Hill if he could take his whole division back to the town the next day and the lieutenant general agreed. Pettigrew protested, insisting that there might be a large number of Federal infantry near Gettysburg, but both Hill and Heth ignored his pleas.[49]

At five o'clock on the morning of July 1, Heth's division marched toward Gettysburg. Brigadier General James J. Archer's brigade was placed in the lead followed by Davis's troops. Archer and Davis had been ordered to reconnoiter the area and occupy the town. The column moved toward the small Pennsylvania town unaware of the forces that were marching to oppose them. The weather was warmer than it had been during the past few days and showed every sense that the day would be very hot.[50]

3. *June–July 1863: Forgotten Courage — the Regiment at Gettysburg*　　　47

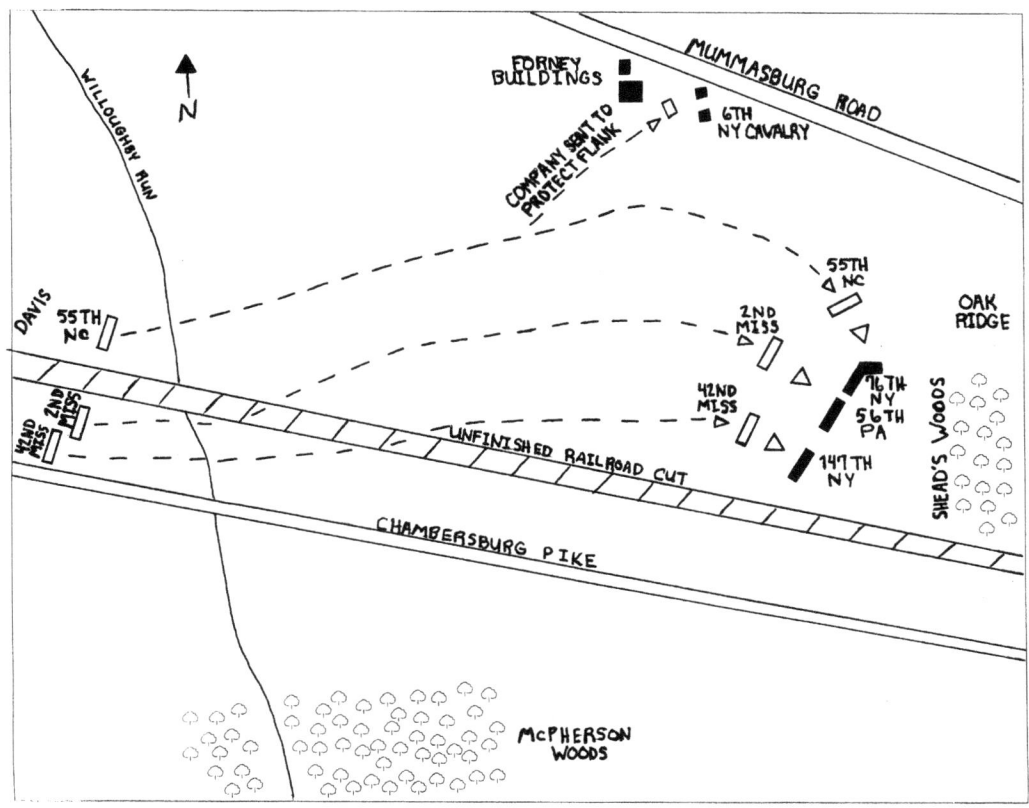

Davis's Brigade advances toward Gettysburg on the morning of July 1, 1863.

As Davis's brigade marched toward Gettysburg, the 11th Mississippi remained behind to guard the division's supply trains. The three remaining regiments, numbering a little over 1,700 men, marched at a leisurely pace and had no indication that they would soon be engaged in the largest battle ever fought in North America. The 55th North Carolina marched with a deep desire to face the enemy once again and had about 640 men ready for action.[51]

The lead elements of Heth's division encountered pockets of Buford's cavalry brigade around 5:30 a.m. Corporal Alpheus Hodges of Company F, ninth New York Cavalry, was at his post when he saw Confederate infantry marching toward his position. He immediately sent word of his sighting to Buford and was soon fired upon by the advancing Rebel column. Finding cover behind the pike bridge that crossed Willoughby Run, Hodges returned fire. Shortly after this initial engagement troopers from the eighth Illinois reinforced Hodges and his small band of men and were able to delay Heth's advance.[52]

As Archer deployed a large number of skirmishers south of the Chambersburg Pike, Davis's unit became aware that members of their division had engaged the Federals. Joseph R. Davis immediately ordered his own line of skirmishers forward to take up a position north of the road. Davis's troops advanced cautiously, joining the rest of Heth's skirmish line, which now extended over a mile and a half front. As Heth's men pushed forward Buford ordered his troopers to take position on McPherson Ridge, which overlooked

Willoughby Run, west of Gettysburg. The cavalrymen were armed with breech-loading carbines and were able to slow the Rebel advance.[53]

The Confederates moved slowly toward the town, but Heth, who had not properly scouted the terrain, was not sure where the main Union battle line was located. Unable to find the Federal forces, Heth ordered Major W. J. Pegram's artillerymen to commence firing into the woods in front of his position. After firing about 10 rounds into the woods Heth ordered his men forward again. Finally, after his forces pushed passed Herr Ridge, the major general through his field glasses spotted Buford's line positioned on McPherson Ridge.[54]

Believing that he outnumbered the Federals, Heth ordered Archer and Davis to move their brigades into Gettysburg and occupy the town. Archer deployed his troops south of the Chambersburg Pike while Davis's men took up position north of the road. The 55th North Carolina was positioned on the extreme left of the line while the 42nd Mississippi was assigned to the right and the secondMississippi occupied the center. The 55th North Carolina moved forward and with the second and 42nd Mississippi regiments formed a line that extended for more than 400 yards. As the men in Davis's brigade moved down Herr Ridge they began to move more rapidly and let out the famed "rebel yell." The Union troopers were unable to repel the Confederate tide moving rapidly toward their position.[55]

The 55th North Carolina and the other two regiments of Davis's brigade, the second and 42nd Mississippi, fought hard near Willoughby Run, and were finally able to press the Federal troopers back toward Gettysburg. A company of soldiers from the 55th North Carolina was sent to the extreme left of the line to resist any possible flanking maneuver by the Federal cavalry. After the Confederate forces wading through Willoughby Run, the Federals intensified their fire. Davis's men were able to move virtually unhindered toward the Union line because their right was protected by a railroad cut that ran through the Willoughby Run valley. The 55th, with the aid of the two Mississippi regiments, was thus able to push Buford's cavalrymen back toward McPherson's Ridge.[56]

The 55th North Carolina company sent by Major Belo to protect the brigade's left flank encountered the sixth New York Cavalry Regiment. The New York troopers' weak skirmish line stretched beyond the North Carolinians' flank, and Major Belo, recognizing the possible threat, sent a company to push the Federal cavalry back. The sixth New York was soon joined by members of the ninth New York, but was unable to slow the 55th North Carolina's advance. The 55th drove the Federals back to the field east of the Forney buildings and formed a line of battle across the road in Forney's Woods.[57]

As several men of 55th moved toward the Forney buildings they were driven back by troopers from the ninth New York. As more of Belo's troops advanced toward the buildings the New Yorkers retreated to the stone wall located at the crest of Oak Ridge. There the Federal troopers waited until Confederate skirmishers came within range of their carbines before they unleashed a volley that pressed the Rebels back beyond the Forney buildings.[58]

With its right protected by the railroad cut and the New Yorkers held in check by a company from the 55th, Davis's troops,, along with those of Archer's brigade, were able to advance unhindered and were on the verge of sweeping the field when reinforcements from Major General John Reynolds's I Corps appeared on the battlefield. As Reynolds's men arrived the 2nd Maine artillery positioned itself on McPherson's Ridge and relieved the 2nd U.s. Artillery, which was almost out of ammunition. Brigadier General Lysander Cutler ordered three of his regiments, the 76th New York, 56th Pennsylvania, and 147th New York infantry regiments to take up position north of the railroad cut. The 4,000 Union troops

3. June–July 1863: Forgotten Courage — the Regiment at Gettysburg

arrived on the field around 10:00 a.m. and prepared to resist Heth's advance. Shortly after Major General Reynolds arrived on the battlefield he was shot by a Confederate marksman and killed instantly. In his work *Lee and Longstreet at Gettysburg*, Glenn Tucker asserts that Benjamin Thorpe shot Reynolds. Tucker mistakenly states that Thorpe was a member of the 26th North Carolina Regiment, but records indicate that he belonged to the 55th North Carolina. Tucker states that Thorpe shot Reynolds from a distance of 800 yards.[59]

As Davis's three regiments advanced toward Cutler's troops their movements were concealed by high grass. As the Confederates moved closer the heads of the Federal soldiers began appearing over the crest of the ridge and the eager troops of Davis's unit quickly fired a fierce volley into the Union line. The commander of the 76th New York, Major Andrew J. Grover, ordered his men to hold their fire because he believed the shots had been fired by remnants of Buford's cavalry brigade by mistake.[60] Lieutenant John E. Cook of the 76th New York described the situation in his report.

Private Benjamin P. Thorp, Company K. Private Thorp is reported to have been one of the best marksmen in the Army of Northern Virginia, and is alleged to be the Confederate sniper who shot and killed Major General John Reynolds at Gettysburg on July 1, 1863. (Courtesy of the North Carolina Division of Archives and History, Raleigh, North Carolina.)

> At about 10:30 a.m., being the extreme advance regiment of the First Corps, we reached the battle-field near the seminary at Gettysburg, and while marching by the flank were opened upon by the enemy, stationed in large force at a distance of about 30 rods, where they were lying down concealed from view in a wheat-field. We were exposed to their fire several minutes before replying. The men were cautioned to hold their fire until the enemy appeared, when orders were given to commence firing.[61]

After several moments of indecision, Major Grover realized the bullets being fired into his ranks were not from Buford's troopers as Davis's men rushed over the ridge. Davis's troops continued forward undaunted by the artillery fire from the second Maine, which now poured down upon them.[62] Because of the lay of the land the 55th North Carolina was the first of Davis's regiments to be seen by Cutler's troops and thus received the first of the Federal return fire.[63]

The second Mississippi regiment advanced straight into the 56th Pennsylvania and the 76th New York regiments and continued firing murderously into the blue battle line. The 42nd Mississippi advanced toward the left of the Federal line where the 147th New York was positioned. While the two Mississippi regiments hit Cutler's men in the front, Colonel Connally moved the 55th North Carolina around to the right of the Federal line and prepared to flank the 76th New York. A few moments later the young colonel gave the order to fix bayonets and charge.[64] Major Grover soon realized that his boys were about to be flanked and ordered the five companies posted on the right to shift back at an angle. Lieutenant Cook stated, "At this juncture, a large force of the enemy appeared upon our right flank, subjecting us [76th New York] to a galling cross-fire."[65]

Upon ordering his men to charge, Colonel Connally began running and was soon about 15 yards in front of the regiment. The color-bearer, Sergeant Marlin Galloway of Company E, was near Connally when the colonel was hit in the leg by a Yankee bullet. The brave young colonel quickly lifted the regimental colors up and urged his men forward. As the colonel wheeled his men around to the right in the "pivotal tactical maneuver" the frenzied troops of the 76th New York fired several more volleys and Connally went down.[66] Major Belo, the only senior officer still standing (Lieutenant Maurice T. Smith had also been shot), described the scene years later in his memoirs.

> Colonel Connally seized the battle-flag and advanced with it in his hands. This drew upon him and the color-guard the fire of the enemy, and he fell, badly wounded in the arm and hip. I was near him at the time and asked if he was badly hurt. He said. "Yes, but do not pay any attention to me. The litter is just here and will take care of me. Take command of the regiment and don't let the Mississippians get ahead of you."[67]

The 55th North Carolina, perhaps invigorated by the loss of their commander, rushed forward and broke the Federal line. Captain Whitehead stated, "we pressed them, onward and onward we sped, raising a real old N.C. whoop." The 76th New York managed to hit two of the 55th North Carolina color-bearers, one being Colonel Connally, but were unable to stop the wave of men pressing onto their line. The North Carolinians succeeded in taking the 76th New York in the flank and rear. The enfilading fire of the North Carolinians was extremely effective, and realizing resistance was futile, Brigadier General James Wadsworth ordered Cutler's men to fall back. During the fierce fight Davis's troops, especially the 55th North Carolina, inflicted a severe toll on the 76th New York. Of the 370 men engaged, the New York regiment had over 30 men killed and 140 wounded.[68]

The 55th North Carolina and the second Mississippi had also forced the 56th Pennsylvania to fall back toward Seminary Ridge. The commanding officer of the second Mississippi, John Marshall Stone, was also wounded, but his men continued to fight. As the 76th New York and 56th Pennsylvania retired to Seminary Ridge, the 147th New York struggled to hold back the 42nd Mississippi, which had begun to press Cutler's remaining regiment back.[69]

As Davis's brigade advanced the second Maine artillery was forced to retreat, having almost lost a gun to several troops from the second Mississippi. The two Mississippi regiments continued to assault the 147th New York while once again the 55th North Carolina moved in from behind. With superb discipline the men of the 55th North Carolina climbed over a rail fence, corrected their alignment, and pressed forward. Captain J. V. Pierce of the 147th New York remarked years later with admiration that the advance of the 55th North Carolina was a portrait of martial beauty.

> Closer pressed the enemy. A regiment — the Fifty-fifth North Carolina — was pressing far to our right and rear, and came over to the south side of the rail fence. The colors drooped to the front. An officer in front of the centre corrected the alignment as if passing in review. It was the finest exhibition of discipline and drill I ever saw, before or since, on the battlefield.[70]

Soon the North Carolinians and the second Mississippi opened a murderous volley aimed at the rear of the 147th New York and having received the order to retreat the New Yorkers fled in a panic toward Seminary Ridge.[71]

Joseph R. Davis reported that the Federals retreated but were able to re-form near the railroad cut and make a firm counterattack.[72] The adrenaline pumped into the bloodstream during battle brought on what many psychologists refer to as "combat narcosis." The men were swept along by a sensation of power and anger. This behavior was facilitated by the close formations of nineteenth-century warfare.[73] In a half hour of fighting the three regiments of Davis's unit engaged on the morning of July 1 inflicted over 515 casualties to Cutler's brigade and had crippled Captain James Hall's second Maine Battery. The victorious Rebels were unable to contain their excitement and began rushing headlong after the retreating Federals.[74]

The men of the 55th North Carolina, and the second and 42nd Mississippi regiments advanced without concern for order and soon became disorganized. The disordered Rebel advance gave the Federals time to stage an effective counterattack. With Connally and Stone out of action the men allowed the heat of battle to cloud their judgment. As Davis's men moved forward only a few of them noticed that the sixth Wisconsin Regiment was rapidly approaching.[75]

As the Confederates rushed madly forward Lieutenant Colonel Rufus R. Dawes of the sixth Wisconsin ordered his men to take up a position in a line parallel to the Chambersburg Pike and the railroad cut. Dawes then commanded his men to rest their rifles on the turnpike fence rails. Once convinced that his troops were ready Dawes gave the order to fire and a devastating roll of musketry was unleashed into the advancing Rebels. The Federal volley staggered the Confederates and caused added confusion in their ranks. However, Davis's troops quickly rallied and ran for cover into the railroad cut. Private William B. Murphy of Company A, second Mississippi claimed years later that the cut was more than 60 yards in length, and about 10 feet in height at its deepest point.[76]

Dawes, unaware of the railroad cut, assumed that the Confederates were retreating and ordered his men forward. As the men of the sixth Wisconsin advanced it became clear that Davis's men had not fled. Dawes reported that "the heavy fire which they began at once to pour upon us from their cover in the cut" dispelled any conception that Davis's troops were in retreat. The advancing Federals continued to push forward even though the North Carolinians and Mississippians unleashed several well-aimed volleys.[77]

As the Confederates moved into the railroad cut about half of the men in the 55th North Carolina were positioned on the embankment on the eastern end of the cut. Major Belo, now commanding the regiment, suggested to Major John Blair, who now led the second Mississippi, that whichever side charged first, would control the field. Belo and Blair agreed, but were ordered to re-form before they had the opportunity to test their theory.[78] As previously stated, during their pursuit of Cutler's brigade Davis's men had become disorganized, and the surprising volley from the sixth Wisconsin caused even more confusion among the Mississippi regiments and the North Carolinians. Eager to reestablish order Joseph Davis commanded his men to retreat through railroad cut, but before his men were able to follow his instructions the sixth Wisconsin, 84th and 95th New York regiments charged.[79]

Davis ordered Major Belo to cover the retreat of the brigade. Once the Federals realized Davis's men were preparing to withdraw they advanced at the double-quick with bayonets fixed. Approximately 900 Federal troops were formed and charged toward the railroad cut. In the ensuing confusion only a portion of Davis's unit heard the order to retreat. The brigade was in a terrible position and confusion reigned supreme. The members of the 55th

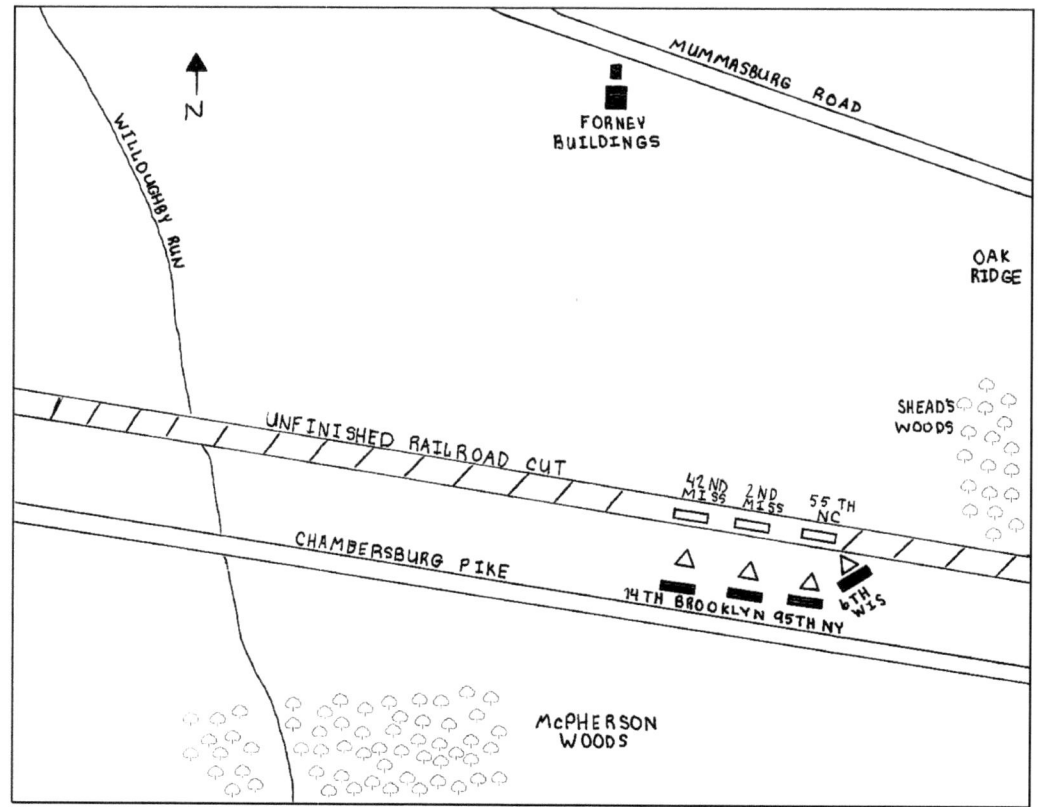

Davis's Brigade in the railroad cut, July 1, 1863.

North Carolina and second Mississippi still positioned on the embankment experienced heavy hand-to-hand combat and fought bravely, but were unable to stop the advancing blue tide.[80]

The fight earlier in the morning with Buford's and Cutler's troops had exhausted Davis's men, and their wild charge after the retreating Federals added to their fatigue.[81] They were in no shape to resist some of the finest soldiers serving in the Army of the Potomac. Remnants of the famed Iron Brigade now rained heavy fire into the cut, but many of Davis's men were able to escape back toward Willoughby Run. Those that remained put up a determined fight and continued to stand their ground. Behind the attacking Federal line streams of wounded Union soldiers fled to the rear or fell dying on the bloody field. Dawes was only able to maintain order by constantly rallying his troops by yelling out "Align on the colors!" The continuous firing from the remaining Confederates, however, began to break apart Dawes's regiment. About 420 men from the sixth Wisconsin advanced from the turnpike fences, but only about 240 made it to the railroad cut.[82]

The remaining Confederates included Major Belo and Captain Whitehead. Whitehead was shot in the back of the neck as he attempted to withdraw from the cut, but refused to surrender and made his escape.[83] Belo, who had been engaged in the heavy hand-to-hand combat on the cut's embankment, escaped serious injury to lead several of his men out of the railroad cut.

One officer on the bank, seeing me directing the men, threw his sword at me, shouting, "Hit that officer." The sword missed me, but struck the man behind me. I directed one of our men to shoot the officer, which he did, thus putting a check on the Federals. By this time the left of the regiment was overwhelmed by numbers, and we had quite a number dead and wounded. I got out with as many as I could, and the enemy did not follow us beyond the cut.[84]

Belo and several other men of the 55th North Carolina were able to fight their way out of the cut, but many more remained in the deadly chasm. The Federals continued to press into the cut even though the Confederates kept up a deadly fire. Finally about 20 Union troops straddled the railroad cut and began pouring enfilade fire into the Rebels. With both gaps in the cut blocked, the remaining members of Davis's Brigade were trapped. After a severe struggle, which included a determined fight for the second Mississippi's battle flag, most of the trapped Confederates surrendered. Several members of the brigade refused to give up and continued the fight until shot dead. Among those captured were privates Calvin Raper and his brother-in-law Jesse P. Sullivan of Company A. Both of these men would die in Federal prison — Sullivan at Fort Delaware and Raper at Point Lookout.[85] Private Murphy of Company A, second Mississippi, described the fate of those captured in a letter written years after the day's fighting had ended.

> We were marched through Gettysburg to Cemetery Hill and held there until about dark, and we were then marched off to West Chester Pa. We arrived in Westchester about 11 A.M. July 2nd.

Those able to escape the Federals were still under mortal danger. As the retreating soldiers from the 55th North Carolina fled from the railroad cut they were fired upon by troops from the 95th and 84th New York regiments. The North Carolinians paused and returned fire, but quickly continued their withdrawal.[86] Dawes reported that seven officers and about 225 men were captured in the railroad cut, but the 55th North Carolina regimental historian stated that the loss was great in killed and wounded and that "a large number were captured in the road-cut."[87] Lieutenant Hoyle of the 55th North Carolina added that his regiment's losses were "heavy in the onset, a great many being captured."[88]

The remaining men of Davis's brigade withdrew back across Willoughby Run and positioned themselves on Herr Ridge. Heth attempted to reorganize his thinned ranks and ordered Davis's men to the rear to collect stragglers. Heth felt that Archer and Davis had fought hard and did not want their troops in the front lines in case the Federals made an assault against his position.[89] Lieutenant Joseph Hoyle described the morning's events in a letter to his wife.

> We moved forward this morning to attack the enemy who is in our front. Our brigade is in front and opened the fight. We found the enemy in position immediately in front of Gettysburg, Pa. We (our brigade) attacked him and after a sharp struggle broke two of his lines and drove him back. But the yankees soon brought up reinforcements on our right, and we, having no forces to cooperate with us on the flanks, after a hard contest, had to fall back. We fell back slowly some distance and awaited reinforcements.[90]

Heth did not believe it "advisable" to order Davis's brigade into action again on July 1, but his recommendation was ignored.[91] Shortly after 2:00 p.m. General Lee arrived on the battlefield west of Gettysburg. Stuart had still not arrived and the general had no idea how many Federals were facing him. Artillery exchanges continued to be heard as Lee moved closer to ascertain what was happening. As the general moved forward to view the field, Rodes's division of Ewell's corps began marching into the area north of Gettysburg.

Lee was still adamant about not wanting a general engagement until his entire army was in position, but Hill's corps had already started the battle.[92]

Lee most likely would have ended the day's fighting had he not witnessed the Federals shifting rapidly to the north. Moments later the Confederate commander understood what all the commotion was for as Rodes's division of Ewell's Second Corps appeared advancing toward the Federal right flank. Lee had ordered Ewell to march his men to Gettysburg and now they were arriving.[93]

General Heth heard the sounds of battle and rushed to find a better place in which to view the engagement. While moving to a more advantageous position Heth found Lee and Hill, who were also viewing the advancing Rebel lines. The major general offered to assist Rodes, but General Lee still did not want a general engagement and instructed Heth to stand down. Heth insisted that an assault from his line would prevent the Federals from reinforcing their lines facing Rodes. Lee once again told Heth to be patient and wait for further orders.[94]

Lee, who did not know how many Federals were moving into Gettysburg, wanted his entire army to be present before he ordered his lieutenants to attack. Without Longstreet's corps up Lee hesitated, but as he saw Rodes's men pour into the Federal line he realized that his army was in fact heavily engaged and he ordered Heth to attack.[95] Sometime between 2:30 p.m. and 3:00 p.m. Heth's division joined the embattled Confederates. Davis's men, still weary from their morning melee, formed on the left of Heth's division and marched up West McPherson Ridge between the Chambersburg Pike and the unfinished railroad.[96]

Davis's brigade first encountered the 149th Pennsylvania and succeeded in pushing the regiment back, capturing over 150 prisoners. The Confederates advanced and were soon supported by Major General Dorsey Pender's division of fresh troops. Davis's men became entangled in heavy fighting and were momentarily pushed back by the large number of Federal troops opposing them. Just as Davis's unit began falling back Brigadier General Alfred M. Scales's brigade smashed into the Federal flank and forced the Union troops to retreat.[97]

The men in Davis's brigade were exhausted but continued to press the Federal troops. Davis stated that "after considerable fighting" his soldiers reached the suburbs of Gettysburg. The Confederate attack succeeded in pushing the Union soldiers through the town to Cemetery Hill.[98] Lieutenant Hoyle described the experiences shared by the men of the 55th North Carolina during the afternoon of July 1, 1863.

> Ewell's forces now came up on our left, and the balance of our corps on our right, and the battle raged furiously along the whole line. Our forces moved steadily on, though the enemy gave back very stubbornly, but against sunset we had drove them back at all points and held the town. The yankee loss was heavy in killed and wounded and prisoners, evidently heavier than ours. This days fight was a decided victory for us. But alas; it has been bought with the life blood of many of our brave boys. Our division was permitted to pass back to the rear to night and rest.[99]

As the fight ended the 55th North Carolina marched back to the woods near Willoughby Run and bivouacked for the evening. Although the day's fighting was over for the men of the 55th another one of its field officers would be seriously wounded before sunset. As he was directing his men where to set up camp, Belo's left leg was hit by an artillery fragment just below the knee. Belo would not return to active duty until January 1864. Private Jeremiah Morrison of Company C, himself wounded in the leg on July 1, stated years later that the day's fighting cost the 55th the majority of their first and second lieutenants.[100]

During the day's engagements Davis's brigade had seven of the nine field officers present for duty killed or wounded. Among these officers were Colonel Connally, who would

3. June–July 1863: Forgotten Courage — the Regiment at Gettysburg

Private George W. Currin, Company K. Private Currin served as a private with the 23rd Regiment North Carolina Troops before joining the 55th on February 7, 1863. He was killed at Gettysburg on the first or third day of the battle. (Courtesy of the North Carolina Division of Archives and History, Raleigh, North Carolina.)

Private James C. Knott, Company K. Private Knott was a farmer living in Granville County before enlisting in the army on May 6, 1862, at age 29. He was killed at Gettysburg on July 1, 1863. (Courtesy of the North Carolina Division of Archives and History, Raleigh, North Carolina.)

live but never lead his regiment into battle again; Major Belo, who would return to take command of the regiment in January 1864; and Lieutenant Maurice T. Smith, who would die of his wounds that very day. Brigadier General Davis especially mentioned Connally, Smith, and Belo among several other officers for displaying "conspicuous gallantry" on the field of battle. The valor displayed by Davis's men did not go unnoticed by their division commander, Henry Heth, who stated, "The good conduct of this brigade on this occasion merits my special commendation."[101] The total number of casualties inflicted on the 55th North Carolina on July 1 is unknown. The official report combines the first and third day of the battle, although the majority of those killed, wounded, or reported missing occurred on July 1. Lieutenant Hoyle stated that his company had 48 present for duty at the beginning of the day's engagement and only 11 remaining as night fell. Hoyle also reported that the regiment went into the fight with about 525 men and when the men bivouacked for the evening there were only 123 still able to fight. Hoyle's estimate may be high when one considers that the official report for all three days of the battle for the regiment was 198 killed or wounded. But this report did not include those captured or missing and Hoyle declared that the 55th had a large number of men captured, which may account for the discrepancy.[102]

Brigadier General Davis spoke highly of the 55th North Carolina, especially its officers, in his official report on the July 1 fighting. His report provides a view of how the battle was perceived at the command level.

> I have the honor to submit the following report of the part taken by my brigade in the battle of July 1, at Gettysburg: Early on the morning of the 1st, I moved in rear of Archer's brigade, with three regiments of my command (the Eleventh Mississippi being left as a guard for the division wagon train) from camp on the heights near Cashtown, by a turnpike road leading to Gettysburg. When within about 2 miles from town, our artillery was put in position, and opened fire. I was ordered to take position on the left of the turnpike, and with the right resting on it, press forward toward the town. About 10.30 o'clock a line of battle was formed-with the Forty-second Mississippi, Colonel H. R. Miller commanding, on the right; Fifty-fifth North Carolina, Colonel J. K. Connally commanding, on the left, and Second Mississippi, Colonel J. M. Stone commanding, in the center — skirmishes thrown forward, and the brigade moved forward to the attack. Between us and the town, and very near it, was a commanding hill in wood, the intervening space being inclosed fields of grass and grain, and was very broken. On our right was the turnpike and railroad, with deep cuts and heavy embankments diverging from the turnpike as it approached the town. On the high hill the enemy had artillery, with infantry supports. The line of skirmishers advanced, and the brigade moved forward about 1 mile, driving in the enemy's skirmishers, and came within range of his line of battle, which was drawn up on a high hill in a field a short distance in front of a railroad cut. The engagement soon became very warm. After a short contest, the order was given to charge, and promptly obeyed. The enemy made a stubborn resistance, and stood until our men were within a few yards, and then gave way, and fled in much confusion, but rallied near the railroad, where he again made a stand, and, after desperate fighting, with heavy loss on both sides, he fled in great disorder toward the town, leaving us in possession of his commanding position and batteries. After a short interval, he again returned in greater numbers, and the fight was renewed, and being opposed by greatly superior numbers, our men gave way under the first shock of his attack, many officers and men having been killed or wounded, and all much exhausted by the excessive heat; but the line was promptly formed, and carried to its former position, and, while there engaged, a heavy force was observed moving rapidly toward our right, and soon after opened a heavy fire on our right flank and rear. In this critical condition, I gave the order to retire, which was done in good order, leaving some officers and men in the railroad cut, who were captured, although every effort was made to withdraw all the commands. This was about 1 p. m. About 3 p.m. a division of Lieutenant-General Ewell's corps came up on our left, moving in line perpendicular to ours, and the brigade was again moved forward, and after considerable fighting, reached the suburbs of the town, into which the enemy had been driven. The men, being much exhausted by the heat and severity of the engagement, were here rested, and about sunset were ordered to bivouac about 1 mile to the rear. In this day's engagement the losses in men and officers were very heavy; of 9 field officers present, but 2 escaped unhurt. Colonel Stone, of the Second Mississippi, and Colonel Connally, of the Fifty-fifth North Carolina, were both wounded while gallantly leading their men in the first charge. Lieutenant Col M. T. Smith, of the Fifty-fifth North Carolina, a gallant and efficient officer, was mortally wounded. Major Belo, of the same regiment, was severely wounded. Lieutenant-Colonel Moseley and Major Feeney, of the Forty-second Mississippi, were both severely wounded. A large number of the company officers were killed or wounded. It is due to the gallantry of a few brave men to state that the Second and Forty-second Mississippi, under the lead of Lieutenant [A. K.] Roberts, of the Second Mississippi, dashed forward, and, after a hand-to-hand contest, in which the gallant Roberts was killed, succeeded in capturing the colors of a Pennsylvania regiment. A number of prisoners were captured, the Forty-second Mississippi taking 150; other regiments perhaps as many or more.[103]

As the sun set and the soldiers of Davis's brigade rested for the night there was still work to be done for some of them. Assistant Surgeon LeGrand Wilson was ordered to ensure that all of the dead were buried and that the wounded were moved to the field hospital.

Wilson stated that it was after midnight before "we finished our sad task, and turned our weary steps toward the division hospital." The assistant surgeon had never experienced the horrors of the battlefield after a day of bloody combat, and declared "if every human being could have witnessed the result of the mad passions of men as I saw it that night, war would cease, and there would never be another battle."[104]

The men of the 55th North Carolina had fought well during the day and had faced some of the best troops in the entire Army of the Potomac. The famed Iron Brigade, a well-experienced fighting unit, had a difficult time pushing Davis's men back to Herr Ridge. The men fought with determination and pride, but were unable to compensate for the mistakes made by their commanders.

Joseph Davis was inexperienced and had allowed his men to rush in complete disarray after the retreating Federals. The brigade commander had no idea how many Union troops were awaiting his men as they approached Seminary Ridge. After being forced back by the sixth Wisconsin, Davis again blundered by positioning his men in the railroad cut. The mistake was understood by at least one company commander, Captain Whitehead of the 55th North Carolina, who stated, "We were in a very precarious condition."[105] The morning melee had been hard on all of the men including the untested brigade commander who under the strains of battle may have believed he was doing all he could to save his men from disaster. Robert K. Krick asserts in his essay "Three Confederate Disasters on Oak Ridge: Failures of the Brigade Leadership on the First Day at Gettysburg," that entering into the deep railroad cut, which proved to be Davis's fatal mistake, could have easily been avoided with even a moderate amount of intelligent leadership.[106]

Another interesting point is that Davis ordered one of his veteran regiments, the 11th Mississippi, to remain near Cashtown to protect the divisional supply wagons. The brigadier general may have assumed that his men would see very little action during the day; however, the second Mississippi had spent all of June 30 on picket duty and therefore would have most likely needed to rest.[107] Davis's decision to leave one of his most combat experienced regiments guarding supplies probably had a drastic effect on the morning's action near the railroad cut.

The failures at the brigade level were not the only mistakes that had dire effects on the 55th North Carolina. A. P. Hill and Henry Heth well understood that Lee did not want a general engagement brought about until his entire army was prepared for action, yet both allowed the first day's action to begin. Heth, who understated in his report that "the enemy had now been felt," allowed his troops to engage the Federals and conduct more than just a simple reconnaissance mission.[108] Whether Hill or Heth sent their troops out to find and attack the Federals is inconsequential; the real failure lies in the fact that, once engaged, Heth did nothing to support his embattled troops.

Several of the men serving in the 55th North Carolina stated after the first day's action that during the morning engagement they continued to wait for reinforcements that never came.[109] Heth possibly hoped to contain the fighting by not sending in more of his brigades. However, to allow the brigades of Archer and Davis to be heavily engaged and to not assist them by ordering more troops to advance is unquestionably an error in judgment.

Although mistakes were made on July 1, 1863, the men of 55th North Carolina fought hard and proved they could stand up against some of the best troops in the Union army. The Iron Brigade was composed of veteran troops who had fought courageously during past battles. The morning melee near the railroad cut had been a bloody engagement, but it had inspired the soldiers in the Army of Northern Virginia to fight.

On July 2 the two armies faced off again, but neither side gained any real advantages. While other North Carolina troops assaulted the Federal positions on Culp's Hill, and Joshua Lawrence Chamberlain's 20th Maine and other Federal units repelled Confederate attempts to capture Little Roundtop, the men of the 55th North Carolina spent the day resting and becoming fully aware of the losses their regiment had suffered the previous day.

After resting throughout the second day of battle Davis positioned his brigade near Seminary Ridge in McMillan Woods. Heth's division, now commanded by Brigadier General James Johnston Pettigrew, was posted on the left of Longstreet's troops and Davis's unit was located at the left center of the division.[110]

The 55th and the rest of Heth's division were in a position almost parallel to the defense line of the Federals. During the evening the Union artillery continued to rain upon the Confederate lines and kept the weary Rebels awake most of the night.[111] Lieutenant Hoyle briefly described his regiment's activities on July 2 to his wife and summed up the outcome of the entire day's battle.

> We rested till late this evening when we were moved round to the right, and took position on our lines, bloody work is before us again. Hard fighting has been going on to day, but, as you see, our division was not in it. The enemy has a very strong position, and our men have failed to route them to day.[112]

By nightfall on July 2 Lee still firmly believed that his men could do anything he asked. Although the Confederate assaults throughout the day had not been properly coordinated and delays had hampered the attacks, the Rebels had moderate successes. Lee still had at his disposal enough soldiers to mount an effective attack. The Confederates had several fresh divisions that had seen no action during the first two days of battle and were eager to engage the Federals. With the morale of his troops high and the addition of determined reinforcements Lee decided that another attack against Meade on July 3 would bring his army total victory. Yet, uncharacteristically the commander of the Army of Northern Virginia did not meet with his primary lieutenants to discuss the condition of their forces. He had no real idea how many troops Meade had in front of him, and so based his decisions entirely on the belief that his army could defeat the Federals like they had just one month before at Chancellorsville.[113]

Lee's battle plan for July 3 remained basically the same as the previous day's scheme. Longstreet's troops would attack the Union left while Ewell's men would strike the Federal right. The commanding general's timetable had called for Longstreet's corps to be in action at daylight; however, Major General George Pickett had not been informed of this, and therefore his men were not prepared for an early morning assault. The breakdown of communication and Federal advances forced Lee to rethink his battle plan.[114]

After the Federals made an effort to recapture their trenches at the base of Culp's Hill around 4:30 a.m. Lee quickly changed his plans and instructed Longstreet to assault the Union center.[115] Longstreet ordered Colonel Edward Porter Alexander, who was commanding the reserve artillery, to shell the Federal positions before the Confederate assault was made. Alexander began placing his batteries in position early in the morning so that his artillery would be ready to commence firing at daybreak. Alexander's cannonade was not merely to soften the Federal lines but to "cripple him — to tear him limbless, as it were, if possible." Once the artillery had demoralized or driven the Federals from their lines the infantry would be ordered to charge.[116]

At 1:00 p.m. Colonel Alexander's artillery opened fire and the largest artillery duel in American history had begun. Positioned near the Peach Orchard were 150 Confederate guns placed in good order by Alexander during the early morning hours. As the Confederate cannonade hurled shells into the Federal lines, the attention of all those on the battlefield was focused on the Peach Orchard.[117]

The Confederate barrage startled the Federals, causing momentary confusion in the blue ranks. One Union lieutenant stated, "we thought that at the second Bull Run, at the Antietam and at Fredericksburg on the 11th of December, we had heard heavy cannonading; they were but holiday salutes compared with this."[118] Although surprised by the artillery assault, the Federals quickly responded in kind. As Union troops tried to make themselves as inconspicuous as possible their artillerymen worked feverishly to limit the Confederate threat.[119]

The 55th North Carolina remained in McMillan Woods, about 100 yards behind several artillery pieces. This position proved to be deadly for several men in Davis's brigade. The Federal artillerymen began shelling the Confederate batteries soon after Alexander had opened on their lines. However, the projectiles fired at the guns in front of the 55th overshot their mark. Captain Whitehead remarked, "most of the shells from the Yankee batteries fell in our ranks. Consequently we had a great many men killed."[120] LeGrand Wilson, who had spent the last two days tending to the wounded, stated that the artillery exchange caused "pandemonium" throughout the Confederate lines.[121]

In his report of the third day's action, Joseph R. Davis remarked that the cannonading continued for two hours, which does not concur with other eyewitness accounts, and that the "fire was heavy and incessant." Davis also claimed that two men from his brigade were killed during the shelling and 21 were wounded.[122] Although the Federal fire only inflicted a few casualties to Davis's brigade, those killed or wounded suffered greatly. Captain Whitehead declared that he saw a shell strike a man who had been lying down to escape injury. The shell Whitehead claimed "seemed to raise him 10 or 12 feet in the air and literally shake him into mince meat, his blood and portions of his body falling on and around me."[123]

Although the heated exchange lasted several hours little damage was done to either side. Both sides lost supplies, horses, and ammunition, but the infantrymen poised to fight were virtually unharmed.[124] About 40 minutes after the cannonading had commenced Alexander noticed that the Federals were withdrawing entire batteries from their positions. Alexander doubted that he had crippled the Federal artillery, but he believed his barrage had been well aimed and demoralizing. Shortly after witnessing the retreating Union batteries the young artillery colonel informed Major General George Pickett to order his infantrymen forward. Distressfully, Alexander wrote to Pickett, "For God's sake come quick. Come quick or I can't support you."[125]

Pickett, eager to order his men to advance, received Alexander's note and understood it as a command to begin his assault. Pickett instructed his brigade commanders to prepare their men and he rode to find Longstreet. Upon locating the lieutenant general Pickett asked if his troops should advance. Longstreet, unable to acquiesce verbally, simply nodded. Although Alexander reported to Longstreet that his ammunition was low and he would not be able to properly support the infantry the assault continued as ordered.[126]

Lee's plan called for three Confederate divisions to make the assault on Cemetery Ridge. Two divisions from A. P Hill's corps — Heth's and Pender's — and Pickett's division from Longstreet's corps would advance and attack the Federal center. Both Heth and Pender had been wounded during the previous day's fighting. Pettigrew, who had no prior experience commanding a division, led Heth's troops into battle. Major General Isaac R. Trimble, a veteran soldier, ordered Pender's men in the assault.[127]

A little after 2:00 p.m. the Confederate guns fell silent. As George Pickett spoke inspiringly to his men, James Johnston Pettigrew did the same. Pettigrew, mounted on his gray horse, stopped in front of Colonel James K. Marshall, now in command of the brigadier general's brigade, and said, "Now Colonel, for the Honor of the Good Old North State, Forward!" Pettigrew's troops marched out, positioned on the left of Pickett's men. Heth's division was posted in the front line and arranged with Archer's, Pettigrew's, Davis's, and Brockenbrough's brigades aligned from right to left, respectively.[128]

As the Confederates advanced the Union troops soon became aware that the silent cannons did not imply that the Rebels were retreating. Union Lieutenant Frank A. Haskell wrote of the sight years later in his history of the battle.

> None on that crest now need to be told that the enemy is advancing. Every eye could see his legions, an overwhelming resistless tide of an ocean of armed men sweeping upon us. Regiment after regiment and brigade after brigade move from the woods and rapidly take their places in the lines forming the assault. Pickett's proud division with some additional troops, hold their right; Pettigrew's their left. The first line at short interval is followed by a second, and that a third succeeds; and columns between support the lines. More than half a mile their front

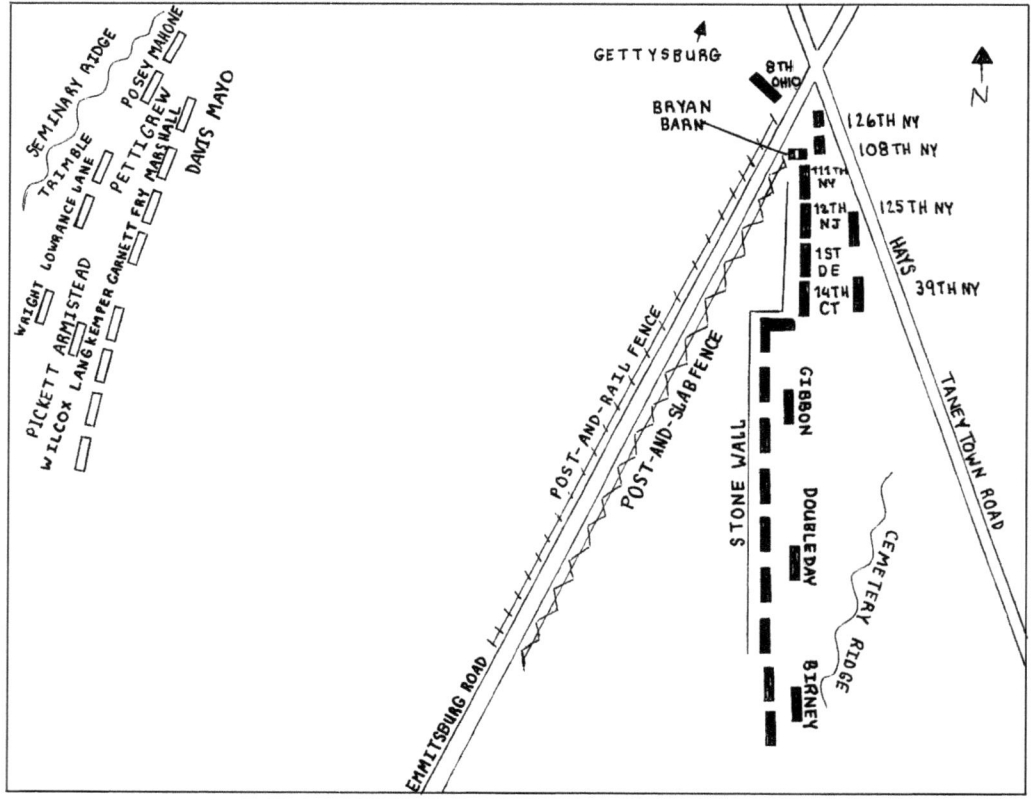

Location of Pettigrew and Pickett's divisions on the afternoon of July 3, 1863.

extends; more than a thousand yards the dull gray masses deploy, man touching man, rank pressing rank, and line supporting line. The red flags wave, their horsemen gallop up and down; the arms of eighteen thousand men, barrel and bayonet, gleam in the sun, a sloping forest of flashing steel. Right on they move, as with one soul, in perfect order, without impediment of ditch, or wall or stream, over ridge and slope, through orchard and meadow, and cornfield, magnificent, grim, irresistible.[129]

Although the approaching Confederate soldiers were mostly dressed in faded, torn uniforms, a few officers being the only Confederates in magnificent attire, the Federals on Cemetery Ridge were impressed by the sheer beauty of the advance. A Federal officer from New York stated years after the battle that there was "a precision of movement and air of discipline that evoked in the highest degree the admiration of each soldier who awaited their coming."[130]

As the Rebel tide advanced the topography of the field proved both advantageous and dangerous. The surface of the ground was rolling with scattered depressions found throughout the field. These depressions shielded the advancing Rebels from artillery

Private Albert Eakes, Company K. Private Eakes was wounded in the left side and elbow and captured at Gettysburg on July 3, 1863. His left arm was amputated while at a field hospital at Gettysburg. Eakes was transferred to a Federal hospital in Baltimore, Maryland, and was paroled on November 12, 1863. He survived the war. (Courtesy of the North Carolina Division of Archives and History, Raleigh, North Carolina.)

and rifle fire. However, as their heads appeared above the crests of the indentations the Union troops could fire a few rounds before the Confederates could respond. Although the field through which Pickett's troops crossed provided some protection from the Union artillery, the path Pettigrew's men were forced to follow was exposed to artillery fire from Cemetery Ridge and Ziegler's Woods.[131]

From their positions in the woods the men of the 55th North Carolina advanced in perfect order. The regiment was temporarily under the command of Captain George A. Gilreath of Company B, and his troops advanced unhindered in splendid fashion.[132] Captain Whitehead joined his comrades until struck in the head by a shell fragment before the regiment began to march.[133] Whitehead's participation indicates that the wounded from the first day's fighting who were still fit to walk were advancing toward the Federal position as well. The Federal troops anxiously followed their orders and held their fire. As Pettigrew's men moved forward they were not parallel to the Federal line. Obeying their instructions the men in the brigadier general's command "spread their steps," and soon were aligned with Pickett's troops. There was a bend to the west in Seminary Ridge, causing Pettigrew's starting point to be farther than Pickett's from the Federal lines.[134]

Davis's men marched side by side in perfect cadence toward the Union position. Davis reported, "not a gun was fired at us until we reached a strong post and rail fence, about three-quarters of a mile from the enemy's position, when we were met by a heavy fire of grape, canister, and shell, which told sadly upon our ranks."[135] The Federal artillery opened on the front and left of Pettigrew's men with 80 or more guns. Although the fire was hot the men on the left of the Confederate advance continued to move forward, climbing over several more post and rail fences.[136]

On the extreme left of the Confederate line Brockenbrough's brigade, commanded by Colonel R. M. Mayo of the 47th Virginia Regiment, received tremendous fire from Major Thomas W. Osborn's artillery positioned on Cemetery Hill and the eighth Ohio Regiment. The men of the eighth Ohio were positioned so that as the Confederates advanced they were able to unload a deadly fire into the Rebel flank. As Mayo's troops advanced they had to turn slightly to the right and were momentarily perpendicular to Osborn's guns. Thus exposed, the Federal major ordered his 31 guns to open with everything they had on the helpless Rebels. Mayo's men staggered, but continued moving forward.[137]

Weakened by the devastating artillery barrage Mayo's men were still able to advance, but as they came within 300 yards of the eighth Ohio infantrymen they were hit hard by rifle fire. Unable to endure the deadly Federal fire, the soldiers in Mayo's command became disorganized. Lieutenant Colonel Franklin Sawyer of the eighth Ohio described the confusion in Mayo's ranks brought on by the Federal onslaught.

> Our fire was poured into their flank with terrible effect for a few minutes before the Second Brigade at the battery opened, but almost instantly on the fire from the front, together with the concentrated fire from our batteries, the whole mass gave way, some fleeing to the front, some to the rear, and some through our lines, until the whole plain was covered with unarmed rebels, waving coats, hats, and handkerchiefs in token of a wish to surrender.[138]

With Mayo's men in retreat the Federals were able to concentrate their fire on the remaining brigades. Davis's flank was now exposed, which enabled the eighth Ohio to fire devastating volleys into the ranks of his command. The Federals poured into Davis's troops but the determined Rebels continued advancing. Davis's command marched forward with the 55th North Carolina on the right, the 11th Mississippi on the left, and the second and 42nd Mississippi regiments in the center.[139]

Brigadier General Alexander Hays commanded the Federals positioned at the stone wall in front of Davis's men. As the 55th North Carolina advanced to within 100 yards of the stone wall, Hays's troops, including the 111th and 125th New York, the 12th New Jersey, and the first Delaware regiments unleashed a deadly volley. As the Confederates began to climb over the fence, which ran along the Emmitsburg Road, Hays gave the order to fire. Nearly 1,700 rifles and 11 cannon discharged in unison.[140] Hays described his men's reaction to the oncoming Confederate tide.

> Their march was as steady as if impelled by machinery, unbroken by our artillery, which played upon them a storm of missiles. When within 100 yards of our line of infantry, the fire of our men could no longer be restrained. Four lines rose from behind our stone wall, and before the smoke of our first volley had cleared away, the enemy, in dismay and consternation, were seeking safety in flight. Every attempt by their officers to rally them was vain.[141]

3. June–July 1863: Forgotten Courage — the Regiment at Gettysburg

Lieutenant Hoyle, who commanded Company F that day, continued forward through the heavy artillery fire. As he approached the stone wall, however, the Federal fire became too much for him and most of his comrades. In a letter to his wife the young lieutenant explained the horrific event in which he had participated.

> We have been shelled nearly all day, and this evening the most terrific cannonading occurred that I ever heard. We had over 100 pieces of cannon engaged and the yankees, I suppose had equally as many. The cannonading continued one hour. Our line was then ordered to move forward and charge the enemy, who were posted behind a stone fence, with their artillery on rising ground in their rear. An open field lay to their front through which we had to advance. We moved forward, exposed to a hot fire of grape shot and shells, yet we moved on. When we came in rang of their small arms their fire became destructive in the extrem yet we moved on till within about 100 yards of their line, when our ranks were so thinned that we could proceed no further. So our line broke in confusion and every man got out the best he could. It must be remembered that while we were going back we were equally exposed as when we were advancing. Our Regt went inthis time with about 120 and came out with 40. The rest suffered equally as much.[142]

The Confederates continued on to within 20 or 30 yards of the stone wall, and as they did the Federals continued to fire murderous close range volleys into their exhausted ranks. The 126th New York Regiment joined in the effort to repel the advancing Rebels and began firing into the approaching Confederates. The 126th advanced to a position nearly perpendicular to the assaulting Confederate lines and unleashed a deadly flanking fire. The Rebels stood their ground and returned fire as best they could. As the rifle and musket fire became more intense the field filled with a smoky haze making visibility nearly zero.[143]

As Davis's men advanced toward the stone wall the "galling fire of musketry and artillery that so reduced the already thinned ranks" made any attempt to continue forward futile.[144] The men in the first line were shot to pieces and "mowed down as grass by the scythe." S. A. Ashe, a Confederate veteran from North Carolina, wrote in his brief history of the Pettigrew-Pickett charge that the cries of the dying and wounded could be heard throughout the field. He also quoted General Trimble as saying that Heth's division "seemed to sink into the earth under the tempest of fire poured into them."[145]

As the majority of Davis's men broke in confusion and retreated back toward Seminary Ridge a few of the brigade's soldiers continued to advance undaunted.[146] These few men, mostly from the 11th Mississippi — though some were from the other regiments including the 55th North Carolina — "impetuously rushed through the hell of fire of all arms to and near the wall continuing the battle there at close quarters for a short time." There is no evidence that any soldiers from the 2nd or 42nd Mississippi advanced past the Emmitsburg Road.[147]

Among these courageous Confederates were at least three members of the 55th North Carolina: Captain Edward Fletcher Satterfield of Company H, Lieutenant T. D. Falls of Company C, and Sergeant J. Augustus Whitley of Company E.[148] Whitley recorded his experience years later in a letter to the *Galveston Daily News*, a newspaper owned by A. H. Belo.

> We charged across the field and crossed a road about one-hundred yards from the federal works (a stone fence). Our line was cut down to a mere skirmish line when we got to the works, about thirty feet on the right of that old barn. Our flag had fallen a few yards back.... I looked back for our support and saw them in full retreat at least 150 yards from me. Captain Satterfield was the only man I saw near me on my left. He and I had started a few paces back, when a shell from our batteries that were protecting the retreat of the second and third lines fell just in front of him, exploded and literally tore him to pieces. I fell behind a small elm, and was soon ordered to surrender.[149]

Captain E. Fletcher Satterfield, Company H. Captain Satterfield was one of three members of the 55th said to have reached the farthest point during the Pickett-Pettigrew charge. (Courtesy of the North Carolina Division of Archives and History, Raleigh, North Carolina.)

Second Lieutenant T. D. Falls, Company C. One of three members of the regiment said to have reached the farthest point during the Pickett-Pettigrew charge. (Courtesy of the North Carolina Division of Archives and History, Raleigh, North Carolina.)

Supporting Whitley's story is a letter from William P. Webb, a family friend, to one of Satterfield's sisters. Webb stated that the young captain was ahead of his company as he advanced, and that several men from his command saw a shell explode near his body. The explosion tore Satterfield's body to pieces, and after the battle Federal troops buried his mutilated remains. The regiment's adjutant, Henry Jordan, a former classmate of Satterfield, informed the captain's family that he heard that Fletcher made it to the stone wall but was killed by an artillery shot.[150]

A letter written to the Satterfield family shortly after the battle sheds some light on what

Sergeant J. A. Whitley, Company E. The third member of the 55th said to have reached the farthest point during the Pickett-Pettigrew charge. (Courtesy of the North Carolina Division of Archives and History, Raleigh, North Carolina.)

soldiers think about before an engagement. The letter describes a premonition Fletcher had before the fighting began that he would be killed during the battle. Apparently Satterfield had a deeply religious conversation with J. D. Williams, a soldier in his own company. Williams informed Satterfield's sister, Sue E. Satterfield, that the realization of his own mortality had made Fletcher adhere to Christian beliefs more strenuously.[151]

As the Confederates began retreating the Federal troops climbed over the stone wall and followed. T. D. Falls stated years later that as he was running back toward Seminary Ridge, the Federals began to chase him and his fellow Confederates. Falls was only able to retreat about 75 yards before being shot and forced to surrender.[152] The men had done their best but the charge had failed.

After the fateful charge had been repelled the Mississippians and North Carolinians of Davis's brigade limped back in utter exhaustion and despair. One young soldier from Mississippi searching for the remaining members of his regiment found General Davis "weeping like a child." The weary soldier asked the disheartened general where his brigade was and Davis, unable to speak, simply motioned upward.[153]

In August, Brigadier General Joseph R. Davis submitted the official report regarding the fighting his men participated in on the third day at Gettysburg. The report is not limited to Davis's brigade, but includes the activities of Heth's entire division. In their history of the 55th North Carolina, historians Louis H. Manarin and Weymouth T. Jordan, Jr., assert that the task of writing the battle report was completed by the brigadier general because Henry Heth had been wounded prior to the attack and was not present during the assault, and James Johnston Pettigrew was killed at Falling Waters on July 14, 1863. The Mississippian's testimony the Heth division's part in the final attack at Gettysburg is primarily a record of his brigade's participation simply because as commander of the unit his attention was focused on it rather than the whole division. Davis's words express the belief that his men did their duty and deserved recognition.

> I have the honor to submit the following report of the operations of Major-General Heth's division in the battle of July 3, at Gettysburg: On the evening of the 2d, this division, under command of Brigadier General J. J. Pettigrew (Major-General Heth having been wounded in the engagement of the 1st), moved to the front, and was formed in line of battle, with Archer's brigade on the right, commanded by Colonel B. D. Fry (Brigadier-General Archer having been wounded and captured on July 1); Colonel Brockenbrough's brigade on the left; Pettigrew's, commanded by Colonel James K. Marshall, of the Fifty-second North Carolina, on the right center, and Davis' on the left center immediately in the rear of our artillery, which was in position on the crest of a high ridge running nearly parallel to the enemy's line, which was on a similar elevation and nearly 1 mile distant, the intervening space, excepting the crests of the hills, being fields, intersected by strong post and rail fences. In this position we bivouacked for the night. Early on the morning of the 3d, the enemy threw some shells at the artillery in our front, from which a few casualties occurred in one of the brigades. About 9 a. m. the division was moved to the left about a quarter of a mile, and in the same order of battle was formed in the rear of Major Pegram's battalion of artillery, which was posted on the crest of a high hill, the ground between us and the enemy being like that of our first position. About 1 p. m. the artillery along our entire line opened on the enemy, and was promptly replied to. For two hours the fire was heavy and incessant. Being immediately in the rear of our batteries, and having had no time to prepare means for protection, we suffered some losses. In Davis' brigade 2 men were killed and 21 wounded. The order had been given that, when the artillery in our front ceased firing, the division would attack the enemy's batteries, keeping dressed to the right, and moving in line with Major-General Pickett's division, which was on our right, and march obliquely to the left. The artillery ceased firing at 3 o'clock, and the order to move

forward was given and promptly obeyed. The division moved off in line, and, passing the wooded crest of the hill, descended to the open fields that lay between us and the enemy. Not a gun was fired at us until we reached a strong post and rail fence about three-quarters of a mile from the enemy's position, when we were met by a heavy fire of grape, canister, and shell, which told sadly upon our ranks. Under this destructive fire, which commanded our front and left with fatal effect, the troops displayed great coolness, were well in hand, and moved steadily forward, regularly closing up the gaps made in their ranks. Our advance across the fields was interrupted by other fences of a similar character, in crossing which the alignment became more or less deranged. This was in each case promptly rectified, and though its ranks were growing thinner at every step, this division moved steadily on in line with the troops on the right. When within musket-range, we encountered a heavy fire of small-arms, from which we suffered severely; but this did not for moment check the advance. The right of the division, owing to the conformation of the ridge on which the enemy was posted, having a shorter distance to pass over to reach his first line of defense, encountered him first in close conflict; but the whole division dashed up to his first line of defense — a stone wall — behind which the opposing infantry was strongly posted. Here we were subjected to a most galling fire of musketry and artillery, that so reduced the already thinned ranks that any further effort to carry the position was hopeless, and there was nothing left but to retire to the position originally held, which was done in more or less confusion. About 4 p.m. the division reached the line held in the morning, and remained there thirty hours, excepting an attack from the enemy. No demonstration was made on any part of our line during that or the following day, on the night of which we began our retreat to Hagerstown. In the assault upon the enemy's position, the coolness and courage of officers and men are worthy of high commendation, and I regret that the names of the gallant men who fell distinguished on that bloody field have not been more fully reported. In this assault, we are called upon to mourn the loss of many brave officers and men. Colonel B. D. Fry, Thirteenth Alabama, commanding Archer's brigade, and Colonel James K. Marshall, of the Fifty-second North Carolina, commanding Pettigrew's, were wounded and taken prisoners while gallantly leading their brigades. The number killed and wounded was very great, and in officers unusually so, as may be seen from the fact that in Archer's brigade but two field officers escaped, in Pettigrew's but one, and in Davis' all were killed or wounded. Brigadier-General Pettigrew had his horse killed, and received a slight wound

in the hand. Not having commanded the division in this engagement, and having been exclusively occupied by the operations of my own brigade, this report is necessarily imperfect, and I regret that I am unable to do full justice to the division.[154]

The official report stated that Davis's brigade had a total of 897 men killed or wounded, with the 55th North Carolina's casualties numbering 198: 39 killed and 159 wounded.[155] These figures, however, do not include those soldiers listed as missing. In a

Private Marion H. Hester, Company K. Private Hester enlisted in the Confederate Army on May 6, 1862, at the age of 22. He was wounded in the right leg and captured at Gettysburg on July 3, 1863, and was paroled on August 23, 1863. He returned to the 55th North Carolina on and unspecified date and survived the war. (Courtesy of the North Carolina Division of Archives and History.)

3. June–July 1863: Forgotten Courage — the Regiment at Gettysburg   67

report filed with the *Weekly State Journal*, Robert W. Thomas of Company K, who temporarily commanded the regiment from August 1863 to January 1864, compiled a list almost twice as long as the official one. Thomas, who was himself wounded on July 3, claimed that the losses of the 55th during the battle of Gettysburg totaled 377, with 34 killed, 159 wounded, and 184 missing. The report sent to the *Weekly State Journal* by Thomas provided a detailed list of those killed, wounded, or reported missing from each company.[156] Among those listed as missing was Captain Gilreath, who had led the regiment into battle. Gilreath was killed during the charge on July 3. After Gilreath's death Lieutenant Marcus C. Stevens of Company G was the ranking officer who commanded the regiment until July 14. Captain Whitted, after recovering from his wounds, led the 55th until Thomas assumed command in August.[157]

Lieutenant Hoyle described the losses in a letter to his wife. Although his estimates are incorrect, his assessment presents a view of how devastating the men perceived the battle to have been, and how costly it was for the regiment. Hoyle also hints at the fact that many of the men knew retreating back across the Potomac River would be difficult.

> Our troops are badly cut up. Brigades now are not larger than Regts were befor the fight. I have 14 in my co. now. Our Regt has about 100. We also damaged the yankees a great deal, but I cannot say who was hurt worst. If we get back cross the river I will write you again.[158]

Private Robert B. Elixson, Company K. Private Elixson served his regiment as a mechanic early in the war before returning to the ranks on an unspecified date. He was wounded in the hand and captured at Gettysburg on July 3, 1863. Private Elixson died at the Federal prison Point Lookout, Maryland, on September 17, 1864. (Courtesy of the North Carolina Division of Archives and History, Raleigh, North carolina.)

Private Thomas B. Daniel, Company K. Private Thomas was wounded in the head and captured at Gettysburg on July 3, 1863. He returned to his command on an unspecified date and survived the war. (Courtesy of the North Carolina Division of Archives and History, Raleigh, North Carolina.)

The battle of Gettysburg devastated the 55th North Carolina. Particularly damaging was the effect the three-day engagement had on the officer corps. In past engagements several officers, including Captain Peter Mull, had been wounded. These casualties, however, were in no way as costly to the regiment's unity as those suffered during the battle of Gettysburg. Of the regiment's top officers only Major Belo would return to active duty after the battle. As previously stated, Colonel Connally was severely wounded and would never command his troops again. Lieutenant Colonel Maurice Smith was killed on July 1, and Adjutant Henry Jordan was taken prisoner.[159]

The regimental company commanders also suffered greatly at the battle of Gettysburg. Of the unit's 10 company commanders, only one, Peter Mull, escaped death or injury, and that was because he was still recovering in a Richmond hospital from the wounds he had received at Washington. Captain Gilreath of Company B and Captain Satterfield of Company H were killed in action, while Captain Upchurch of Company A died in prison on November 9, 1863, of dysentery.[160] The remaining six were either wounded or taken prisoner. Many of the regiment's lieutenants were also killed, wounded, or taken prisoner.[161]

Captain Robert W. Thomas, Company K. Captain Thomas commanded the regiment on and off after Colonel Connally and Lieutenant Colonel Belo were wounded. After Lieutenant Colonel Belo was wounded at Cold Harbot, Captain Thomas would again serve as regimental commander from time to time. (Courtesy of the North Carolina Division of Archives and History, Raleigh, North Carolina.)

Private James Wesley Adcock, Company K. Private Adcock was wounded in the thigh and hip and captured at Gettysburg on July 3, 1863. He was paroled on August 1, 1863, and returned to his command on an unspecified date. He survived the war. (Courtesy of the North Carolina Division of Archives and History, Raleigh, North carolina.)

3. *June–July 1863: Forgotten Courage — the Regiment at Gettysburg* 69

Though many of the unit's most promising young officers never fought again, the 55th would continue the struggle for Southern independence.[162] The 55th North Carolina's participation in the July 3 charge has gone relatively unnoticed by contemporary, as well as modern historians. In his short historical sketch of the Pettigrew-Pickett charge, S. A. Ashe does not even mention the regiment. Though he does specifically mention other North Carolina regiments, his report mainly discusses the role of Heth's division.[163] In the most recent study completed that focuses on the third day of fighting, historian Jeffry D. Wert mentions the 55th twice. This recent work, *Gettysburg: Day Three*, also incorrectly asserts that all three of the men from the regiment that reached the stone wall were killed, when in reality only Captain Satterfield died. The other two members, T. D. Falls and Whitley, were captured and lived to tell about their experiences.

The controversy over who was to blame for the failure of Pickett's assault on July 3, 1863, began almost immediately after the battle. The Virginians

Captain Silas Dixon Randall, Company D. Captain Randall was appointed captain on March 29, 1862. He was wounded in the face and captured at Gettysburg on July 1, 1863, and was not paroled until March 14, 1865. He survived the war. (Courtesy of the North Carolina Division of Archives and History, Raleigh, North Carolina.)

who served under Pickett claimed that the soldiers in Pettigrew's attacking wing had wavered and retreated as soon as they came under fire. This withdrawal left the Virginians' left flank exposed to Federal fire. The North Carolinians refused to accept the role of the scapegoat, but Virginia, being the main seat of war in the east, left them at an unfair advantage. Private William C. Gardner of Company E, himself injured on the first day of fighting, wrote in a letter to a friend that Virginians had "no sympathy for a north carolina soldier." He also added that the fighting men of the Old North State had little concern for them as well.[164]

Most contemporary commentaries, the majority of which were written by men who served on Lee's or Longstreet's staff, claimed that the collapse of Pettigrew's troops was the main cause for the assault's failure. In her work *Pickett's Charge in History & Memory*, a more recent study, historian Carol Reardon asserts that history has been less than flattering to Pettigrew's men. Reardon declares that several of Lee's officers refused to accept the fact that Pickett's charge was doomed from the start, and that the general was at least partly to blame. In order to clear Lee many Virginians asserted that Longstreet was guilty of insubordination and that Pettigrew's diverse division wavered at the crucial point in the assault, thereby enabling the Federals to focus their complete attention on Pickett's troops. With the blame thus placed on Longstreet and on Pettigrew's men, any suspicion that Lee had faltered at Gettysburg was easily disputed, though not everyone was convinced.[165]

After years of allowing Virginians to assert that they alone almost broke the Union line on July 3, ex–Confederates from North Carolina, Mississippi, Tennessee, Florida, and Alabama began speaking out. North Carolinians in particular declared that soldiers from the Old North State went farther than any other Confederate did on July 3. In 1904, the North Carolina Literary and Historical Society published a response to counter Virginia's assertion that Pettigrew's men did little during the Confederate charge on July 3. The pamphlet *Five Points in the Record of North Carolina in the Great War of 1861–5* included a map that pinpointed the location reached by the three soldiers from the 55th North Carolina.[166]

The argument over which state ultimately reached the "high water mark" at Gettysburg will most likely continue for years to come, but there is no denying that soldiers from North Carolina advanced to within feet of the stone wall. Captain Samuel C. Armstrong, who served with the 125th New York Volunteers at Gettysburg, stated 20 years after the battle that those soldiers from North Carolina that participated in the assault had nothing to be ashamed of because they were as courageous and patriotic as any soldier from Virginia. Colonel Birkett D. Fry, who commanded Archer's brigade on July 3, declared that at least one of Heth's brigades went as far as Pickett's men, and in no way caused the charge to fail.[167]

After years of hearing that his brigade faltered during the Confederate charge on July 3, 1863, Joseph R. Davis responded by writing a letter to Colonel John B. Bachelder, who had taken it upon himself to compile a documented history of the battle of Gettysburg. After clearing up the rumor that his brigade was captured on July 1, Davis proceeded to explain his troops' activities on the third day of battle.

> In the 3d days battle great injustice has been done by the so called history. My brigade went as far as Pickets, and made as gallant a charge as any in the attacking column. It is a popular delusion that pickets division, went farther than Heth's, to which I belonged. Many of my men, including my A. A. General and an Aid fell within the Federal lines.[168]

The 55th North Carolina's regimental historian asserted that Captain Satterfield, Lieutenant Falls, and Sergeant Whitley went farther than any other Confederate on July 3, 1863, and stated that the Gettysburg National Park Commission had substantiated this fact by marking the location for all to see.[169] This assertion is difficult to prove, but the fact that Satterfield's body was found so close to the stone wall and that Falls and Whitley were captured near the Bryan Barn is proof that at least three members of the 55th did continue to advance under extreme fire. Lieutenant Hoyle's claim that the majority of the regiment broke in confusion after advancing to within 100 yards of the stone wall is probably correct also. The argument over which regiment and which state went the farthest at Gettysburg clouds the real story. What must be known, but unfortunately has been overlooked by such historians as Edwin Coddington, Clifford Dowdey, and Douglas Southall Freeman, is the fact that the 55th North Carolina fought courageously during the three-day battle in Pennsylvania. After being bruised and battered on July 1, the regiment was still able to go the distance under heavy Federal fire on the final day of battle. The 55th was one of the first regiments to be engaged at Gettysburg and one of the last to leave the battlefield on July 3. Before Gettysburg, the men of the 55th had seen only minor skirmishes; yet they were able to stand beside some of the Confederate army's best regiments and equal if not exceed them in combat performance. As Lieutenant Hoyle stated in a letter written after the battle, he and his fellow soldiers were "in the very jaws of death," but they continued to perform their duty.[170]

As the weary Confederates fell back to their positions on Seminary Hill, General Lee met his defeated troops with the words "It is all my fault." The responsibility for the devastating Confederate charge that Lee had so adamantly desired on July 3 was indeed the general's. Lee's invasion of the North had, as historian Michael Palmer asserts, "failed well before Pickett's Charge." The choice of which troops should participate in the grand assault was not well thought out.[171] The decision to use Heth's battered division to attack the Federals is clearly a mistake on the part of the army's high command. Davis's brigade had suffered greatly on the first day, yet they were placed in line near the left flank, an important position. Were Lee and his principal lieutenants unaware of the heavy fighting Davis's men had participated in on July 1? The only explanation is the fact that the command structure was flawed and plagued with replacements. Hill's men were under the command of Longstreet, who most likely had no real understanding of how devastated Davis's command had been on the first day's fight. Also, Heth was out of action and Pettigrew was inexperienced in commanding a division in battle. Even with fresh troops the Confederate assault on July 3 would probably still have failed.

On July 4, 1863, the soldiers who had bravely fought to preserve the Union for three hard days at Gettysburg celebrated their country's 87th Independence Day. As the Federals exuberantly made the best of their first victory in the eastern theater in nearly a year, the Confederates braced for the attack they were sure was coming. When Lee felt confident enough that Meade was not planning a counterattack he began his slow retreat south. On the evening of July 4 the battered Rebels began pulling away from Gettysburg. As night fell the 55th North Carolina joined the rest of Lee's army and began moving south. Heth's battered division had been assigned to protect the rear of the retreating army. Lieutenant Hoyle described that summer night to his wife.

> Stay in our position till dark this evening, when we commenced falling back. A heavy rain fell this evening, and the roads are extremely muddy. Added to this the darkness of the night, makes the most difficult and laborious marching I ever experienced. We marched all night.[172]

As the Confederate troops continued their retreat into Virginia those soldiers unfortunate enough to be wounded during the three days of fighting were suffering. Immediately after Pickett's Charge, the cries from those wounded Confederates still on the field could be heard by both sides. As night fell Federal troops reported that "there were hundreds, if not thousands, of Rebels still out there, desperate for attention." The Union soldiers positioned on Cemetery Hill found it difficult to sleep with the constant moaning emanating from the dark field.[173]

On July 4 at 5:30 p.m. Brigadier General John Imboden, who Lee had chosen to escort the wagons, began moving toward Virginia. The wagons could not carry all of the wounded, so over 6,800 injured Confederates had to be left behind, including Colonel Connally, who was captured near Cashtown on July 5. Many of these men were left simply because the retreat south would kill them. The wagons moved slowly toward Virginia and the constant bumping and rocking made the journey extremely torturous for many of the wounded Rebels.[174]

Assistant Surgeon LeGrand Wilson was also ordered to accompany the wagons as they moved southward. Wilson gathered some needed supplies, which included, among other items, morphine, bandages, and surgical instruments. The Mississippi surgeon was assigned to assist the wounded soldiers in the rear half of the wagon column. Wilson stated that the extreme heat made traveling miserable, especially for the wounded. Although a cooling rain relieved some of the misery, the inclement weather also hampered the Confederate retreat.[175]

One of these wounded Confederates was Captain Howell G. Whitehead. Whitehead and several other wounded Rebels were "closely packed" in wagons on July 4, and withdrawn during the evening. The retreat was tremendously painful for many of the wounded and Whitehead asserted he "suffered greatly." The following day Federal cavalry units, commanded by Captain Jones of the first New York Cavalry, attacked the wagon column being escorted by General Imboden near Greencastle, Pennsylvania. The Union troopers captured Captain Whitehead and more than 500 other Confederates, including several men from the 55th North Carolina. Of the Rebels who were taken prisoner, about three hundred were wounded. The Union attack also cost the Confederates nearly 100 wagons and several artillery pieces. The fact that the wounded Confederates were now in Federal hands did not make their traveling any easier. Whitehead stated, "I can say with truth that I suffered more that night than all my life before, completely broken down and nearly starved to death."[176]

Major Belo, who had been wounded in the leg on July 1, was also traveling with the wounded when the Federals attacked. When the Union troopers spotted Belo they thought he was a general because of his major's star, which resembled that of a brigadier general in the Federal army. The major's servant, who was riding one of Belo's horses and leading another, tried to help Belo escape. Before Belo had the chance to mount his horse, Confederate cavalry arrived and forced the Federals to retreat.[177]

After arriving at Williamsburg the Confederates were again attacked by advancing Federal cavalry. Belo, always the soldier, gathered all of the able-bodied Rebels and took up position in nearby trenches. Colonel Stone of the second Mississippi and Major R. O. Reynolds of the 11th Mississippi assisted Belo. Their efforts succeeded in driving the Federals back.[178]

July 5 brought continued marching for the soldiers of the 55th. As night fell the regiment bivouacked near Waynesboro, Pennsylvania. Before darkness fell on the following day the regiment was out of Pennsylvania and camped near Hagerstown, Maryland. Hoyle stated, "the marching is setting very severely upon us." After passing through Hagerstown on July 7, the men were allowed to rest, and spent the following day in their camp. The day spent in camp provided the men with some much-needed rest. The delay was by no means an indication that Lee no longer feared an attack. Lieutenant Hoyle claimed that the only reason the regiment was able to stay in camp on July 8 was because the Potomac was "so full" the troops were unable to cross. The rain that had hampered Lee's retreat had also swollen the Potomac River.[179]

The 55th North Carolina remained near Hagerstown for several days. Several minor skirmishes had occurred, but the regiment was not engaged. The Confederates were unable to cross the Potomac for several days because Union cavalry under the command of Major General William H. French had destroyed the pontoon bridge at Falling Waters on July 4. Lee was forced to wait, all the while expecting Meade to attack.[180]

As Lee's back remained pinned against the Potomac, Meade inched closer to the Army of Northern Virginia. During the time Lee's army remained positioned near the Potomac, Federal cavalry continuously made minor demonstrations against the Rebel pickets. On July 10 the 55th was ordered to form a line of battle and was posted in the rear of where the fighting was occurring. The men remained in reserve until the evening and then were ordered back toward the river. On July 11, Davis ordered the men in his brigade to form again and fortify their position. Lieutenant Hoyle wrote that the Federals were in front of their position and that the North Carolinians were engaged in minor skirmishes. Hoyle also stated that the men expected a battle soon.[181]

On July 12 the Federals in front of the 55th drove back the regiment's skirmishers and advanced to within sight of the Confederate line. The soldiers behind the Rebel lines prepared for an attack they were sure was imminent. In reality Meade had planned to attack Lee on July 12, but his principal lieutenants felt that an assault would fail.[182] The day passed without any major attempt by Meade to attack the Rebels, but the Federals would not wait long.

Lee waited for Meade to make a major assault against his position, and the early morning skirmishes convinced the general that the Federals were coming. Meade, however, had realized that Lee was prepared to repel any attack and decided to spend the day reconnoitering the Confederate lines. Lee, growing more impatient as the day went on, was informed that the Federals were still entrenching. Unwilling to wait any longer, Lee ordered his troops to cross the Potomac. The engineers had finished the pontoon bridge and the river had receded enough for the army to move. As darkness fell on July 13, Lee's army began crossing back into Virginia. By eleven o'clock the following morning all of Lee's troops, except Heth's and Pender's divisions, were across the Potomac.[183]

On the evening of July 13, Heth's division began moving toward the pontoon bridge at Falling Waters. The 55th continued to be engaged in minor skirmishes, but as darkness fell they retreated with the rest of Heth's men. Heth stated that the evening "was the most uncomfortable night I passed during the war; it rained incessantly; the roads were eight or ten inches deep in mud and water." Lieutenant Hoyle agreed with the major general, declaring "Our forces drew off this evening at dark toward the Potomac. It is raining and the roads are desperately muddy. This night has been the worst marching I have done yet."[184]

Heth's men marched to the elevated ridge about a mile and a quarter from Falling Waters. The men in the major general's division then formed a line of battle on both sides of the road and stretched out along the crest of the ridge facing toward Hagerstown. After placing artillery the division prepared to protect the rear of Lee's army as it crossed the Potomac. By eleven o'clock the following morning Heth received orders to move Pender's division across the river. Heth was then told to move his troops across as soon as Pender's men were safely on the south bank of the Potomac. Joseph Davis's brigade was chosen to remain in line of battle to protect the final crossing.[185]

Shortly after receiving the order to move his men across the Potomac, Heth's troops were attacked by Federal cavalry. At first Heth had thought the cavalry to be a squad of Confederates that had passed by his position several hours earlier. In fact, the major general was about to send one of his staff officers to arrest the trooper who was carrying an American flag. Heth mistakenly thought the man holding the flag was a Rebel officer who was dangerously flaunting a captured Federal flag in front of his men. Heth soon realized his blunder when he heard the Federal cavalry commander order his men to charge the Confederate line.[186]

The small cavalry detachment of the sixth Michigan Cavalry, commanded by Major Peter A. Weber, charged Heth's position.[187] Lieutenant Hoyle reported the incident to his wife.

> Our Division halted and formed in a line faced to the rear, this morning, about 1½ miles from the river, to protect the rear while crossing (we are crossing on a pontoon bridge) We stacked arms and lay down to rest but we did not lie long till the yankee cavalry dashed in among us befor we knew it, completely Surprising us. We had to get our arms and form as best we could while the bullets were whizzing among us. We formed after a little and held them in check till we could cross the river.[188]

Davis's men fought desperately to fend off the Federal troopers. Many of the men used their rifles to knock riders from their horses. Some of the Confederates even used axes and fence rails to fight off the mounted Union men. The remnants of the sixth Michigan Cavalry were forced to retreat minutes after they had first charged. Few of the Federal troopers escaped without injury.[189]

Brigadier General Judson Kilpatrick, who was in command of the cavalry force that was in front of the Confederate line, renewed the attack assisted by Brigadier General John Buford. Buford's men attacked the rear and right flank of the Rebel line while Kilpatrick advanced on their front. Heth's men were finally able to cross the Potomac, but they had suffered greatly.[190]

The official casualty reports state that the 55th North Carolina had three men killed and four men wounded between July 5 and July 14. Davis's brigade had a total of 12 killed and 16 wounded during the same period.[191] The official reports do not include those soldiers listed as missing. In their North Carolina Civil War Roster Project, Lewis Manarin and Weymouth Jordan, Jr., state that the regiment suffered four killed, three wounded, and 36 captured.[192] Lieutenant Hoyle stated, "We lost a good many men in this affair, mostly prisoners." Buford's report puts the total captured at around 500, which corresponds with A. P. Hill's report. Hill's report, however, stated that most of those captured were stragglers.[193]

The losses at Falling Waters further injured Heth's already weakened division, the loss of James Johnston Pettigrew being the most notable casualty. The 55th North Carolina's officer corps suffered as well. Lieutenant Thomas J. Hadley of Company A and Lieutenant Wilkins Stovall of Company K were both wounded during the battle at Falling Waters. Hadley would recover and serve again. Stovall was taken prisoner and sent to Johnson's Island.[194]

The encounter at Falling Waters apparently caused many of the soldiers in Davis's brigade to lose confidence in their divisional commander. Several months after the battle Joseph R. Davis wrote a letter to President Jefferson Davis describing the negative effects the fight had on his brigade's opinion of Henry Heth.

> Our Major General I am sorry to say has lost the confidence of the men of this Brigade on account of the Falling Waters affair. I doubt if he was to blame, but some one blundered and many more men were lost than is admitted. In my small command the loss was over one hundred and other Brigades suffered much more.[195]

The 55th marched with the rest of Davis's command through Martinsburg, Virginia, and bivouacked near Bunker Hill, some 12 miles north of Winchester.[196] The regiment remained in camp near Bunker Hill until July 21 when it was ordered to continue moving south. Minor skirmishes occurred throughout the retreat and the 55th fought briefly near Culpeper Court House. Private Wilkerson informed his mother that during the minor engagement one lieutenant was killed and several other men were wounded. Wilkerson also told his father "our cannon soon made them leave the mountain whare thay was shelling us from." Meade had crossed the Potomac on July 19, but was unable to catch the Confederate army off guard. As July ended, the men in the 55th found themselves stationed around Culpeper Court House.[197]

The invasion of Pennsylvania had been devastating for the 55th North Carolina. Nearly 50 percent of the men of the regiment were killed, wounded, or captured. Private Wilkerson described his company's situation in a letter to his mother on July 28, 1863. Wilkerson informed his mother that his company was "down to nothing" and that the only officer still able to serve was Sergeant William Chandler. The company's captain, Robert W. Thomas, was wounded in the head at Gettysburg and hospitalized on July 24 with typhoid fever. Lieutenant Stovall, as mentioned above, was captured at Falling Waters, and Lieutenant William H. Webb was wounded in the leg and captured at Gettysburg.[198]

Company K was not the only unit of the 55th decimated during the Gettysburg campaign. Lieutenant Hoyle informed his wife that as of July 20, there were only 14 men left in Company F. Among those wounded and captured were second Lieutenant Peter P. Mull, not to be confused with Captain Peter M. Mull, and third Lieutenant Archibald Williams. Mull would remain a Federal prisoner until March 1865, but Williams would return to duty and be promoted to first lieutenant in September 1864.[199]

As Lee's army tried to regain its strength the 55th North Carolina desperately needed to reorganize. In an attempt to enforce discipline the regiment began having roll call four times a day and drilled three times a day. Food, which had been so plentiful during the days preceding the battle of Gettysburg, had now become scarce. Wilkerson told his mother that the men couldn't get any bacon and hadn't had any since June. The troops were, however, able to obtain some beef, but continued rations of it seemed to have upset the soldiers.[200]

The battle of Gettysburg and the hurried retreat south afterward caused many of the men in the 55th North Carolina to lose their knapsacks and some clothing items. Wilkerson was lucky enough to still have most of his belongings, but he lost his army coat, which he had had since his training days at Camp Mangum. Many members of the regiment received some clothing and shoes at the end of July, though Private Wilkerson was not one of them. Like many of the other men fighting in Lee's army, Wilkerson needed shoes, and the filthy condition of the men made the young private remark that it "seems like the lice will devour us." Some of the soldiers who could afford to were able to get their clothing washed. The men had to pay twenty-five cents and furnish the soap.[201]

As the weary retreat began to end, Wilkerson, like many other men serving in the Army of Northern Virginia, was not doing well. The young private was sick, yet he continued to do his duty. The men of the 55th were tired, some of them sick, almost all of them filthy, and only receiving half rations.[202] The constant drilling to keep the men disciplined only added to the low morale. The summer of 1863 proved to be a very bloody affair for the men of the 55th North Carolina. Although glad to be back in good old Dixie, the soldiers knew that the next day could bring the horrors of battle back again. Unfortunately for the 55th, some of the bloodiest fighting of the Civil War was still to come and they would once again find themselves in the midst of death.

4

August 1863–March 1864: Politics, Winter, and God

"We have bowed down in the dust of true repentance"

After the Gettysburg campaign the number of troops in the Army of Northern Virginia was severely diminished. The thousands killed or wounded during the battle and subsequent retreat were not the only reasons Lee's army had shrunk after Gettysburg. The defeat had lowered the army's morale, and many soldiers felt the war was lost and decided to go home. Although soldiers from every Confederate state deserted, the highest numbers of deserters were from North Carolina. By the end of the war 23,694 soldiers from North Carolina had deserted the Confederate armies. This number nearly doubled that of Tennessee, which had the second highest number of deserters.[1]

The actual number of men deserting the 55th North Carolina during this time is unknown. Private Wilkerson wrote a letter to his father in August indicating that several members of Company K had gone home during this period, writing that the men were "deserting Study." Lieutenant Hoyle informed his wife "every body is sicker of the war than they ever was before, and I fear many will run away."[2] The regiment's morale remained low throughout the rest of the summer.

On August 1, 1863, in an effort to stem the tide of desertion, President Davis issued a proclamation that all soldiers who were absent without leave, or had failed to report to their respective regiments, would receive a full pardon if they returned to their commands in 20 days.[3] New conscripts, recruits, Davis's proclamation, and Lee's efforts to provide his men with furloughs helped refill the depleted ranks of the Army of Northern Virginia. Early in August, Hill's Third Corps had 11,207 men present for duty. By the beginning of October he had over 16,000 men ready for action. The fact that deserters from almost every division were being shot probably motivated some of the men to stay with their commands.[4]

The defeat at Gettysburg was not the only reason the morale of the men serving in the 55th North Carolina was low throughout August and September. The lack of supplies and nutritious food added to the displeasure of many of the soldiers. Private E. H. Jones of Company H informed his father that the only food the men were given was fatty bacon, beef, and bread. Jones stated that it was "impossible to get any nourishment." Jones also wrote that the poor quality of food was starting to have a negative effect on the fighting men.[5] Insufficient food continued to be a problem but several of the men finally received new clothing and shoes. On August 8, Private Wilkerson received a pair of pants and several pairs of socks. Wilkerson also was issued a pair of "very good Shoes," which he had needed since the retreat from Gettysburg.[6]

Although the soldiers' rations were less than desirable, most of the men of the 55th continued to support the war effort. Bell Irvin Wiley, who wrote about the lives of the common soldier, asserted that, in general, the Confederate soldier did not concern himself with politics. Wiley also claimed that most Southern soldiers cared little about gubernatorial elections in their home states.[7] Joseph Allan Frank, in his work *With Ballot and Bayonet: The Political Socialization of American Civil War Soldiers,* contends that politics was "the defining feature of the people's armies of the North and South." Frank also asserts that, as the war dragged on, soldiers' political convictions became more important.[8] Although Frank does not contend that the majority of Civil War soldiers were concerned with political problems and events, he does assert that Southerners were as committed to their convictions as Northerners.

In the summer of 1863 affairs at home began to harden the resolve of North Carolina soldiers everywhere. Throughout July and August nearly 100 protest meetings occurred in North Carolina. These rallies were primarily concerned with the Confederate government's conscription laws and President Davis's demand that all recruitment be controlled by the central government in Richmond. The suspension of *habeas corpus,* which was implemented after October 1862, also angered many citizens of the Old North State. Fearing a military dictatorship, some North Carolinians began calling for an end to the war. William W. Holden, owner of the popular newspaper the *Raleigh Standard,* asked all Confederate states to convene a peace conference to negotiate an end to the Civil War.[9]

The opposition to the peace movement was spearheaded by Zebulon B. Vance, himself a Confederate officer. Vance and his followers believed the result of pulling out of the Confederacy and making peace with the North would result in nothing but more suffering and greater loss of freedom for their state. As news of the civil unrest in their home state reached the North Carolina regiments, they quickly acted to show their support for the war.[10]

In August the North Carolina troops serving in the Army of Northern Virginia banded together in an act of solidarity. The Tar Heel soldiers held a convention composed of delegates from every North Carolina regiment serving in Lee's army. The soldiers of each regiment elected delegates and those selected included captains, lieutenants, sergeants, corporals, and privates. The colonel of the fourth North Carolina Regiment, Bryan Grimes, was chosen to serve as the president of the convention. Lieutenant Thomas J. Hadley, who had recently been wounded at Falling Waters, and Lieutenant Charles R. Jones of Company G represented the 55th.[11]

The convention voted on a set of resolutions that had been drafted by an appointed committee, which contained one member from each of the nine brigades that contained North Carolina regiments. Lieutenant Hadley was chosen to represent Davis's brigade. The resolutions presented at the convention included a repudiation of those individuals in North Carolina who were proposing to accept a peace proposal based on submission or reconstruction. The resolution asserted that the men serving in the army would only accept an honorable settlement to the existing conflict.[12] The committee's third resolution was a flat attack on Holden and his peace movement.

3d Resolved, That while the soldiers are fighting, suffering and dying for our independence, it is wrong that some at home should be continually dampening their ardor, casting a chill and gloom on their hopes and unnerving them for the contest by untimely repinings and base leanings toward submission; that would be untrue to our principals, untrue to our wives and children, who would be the greatest sufferers by submission, untrue to our noble dead, untrue to our interest, untrue to our State, untrue to our Confederacy, and untrue to the cause of freedom, now submit to the domination of such as rule the Northern people, and that we fear their rule more than we fear their wrath.[13]

The delegates at the convention also expressed "mortification" that their own citizens had met to oppose enforcement of the conscription law. The North Carolina troops asserted their support for conscription, stating that those who opposed the law were merely afraid to fight and were in fact traitors to the cause of freedom.[14]

The North Carolina troops serving in Lee's army in the summer and fall of 1863 surely prove that Bell Wiley's contention that Southern soldiers cared little about politics was mistaken, at least in respect to Tar Heels. With the support of the combat troops, whom North Carolina (as well as several other states) allowed to vote by proxy, Zebulon Vance defeated William Holden in the state's gubernatorial election in 1863. Vance's election was a mandate from the state's soldiers that the war must continue until the South had won its independence.

As political battles waged in their home state, the men of the 55th remained near Culpeper Court House. Meanwhile, the Army of the Potomac's movements north of the Rappahannock forced Lee to shift his army to the Rapidan. On August 3 the 55th North Carolina, along with the rest of Hill's corps, moved to an area north of Orange Court House. Lee informed Richmond that the terrain around Culpeper offered no advantages for battle. The general also stated that if Meade's army advanced toward the Rapidan he would be in a position to check their march.[15]

The 55th spent the month of August drilling and picketing the fords of the Rapidan. A few minor skirmishes occurred, though it is not known if any members of the 55th participated in them. A. P. Hill reviewed Heth's division late in August and the *Richmond Daily Dispatch* declared "the respective brigades were in excellent condition." On September 12 General Lee reviewed the fighting men of Hill's Third Corps. These reviews were part of the high command's attempt to raise the army's morale.[16]

By the end of August, Heth had 264 officers and 3,686 men present for duty, and by the end of October the major general's division had 425 officers and 5,044 men present and ready for action.[17] The increases were mainly attributed to new recruits, conscripts, and wounded soldiers returning for duty. As the dreadful summer of 1863 ended and the falling leaves ushered in another autumn, the Third Corps received some much need supplies. The men had been eating fatty bacon, beef, and bread for weeks, but now they were treated to apples, blackberries, potatoes, and other vegetables. More clothing and shoes also arrived and Hill's troops began to look like a fighting force once again. These supplies did not include blankets, which many of the men in the 55th North Carolina desperately needed, especially as the weather turned colder near the end of September.[18]

The men of the 55th continued performing picket duty throughout August and September. Fraternization between Federal and Confederate pickets became an everyday occurrence. Meade kept his army close to Lee, but did not attack. The Federal commander felt that the Confederate lines were too strong and any assault would result in a considerable loss of life.[19] As the stalemate continued the fighting men of the 55th prepared for an attack they believed was imminent. Still the Federals showed no signs of any kind of major assault. With the exception of minor skirmishes and a few cavalry engagements all remained quiet.[20] Lieutenant Hoyle alerted his wife of his belief that the Federals would move upon the Confederate positions in the coming days.

> All has been compartively still for the last two days here, but the enemy is still in our front beyond the river, and some reports say in heavy force. If this be the case, which is doubtful, they may advance and a fight ensue any day. If we have to enter the field of blood and carnage again, I hope God's good grace will keep us as it has in times past. Dear Sarah, my own bosom friend, be comforted then, and put your hope and trust in the Lord, who only can reconcile us to our lot, and turn our sorrow and grief into praise and rejoicing.[21]

Meade had remained obstinate against assaulting Lee's line. However, the Confederate decision to transfer Longstreet and most of his corps to Tennessee made the Federal commander consider an advance. By September 8 Longstreet's troops were on the move and preparing to travel by rail to Tennessee.[22] The move brought no immediate reaction from the Federals and the men of the 55th continued to bide their time in camp or on picket duty relaxing and thinking of home. Lieutenant Hoyle penned a poem to his wife that reflected the thoughts and dreams that entered the soldiers' minds as they watched for Union advances or slept through the night.

> When all is Silent in the night,
> And my eyes in Sleep are closed,
> Then comes flushing, pure and bright,
> Thy image lovely as an angel robed.[23]

At the end of September the weather in northern Virginia began turning cold and had some effect on the welfare of the men in the 55th. The concerns of Federal attacks continued throughout the month, but according to Lieutenant Hoyle the morale of the troops was higher than it had been since they had returned from Pennsylvania. Desertions continued to be a problem, but the continued vigilance of the Confederate high command to treat deserters with the most severe consequences was producing the desired effect.

> The weather is cold up here now, and we have frost plenty, and some of our men are poorly provided for cold weather. Some have no blankets at all, and I fear we will not get any from the government soon. I have two of Capt. Mull's blankets, and one of my own and a bed tick, so I fare very well in this line. There was some cavalry fighting up here last week. We were ordered out, and expected the general fight was coming on, but the yankees soon went back, and all is now quiet again. It is hard telling what the enemy aims to do here. It is quite sure they have a heavy force in our front, and yet they do not advance. Though they may come when we least expect it. I think our army is now in a great deal better spirits than they have ever been since we came out of Pa., and if the deserters know how cheerful our brave soldier's now are, I think some, at lest, would come back. And I would here say that deserters are faring but midling here now. 10 or 12 have been shot lately. One was shot in sight of our camp last week, but we being on picket at the time, I did not see it. I believe that hundreds of the deserters will now be shot. It seems very hard, but the cause demands it.[24]

The monotony of picket duty was somewhat relieved when the soldiers serving in Lee's army heard that General Braxton Braggs's Army of Tennessee had defeated the Federals on September 20 at the Battle of Chickamauga. Longstreet had assisted Bragg, and the Army of Northern Virginia felt they could claim some of the credit for the victory.[25] When the

Federal high command decided to transfer the XI and XII corps to Tennessee to resist the Confederate advances in the West, Lee decided to once again conduct an offensive campaign. Why Lee decided to attack Meade is not clear. Historians cannot agree on whether Lee wanted to gain time, gain space, or gain a battlefield victory.[26] Why Lee chose to attack Meade is not the concern of this study, but the subsequent battle at Bristoe Station involved the 55th North Carolina.

By the beginning of October, General Meade had moved his army from Culpeper Court House to the Rapidan River. Lee, whose Army of Northern Virginia was on the south bank of the river near Orange Court House, met with his senior lieutenants on Clark's Mountain to discuss his proposed offensive strategy. The Confederate commander felt that his best chance of success was to strike Meade's right flank. On October 9 the Confederate army began to move, leaving half of J. E. B. Stuart's cavalry behind to protect the army's rear. Two days later Hill's men, including the 55th North Carolina, entered Culpeper, which was now deserted. On October 10 Meade had learned that Lee was attempting to attack his right flank. The Federal commander, who had known since October 3 that Lee was planning some type of movement, immediately ordered his men to retreat from Culpeper along the Orange & Alexandria Railroad.[27]

Warrenton, Virginia, was Lee's objective, and he and Ewell arrived there during the afternoon of October 13. Hill was ordered to move to Warrenton by leading his men on an encircling march northwest to Sperryville, then east to Warrenton through Amissville and Waterloo. Once Hill arrived Lee hoped to strike Meade's army somewhere along the Orange & Alexandria Railroad. Hill's corps finally reached Warrenton near sundown on October 13. With the Federals in retreat, many Confederate soldiers believed another victory resembling that of Second Manassas in August 1862 would soon occur.[28]

On October 13 the majority of the Army of Northern Virginia was centered around Warrenton. Major General Wade Hampton's cavalry division, of Stuart's corps, was positioned on the right; Ewell was in the center; and Hill's troops were on the left. Lee's army was positioned facing north and east, and Meade's troops were retreating along the Orange & Alexandria Railroad moving northeast.[29] On the morning of October 14 Hill's corps moved away from Warrenton around 5:30 a.m. Major General Richard Anderson's division was in the lead followed by Heth. The Third Corps marched through New Baltimore. Upon hearing that the Federals were moving north, almost parallel to his line, Hill ordered Anderson's division to continue forward toward Buckland Mills, a few miles away, and instructed Heth and Major General Cadmus Wilcox to march their divisions east toward Greenwich. Anderson, it was hoped, would be able to catch the Federals and attack them while they were in retreat. Unfortunately the troops north of Hill's line were only scattered remnants of Union cavalry fleeing from Major General Fitz Lee's troopers. Unable to engage the Federals, Anderson quickly altered his course and regrouped with Hill's main force.[30]

Around 10:00 a.m. most of the Third Corps had reached Greenwich, Virginia. Evidence that the Federals made a hasty retreat was seen everywhere. Fires were still burning and the road to Bristoe Station was covered with Federal knapsacks, blankets, and even guns. Filled with enthusiasm the Confederates under Hill's command rapidly advanced toward Bristoe Station. Unfortunately Hill, as at Gettysburg, had not properly reconnoitered the area and was not sure exactly how many Federals were approaching. Hill rode ahead of his men and from a high point observed Federal troops crossing Broad Run. The Union soldiers that had crossed the run were moving northward up the railroad toward Manassas, while those on the southern bank were resting and waiting for their turn to cross the fords. The lieutenant general, without scouting out the area, quickly ordered Heth to advance his division and form in a line of battle. Hill's haste would cost the lives of hundreds of Heth's men.[31]

Heth ordered his men forward with Brigadier General John R. Cooke's brigade to the right of the Greenwich Road and Brigadier General William W. Kirkland's brigade to the left. Brigadier General Henry W. Walker's command was placed in support of Kirkland's force and Davis's unit was held in reserve, and ordered to support Major Thomas Poague's battery. Heth's men advanced, prepared to defeat the retreating and confused Federals.[32]

As Heth's men advanced, Federal "skirmishers" appeared on his right flank. Heth and Cooke were concerned with the Federal presence on their flank, but Hill informed them that Anderson's men would protect their right. Cooke is said to have responded to his order to advance by saying "I will advance and if they flank me, I will face my men about and cut my way out." Cooke ordered his men forward and attempted to force the Federals back.[33]

As Cooke's men moved forward Major General Gouverneur K. Warren's II Corps was positioned on the Confederate right behind a railroad embankment. As the Confederates advanced, Warren ordered his artillery to open on their position. Under a heavy cannonade Heth's men moved forward, but the Federal fire only intensified. Some of Heth's men were able to reach the railroad and drive the Federals back, but the relentless fire from the Union lines was too much for the courageous Rebels. After the short battle Heth had lost 1,381 men and another 445 were missing. These casualties included Generals Cooke and Kirkland, who were wounded while advancing with their troops.[34]

Davis's brigade had remained in reserve, but had been ordered in to support Cooke's troops. The 55th North Carolina had been positioned on the left of Davis's command. Davis's men were sent into the attack posted on Cooke's right. The regimental historian stated, "A piece of forest was in front [of their position] and consequently our loss was slight as compared to the loss of some of the regiments of Cooke's Brigade." Davis's casualties were reported as eight men killed and 37 wounded. No official casualty report was filed for the 55th, but Louis Manarin and Weymouth Jordan, Jr., list the regiment's losses at three men killed and two captured.[35]

Although the 55th took part in the engagement it saw little action. Private George W. Pearsall of Company G wrote his wife explaining that at times the fighting was intense, but that the soldiers of the regiment around him "did not fire nor lose no men." Pearsall felt that the regiment should have been sent into to the melee to support their embattled comrades. However, the eager private was happy to remain out of the fight, writing "thank god we was not in reach of the muskits, but a fiew minuts they pepard round me very fast."[36] Lieutenant Hoyle also described the day's action in a letter to his wife. Our Division came up with the yankees this evening at Bristol Station, 5 miles from Manasses, and a fight ensued. We opened the fight by shelling their camp and wagons. Then we advanced upon them, our Brigade being held in reserve, they were strongly posted behind the rail road, and after a fierce charge, our men were compelled to fall back, but we soon formed and advanced again far enough to hold the field, and here we lay (on the battle field) all night. The yankees shelled us furiously after this last advance for a short time, but dark soon came on, when the noise of battle sunk into silent repose. Nothing broke the stillness of night, but the cries and groans of the wounded. Sad, indeed, it is to lie upon a battle field.[37]

The day after the battle Lee and his two lieutenants, Hill and Heth, rode over the battlefield. The Federals had retreated across Broad Run on the night of October 14, leaving the ground littered with Confederate and Union dead. Hill described the attack to his commander and assumed full responsibility for the failure. Lee, not one to allow his anger to be unleashed, simply replied, "General, bury your dead."[38]

On October 17 Lee's army began marching back to the line of the Rappahannock. While falling back toward the river Davis's men participated the destruction of the Orange & Alexandria Railroad to the Rappahannock. For a few days Davis's brigade was positioned along the river picketing the fords. By the end of October the 55th North Carolina was camped near Brandy Station, about nine miles from Culpeper, Virginia. A rumor spread throughout the camps of the regiment that Hill's corps would soon be sent west to assist General Braxton Bragg's Army of Tennessee, but concerns over this possible move quickly faded.[39]

The armies remained quiet until Meade sent a detachment of troops across the river at Rappahannock Station and Kelly's Ford and engaged the Army of Northern Virginia on November 7. Although the 55th marched to Culpeper and prepared to face the Federals they did not participate in these engagements. On November 8 the Army of Northern Virginia marched back toward the Rapidan. The 55th went into camp around Orange Court House with the rest of Davis's unit.[40] Lieutenant Hoyle supplied a descriptive account of the regiment's movements in reaction to the Federal threat.

> I wrote you in my last, that all was quiet, but even while I was writing fighting was going on down the river, and that same night we had orders to be ready to march at day break next morning. And accordingly early on the morning of the eighth we commenced falling back. After marching 6 or 7 miles and 2 miles before we reached Culpeper, we formed line of battle and all day awaited the approach of the enemy, but none came except a force of cavalry on our left and they were repulsed by our skirmishers. Night coming on, we resumed our retrograde movement passing through Culpeper at dark. We continued our march at night and suffered considerably both from cold and fatigue. On the morning of the 9th we halted and got something to eat. We then resumed our march, and crossed the Rapidan in the evening and took up camp in our old position at Rapidan Station.[41]

Although the Confederate army began preparing its winter camps, General Meade was not ready to end the campaigning season. On November 26 he began moving his army into position to attack Lee. Five Federal corps crossed the Rapidan and prepared to strike the Army of Northern Virginia. Lee, being informed of Meade's movements, moved his army and entrenched along Mine Run. After several days of minor skirmishing and indecision Meade pulled his troops back across the river. Lee, tired of waiting for the Federals to strike, ordered an attack for the morning of December 2. The 55th was in line with the Confederate force that was prepared to attack Meade's left flank.[42]

On the morning of November 27 the 55th marched toward Fredericksburg. The condition of the roads made the march difficult, but the men managed to locate the Federals around two o'clock in the afternoon. The men formed into a line of battle and sent out skirmishers. The Federals pulled back and the Rebels discovered that the Union's main body had withdrawn. The soldiers spent the night in battle formation. The next day the 55th North Carolina, with the rest of Heth's division, fell back and spent the day fortifying their position. The regiment spent the day behind breastworks and never advanced. Davis's brigade spent the next few days behind fortifications expecting a general engagement at any moment. The Federals never attacked and the 55th returned to their camp near Orange Court House on December 3.[43] Lieutenant Hoyle described the regiment's activities as they marched to counter the Army of the Potomac's latest offensive moves.

> I have the pleasure of writing you a few lines this morning, informing you that we are back at our old camp near Orange. The yankees have all gone back across the river, and we returned to our old camp yesterday. I will give you a narration of our expedition. On the morning of Friday the 27th inst, we left camp, directing our march on the plank road toward Fredericksburg. The yankees had crossed the river the day before 5 or 6 miles above Chancellorsville, and now had possession of the plank road, opposite the place at which they crossed. Giving to the hard frozen conditions of the ground our march was attended with some difficulty in the morning. Many a fellow caught a fall over the slick frozen ground. We continued our march till about 2 in the evening when we came up with the enemies advance. Our division was in front. We were formed in line of battle on each side of the road, and some artilery and skirmishers were thrown out to the front, and a considerable skirmish ensued. The yankees gave way after a brisk fire, and we pushed forward after them. Having driven them some half a mile till dark, we halted and lay in line all night. We lost 2 men killed (that I have heard of) and several wounded in this affair. The dead yankees were left on the field and fell into our hands. On the next morning (28th) we fell back about 2 miles to get a position. Our division was placed in the reserve now, and we were engaged all day in maneuvering and fortifying. This was a very rainy day, yet we worked nearly all the time, if you would call gouging with our bayonets and scraping dirt with our hands work.[44]

The men in the 55th experienced "hard times" during November and December. Their daily ration consisted of flour and beef. The monotony and harsh realities of camp life wore down the resolve of Private George Woodard, who asked his sister to have his brother-in-law, William Batts, hire a replacement for him. On December 23 the regiment moved about six miles away from their temporary camp near Orange Court House and began construction of their winter quarters.[45]

Christmas 1863 found the men of the 55th North Carolina bivouacked near Orange Court House, hundreds of miles from their loved ones. Like most of the soldiers, Private Woodard expressed his desire to be home for the holidays. In a letter to his brother, Woodard wrote, "I wish I was with you all today to help you eat some good meat and bread, and some good egg-nog. It is very cold here." The men had spent their days constructing their winter quarters, but on Christmas Day it was "very slow."[46] Although members of the 13th North Carolina located a large amount of whiskey, which they proceeded to get intoxicated from, Private Woodard of the 55th declared that he couldn't find anything to drink to help him celebrate the holiday.[47]

The year 1863 had not been a good one for the Confederacy. Even though Lee's army had soundly defeated the Army of the Potomac at Chancellorsville, and the Army of Tennessee's victory at Chickamauga had raised the men's spirits, the resounding defeats at Gettysburg, Vicksburg, and Chattanooga had been disastrous. The previous winter the Army of Northern Virginia had celebrated its victories over General Burnside, but now the feeling of hopelessness began to creep into the thoughts of many of the fighting men.

The lack of supplies also had many of the men feeling demoralized. The men in the 55th were receiving little to eat or drink. Private Woodard summed up the feelings many of the Rebel troops had when he informed his brother, "I think [the] Southern Federacy is broke, for it seems to me." The irritated private claimed that the men were receiving very little meat and that the poor quality of food was having an adverse effect on his health. In addition to the shortage of food several of the soldiers were still without proper clothing. Woodard had no shoes and needed pants, shirts, an overcoat, and a pair of boots. The weather made army life hard and the young private wrote, "I suffer very much with cold."[48]

As the soldiers struggled with the cold and hunger, their beloved governor was working feverishly to have them reassigned to an all–North Carolina brigade. Earlier in October the members of the first and third North Carolina regiments had petitioned Secretary of War James A. Seddon to be placed into a North Carolina brigade. Seddon had informed these men that all of their state's brigades were full, so he would be unable to grant their request. In December Governor Vance once again requested that the first and third regiments be placed in a North Carolina brigade. Vance proposed that these two regiments be placed in a new brigade that would also include the 55th and 33rd North Carolina regiments. Seddon referred the matter to Lee who, although sympathetic to the soldiers' request, stated that the creation of a new brigade would destroy the commands of Joseph R. Davis and George H. Steuart and weaken Brigadier General James H. Lane's command.[49]

Although Lee was adamantly against creating a new North Carolina brigade he did suggest that he would be willing to place the 55th in Steuart's brigade, which contained three Virginia regiments and two North Carolina regiments. Lee stated that he would consider this move, but expressed reservations about the effect it would have on Davis's command. Although several North Carolinians hoped to have some change made, the logistical hassles and negative effects the moves would entail proved too much for the Confederate high command and the brigades remained as they had been.[50] It is not known whether members of the 55th were involved in petitioning officials in Richmond to be taken out of Davis's brigade. The only related reference is found in a letter dated June 10, 1863, from Dorsey Pender to his wife. Pender stated that Colonel Connally had asked the major general to assist his efforts to be transferred out of Davis's command. The letter does not imply that Connally was dissatisfied with his then current post, but asserts that he hoped to be placed in command of his own brigade.[51] There is also evidence that Connally and his superior officer, Joseph R. Davis, harbored no ill will towards each other. In fact, Davis recommended that the young colonel be promoted to the rank of brigadier general stating, that Connally was an "intelligent officer." This recommendation, however, did not occur until March 1864, well after Connally had been wounded while gallantly leading his regiment at the battle of Gettysburg.[52]

As the new year began Alfred Belo returned to take command of the 55th North Carolina. Belo had been out of action for over six months, and even though he still needed a cane to help him walk he was ready to accept the responsibility of leading his old regiment. Belo was given the rank of lieutenant colonel and replaced Captain Robert W. Thomas, who had commanded the regiment since August.[53]

Belo's return brought some light to the dreary winter camp of the 55th, but the men remained in want of better food and warmer clothing. There was little for the men to do during the cold winter months. Most of the soldiers spent their days playing cards, checkers, dominoes, and chess. Occasionally the soldiers were able to join together and listen to their regimental band or their brigade band play "I'm Going Back to Dixie," "Sweet Evalina," and other musical favorites. Assistant Surgeon Wilson wrote that these musical diversions were "worth more to the brigade as a 'health promoter' than the two Surgeons would have been with well filled chests of medicine."[54]

During January the weather remained mild and comfortable enough for the soldiers to drill one hour each day. These drill sessions helped keep the men prepared for military action and provided a much-needed opportunity to exercise. The decent weather did not last and by the end of the month the cold and snow returned. The snow curtailed the brigade's drilling sessions, but the men found other ways to occupy their time.[55]

During the last week of January the men in Davis's brigade participated in their first battle of the new year. The abundance of snow was apparently too tempting to several of the soldiers and they proceeded to form battle lines and attack their fellow regiments. Their rifles remained stacked, but they were able to find plenty of ammunition scattered all over the Virginia landscape. The snowball melee soon turned into a full-scale battle as brigade fought brigade. Several units unfurled their battle flags as if in real combat and charged their "enemies." LeGrand Wilson stated that General Lee, who sat mounted on his horse Traveler, viewed the determined, yet amusing snowball war, and was probably glad to see his men enjoying themselves.[56]

The 55th spent most of the winter months in camp and their daily lives continued to be harsh. The rations for soldiers holding the line near the Rapidan

Musician Henry C. Adcock, Company K. Henry Adcock enlisted in the Confederate Army on March 1, 1862, at the age of 18. He served as a private and a teamster before being appointed a musician sometime between July 1862 and June 1864. Adcock spent his time entertaining and motivating his fellow soldiers. The 55th North Carolina Division of Archives and History, Raleigh, North Carolina.)

remained low in quality and quantity. Private William Meade Dame of the Richmond Howitzers, who was stationed near Morton's Ford, remembered that he and his fellow Confederates were reduced to making salads from dandelions and other green weeds. Private Dame also stated "the unbroken diet of just bread and meat — generally salt meat at that — gave some of the men scurvy." Lieutenant Colonel Belo stated that the daily ration for the men in the 55th consisted of a pound of cornmeal and a quarter pound of beans. Some of the men who could afford to bought cornfield peas at a dollar a quart, Confederate currency, and occasionally the men were lucky enough to get their hands on some coffee, usually captured from the Federals. Although according to Belo the men only received beans and cornmeal as their daily ration they were able to acquire bacon and make bread.[57] Belo described how the men of the 55th spent their days during the cold winter months.

> The order of life was this: breakfast of cold bacon and left-over rolls; then drilling and camp duties; dress parade and dinner about four. A pipe and coffee served a very useful purpose, and it was all we could offer to a man if anyone came to see us, and we had a hard time to keep up the reputation for Southern hospitality.[58]

The cold weather and the low amounts of food also caused a decline in the health of the regiment. In February, Private Pearsall had contracted a severe cold, writing to his wife, "I have begin to coff again very bad." The weary soldier asked his wife to send some potatoes and whatever else she could afford. Although sick and hungry Private Pearsall still concerned himself with matters at home. He instructed his wife to buy some corn to feed their horse and plant turnips to sell. The welfare of his wife and children was still more important to him than his own health and well-being.[59]

The limited nourishment and the struggle to keep warm during the cold winter days became too much for Private Woodard. On January 23 he wrote a letter informing his brother "I ain't fitten for service." Woodard also wrote that his lieutenant was trying to get him discharged from the army on account of his poor health. By the end of January the young private's health was deteriorating and by February 11 he wrote home declaring "I am well at this time, all except the diarrhoea." Although Woodard told his family that he was well, the disease he suffered from in February ultimately ended his life prematurely. On March 23, 1864, Private George W. Woodard died in a Virginia hospital.[60]

In August 1864 George Woodard's family received receipts from the quartermaster at Gordansville, Virginia, for his personal effects. Although Private Woodard may have had more personal wealth than many of the other soldiers, considering that in the last few months of his life he was hoping to pay for a substitute to take his place in the army, his personal belongings provide some indication of what the men of the 55th owned. When Private Woodard died he had one pair of pants, drawers, shoes, and socks, and one coat. He also owned one hat and one haversack. The total appraised value of these items was $22.25. Woodard had a little money, $12.50, and had one promissory note totaling $64.00.[61] Like most of his fellow soldiers Woodard had very little to spare and did not even own a blanket to keep him warm during the cold winter months. The camp around Orange Court House was in almost every respect George Woodard's Valley Forge, and as the latter was for so many forgotten Continental soldiers of 1776, the young private's last refuge.

By the end of February the weather had become "more pleasant again." The men of the 55th spent time writing and receiving letters from family and friends. Letters from home, unless describing some type of hardship, probably always raised the fighting men's spirits, but they also made the longing for home even more profound. Lieutenant Hoyle's letter to his wife late in February provides insight into how welcomed words from loved ones were, but also how they made the men wish they could leave the army and go home. He wrote:

> Dear Sarah, I have just received your letter of the 17th and, as you say, it allways makes me feel glad to get a letter from you, and oh how I long for the time when I can hear from you through your own dear lips. How happy could I then live.[62]

Desertion continued to be a problem for the Confederate armies during the winter months of 1864. Although Lee had allowed hundreds of furloughs to be granted, the harsh conditions and the lack of food had many of the soldiers contemplating whether they wanted to suffer a terrible slow death or escape to the protection and care of home.[63] In the 55th at least four men were apprehended in February while attempting to desert. Lieutenant Hoyle informed his wife that one of these poor souls from Company B was to be shot; the other three were sentenced to hard labor. In a letter to his wife Hoyle explained that he had done everything he could to get these men reduced sentences.[64]

Joseph Hoyle, who in the fall of 1863 believed deserters should be shot, had a change of heart after witnessing the sentence being implemented right before his eyes.

> Dear Sarah, I had to witness one of the most affecting sights to day, I believe I ever did in my life before. That was the shooting a man in our regiment for desertion. The whole brigade was marched out in a square to see it. Although I was out I could not look at him when they shot him, so I turned my eyes off him when they went to fire. I felt very solemn indeed, and all appeared very serious. I will agree with you now that it is not rite to shoot a man.[65]

In February, Brigadier General Joseph Davis called for his troops to reenlist and promise to continue the fight for Southern independence. Although a select few had seen enough of the horrors and hardships of war the regiment as a whole was still firmly behind the cause. Davis's brigade reenlisted in overwhelming numbers, and Lieutenant Hoyle hoped this show of solidarity would brighten the spirits of those at home who felt the war should be ended as soon as possible regardless of victory or defeat.

> I must tell you about us all re-enlisting for the war last Saturday. The whole Brigade was ordered out and General Davis gave us a stirring speech upon the subject. Our Regt. seemed somewhat backward at first, but on a second speech by Genl Davis, nearly all the Regt came out. All my company re-enlisted but one, namely, Jesse Tallen. Re-enlisting is going on very extensively in this army. And surely this will have some effect upon many of our people at home who are whipped already. This patriotic move on the part of our soldiers speaks in the soundest terms that our soldiers are not whipped, and I think that much good will result from this patriotic movement. We soldiers want peace as much as any body, and if any people in the world know the value of peace we do, and our friends need not think that we desire the war continue by re-enlisting, but we know that the stronger position we can show, the sooner we will have peace. We know we will have to fight any how till the war ends. Then let us all rely upon the god of hosts and strive to do our duty and deliverence will come.

During its stay near Orange Court House the 55th North Carolina had twice been ordered out of camp armed and ready to fight. On February 6 Meade made a demonstration across the Rapidan at Morton's Ford and engaged Lee's army. The following morning, however, the Federals had retreated north of the Rapidan inflicting minor casualties to the Army of Northern Virginia. Then, during the final days of February and the beginning of March, Brigadier General Judson Kilpatrick made an ill-fated attempt to raid Richmond. The purpose of this raid was to free Federal prisoners and possibly take part in some type of covert operation.[66]

According to Lieutenant Colonel Belo, the 55th was sent to Gordonsville, Virginia, to cut off Kilpatrick's troopers. While at Gordonsville, Belo ordered the men to perform picket duty. Belo posted his pickets along the different roads leading to Richmond, and established headquarters at their forks. The next morning Belo ordered his men to form a column and march toward Richmond. The weather had turned bad and the roads were not in very good condition. The regiment camped during the late afternoon and finally had the opportunity to eat. The rest of the day and all through the evening the men were on alert, being informed that the Federals could attempt to break through their line at any time. After spending a cold night without the comfort of shelter the regiment was ordered back to their original camp near Orange Court House.[67]

The regiment's historian, Charles M. Cooke, described the 55th North Carolina's role in the "Dahlgren Raid."

> Soon after his [Lieutenant Colonel Belo] return to the regiment, our brigade, one severely cold night, was ordered out of camp and marched to Gordonsville. As soon as it reached that point,

the Fifty-fifth Regiment was sent out to picket the roads on the south. The rain was falling and sleeting and the clothing on the men was frozen. The next day the regiment with the brigade was marched some distance to the southwest and bivouacked for the night with orders to have very few fires, the purpose being to intercept a raiding detachment of the Federal army, but the detachment went around us, and after enduring the intensest suffering that night, the regiment returned to camp.[68]

Besides occasionally being ordered to perform picket duty the regiment spent the winter at their campsite in virtual boredom. Without the constant commotion that accompanied the campaign season, the men were able to reflect on how the war had affected them physically, emotionally, and spiritually — and it was the latter that concerned many of the soldiers as they bided their time in camp.

Historians have debated the notion that religious beliefs can affect combat motivation. Gerald Linderman and Bell I. Wiley have argued that as the war became more strenuous the influence religion had on a soldier declined. Other historians, such as James Silver, have asserted that the most dominating influence that sustained Confederate morale was the church. The fact that death was a common occurrence during the war probably kept many soldiers close to their faith.[69]

Religion had always been a concern for many of the men of the 55th. When the regiment was first established in May 1862, Lieutenant Hoyle, then a private, informed his wife that there were regimental prayer meetings morning and night. Hoyle described how the meetings were set-up explaining that the men sat in a square, leaving one side open, while the minister delivered his sermon standing in the open end of the formation.[70] By the beginning of 1864 many of the soldiers in the 55th were still practicing their faith. To spread the teachings of Jesus Christ the men of Davis's unit built a chapel near their campsites. Fifty volunteers agreed to assist in the construction and after several days of industrious labor the spacious chapel was completed.[71]

Religious revivals were nothing new to the Southern fighting man. They are believed to have begun in Stonewall Jackson's corps toward the end of March 1863. Once the 1863 campaigning season began, however, evangelistic activities were put on hold. By the fall of 1863 the tide of revivalism had started again, and it reached "unprecedented heights" during the winter of 1863–64. Soldiers would stand in the pouring rain or in heavy snow without any shoes just to listen to lengthy sermons. While in winter quarters, listening to the word of God had become the main social activity for many of Lee's troops. Although both Federal and Confederate fighting men experienced a rush of religious sentiment during the war, it is thought that the occurrence was more dramatic in the Southern armies.[72]

The 55th North Carolina and the three Mississippi regiments of Davis's brigade were very much involved with the winter revivalism that had permeated Lee's army. On March 16, 1864, J. Henry Smith, a Presbyterian minister, informed the *North Carolina Presbyterian* that Davis's unit was "enjoying a great and glorious revival." Smith also added that the men were meeting every day and had been doing so for more than a month The minister felt confident that the Christian spirit had been accepted by many of the soldiers, stating "I think at least one hundred were asking 'what must we do to be saved.'"[73]

The 55th alone had three separate prayer groups, and men like Lieutenant Hoyle were trying to organize two more. The Christian influence, at least from the young lieutenant's point of view, had taken a strong hold on the soldiers in his regiment.

> We had preaching to-day in the Brigade. I have already written you about the deep religious concern in our Brigade. I am now holding prayer meetings every night in the different companies of our Regt., and a great deal of interest seems to be manifested. There are now three prayer-meetings in our Regt, and I think I can organize two more. I also intend to try to hold a prayer meeting for the Regt. daily, at some hour in the day time. Pray the good Lord to be with us. I feel happy in working for my master, and I pray he will bless us all. Dear Sarah, I do not forget to pray for you all at home for you are the objects nearest my heart.[74]

Ministers also used revered Confederate heroes, like Stonewall Jackson, to encourage the Christian spirit among the men. Reverend B. Tucker Lacy, who had served as the unofficial chaplain of Jackson's Second Corps, and had been a friend of the late lieutenant general, now served with Hill's corps as a missionary. Lacy preached to Davis's brigade on the evening of February 21. Lieutenant Hoyle, himself very attentive to the religious activities of his company, expressed the reverend's sermon and how he had evoked the pious Jackson as an inspiration for the men.

> Dr. Lacy, our corps missionary gave us two very good sermons yesterday. And to-day, he gave us a very excellent address on the life and character of General Jackson. The speaker dwelt with emphasis upon the Christian habits of Jackson, showing that he was a devout Christian as well as a brave soldier.[75]

In April 1864 the Army of Northern Virginia experienced a grand assembly to celebrate Holy Communion. In a large field near the Rapidan River, thousands of soldiers gathered to listen to a number of chaplains preach the word of God. The chaplains led the men in singing hymns and then prayers. The service concluded with the blessing of the bread, which was actually pieces of hardtack, and the wine. Once all those who wished to take part in the Lord's Supper had finished, one of the ministers delivered the benediction and the men returned to their camps, with, as one soldier later wrote, "glowing faces."[76]

Reverend Thomas Dwight Witherspoon, who had been appointed chaplain of Davis's brigade in June 1863, organized the meetings which the Mississippians and North Carolinians attended. Witherspoon, whom J. Henry Smith described as being "an able, earnest and laborious chaplain," had fought bravely at Gettysburg, but was asked by his fellow soldiers not to risk being killed or wounded. The energetic chaplain had asked volunteers to build a chapel, and they did so throughout the bitter cold days of winter. When finally completed, the chapel was 30 by 40 feet and contained two large chimneys.[77] LeGrand Wilson described the activities at the house of prayer.

> All through that long, dreary winter I visited that chapel at different hours of the day, and I never found it empty, someone was always praying, and toward the close of the day, at the day, at the twilight hour, on raising the curtain and entering the sanctuary, you would find from ten to twenty silent worshippers kneeling in different parts of the chapel in silent prayer, not a word nor a whisper, only now and then a sob.[78]

Lieutenant Hoyle, who had taken a keen interest in the spiritual well being of the regiment, declared that the services were always "well attended."[79]

Several of the officers, including Belo, attended services with Lee and A. P. Hill at a church in Orange Court House. Belo stated that the months he spent recovering from his wounds gave him time to reexamine his life and he realized that he had been neglecting his spiritual life. The lieutenant colonel decided to be confirmed, and became a member of Christ Church in Richmond. The horrors of war had aided Belo in his return to God and he declared that he had "pondered over the questions of life and death and come to the conclusion to be confirmed in the spring."[80]

The common soldiers and the commanding officers continued to adhere to their religious beliefs or turn to a higher power for many different reasons. The soldiers were quick to support revivals mainly because the words being preached were not unknown to them. The familiarity of the gospels and the prayers being spoken reminded many of the soldiers, who longed to be home, of their lives before the war. In his essay *Christian Soldiers? Perfecting the Confederacy,* Reid Mitchell asserts that most Confederate soldiers "wanted answers out of God about death, suffering and hardship more than about Southern independence or Confederate defeat."[81] With respect to the letters left by veterans of the 55th North Carolina, Mitchell's claim seems more accurate than those works that correlate religious fervor in the Confederate army with the "Lost Cause" and Southern nationalism.[82]

Many men who served with the 55th had been devout Christians since their regiment had been formed. During the first week of the regiment's formation Joseph Hoyle wrote a letter to his wife and declared that the men spent time praying every night.[83] By July 1862 the regiment was holding religious services twice every Sunday. The regiment's chaplain, William Royall, informed the *Biblical Recorder* that he had witnessed many of the men "throw away the 'cards'" and instead read the Bible. The chaplain also stated that "it is impossible to realize how eagerly the men desire religious reading."[84]

Many of the soldiers fighting with the 55th continued to follow their faith, and were quick to thank God every time they survived a battle. When 200 members of the 55th participated in the Confederate attempt to recapture Washington, North Carolina, on September 6, 1862, Private Hoyle wrote to his wife that God had protected him and that "I did not feel frightend in the least, in fact I never thought that a bullet would hit me." After retreating back toward Seminary Ridge on July 3, 1863, Hoyle declared, "God's good grace again Shielded me, and I came out unhurt."[85]

Lieutenant Hoyle was not the only member of the regiment to associate his survival with God's grace. After the battle of Bristoe Station, Private Pearsall wrote home to his wife declaring "I am very thankley to god to think that I am spaird to drop you a few lines one time more."[86] These two young men would write several more letters home during the upcoming Overland campaign and have plenty of more times to thank God for sheltering them from the Angel of Death, who would unfortunately visit thousands of their comrades as Lieutenant General Ulysses S. Grant brought the mighty Union army south.

5

April–June 1864: Preparing for the Death Angel

*"Old grant is retreting and I think it is time for if he
ant whiped now thair is no chans to whip him"*

In February 1864 Ulysses S. Grant was promoted to the rank of lieutenant general. Grant had proved his worth in the West, and now President Lincoln wanted him to command all the Union armies. Although his chief lieutenant, Major General William T. Sherman, preferred that Grant stay in the West, away from the intrigues and pitfalls of the capital, Grant decided to make the eastern theater his seat of operations.[1]

For Grant the objective was clear: destroy the Confederate armies and the Southern will to fight. His overall strategy for 1864 is summed up in his own words written years after the conflict: "my general plan now was to concentrate all the forces possible against the Confederate armies in the field."[2] The Union commander wanted to prevent the Rebels from being able to reinforce each other, so he implemented a plan to coordinate Federal advances against the Confederacy on several fronts. Meade was to strike the Army of Northern Virginia while Sherman assaulted General Joseph E. Johnston's army in the West. Sherman was also ordered to penetrate the interior of the Confederacy and destroy whatever war resources he could lay his hands on.[3]

While the two main Federal armies attacked the principal Confederate forces, Major General Benjamin Butler's Army of the James was ordered to cut the railroad between Richmond and Petersburg and to threaten the Confederate capital from the south. Major General Franz Sigel's forces in the Shenandoah Valley and West Virginia were to move up the valley and keep the Rebel forces there occupied while cutting Lee's communications to the area. Grant's last move had Major General Nathaniel Banks's Army of the Gulf advancing toward and capturing Mobile, Alabama, then moving north toward either Selma, Alabama or Atlanta, Georgia. Though these three commanders ultimately failed to achieve what their commander had desired, Meade and Sherman continued to chip away slowly at the Confederacy's ability to wage war.[4]

While Grant and the Union high command planned their campaign, the 55th North Carolina remained camped near Orange Court House. Desertion had continued to plague the Army of Northern Virginia and several men from the 55th had joined other disheartened fellow Confederates and went home. In March two members of the regiment were sentenced to be executed for desertion. The following month two more men from the 55th were sentenced to be shot, but Lee asked President Davis to allow these soldiers to return to their command. As many Confederates continued to leave their camps without leave, the 55th prepared to begin performing picket duty along the Rapidan.[5]

April brought rain to the Rapidan area, but the fighting men along the river were not depressed by the gloomy gray sky. Lieutenant Hoyle summed up the feelings many of the men had as the rain continuously fell and dampened the land around them.

> Although it puts us to some inconvenience, yet we are not sorry to see it rain, as we know it keeps off the fight some longer. When it is raining, you will frequently hear some one say "This rain has prolonged many a man's life," and it is a true saying, as we expect the yankees to move upon us whenever the roads get in condition. (or may be we will move upon them, I don't know).[6]

The dreary weather and the winter hardships had not completely demoralized the soldiers and a "spirit of hopefulness and confidence" pervaded the army. Although Lieutenant Hoyle was glad to see the rain delay the start of the campaigning season, he was quick to write that he believed the men would do their "whole duty when the time comes."[7]

The religious fervor that had spread throughout the Confederate armies continued to be experienced by the men in the 55th. Although picket duty somewhat hampered the religious activities, the men of the regiment continued to express their belief in God's grace. They had received copies of the New Testament, which probably helped them engage in religious thought while away from camp.[8]

Several of the men continued to be in poor health, but the variety of food they received had improved somewhat. Private Wilkerson wrote to his parents that the men were "fairing very well now," writing that he was receiving "aplenty of good coffee" to drink and cornmeal, rice, and bacon to eat. Wilkerson also acquired a new pair of shoes and was very excited to tell his parents that they were made in London. He also wrote that the "huts" the men used for shelter were not comfortable. Wilkerson's main complaint was that they were small and that at times the smoke from their fires became overwhelming.[9]

Throughout April the situation along the Rapidan remained calm and relatively peaceful. The soldiers in the 55th spent their days on picket duty and drilling. They expected a Federal attack any day, and were preparing to drive their enemy from Southern soil. In April, Davis's brigade was enlarged when the 26th Mississippi Regiment and the first Confederate Battalion were added to the thinned ranks.[10] These additional troops probably raised the brigade's confidence as the campaigning season drew ever closer. Lieutenant Hoyle described what his regiment was doing and how the men felt as the days of battle edged nearer.

> We often hear the yankees are coming, but still they don't come, but I expect they will come some of these days. We are drilling daily, and doing picket duty along the river. Our Brigade has been increased by another Regt (26th Miss), and a battalion (Alabamians) recently. We had a brigade drill yesterday, and our Brigade made a very fine showing. I think we will do our whole duty should the enemy come. But I must stop talking at this rate lest you think we are anxious to get into a fight, we are not anxious but if fighting must be done we are willing to do our part — I even pray the good Lord that we may have no more shedding of blood, but we have to say "his will be done."[11]

By the end of April the 55th was still performing picket duty along the Rapidan and remained near Orange Court House. The simple pleasure of receiving a new shirt from one's wife or family continued to brighten the spirits of the men as they waited for Grant to attack. Lieutenant Hoyle, pleased to find that his wife had stitched two interlaced hearts on his shirt pocket, expressed a great desire to be home, but also kept his thoughts focused on the war. With the knowledge that the horror of battle would soon be revisiting his life, the young lieutenant expressed the deep love he had for his wife by composing a short poem that assured her, maybe for the last time, that she was always in his thoughts.

> Often when sleep closes mine eyes
> And forgetfulness takes all care away,
> Then come that dearest one, my wife
> And nestles near, near my side,
> Her gentle hand is laid in mine,
> Her dear lips to mine are pressed,
> O then I am happy in dream land.
> But I awake, alas my happiness is gone.
> My Dear one has flown away, and I
> Again am alone — Thus time
> Passes away in dreamy flight.[12]

The roads had begun to dry and the ever-looming clouds of war were closing in on the men stationed along the river. Many of the men expressed the opinion that the upcoming summer campaign would be the last of the war. Hoyle wrote that his regiment had made its final preparations for the upcoming campaign.

> We sent off our tents yesterday and are now fairly out of doors to take the weather as it comes There is but one tent allowed to a Regt — now, and that one is for the Col — I think we will have active operations in this army ere long if the weather keeps dry — All our men are in good spirits, and if you could see the jolity and merriment among us, you would think that fighting was the least thing in our thoughts.[13]

On the night of May 1 the men of Davis's brigade held a large prayer meeting. The purpose of the meeting was to pray for the Confederacy in its time of need.[14] Although concern for their embattled nation was on every soldier's mind, the primary reason for the large turnout was the upcoming campaign. The fighting men of Davis's brigade could easily recall the murderous battles of 1863, and so in their time of need they turned to their God for protection and redemption.

Lee had done what he could to prepare his army for the Federal onslaught. By the end of April, Longstreet had returned to the Army of Northern Virginia, and Lee wanted to meet with his "old war horse." On May 2 Lee met with his principal lieutenants atop Clark's Mountain. Lee informed his corps commanders that he believed the Federals were preparing to commence operations against the Army of Northern Virginia. The commanding general felt that the Union army would cross the Rapidan at Germanna Ford or Ely's Ford, and he advised his lieutenants that they should have their men ready to move. Longstreet agreed, stating, "we cannot afford to underrate him [Grant] and the army he now commands." Longstreet continued, declaring "we must make up our minds to get into line of battle and to stay there; for that man will fight us every day and every hour till the end of this war." Longstreet, who had been friends with Grant at West Point, understood how effective Grant could be.[15]

The Army of Northern Virginia's weakened command structure had not changed since Gettysburg. Many unqualified and inexperienced officers remained in charge of thousands of soldiers. The leadership may still have been diluted, but the fighting units had grown in combat experience. Davis's brigade had improved tremendously since the spring of 1863. Not only did the influx of additional troops add to the overall strength of the brigade, but the unit had gained valuable battlefield experience at Gettysburg and had participated in engagements at Falling Waters and Bristoe Station. Davis and his men now had a better understanding of combat, and, although many of the men still feared the deadly reality of battle, they had experienced it and now knew what to expect. The brigade commander had also gained valuable combat experience during the latter half of 1863. Although Davis had grown as a brigade commander he would be away from his unit when Grant's Overland Campaign began in early May. The death of his nephew, President Davis's son Joe, on the last day of April, required him to remain in Richmond as the Battle of the Wilderness began. He would not be with his troops on May 5.

On the morning of May 3 a Federal cavalry division and several engineers under the command of Brigadier General David M. Gregg escorted 12 canvas boats and 14 wooden pontoons toward Ely's Ford. The troopers camped near Richardsville, Virginia, about two miles northwest of Ely's Ford, and proceeded to scout the roads leading to the crossing. Gregg had been ordered to ensure that the roads to the Rapidan fords from Culpeper were secure. During the evening an effort to secure the routes to Germanna Ford was also under way. The next day Grant would attempt to attack Lee's right flank.[16]

The increasing amount of activity seen by Confederate observers, and the general himself, on May 2 had alerted Lee to the fact that the Federals were preparing to move; the only question was in which direction. Refusing to make any hasty moves that could prove disastrous to his army, Lee waited for the Federals to decide. While he waited impatiently, the commanding general decided not to attempt to fortify all of the possible river crossings. Lee instead chose to "saturate the country beyond each of his earthworks with cavalry." Once the Federals began moving the Confederate troopers were to alert the army and Lee would do his best to concentrate his forces and strike Grant as he crossed the river or soon thereafter.[17]

Grant had hoped the waterways along the Potomac River and the Chesapeake Bay would make the logistics of supplying his army easier. But the terrain along the chosen route, especially a dense wooded area known as the Wilderness, would prove hard to overcome. Meade's chief of staff, Andrew A. Humphreys, devised a plan that would swiftly move the army through the Wilderness by the afternoon of May 4. The right wing of the army would cross the river at Germanna Ford while the left wing crossed through the Rapidan at Ely's Ford. Both wings would then unite near Mine Run. If properly coordinated, the Union troops would be able to threaten Lee's flank and possibly position themselves between the Army of Northern Virginia and Richmond. The Federal high command, however, rejected Humphreys' timetable and proposed that the army rest in the Wilderness on the afternoon of May 4 to allow time for the wagon train to catch up. This pause would have dire consequences for the Federal army.[18]

Shortly before midnight on May 3 more than 115,000 Federal troops moved southeast in an attempt to surprise Lee's army. The V Corps, commanded by Major General Warren, marched toward Germanna Ford, followed by Major General Sedgwick's VI Corps; Brigadier General James H. Wilson's cavalry division accompanied these two Union corps. Major

General Winfield Scott Hancock's II Corps, with Gregg's cavalry division, proceeded toward Ely's Ford; Brigadier General Alfred T. A. Torbert and his cavalry division were posted north of the Rapidan to prevent the Confederates from crossing and attacking the Federal rear; and Major General Burnside's IX Corps was posted at Warrenton to control the area until Meade's forces were safely across the river.[19]

Lee knew that the Federals were crossing and he was eager to strike them, but the Army of Northern Virginia was not prepared to attack. Unsure of where Grant intended to cross, Lee was forced to keep his army spread out to counter the Federals wherever they chose to ford the river. Confederate generals Hill and Ewell had their corps in position along the Rapidan, but Longstreet's troops were still stationed near Gordonsville. With Longstreet more than 20 miles away, the Confederate commander ordered Ewell and Hill to advance closer to where the Union army was crossing as a delaying action.[20]

In his essay *Escaping the Shadow of Gettysburg: Richard S. Ewell and Ambrose Powell Hill at the Wilderness*, Peter S. Carmichael asserts that Lee's decision to leave his men in their camps on May 3 was one of the general's "greatest military blunders." Carmichael maintains that had Lee, who thought Grant would cross the Rapidan at the right of the Confederate army, moved his troops on May 3 they would have been able to strike the Federals as they forded the river. Leaving Longstreet more than an entire day's march away from the Rapidan proved costly for the Army of Northern Virginia.[21]

Carmichael's argument, which attempts to correct the historic perception that Hill and Ewell blundered during the Wilderness campaign, overlooks the fact that although Lee assumed Grant would attempt to assault his right flank, he was not certain. Had Lee moved his army to the right, as Carmichael thought he should have, he would have exposed his left flank and possibly, had Grant moved to the left, lost his entire army. It is easy to argue that Lee should have followed his instincts and shifted his troops to the right; however, Lee, although audacious, was not foolish enough to rely completely on his own intuition and chose correctly to wait.

As the Federals crossed the Rapidan, Lee moved cautiously. Lee still did not know if Grant had moved his entire force to the right of the Confederate line. Lee, fearing that more Union troops were positioned across the river to his left, hesitated. Lee, whose force totaled about 64,000 men, understood that he was outnumbered and could not afford to make any rash decisions. Although Lee reacted prudently he had been proactive. As stated above, he had already instructed his corps commanders to have their men ready to move. By the time the Federals began fording the Rapidan the soldiers in the Army of Northern Virginia had already cooked three days' rations, packed their gear, and prepared to march. Also, around one o'clock on the morning of May 4, with intelligence coming in that the Federals were moving, Lee sent a message to Ewell ordering him to be ready to move by dawn. Lee also informed Ewell that the Federals were probably moving to the right.[22]

By the time the sun had risen the Confederates knew in which direction the Union army was moving. Stuart's cavalry had a few minor skirmishes with the Federals at the fords, but quickly retreated because they were instructed only to survey the Union troops, not engage them. By 9:30 a.m. Confederate signalmen atop Clark's Mountain relayed the fact that the Federals were moving to the right toward Germanna Ford and Ely's Ford. Lee, now sure that Grant was moving his entire force, except for some cavalry units, to the right, began moving his army.[23]

Lee decided to march his army east and counter Grant's move. The Confederate commander first ordered Ewell to march his corps east along the Orange Turnpike, leaving behind a brigade and six regiments to protect the rear. Lee then instructed Hill to move his forces in the same direction following the Orange Plank Road, leaving Anderson's division behind to patrol the river. Around 11:00 a.m. Longstreet began moving his troops north to an area just below the headwaters of Mine Run. Lee's army was on the move and the Wilderness campaign had begun.[24]

By eight o'clock on the morning of May 4, Davis's brigade, now under the command of Colonel John M. Stone of the second Mississippi, was ordered into line and prepared to march. A little after noon the unit marched out of its winter camp east toward Fredericksburg. Heth's division was at the vanguard of Hill's corps as it moved east on the Orange Plank Road. Hill's men, who were so poorly dressed they hardly resembled an army on the march, continued east at a steady pace. Shortly before sunset after marching nearly 20 miles, Hill's men halted near a small borough called New Verdiersville, just a few miles from Mine Run. Hill's troops were now about as close to the Wilderness, which lies between Spotsylvania, Virginia, and Fredericksburg, as the Federals, and the dense wooded area was where Lee hoped to strike Grant.[25]

On the morning of May 5, Ewell's Corps moved east along the Orange Turnpike and ran into Warren's V Corps. It had become distressingly clear to the Federals that Lee had not, as Meade had presumed, gathered his troops behind Mine Run in a defensive posture. The Federals' decision to wait for their supply wagons instead of swiftly marching through the Wilderness had placed the Union army in a perilous position. Although, as at Gettysburg, Lee had instructed his corps commanders not to force a general engagement until Longstreet's troops were present, the situation in the Wilderness quickly escalated into a confrontation. Ewell's men were attacked and he had no choice but to respond in kind.[26]

While Ewell and Warren faced off against each other, Hill's troops were moving along the Orange Plank Road. The Third Corps continued moving east along the road led by Heth's division. Lee had ordered Hill and Ewell to regulate their advances so that they would be moving forward together. Unfortunately as the two corps marched east the roads they traveled upon began to diverge and they were soon several miles away from each other. Heth's men continued forward and around 10:00 a.m. Colonel Stone's skirmishers came into contact with Federal cavalry. Heth's troops slowly pushed the Federals back to where the Orange Plank Road and Brock Road intersect. Around 1:00 p.m. Heth's men encountered a larger force that had formed west of the intersection. Here Heth's division paused and awaited orders to advance. Lee still did not want a major engagement and so asked Heth if he could occupy Brock Road without becoming engulfed in a serious fight. Heth sent word that he would need to attack with his whole division, but before his message reached Lee the Federals advanced.[27]

The Wilderness was an extremely difficult location to fight a battle. The thick underbrush limited visibility and made any type of movement difficult. Davis's troops were positioned on the left of the Orange Plank Road, with the 55th North Carolina posted in the right-center of the brigade on the top of a small hill. The 26th and 42nd Mississippi regiments were on the extreme left, and the first Confederate Battalion and the second and 11th Mississippi regiments were to the right and left of the North Carolinians. The 55th's regimental historian described the unit's location.[28]

> It [the 55th] was in a dense forest of small tress; the hill in our front sloped gradually to a depression or valley which was a few yards wide, and then there was a gradual incline on the opposite side until it reached a point of about the same altitude as that occupied by us, about 100 yards from our line.[29]

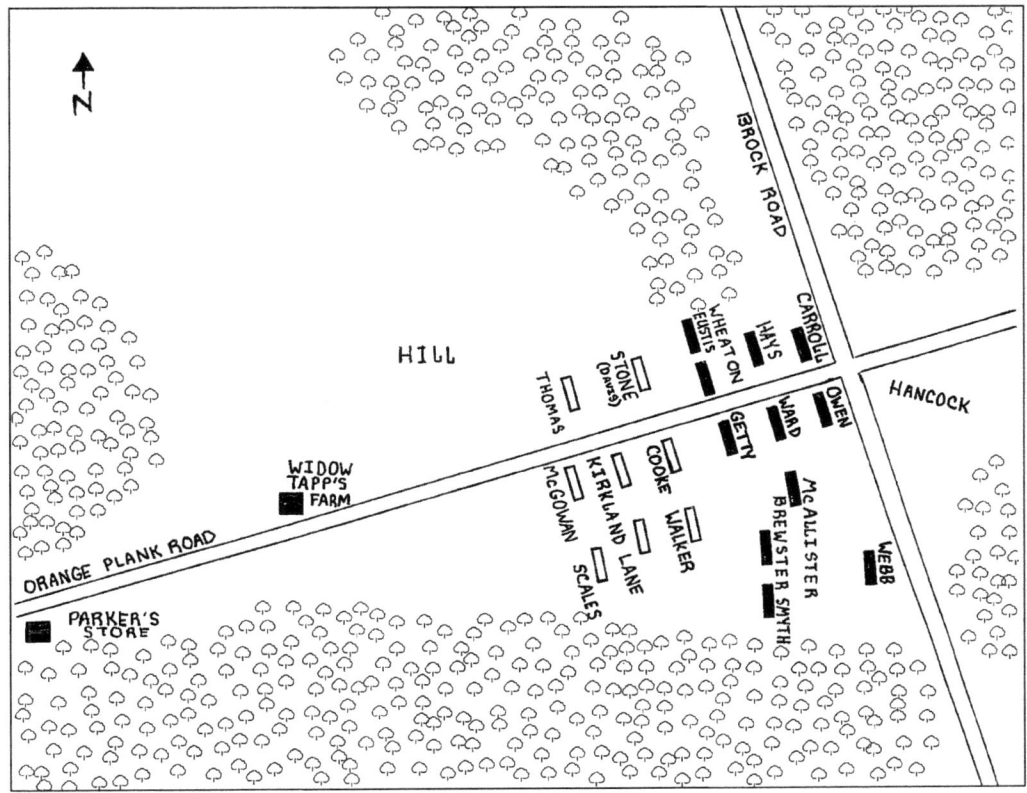

Hill's Corps on the Orange Plank Road, May 5, 1864.

Colonel Stone ordered Major Alfred M. O'Neal, of the first Confederate Battalion, commander of the brigade's sharpshooters, to position his men on the eastern bank of Wilderness Run. It is not known how many men the young major had in his command that evening. At full strength his force consisted of about 200 riflemen who, in O'Neal's words, were "most desperate fighters." O'Neal's sharpshooters—men from each of the brigades regiments—quickly prepared to advance down into the creek bottom. Before they were able to effectively be deployed the Federals attacked, forcing O'Neal to reposition his men on the eastern bank of Poplar Run, about a fourth of a mile southwest of their intended line.[30]

Brigadier General George W. Getty's division held the area opposite Heth's men. Around 3:30 p.m. Getty ordered his men forward and Heth's skirmishers were driven back to the main battle line, but the Federals failed to break through the Confederate line. The Federals assaulting Davis's line were members of the 10th Massachusetts and second Rhode Island regiments, supported by the seventh and 37th Massachusetts regiments. Lieutenant Elisha Hunt Rhodes of the second Rhode Island stated that the "woods and brush were so thick and dark that the enemy could not be seen, but we knew they were in our front from the terrible fire we received." The trees and darkness may have hampered the Federal advance, but the terrible conditions also allowed them to move to within 100 yards of Heth's line before being seen.[31]

Getty's Federal troops continued to assault Heth's position, but were never able to push the Confederates beyond the crest of the hill in front of their line. Shortly after Getty's troops had begun their assault Major General David B. Birney's division, posted on the right, and Brigadier General Gershom Mott's division, positioned on Getty's left, joined in the attack.[32]

The Federals were pushed back several times but continued to regroup and assault the Confederate lines. Shortly before 5:00 p.m. Mott's troops had broken, and General Hancock ordered Brigadier General John Gibbon to send reinforcements in to support Birney and Getty. Gibbon hastily sent two brigades in against Heth's troops to support the wavering Federal position. In addition to these troops Hancock sent orders to Brigadier General Francis C. Barlow to join the attack. By 5:00 p.m. nearly 30,000 Federal troops were assaulting Heth's division of little more than 7,000 men, and his command was reluctantly forced back to their original entrenched lines. Lee, after seeing the attacking force for himself, ordered Major General Cadmus M. Wilcox to send his division in to support Heth.[33]

Although four divisions were bearing down on Heth's position his embattled troops were determined to resist the Federals as long as they could. Lieutenant Cooke of the 55th North Carolina asserted that his unit held firm primarily because the "officers and men of the regiment realized that the safety of the army depended upon our holding the enemy in check until forces left behind could come up, and there was a fixed determination to do it, or to die." Just as Heth's men were concluding that they would never be reinforced, two of Wilcox's brigades, those of Brigadier Generals Samuel McGowan and Alfred M. Scale, moved into to position to support them. Scales's troops provided support on Heth's right and McGowan moved his men into position in the center.[34]

Although Wilcox's troops assisted the men positioned in Heth's center and right, Colonel Stone's embattled soldiers received no support. During the long afternoon Stone's command had repelled seven successive Union assaults, and continued to hold firm. One of Stone's men stated, "the undergrowth was very thick, and during the fight all the bushes as large as a man's wrist were cutdown about two and one-half feet above the ground with musket balls." The fighting in front of the 55th North Carolina became severe at times. Private Pearsall wrote several days after the battle that he had sat in one place all day and had shot his rifle 61 times. The young private also claimed that the Federals were "not more than 2 hundred yards" from his line. The constant attacks by the Federals had many of the men in the 55th fearing "they would annihilate us before nightfall."[35]

As the situation worsened with every passing minute the officers in Stone's command met and decided that they had no alternative but to charge the Federal position. Colonel Belo instructed his adjutant to inform the men of the 55th that a charge was necessary and to be prepared to move at once. Belo also instructed Lieutenant Cooke to ensure that Company C, at that time responsible for carrying the regimental battle flag, keep the regiment's colors well to the front. The soldiers did not fully support the idea, but were ready to put forth all the strength they had left and advance. The thinned and weary ranks prepared to face almost certain death. Most of their ammunition was gone and the soldiers quickly fixed bayonets. Fortunately for the men of the 55th the charge was not necessary. Nightfall had made what little visibility that had existed disappear, and just as the men in Stone's command thought they'd break, Brigadier General E. L. Thomas's brigade arrived to assist them. The fighting that had lasted all afternoon and most of the evening finally ended for Davis's men.[36] Lieutenant Cooke described the situation at the end of the long day's fight in his history of the regiment.

The order for the charge was not given, and about sunset the firing had nearly ceased in our front, and Thomas' Georgia Brigade of Wilcox's division came in and relieved us, and we were sent to the right of the road where we rested for the night. We had held the enemy in check. Not one yard of our line had given away one foot during the three hours the fearful onslaughts had been made upon us."[37]

The 55th and the rest of Davis's brigade were exhausted after hours of horrific fighting. The combat around Orange Plank Road was, as one historian asserts, "some of the war's most intense, unrelieved slaughter."[38] The 55th had suffered greatly during the day's battle. Lieutenant Hoyle wrote that the men had "suffered severely" and that his company had a "great many" wounded. In all Company F suffered over 50 percent casualties. Private Pearsall of Company G declared "my co wint in with 30 men and come out with 8 only and only 2 takin prisner the rest all kiled and wonded." The weary private also claimed that the regiment had gone into the fight with 350 men and only had 120 after the firing ceased. The regiment's historian asserted that the 55th had 340 men, including non-commissioned officers, as the battle opened and declared that "34 lay dead on the line where we fought and 167 were wounded." Lieutenant Colonel Belo wrote after the battle that his regiment had suffered 200 casualties, a number in agreement with Lieutenant Cooke's postwar assessment. Among those killed was Belo's 19-year-old brother, Henry Belo of Company H. Belo had been informed on the battlefield that his brother had been seriously wounded but, always the soldier, the resilient officer continued performing his duties and kept his regiment in line. In fact Henry Belo had been shot in the face and neck and was killed instantly.[39]

The fighting along the Orange Plank Road had ended in a deadlock, neither side having gained any ground. The fighting along Ewell's line also ended in a relative stalemate, but the Confederates had to put every available man into the battle. Hill was faring no better for he too had put everything he had into the contest. Darkness had saved the Third Corps, but Hill could not hold out another day against the Federals. Lee understood the situation well and hoped and prayed that Longstreet would arrive before sunrise.[40]

As the men of the 55th tried to rest after a day of intense combat they probably felt a sense of pride. Virtually alone for several hours, Stone's men had held out against repeated Federal assaults. Had the Union troops been able to push the North Carolina and Mississippi troops back they would most likely have succeeded in rolling up Heth's left flank and routed Hill's corps. The determination of the men of the 55th North Carolina and the rest of Davis's brigade was an important element in preventing a Federal victory on the Orange Plank Road. A. P. Hill believed the effort made by Heth's troops had been magnificent and stated that their "fighting is the theme of the entire Army."[41] Their contribution to the battle on May 5 has been overlooked, but had they retreated the entire Overland Campaign might have ended in a few weeks instead of dragging on for almost an entire year. Had Hill's corps suffered a defeat on May 5, Lee would have had no other option but to fall back to the defenses around Richmond, and as the general himself stated, it would then have been just a matter of time.

Throughout the night of May 5 sporadic skirmishes broke out up and down the battle lines, and with the constant moaning of the wounded the fighting men got little sleep.[42] As the men tried to rest Heth worried that his troops were so spread out and disorganized that if the Federals attacked in the morning, which he believed they would, his men would be unable to hold their position. Heth went to see A. P. Hill and asked that he be allowed to reposition his men, but the lieutenant general refused, stating that Longstreet would be up in the morning. Heth went to speak with his commanding officer several more times during the night to try to convince Hill that his and Wilcox's troops needed to be reorganized. On the third such occasion Hill became very upset and told the major general "Damn it, Heth, I don't want to hear any more about it; the men shall not be disturbed."[43]

Hill was not concerned about reorganizing his forces because Lee had informed him that Longstreet would be on the field to relieve his troops. At first, Lee had ordered Longstreet to attack the Federal left flank, but the day's fighting had so weakened Hill's lines that the general decided to have Longstreet move into position directly behind the Third Corps. Lee had sent his aide, Charles Venable, to inform Longstreet of his new objective. Now Lee and his other two corps commanders waited for Longstreet. If Longstreet did not arrive in time, the ever-increasing Union force would crush the Confederate lines around the Orange Plank Road. As dawn neared Hill found it difficult to suppress his anxiety. He began to believe that perhaps he should have allowed Heth and Wilcox to redress their lines.[44]

Hill may not have been apprehensive about the condition and deployment of his troops, but Colonel Stone had reason to be concerned. When Lieutenant Robert Ward of Company B, 42nd Mississippi, accompanied by a small picket detail, advanced to probe the Federal position they had only progressed about 40 yards before they almost walked into the Union lines. Ward and his fellow Confederates quickly returned to their brigade and spent the night on picket duty within their own lines. With his pickets unable to establish a forward position, Stone and the rest of Davis's brigade would have little or no warning if the Federals attacked. Stone understood that because of the lack of organized battle lines, defending his position would be almost impossible.[45]

Grant was determined to strike Lee again in the morning, but this time his forces would not attack in piecemeal. Grant planned to have Hancock renew his assault against Hill, and Burnside would be sent in to assist his forces. Grant had wanted the assault to begin at 4:30 a.m., but Meade felt the men needed more time to rest. Grant compromised and rescheduled the attack for 5:00 a.m. starting it later, he feared, would allow Lee to take the initiative.[46]

At five o'clock on the morning of May 6 the Federals made their move. Hancock's II Corps supported by Burnside's IX Corps advanced rapidly into the Confederate lines around the Orange Plank Road. Wilcox's troops, slightly closer to the Union lines than Heth's, were the first to be hit. Still exhausted and in disarray from the previous day's fighting, Wilcox's men were swiftly driven back. Heth's men, well aware of the force advancing upon them, retreated to re-form their line. The Federals pushed the Rebels back in confusion and continued to move forward.[47]

As the Federals advanced, the 55th North Carolina was ill-prepared to resist them. Wilcox's men, who had been posted on the left of Stone's command, fell back in such disorder that the Mississippi and North Carolina troops were not fully equipped. Most of Davis's command had not had time to form a battle line and were quickly forced back. The men of the 55th still had their arms stacked and made a hasty retreat as the blue tide crashed down upon their position. Along with the 55th the first Confederate Battalion also made a rapid move to the rear. Stone was, however, able to rally his Mississippi regiments and they re-formed to face the oncoming Union troops. With the support of Lieutenant Colonel William T. Poague's battalion of artillery, Heth's men were able to hold out against the Federals until Longstreet arrived.[48]

Lieutenant Colonel Belo was able to re-form his troops along with the first Confederate Battalion and both units were placed in reserve north of Tapp's farm. The majority of the soldiers in the 55th remained inactive for the rest of the day. Lieutenant Hoyle informed his wife that his regiment did not participate in the fighting that occurred on May 6. The regiment as a whole may not have seen much action on the 6th but at least one member of the command did. During the confusion that arose after Wilcox's troops scrambled into Stone's line, Private Pearsall became separated from his regiment. Although the 55th remained in reserve Pearsall eagerly joined the Mississippians and participated in the day's action.[49]

As Stone's men were attacked by the Federals, and the 55th North Carolina and the first Confederate Battalion retreated in confusion, Private Pearsall "got with" the 11th Mississippi. As Longstreet's troops appeared on the battlefield the tide began to shift slightly. Around 10:00 a.m. Longstreet was informed that the Union left extended only a short distance beyond the Orange Plank Road. The lieutenant general, eager to strike a decisive blow, decided to send a detachment, under the command of Lieutenant Colonel G. Moxley Sorrel, to assault the Federal left flank. Independently, Colonel Stone decided to join this attack and commanded his four Mississippi regiments, and at least one member of the 55th, in this assault.[50]

The flank attack resulted in a complete success and the Federals were forced to retreat. Private Pearsall described the day's events to his wife in a letter written five days after the battle of the Wilderness ended, declaring "I got with the 11 Missippa and went in a charge the 6 [May 6] in the morning and backed the yankees considerbal and I nevor saw as meney ded yanks in my lif they wair laid threw the woods for 2 miles."[51]

Pearsall and the rest of Stone's men fought courageously and contributed to the success of Longstreet's flanking attack. Although most of the 55th most likely did not participate in this engagement, other sources indicate that Stone's brigade, including the 55th, reunited sometime in the afternoon, which would imply that Private Pearsall was not the only North Carolinian to fight on May 6th.[52] Colonel Venable of Lee's staff commented on the fighting spirit of Stone's troops years later.

> As an evidence of the spirit of the men on this occasion, the Mississippi brigade of Heth's division, commanded by the gallant Colonel Stone, though the division was placed further to the left, out of the heat of battle, preferred to remain on the right, under heavy fire, and fought gallantly throughout the day under Longstreet.[53]

Unfortunately for the Confederates, several key officers were killed or wounded so severely that they were unable to lead troops for some time. Longstreet was shot in the neck and left shoulder by remnants of Brigadier General William Mahone's troops while trying to stop them from firing on fellow Confederates. In the same incident Brigadier General Micah Jenkins was shot in the head; he died later that day. Although wounded, Longstreet continued to focus on the task at hand. He wanted to follow up the flanking assault and drive the Federals "back across the Rapidan," if possible. His forces, however, had become fragmented in their advance and any assault would have to wait until the troops were reorganized.[54]

After several hours of indecision the Confederates were surprised to realize that the Federals were making a counterattack. Around 2:00 p.m. Burnside's IX Corps struck Longstreet's northern flank. Believing the Rebels were finished for the day, Hancock's troops remained behind their earthworks. Lee had other ideas and planned another attack. Lee devised a plan to attack straight up the Orange Plank Road and strike the Federals in a determined frontal assault. Initially, Lee's troops pushed Hancock's men back. But as the Federals gradually fell back to their earthworks they were able to halt the Rebel advance. Federal artillery and the dense foliage caused confusion in the Southern ranks and they ultimately had to fall back.[55]

Late in the afternoon Burnside was ordered to renew his attack, and at first his troops appeared to be winning the day. Confederate reinforcements, however, quickly ended the major general's hopes for success. Among the several units sent in to repel Burnside was Stone's command. Stone's troops, with the aid of several other Confederate commands, were able to drive back the Federals and then hold firm against repeated Union attempts to break their line. As the day ended, neither side had gained much, and, other than more loss of life, the results were the same as in the fighting that had occurred the day before.[56]

Grant characterized the horrific struggle in the Wilderness by stating, "More desperate fighting has not been witnessed on this continent than that of the 5th and 6th of May." The Union commander was not happy with the overall results of the battle. Having moved his army across the Rapidan, though, had made the ensuing battle a tactical victory for the Federals. The total casualties for the battle of the Wilderness were more than 22,000. Thomas Livermore, a Civil War veteran, stated that the Confederates suffered 7,750 killed or wounded while the Federals had 14,283 casualties and 3,383 missing.[57] Several sources, however, assert that Confederate casualties exceeded 11,000.[58]

Private John H. Dean, Company K. Private Dean enlisted in the army on May 6, 1862, at the age of 27. He was killed at the Wilderness on May 5, 1864. (Courtesy of the North Carolina Division of Archives and History, Raleigh, North Carolina.)

Stone's men rejoined the rest of Davis's brigade and their brigadier general, who had assumed command of the 55th and the first Confederate Battalion earlier in the day. The losses for the 55th North Carolina during the two days of fighting were 43 killed, 119 wounded, 16 captured, and four missing.[59] The combat had been fierce, but Grant was determined to fight Lee wherever he could. Longstreet's prediction that the new Federal commander would continue to attack the Confederates every day until he had a complete victory was accurate. Grant, even though his army was wounded, would not retreat back across the Rapidan. He was going to destroy Lee's army, and if he had to fight every hour of every day he would do so to put an end to the bloody conflict.

In such horrific combat any man willing to stand his post and do his duty merits the respect and thanks of his fellow citizens. At the Wilderness, courage under fire was the rule not the exception, but as in many battles, individuals can make a lasting mark on those who witness their bravery. Several members of the 55th North Carolina stood above their fellow soldiers and were rewarded by having their names placed on the Confederate Roll of Honor. In October 1862, the Confederate Congress passed a law authorizing the distribution of "medals and badges of distinction as a reward for courage and good conduct on the field of battle." The act detailed what type of service warranted acknowledgment by the government.

> The Congress of the Confederate States of America do enact, That the President be, and he is hereby, authorized to bestow medals, with proper devices, upon such officers of the armies of the Confederate States as shall be conspicuous for courage and good conduct on the field of battle, and also to confer a badge of distinction upon one private or non-commissioned officer of each company after every signal victory it shall have assisted to achieve. The non-commissioned officers and privates of the company who may be present on the first dress-parade thereafter may choose, by a majority of their votes, the soldier best entitled to receive such distinction, whose name shall be communicated to the President by commanding officers of the company; and if the award fall upon a deceased soldier the badge thus awarded him shall be delivered to his widow, or, if there be no widow, to any relation the President may adjudge entitled to receive it.[60]

The difficulties of acquiring medals prevented the Confederate government from honoring those fighting men who distinguished themselves in battle with such awards. To compensate for this the Adjutant and Inspector General's Office in October 1863 decreed that a list of those soldiers who displayed outstanding valor in combat be kept in his office. Adjutant and Inspector General Samuel Cooper proclaimed:

> I. That the names of all those who have been, or may hereafter be, reported as worthy of this distinction, be inscribed on a Roll of Honor, to be preserved in the office of the Adjutant and Inspector General for reference in all future time for those who have deserved well of their country, as having best displayed their courage and devotion on the field of battle.
> II. That the Roll of Honor, so far as now made up, be appended to this order and read at the head of every regiment in the service of the Confederate States at the first dress-parade after its receipt, and be published in at least one newspaper in each State.
> III. The attention of the officers in charge is directed to General Orders, Numbers 93, section Numbers 27, of the series of 1862, Adjutant and Inspector-General's Office, for the mode of selecting the non-commissioned officers and privates entitled to this distinction, and its execution is enjoined.[61]

Ten members of the 55th North Carolina, one from each company, received this respect for their efforts during the battle of the Wilderness. Their names are listed below.

> Corporal Haywood Scott, Company A (Mortally wounded)
> Private Samuel Benge, Company B
> Sergeant John D. Boggs, Company C
> Private Miller H. Randal, Company D
> Private William B. Fleming, Company E
> Sergeant Westly A. Williams, Company F
> Sergeant Marshall P. Grantham, Company G
> Private Andrew W. McGee, Company H
> Private Berry Pearce, Company I
> Corporal Charles L. Stovall, Company K[62]

On May 7, Grant ordered Meade to move one Federal corps to Spotsylvania Court House. The Federal commander's objective was to hold the important crossroads that were located on the route from the Wilderness to Hanover Junction. If Grant wanted to position his army on Lee's right flank, placing the Union army between the Confederate forces and Richmond, he had to control these access roads. Lee believed Grant was preparing to march and had sent out reconnaissance detachments to ascertain whether the Federals had moved. Lee, reasoning that Grant would try to post the Army of the Potomac between the Confederate army and Richmond, ordered the First Corps, now commanded by Major General Richard Anderson, to move toward Spotsylvania.[63]

Although the Army of Northern Virginia had stalled Grant's advance, the cost had been substantial. The nearly 8,000 casualties, plus the fact that Longstreet was out of action for the time being and Hill was debilitated by illness, greatly hampered Lee's ability to wage an offensive war. Left with limited options the Confederate commander had to put his army back on the defensive. The Army of Northern Virginia was ailing but the morale of the troops remained high. Throughout May 7 Confederate and Federal cavalry clashed, but no serious engagements erupted.[64]

Anderson's troops began their march to Spotsylvania during the night of May 7–8 unimpeded; the Federals, however, were hampered by Confederate cavalry and by their own forces clogging up the roads. On the morning of May 8 Anderson's forces reached Spotsylvania, and promptly began building breastworks to hold off any Federal assault. The Confederates were able to construct formidable works extending five miles, covering Spotsylvania in what resembled a giant inverted U. By the time the Federals arrived the Rebels had already dug in and were prepared to fend off the Union advance; Lee had won the race to Spotsylvania Court House.[65]

A. P. Hill's condition had worsened and the lieutenant general was unable to command his forces as they marched toward Spotsylvania Court House. Although extremely ill, Hill made a point of visiting Davis's brigade during the day on May 7 to thank the soldiers in the unit for their courageous behavior during the battle. With Hill out of action Lee placed Major General Jubal Early in temporary command of the Third Corps. Early would lead the command during the battles around Spotsylvania Court House. The Third Corps moved slowly at first, only moving about 200 yards in the first two hours. Eventually the Confederate troops began moving at a better pace.[66]

During most of the following day Heth's division remained on the Wilderness battlefield and assisted in the burying of the Confederate dead. While Heth's men concerned themselves with honoring the dead, Anderson's men fought off repeated attacks by General Warren's Federal troops around Spotsylvania. On May 9, around 6:00 a.m., Early's command began marching toward Spotsylvania Court House, traveling southeast along the Shady Grove Church Road and arrived later that afternoon. Upon arriving, the men immediately began constructing earthworks east of Spotsylvania and to the right of General Ewell's position. Minor skirmishes occurred as the two opposing armies entrenched. The soldiers of the 55th North Carolina would get little sleep as they prepared for the Federal onslaught they were sure was coming in the morning.[67]

By late afternoon the Confederates had almost completed their fortifications. Rebel sharpshooters were detached to keep the Union troops behind their earthworks. Major General John Sedgwick was unconcerned by the Confederate snipers and jokingly stated "they couldn't hit an elephant at this distance." A few moments later, while calming his troops, the Federal general was shot in the face by a Confederate sniper and killed. As the hours of the day passed, the Federals were still hoping to assault the Confederate left.

Hancock's troops, which were probing the Confederate lines and prepared to strike Lee's left flank if the opportunity presented itself, were forced to retire because the darkness and the thick woods around the area lowered the chance for success.[68]

During their march to Spotsylvania the 55th North Carolina participated in several minor skirmishes, but no heavy fighting occurred during its advance. Throughout the fighting on May 9, Heth's division was kept in reserve. The men of the regiment had found little time during the past five days to eat or sleep, and they could expect more of the same in the next few days.[69]

On the morning of May 10, exactly one year since the death of Stonewall Jackson, Grant ordered Hancock to continue his flanking maneuver across the Po River near the Block House Bridge. Once Anderson's lines had been smashed, Warren and Major General Horatio G. Wright were to attack the Confederate positions at Laurel Hill. As these attacks were raging Burnside was to resume his march down the Fredericksburg Road into Spotsylvania. With the proper coordination, Grant believed he could defeat Lee's entrenched army.[70]

Lee was not about to allow Grant to roll up his left flank. Instead of sitting idle while the Federals prepared to attack Anderson's line, Lee set into motion a plan to regain the initiative and destroy Hancock's force. By the evening of May 9, Major General William Mahone's troops had constructed a barricade of earthworks above and below the Block House Bridge to Anderson's flank. Lee's scheme called for Mahone to hold down Hancock, while Heth's division crossed the Po, turned north and struck the Federal's flank.[71]

In the early hours of May 10, the 55th North Carolina, with the rest of Heth's division, began the intended flanking maneuver. Heth's column moved around the left of the Confederate position on a pathway that ran westward toward the Po. Hancock was informed that the Rebels were entrenched near the Block House Bridge and would be able to contest any Federal attempt to cross. To find out more about the Confederate position, Hancock sent several reconnaissance detachments out to probe the Rebel lines. Major James C. Briscoe, of Birney's staff, was dispatched south from Waite's Shop to reconnoiter the area. Briscoe had with him the fourth and 17th Maine regiments and began moving south toward Glady Run. After fording the stream, the major's troops encountered remnants of Major General Wade Hampton's Confederate cavalry, which he promptly forced back. Briscoe continued forward but was soon surprised to find skirmishers from the 11th Mississippi in his path. The small Federal column had unexpectedly marched into Henry Heth's entire division.[72]

Briscoe's small force decided against attacking an entire Rebel division and proceeded to retreat across Glady Run. Heth's troops chased the fleeing Federals, who made a short stand on the northern bank of the stream near Talley's Mill. Brigadier General Birney was alerted that the Rebels were pushing Briscoe's troops back and quickly sent in two more regiments for support. The infusion of fresh Union soldiers slowed Heth's advance toward Waite's Shop. As the Confederates approached Talley's Mill they found a home that had been abandoned when the firing began. Many of Heth's tired troops helped themselves to the icehouse near the home and refreshed their bodies with cold drinks of water. After a short pause the Rebels continued their advance.[73]

By noon Briscoe's men and the two regiments sent in to assist them were wearily retreating back to Shady Grove Church Road, where Brigadier General Francis Barlow's men had built fortifications. Heth moved his division into position and with the aid of Early, who had joined the battle, deployed his troops for the attack. The Union troops now took up position behind their breastworks and awaited the Confederate assault.[74]

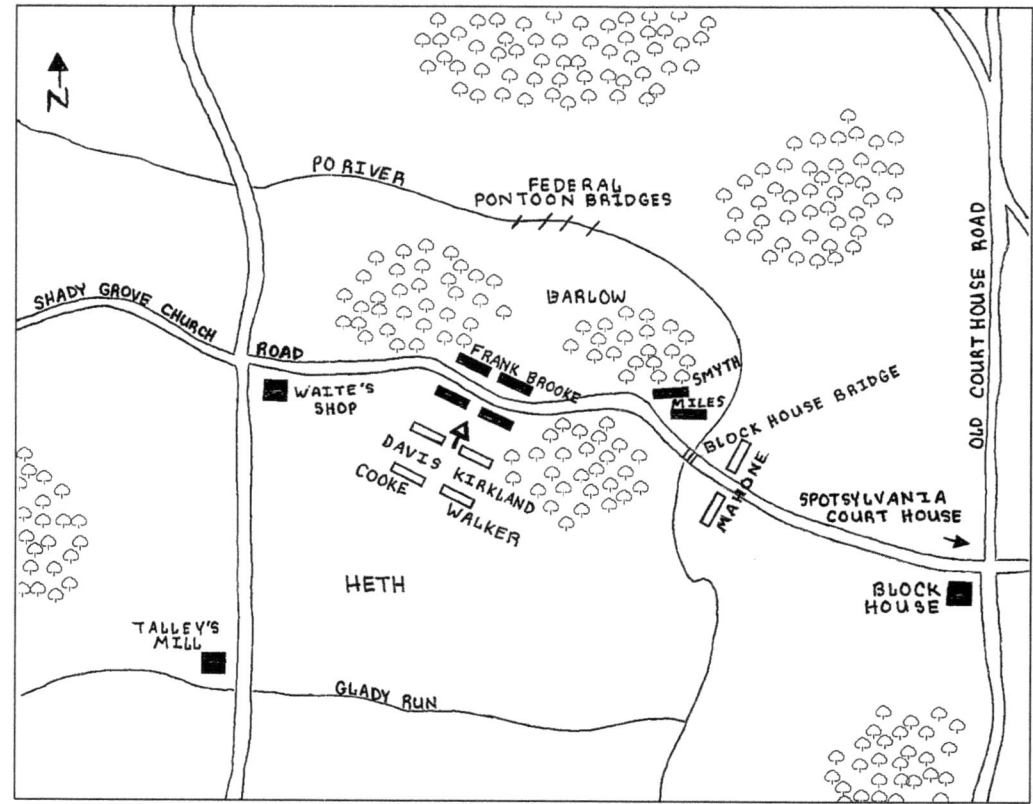

Heth's advance against Barlow, May 10, 1864.

The 55th North Carolina participated in this assault and helped push the Federals back. The regiment, with the rest of Heth's troops, moved forward in "skirmishing order," followed by an advancing line of battle. The Rebels climbed over the forward trenches below Shady Grove Church Road — which had been quickly abandoned by the Federals — then charged into a deadly volley of rifle fire. The men in the 55th were momentarily staggered, but quickly re-formed and made another determined charge. Colonel Belo described the fighting years later.[75]

> About 2 p.m. we struck the enemy. The Matt, the Tay, the Po and the Ny were branches of the Mattapony River. The enemy had crossed these different branches; we drove them successfully over three of them. My colors were shot down three times. The last time we were charging a line of breastworks; a cannon in front was trained on our colors and when we were within a hundred yards was fired with terrible effect. This was the only time I think it was lawful for the commander to take the colors. While we were resting from this charge General Early rode up and said, "Well, men, we must charge them once more and then we'll be through." Some of the Mississippians on my right said "General, we are all out of ammunition." He said, "Damn it; holler them across." So we started with a yell and did holler them across.[76]

It is doubtful that the Federals retreated after hearing the "rebel yell." The determination of the men in Heth's division did, however, gain the respect of Early, who commented that the major general's troops "behaved very handsomely."[77]

Davis's brigade, after several attempts, succeeded in driving the Federals out of their breastworks. Private Pearsall wrote that "we charged them out of three lines of brest works but didnot kill half as meney as we did the 5 [May 5] for they can out run eney folks I evor saw." In a letter sent to his wife Lieutenant Hoyle's account differs slightly from Pearsall's. Hoyle wrote, "We charged the enemy, and drove them from two lines of their breast works. Our loss was heavy again."[78]

During the assault the 55th captured a Federal artillery piece, the first gun lost by Hancock's II Corps in almost a year.[79] Lieutenant Cooke described the battle in his history of the 55th North Carolina.

> We charged and captured a piece of artillery and drove the enemy across the Mattapony. The Regiment upon this occasion behaved with great gallantry, charging for half a mile up the hillside through an old field. Though subject during this charge to a fire from bothartillery and small arms, the loss was not very great; we were charging up hill and the fire of the enemy went over our heads. On this charge three color bearers were shot down in succession before we captured the artillery.[80]

Although Cooke's account states that losses were minimal, which contradicts Hoyle's version, it must be understood that Hoyle may have been referring to his company and not the entire regiment.

The historian of the II Corps, Francis A. Walker, believed that Heth's men fought well during the engagement, known to Davis's brigade as the battle of Talley's Mill. Walker wrote years later in his history of the II Corps, in a statement that can only be understood as a rebuttal to claims that the Union troops were heavily outnumbered during the fight around Talley's Mill, that "the forces were far from being unequally matched. A Confederate division was, in general, much larger than a division of Union troops; but Heth's column had suffered heavily in the Wilderness; while Barlow's was at this time much the strongest division of the Army of the Potomac."[81] For the historian of a Federal corps to defend Heth's troops at the expense of his own men clearly shows that Walker obviously felt that the Confederate soldiers engaged near Talley's Mill on May 10 fought extremely well. It should also be added that in Hancock's official report the Federals posted along Shady Grove Church Road had been ordered to retreat. Hancock, fearing Mahone's nearby troops would join Heth's assault, decided to pull his men out as orderly as possible. The Rebel assault, however, did force many of the Federals to retreat before being ordered to do so.[82]

Throughout the rest of May 10, Grant continued his attempts to break through Lee's line. Around 4:00 p.m., Warren attacked Major General Charles W. Field's entrenched position northeast of the Block House Bridge, but nothing was gained. Heth's troops remained in reserve as the Federals continued to probe the Confederate line. Another Union assault, commanded by Wright, struck Ewell's line and two assaults under Colonel Emory Upton and Brigadier General J. Hobart Ward succeeded in breaking through Lee's fortifications. Fortunately for the Confederate troops, proper support was never sent in and the Federals were forced to retreat.[83]

During the late afternoon of May 11, Union and Confederate cavalry clashed near Yellow Tavern. During the melee, which ended in a decisive victory for the North, J. E. B. Stuart was mortally wounded while rallying his troopers. The brilliant cavalier died the following evening in Richmond. The death of Stuart had a resounding negative effect on the morale and capabilities of the Army of Northern Virginia.[84]

Throughout the day Heth's troops moved from their position west of the Block House

Bridge to an area around Spotsylvania Court House near the Massaponax Baptist Church. Lee continued to wait for Grant's assault and instructed his men to strengthen their defenses. The men in the 55th North Carolina had little time to do anything else, including writing letters home. In a brief message written to his wife on May 11, Lieutenant Hoyle simply stated, "I have but little opportunities to write, and less to send off what I do write." As the morning turned to the afternoon a heavy rain and a brisk wind pelted the men as they worked at mending their earthworks. Although the troops remained relatively quiet throughout the day, minor skirmishes and artillery barrages occurred sporadically.[85]

Throughout May 11 Heth remained in position along the Fredericksburg Road behind Confederate earthworks. The limited activity of the day must have convinced some of the Confederates that Grant, like so many of his predecessors, was retreating. Private Pearsall wrote his wife ecstatically after being informed that the Federals were falling back.

> I just herd such good nuse I thout I would try to finish it the report is old grant is retreting and I think it is time for if he ant whiped now thair is no chans to whip him.[86]

Pearsall's claim that Grant was preparing to pull out may seem surprising, but during the evening of May 11 Lee had instructed Heth to be ready to march at a moment's notice. Lee believed the Federals might be planning to retreat to Fredericksburg.[87] In all likelihood, Heth informed his brigade commanders to be ready, and word probably filtered down to the common soldiers in the ranks. It is interesting to note that even a weary private understood that if Grant was not defeated, the South had no chance for victory.

By the morning of May 12, the Confederate line was in the shape of an arc, five to seven miles in length. In the center of the Confederate defenses a large salient protruded north about three-fourths of a mile. The men referred to this position as the "Mule Shoe," and the area directly in front of this salient was an open field. Hill's troops were positioned on the right of this bulge and were exhausted after days of marching, fighting, and entrenching.[88] Although Grant made no attempts to assault the Confederate lines on May 11, he had prepared to commence another offensive the following morning.

On May 12 around 4:30 a.m. Hancock ordered his division commanders to their units. A mass of troops larger than the Confederates had assembled for the Pickett-Pettigrew charge formed and began moving forward. After subduing several Rebel pickets the Union tide advanced toward their main objective point: the Mule Shoe salient. As the Federal troops came into view one Louisiana soldier declared, "as far as the eye could reach, the field was covered with the serried ranks of the enemy, marching in close columns to the attack." As the Confederate artillery opened the Federals began to advance at the double-quick. The massive blue wave crashed into the Rebel works and a bloody hand-to-hand to battle ensued. After little more than 15 minutes of fighting the Federals pushed through parts of the eastern portion of the salient.[89]

As the Federals pored over the Confederate works hundreds of ragged, weary Rebels were taken prisoner. Among those captured was Major General Edward "Allegheny" Johnson, a division commander in Ewell's corps. Grant's headquarters became overjoyed when reports began to come in informing the commander that the Confederate line had been broken. The Federal advance, however, was stopped some time later by the swift and timely movements of Brigadier General John B. Gordon, who was commanding Early's division, and other Confederate forces. Lee had stalled Grant's advance, but the Union V and VI corps still remained poised to strike the Rebel line.[90]

Gordon's troops were able to push the Federals back to the outer trenches, but the Confederate counterattack was stopped there. Around 6:00 a.m., Meade ordered Wright's VI Corps to attack the Confederate right where Rodes's division was positioned. Confederate artillery hampered the Federal assault. In one area the line bent in two spots, which were approximately 50 yards apart. It was at this location, referred to as the "Bloody Angle," that some of the war's most horrific fighting occurred. The dead of both armies piled up three, even five, deep in some areas. The hand-to-hand fighting was terrible and the carnage unbelievable as the soldiers of each army fought almost continuously for nearly 20 hours.[91]

Several hours after noon the fighting at the Bloody Angle had ground to a stalemate. The opposing commanders now felt the need to exploit other locations. Remarkably both generals thought of attacking each other at the "salient's eastern leg." Lee believed he could strike Burnside's thinly guarded left flank while at the same time Grant wanted to assault what he perceived to be a weakly defended spot in the Confederate line.[92]

Burnside, after repeated pressure from Grant, had finally begun his offensive around noon. While Union and Confederate artillerymen traded shots Lee arrived near what became known as Heth's Salient, a bulge in the Rebel line that pointed west toward the lower end of Burnside's line. Lee instructed the brigades of Brigadier General James H. Lane and Colonel David Weisiger to move to a position southeast of Heth's Salient and strike Burnside's

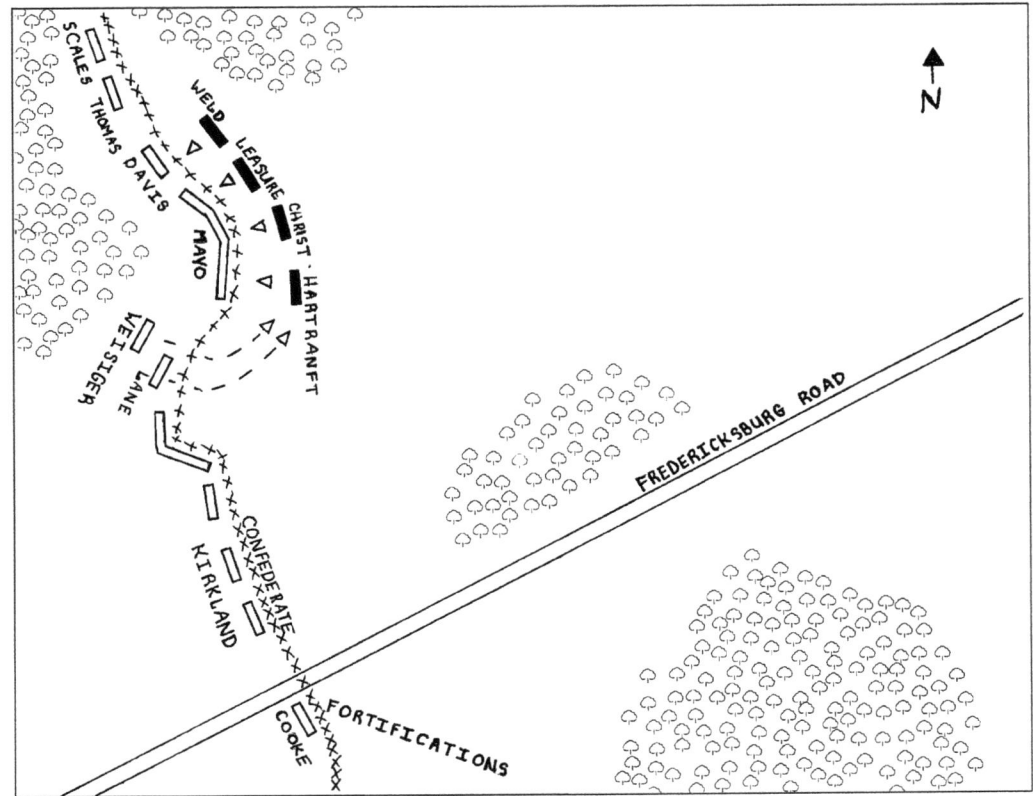

Burnside's attack against Heth's salient on May 12, 1864.

flank. At approximately the same time Weisiger began advancing into the Federal flank, Brigadier General Orlando B. Willcox's division, of Burnside's IX Corps, attacked Heth's Salient.[93]

As Willcox's men advanced toward the Confederate line, occupied by the brigades of Davis and Mayo, they first encountered skirmishers from Davis's command. Major General Thomas L. Crittenden's brigade advanced directly in front of Davis's position, which was directly above Heth's Salient. The line was heavily contested throughout the day, but the Rebels continued to hold. Finally, well past midnight, the Confederate engineers completed the new line across the base of the Bloody Angle and the day of carnage ended as the weary Rebels fell back to their new trenches.[94]

The 55th North Carolina remained behind their fortifications throughout the day's battle. Because its position was to the right of Hancock's assault and well protected during Crittenden's attack, its losses were "comparatively small." Several members of the regiment were not even involved in the day's action. Private Pearsall and Lieutenant Hoyle both informed their wives, in letters written several days after the battle for the Bloody Angle, that they had not been engaged since May 10. Davis's entire brigade suffered minimal casualties, and the majority of those killed or wounded were from the 150 skirmishers in front of their line. Twenty guns posted behind their line, which continuously shot holes through the oncoming Federal lines, assisted the Confederates near Heth's Salient.[95]

On May 13 Lee, whose options were now limited because of the appalling casualties his army had sustained since Grant crossed the Rapidan nine days before, ordered his men to strengthen their defenses and rest. Grant spent the day re-forming his army and trying to ascertain where Lee's line was weakest. As the sun brought an end to the darkness the carnage of the previous day's battle became evident. The dead lay piled up almost to the top of the tarnished earthworks. As the daylight hours drifted by, soldiers in both armies tried to eat, but many were too tired and simply lay down to rest.[96]

Grant still hoped to strike Lee's army and after spending the day gathering information concerning the condition of the Confederate line he planned his next assault. The Federal commander realized that Lee's line was weak on the right, where Hill's troops were posted. During the night of May 13–14, Grant sent Warren's and Wright's forces around to take position near Lee's right. As the morning drew near, Lee ordered pickets out to probe the Union lines. By 10:00 a.m. Grant's V and VI corps were in place, but the commanding general hesitated. Had Grant attacked Lee at that moment his planned offensive may have succeeded. Lee, unaware of the number of troops that had stealthily moved to his right, had neglected to reinforce Hill's position. The Federals gained relatively nothing from the clashes near Myers Hill, and Grant had to accept that he had missed a great opportunity to crush Lee's army.[97]

Throughout May 14 and 15 heavy rains had made movement difficult and combat even harder. The inclement weather brought activity around Spotsylvania to a virtual standstill. Lee's men addressed their defenses and rested while Grant pondered his next move. For Lee the decision was simple: he had little choice but to remain on the defensive. By May 15, the soldiers in both armies were drained physically and emotionally. The constant need to remain in a state of preparedness had brought on fatigue and exhaustion. Private Pearsall informed his wife "I am well as to helth but the worst broke down I evor was in my life." Pearsall, like all those who survived the bloody carnage of the Wilderness and Spotsylvania, was happy to be alive, writing, "it is grate pleasur to me that I have gon threw the hevy batls safe so far and I trust in god I may go threw safe." Interestingly, Pearsall instructed his wife to keep the letter he had sent because "this is yankee paper." The young private or friends of his may have joined in with those who rifled through the pockets of dead Federal troops during the past several days.

The situation around Spotsylvania Court House remained relatively peaceful throughout the next several days. By May 18 the roads had dried enough for fighting to resume. Grant had decided to attack Lee once again. The Federal commander proposed to send Hancock and Wright against the Confederate left, west of the Mule Shoe salient. While the II and VI Federal corps assaulted Lee's left, remnants of Burnside's IX Corps were to strike the salient. The attacks began at 4:00 a.m. and did not go well for the Union troops. Hancock's and Wright's men encountered stiff resistance from the Confederate left, and Burnside's soldiers fared no better. As the Federals under the command of Colonel Stephen M. Weld, Jr., advanced just north of Heth's Salient, Davis's unit, posted in front of them, patiently took aim and waited. Weld's men advanced in such a manner that their entire line was exposed to Davis's command. As the unsuspecting Federals approached, the Mississippians and North Carolinians opened fire. The Union line staggered then fell back. After only a few short hours the Union offensive was called off. The Confederate line had held again.[98]

The attack had done little damage to the Confederate army and was barely felt by the men in the 55th North Carolina. The most miserable aspect of the day's fighting for the regiment was the Federal artillery barrage. Private Pearsall wrote, "our Regt was not engaged but under the fire of the hevist canonading I evor herd the bumes fell all around me and threw the dirt all over me." Other than being a nuisance, the Union artillery did little harm and inflicted no casualties on the 55th. Lieutenant Hoyle also commented on the cannonading, stating on the following day, "Yesterday the yankees shelled us heavily, but did us no damage.[99]

On May 19, the last day of the battles for Spotsylvania Court House, Lee ordered Ewell to attack the Federal position around the Harris and Alsop farms. The main reason for the assault was to ascertain if Grant had left his right flank unprotected. The battle of Harris Farm ended with little gained by the Confederates. The 55th remained inactive throughout the day waiting anxiously for word on Ewell's assault. Lieutenant Hoyle, suffering from diarrhea, believed the Confederates had prevailed, stating "A heavy fight took place on our left yesterday evening, but I do not know for sure how it went, reports say our men were successful." The calmness of the regiment's line did not ease the men's apprehension. In a letter to his wife written on May 20, Hoyle's words clearly indicate that after more than two weeks of virtually non-stop carnage and death the belief that another battle was soon to follow had become almost second nature. The young officer declared, "All has been quiet along the lines to day though the storm of battle may break cross at any time."[100]

The battles for Spotsylvania Court House cost the Federals over 18,000 men killed or wounded and the Army of Northern Virginia approximately 12,000. Grant, satisfied that he could not break Lee's line, decided on another flanking move to the right. Early in the morning of May 21 Hancock's battered corps moved out and marched southeast to successfully turn Lee's right flank. But the ever-intuitive Confederate general would not sit idle while the Federals were on the move. Lee had decided to fall back to the North Anna River, a natural barrier, about 23 miles north of Richmond, and by 4:00 a.m. Ewell's corps began moving to counter any Federal threat. Ewell's troops were closely followed by Anderson's First

Corps while most of Hill's force remained behind to check any possible Federal attacks against the Confederate rear.[101]

Around 9:00 p.m., Davis's brigade began moving south, marching about seven miles before resting for the night. Lee's troops once again beat Grant and began preparing for a Federal assault around Hanover Junction. Hill's corps arrived on the morning of May 23 and quickly entrenched along the Virginia Central Railroad, which was located on the left of the Confederate line. Later that day, Heth's division was sent in to support Wilcox's troops as they tried to halt the Federal advance across the North Anna near Jericho Mills. The Federals, under the command of Gouveneur Warren, were hit hard by Wilcox, but were able to maintain their foothold on the southern bank of the river. According to Lieutenant Hoyle the 55th North Carolina did not participate in this counterattack. Davis's brigade did see action, but it is not known for certain which regiments were engaged. In a letter to his wife, dated May 23, which corroborates Hoyle's assertion, Private Pearsall does not mention being engaged, but does state "they ur fiting now but little wais from me." The engagement near Jericho Mills did not begin until well after 4:30 p.m. and so it is possible that Pearsall wrote his letter earlier in the day before the assault occurred.[102]

According to Joseph Hoyle the 55th began a forced march on May 21 and continued day and night until being placed in front of the Army of the Potomac, taking up position on the east bank of the South Anna River near Hanover Junction. The young lieutenant also found himself, once again, in command of Company F.

> I have suffered a great deal from hard marching for a few days past. I do not think I was ever nearer worn out, but we have been resting now for a couple of days, and I am feeling about right again. I will give you some account of our late movements. On Saturday, 21st, the yankees left Spotsylvania C. H. and moved in the direction of Fredericksburg. That night we also left and moved in the direction of Hanover Junction. We marched nearly all night, resting only an hour or two before day. Early Sunday morning we again commenced marching and marched hard all day. We camped this night on the Central Rail Road, 10 miles above Hanover Junction. Early Monday morning we again took up the march and marched three or four miles till we crossed South Anna River, about 3 or 4 miles from the junction. Here we rested till evening, when we fell in and retraced our steps up the road 2 or 3 miles to meet the yankees who were about to strike the road at this point. A sharp fight took place here by Wilcox Division. Our Division was exposed to the shelling but was not engaged and suffered none. After night came on we fell back to the South Anna River, and took position on its east bank. Where we are now. Our army is again in position in front of Grant and tis said hard fighting was done on the right of the lines yesterday. Skirmishing is going on in our front to-day and an attack is looked for at any time. The captain has been sick since we left Spotsylvania, and I am placed in command of the company again.[103]

By May 25 Davis's brigade was entrenched between the North Anna and Little rivers. Although the two armies continued to engage each other for the next several days, with no significant achievements being made, the 55th North Carolina remained behind their defenses, occasionally performing picket duty. A few days later Grant's whole force was back across the North Anna River and moving east. Once again Grant hoped to turn the Confederate flank, and Lee began shifting his troops to keep his army between the Federals and Richmond.[104]

The 55th North Carolina began moving toward Richmond on May 27 and continued marching slowly throughout the following day to "keep opposite the enemy." The spirit of the men remained high and they understood that their move was not a retreat. Lieutenant

Hoyle described how the soldiers interpreted the battles that occurred during May and their move toward Richmond.

> Although we have fell back on Richmond, yet we have not been whipped back on the other hand we have whipped the enemy wherever he has attacked us. So the yankees have got here not by driving us back, but by moving around our flank. I do not see that Grant has gained any advantage, although he has got nearer Richmond, for it must be born in mind that he might have got this near by coming up the Peninsula without loosing a man, while he has already lost about 60,000 men. Our soldiers are in hopeful spirits it seems that Grant is now mustering all his strength for a final struggle, and we hope this will end the war.[105]

During the evening of May 29, the 55th moved a few miles closer to Richmond and worked throughout most of the night "making brest works." The regiment was then set up in a line of battle and prepared to force back any Federal attack. The men continued to perform picket duty and Private Pearsall got a little closer to several Federal bullets than he would have liked to. Pearsall wrote in a letter to his wife that "me and the yankees pickets has taken several fair cracks at each other they have come very clost to me the balls has pased between my legs and one went under my arm but thank god it has bin his will so far that I have escape."[106]

Private William Ellis Royster, Company K. Private Royster was mustered into the army as a corporal, but was reduced to ranks sometime between April 1863 and June 1864. Private Royster served as a teamster and a carpenter during the war and survived. (Courtesy of the North Carolina Division of Archives and History, Raleigh, North Carolina.)

As the Confederates fortified their position near the Totopotomoy Creek, most of the soldiers received rations of a piece of bacon and three biscuits. For some of Lee's fighting men this was the first taste of food they had experienced in several days. Private Pearsall wrote that the men in his regiment were receiving double rations of meat and some tobacco. The hungry and exhausted Rebels dug in making good use of the ridges that overlooked the stream; they prepared to fend off any Federal assault. The Federals had entrenched along a line that ran from the Pamunkey River south to the Totopotomoy. During the last days of May both armies engaged in minor skirmishes and several cavalry fights occurred as the two commanders tried to ascertain the strength and position of their enemy.[107]

By May 30 the Confederates were almost certain that Grant was attempting to extend his line east to the Chickahominy River. With the Army of the Potomac slowly approaching Richmond, President Davis endorsed Lee's request for additional troops. Lee understood that if Grant reached the Chickahominy the Federal left flank would be protected. If the Federal left was protected, Grant could shift troops to other locations as needed, which meant that even with more men Lee would still, for all practical purposes, be forced to stay on the defensive. Also, as the Federals extended their line, the Army of Northern Virginia, already thinned from almost a month of continuous fighting, would be stretched out and made even weaker.[108]

Lee, in an effort to prevent Grant from moving farther southeast, decided to attack the Army of the Potomac. The Confederate commander believed that if he hit Grant hard enough the Federals would be forced to reinforce their current lines, and thus be unable to continue moving toward the Chickahominy. Lee ordered Early, who at the time was in temporary command of Ewell's corps, to assault the Federal V Corps near Bethesda Church, a few miles from Cold Harbor. Early's attack was repulsed and did nothing to prevent Grant from extending his line.[109]

Before Early and Warren's engagement near Bethesda Church, both Grant and Lee had sent out cavalry units to determine how many troops were on the move. Grant's main concern was to maintain his supply depot at White House Landing, along the Pamunkey River. Throughout May 30 and 31 Federal and Confederate cavalry clashed as they attempted to probe each other's lines. Between the Confederate and Federal lines was a small dusty hamlet known as Cold Harbor. Both commanding generals realized that control of this road junction was very important strategically. Of the five roads that intersected at Cold Harbor, one offered a possible route leading behind Lee's army. If Grant held that road he would force the Confederates to fight around Richmond. Of the remaining four, one ran indirectly west toward Richmond, two led south toward Petersburg and the James River, and the last was a clear path to White House Landing.[110]

On May 31 Major General Philip H. Sheridan, commander of Grant's cavalry, arrived near Cold Harbor and found Confederate troopers under the command of Major General Fitz Lee occupying the crossroads. Sheridan was able to force Fitz Lee out of Cold Harbor, but was unsure whether he would be able to hold it. After being instructed to hold his position at "all hazards" the cavalry commander braced for an attack and waited for the infantry support he had been told was coming.[111]

The following morning Major General Robert Hoke's division, which had just arrived from North Carolina, and Major General Joseph Kershaw's division attacked Sheridan's troopers at Cold Harbor. The Confederates pressed hard, but one of Kershaw's brigades, commanded by Colonel Lawrence M. Keitt, who was inexperienced, retreated after encountering strong resistance. Although Keitt tried to rally his troops, an effort that cost him his life, they continued falling back and panic spread to other brigades. The Federals held their line until Wright's VI Corps arrived around 10:00 a.m. and relieved Sheridan's exhausted troopers.[112]

In an effort to move his army closer to Lee's and possibly break through the Rebel lines, Grant ordered Wright's VI Corps and Major General William F. "Baldy" Smith's XVIII corps to attack the Confederates now entrenching around Cold Harbor. At approximately 4:00 p.m. the Federals advanced and, at first, succeeded in separating Anderson and Hoke. But the Confederate earthworks provided excellent cover for the Rebels and they were able to halt the Federal advance. Grant's offensive move had been halted, but he was not prepared to give up.[113]

The 55th North Carolina spent the day of June 1 behind breastworks. They had moved from the position they had occupied on May 29, and although two of Heth's brigades participated in the day's fighting, Davis's troops remained behind their fortifications. Like the rest of their brigade the men of the 55th were close enough to the battle to see their fellow Confederates hold back the Federal tide, but did not engage.[114]

During the evening of June 1 Grant ordered Hancock to move his II Corps south to join with Smith's and Wright's troops. The Federal commander planned to begin the following day by launching an attack spearheaded by Hancock. The weary II Corps needed rest, though, so the assault was postponed until 5:00 p.m. By midafternoon Grant was convinced that his troops needed more rest and decided to reschedule the attack against Lee's right for dawn on June 3. After sending orders to his lieutenants to have their men prepared to strike the Confederates in the morning, Grant allowed Meade to arrange the battle plans.[115]

Realizing that Grant was weakening his right flank, Lee made plans to attack while the Federals were moving southeast. Around 3:00 p.m., Early, supported by Heth's division, crashed into the Union far right, which at the time was being occupied by Burnside's and Warren's corps. The Confederates succeeded in driving back the Union troops toward their defenses around Bethesda Church. Although the Union troops were able to halt the advance, the Rebels swallowed up numerous Federal prisoners.[116]

The 55th North Carolina actively participated in Early's strike against the Federal right on June 2. Davis's troops charged into the Armstrong field expecting to be supported on their right by Rodes's division. The 55th reached the battle late in the afternoon as the Federals were making this counterattack. The 55th and the rest of Davis's command charged the Federal lines around sunset and succeeded in stopping the Union advance. Many of the men in the 55th became entangled in a deadly fight with some of Brigadier General Robert B. Potter's Federal troops. Lieutenant Cooke stated, "it was a fearful charge. The Ground was unfavorable on account of a thick under-growth and the loss was considerable." At first they were able to push the Federals back, but Rodes failed to order his men forward. With their right flank exposed Davis's brigade was hit by severe enfilading fire and could not continue forward. The brigade made an orderly retreat north of the Shady Grove Road and entrenched on Rodes's left.[117] Major General Heth's report of the assault underscored his anger that Rodes had refused to advance.

> The consequence was that after Davis had driven the enemy a quarter of a mile his right flank was assailed, and his brigade driven back some 200 yards. In this fight our loss was heavy considering the numbers engaged.[118]

Apparently not everyone in the 55th participated in Heth's "brief, but furious" attack on June 2. Lieutenant Hoyle wrote that he was "out on the skirmish line" when orders for his regiment to advance were received and so he and several others did not charge the Federal position. Although he did not directly participate, Hoyle did describe the battle in a letter he sent home to his wife.

> Our division in conjunction with Ewell's forces moved on the enemies flank, and drove them with considerable loss from their breast works. Our loss was light. In our Co were killed none, wounded Andrew Marlicks in thigh J. A. Canipi on leg, slight, Wm. Hicks on knee, slight. I joined the Brig- after dark, being in line behind the yankee breast works. Our loss was light.[119]

Private Wilkerson was also sent out with the skirmish line and did not advance with his regiment. Wilkerson explained that his detachment engaged the Federals but was forced back by Union cavalry.

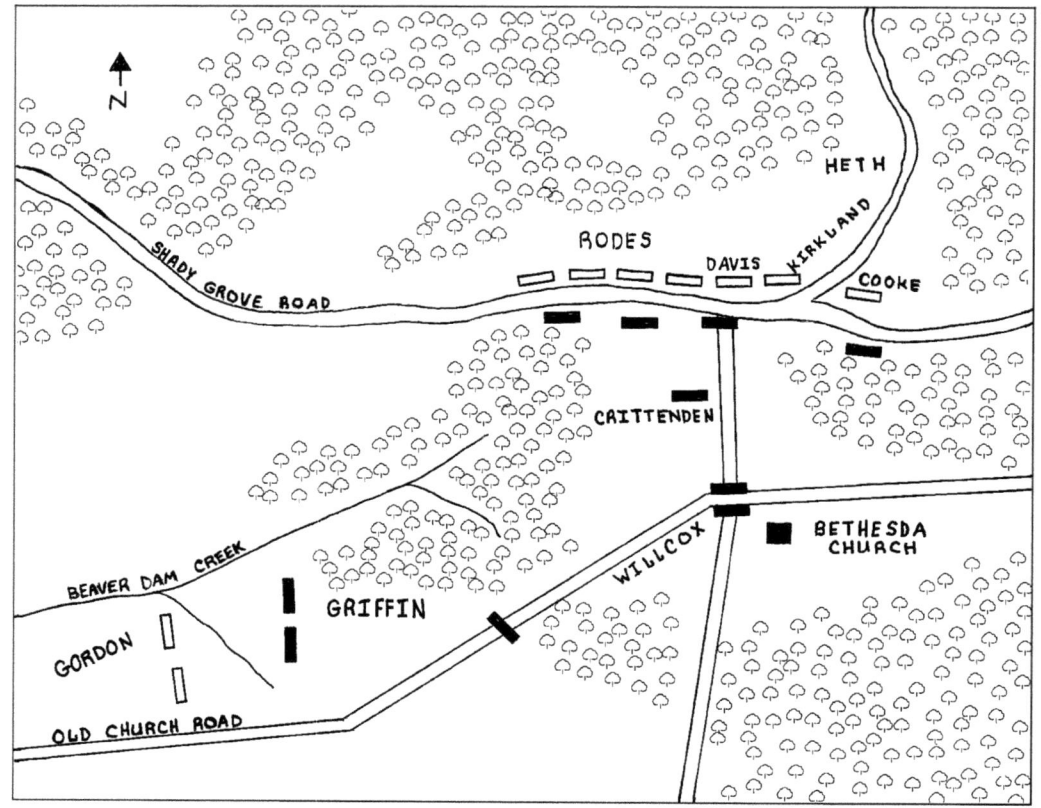

Heth's location on the evening of June 2, 1864.

> I was detailed to go out on skirmish thursday so we went over the yankee breast works 2 or 3 miles before we over took any of them an we had some fighting, and the yankee calvire like to cut us of so we fell back an when we got back to our works all of our men had moved to the right so it wont long before they ware in a fight.[120]

Among those wounded was Lieutenant Colonel Belo. The regimental commander commented on his injury years later, stating "about five o'clock we were ordered to charge the line in front and on getting within a few yards of the works a minie ball struck me in the left arm, turning me completely around."[121] The loss of their commanding officer was demoralizing to the regiment. Cooke expressed in his history of the 55th how devastating Belo's loss was.

> The loss to the regiment was irreparable. He had been with the regiment in all its hard-fought battles, and had the absolute confidence of every man in the regiment. He was cool and intrepid. He never lost his head in the midst of the fiercest conflict, nor failed to discover and seize the advantage of a position. He had a genius for organization, and appreciated every detail that contributed to the effectiveness or character of a military organization.[122]

June 2, 1864, would be the last time Belo commanded the 55th North Carolina. His wounding, which required the removal of several inches from his left arm, kept the gallant officer from returning to his duties.[123]

Although suffering from diarrhea, Private Pearsall continued performing his duties the best he could. In a letter written the same day that his regiment attacked the Federal right, Pearsall described what the 55th had been doing during the past several days and expressed sympathy for the Union troops.

> Dear we have bin under hevy firing evor sens yestaday 12 oclock but we have not been engaged.I saw a ofel site yestaday evning the yankees charged in front of Cooks [Cooke's] brigade a bout 5 hundred yards on my left and they wair slaid by Cooks men I cant tell the number that was kiled and wonded but I don't think the 10 one went back they got in a bout 100 hundred yards of our brest works before they turned back I was sarry for them to see them faling so fast as they com runing threw the field we lost no men our pickets is firing in our front prity thick.[124]

Later that afternoon Private Pearsall charged the Federal position with the rest of his regiment. During the advance Pearsall was shot in the head and killed instantly. Several days after the battle his wife received the news by letter. Sarah Pearsall was informed that her husband had been buried in his blanket during the night of June 4. Pearsall's friend, John W. Powell, informed Mrs. Pearsall that George was well liked and would be missed terribly by the men in his company.[125]

The following morning Grant launched a massive assault all along the Confederate line. A little after 4:30 a.m. over 50,000 Federal troops advanced toward the well-entrenched Confederate line. The Federal commander believed if his men could break Lee's line and force the Rebels back toward Richmond, the destruction of the Army of Northern Virginia would be only a matter of time. Unfortunately for the Union troops, Lee's soldiers had strengthened their fortifications and were poised to repel any assault. Before the blood and carnage of battle was finally over, nearly 7,000 Union soldiers lay dead or wounded on the field. Grant's tremendous charge had failed.[126]

During the June 3 Federal assault the 55th North Carolina remained well protected by breastworks and was positioned on the left of the Confederate line. Cooke's brigade did most of the fighting on this line. Lieutenant Hoyle described the regiment's action during the Federal attack.

> Early yesterday morning [June 3] the enemy attacked portions of our lines, but were repulsed and kept back all day. Our Brig. was not engaged during the day except skirmishing. Andrew Williams of my Co. was severely wounded in the thigh. No body else was hurt in our company. Cooks Brigade, on our left was heavily engaged during most of the day. Their loss was notheavy.[127]

Later in the day the 55th was moved to a position on the right of Lee's line and camped in a field near Gaines' Mill. The month of constant marching and fighting wore down the soldiers of both armies. Private Wilkerson wrote his mother "I wish this fighting would stop it seem like the war stop if we could get in camp." The terrific carnage and destruction of the past month had many soldiers believing the war was finally near its end. Wilkerson informed his mother that many of the soldiers felt the conflict could not continue for long and wrote, "some think this is the last." Grant, however, was not about to admit defeat and after shaking off the dust and blood of Cold Harbor he began moving again.[128]

For several days after the June 3 assault both armies did little fighting. Shots were exchanged and skirmishers sent out, but no major action occurred. On the evening of June 5 Grant asked Lee to allow unarmed soldiers to scour the battlefield for dead and wounded men. Lee agreed and both armies collected their dead and injured comrades. After spending time reorganizing his command, Grant began to move away from Cold Harbor.[129]

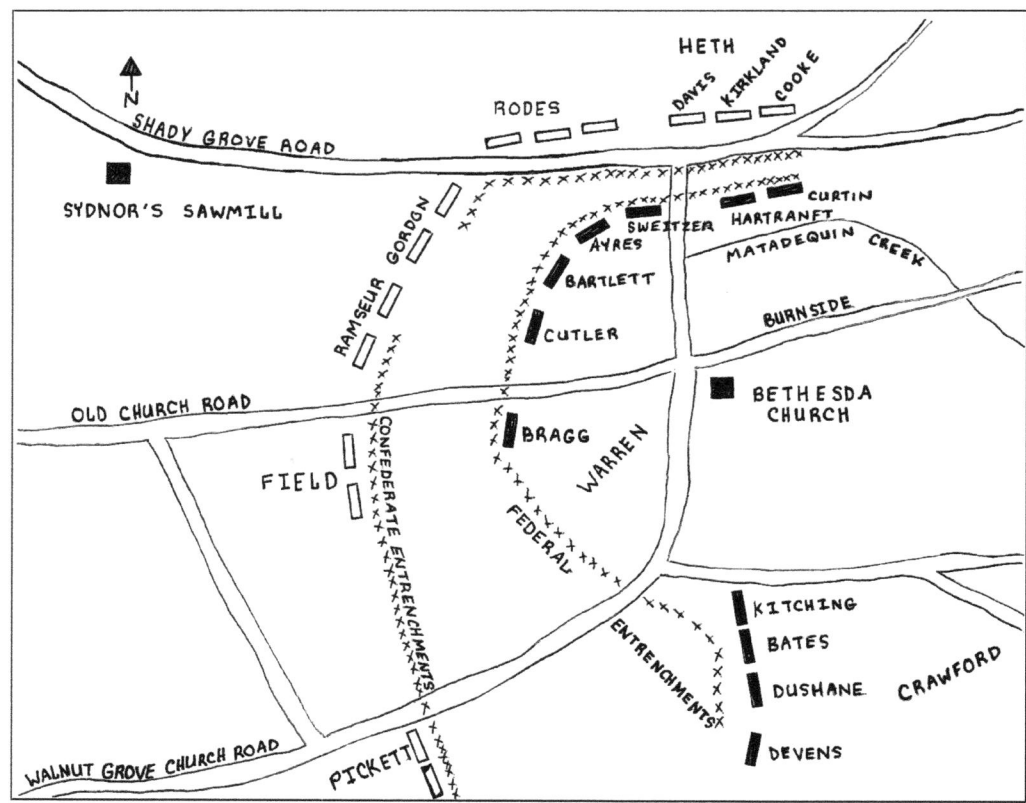

Location of Heth's Brigades on the morning of June 3, 1864, as Burnside and Warren prepare to attack.

The 55th North Carolina returned to the Cold Harbor line and manned their defenses. On the evening of June 12 the Army of the Potomac began moving south toward the James River. Lee hoped that he could catch the Federal army in motion. However, the Confederate commander did not learn of the Union evacuation until the following morning. Lee quickly ordered Hill and Anderson to follow the Federals. Heth's division marched out of Cold Harbor on the morning of June 13 and crossed the Chickahominy and entrenched near Turkey Bend.[130] Private Wilkerson described the regiment's move in a letter to his sister on June 16.

> We over took them [the Federals] in the evening and our skirmishers was fighting some. So we thought we would be in it very Soon. We formed line of battle and throwed up breast works and that night the yankees left again. So tuseday morning we folered on after them and got whare theyankees stayed that night we rested their until wednesday morning [June 15] and formed another line of battle and throwed up more breast works. So orders come very soon to move forward. So we was after the yankees all day yesterday runing through the woods and swamps and formed another line of battle near the long Bridg and made more breast works.[131]

On June 14 around 11:00 a.m. Grant began moving his 100,000-plus army across the James River. His objective was to capture Petersburg, an important railroad hub south of the Confederate capital that, if taken, would give the Federals control of the southern routes

5. April–June 1864: Preparing for the Death Angel 119

to Richmond. The Union troops crossed the James in perfect order and were prepared to move against Petersburg. Lee, not certain Grant was actually moving his entire force toward Petersburg, ordered A. P. Hill's corps to remain north of the James while moving the majority of his army across the James on June 16.[132]

The Federals proceeded to attack Petersburg for several days starting on June 16, but were beaten back by General P. G. T. Beauregard. The 55th did not participate in the defense of Petersburg, still being positioned north of the James. On June 18 part of Davis's command was sent across the James and ordered to take up position along the Howlett Line, six miles west of Bermuda Hundred. This move, an effort to strengthen the protective line around Petersburg, involved the 11th Mississippi and at least part of the 55th North Carolina. Lieutenant Hoyle informed his wife that he had been moved south of the James, but was sent back across to intercept some Federal troops that were moving up the northern bank of the river. Hoyle reported that his men were posted below Chaffin's Bluff along the James.[133]

The 55th performed picket duty along the James and was occasionally shelled by Federal gunboats, but its time spent near Chaffin's Bluff was relatively peaceful. The Union troops were close to the Confederate lines but Hoyle wrote, "the yankees take care not to come out from their gunboats." Their stay near the bluff did not last long. Early in July the 55th crossed to the south bank of the James. By July 5 it was within sight of Petersburg.[134]

6

July 1864–April 1865: Fading into Legend

"I am tired of this war"

From the Wilderness to the North Anna River, Lee's soldiers had fought against a force that outnumbered them nearly two to one, but somehow the Army of Northern Virginia remained intact. The 55th North Carolina, although not engaged in every battle, had participated in some of the most horrific combat experienced during the Civil War. By the first week of July 1864 the tired and thinned regiment had taken up position with the majority of Lee's army in a protective line around Petersburg. Several members of the 55th were sent to guard the Weldon Railroad, but the majority remained entrenched around Petersburg. The last several months had been a time of constant fatigue, and by July most of the unit could not help believing that every new day would bring another battle.[1]

Lieutenant Hoyle believed the Confederate defenses well maintained and informed his wife that he didn't think the Army of the Potomac would attempt an assault at the present time. He also explained the condition of the regiment and the negative effects the weather was having on the men.

> Day before yesturday we left the north side of the James River and are now in position on the right of the lines around Petersburg, near the Weldon Rail Road. The enemy is about a mile off at this point, but further to our left. The lines are in close proximity and picket firing is constantly going on. Though this has been the condition for some time now, and I think it doubtful whether Grant makes another general attack from his present lines. We are having very dry and hot weather for some time now, and suffer a great deal from the heat, as we frequently have to lie in line through open fields exposed to the sun. And when we march, the dust is excessively hard on us. I do hope, and pray, this hard campaign will soon end, and with it this cruel war also.[2]

While the opposing armies spent their days extending their trenches and fortifying their position, the Confederate soldiers manning the defenses had to be constantly vigilant. Every day an hour before sunrise the Rebels were awake and standing at their post ready to contest any Federal assault. After daybreak about one man in two was able to sleep or relax. Several men in each regiment were ordered to fire their rifles at the Federal lines every five minutes or so. Sharpshooters made any exposure extremely hazardous and the occasional mortar shell kept every man alert. Around a half an hour before dusk all of the troops once again positioned themselves on the fire step and remained there until dark.[3]

Life in the Petersburg trenches was not pleasant. The Virginia summer heat, the constant nagging of swarms of flies, and the smell from over-used latrines made the defenses a virtual hell on earth. The rain brought relief from the heat, but after days of constant rain the trenches would fill up often two feet deep with water making life miserable for the fighting men on the line.[4] T. P. Buford, a member of the 11th Mississippi, wrote the following account of life in the Petersburg trenches:

> Imagine, if you can, yourself down in a dirty ditch, living and sleeping in it day and night; a space cut in the side to cook in, another space cut in the side to spread your blanket on, the ditch deep enough so that the watchful eye of the enemy could not see you at times from the front. You must be careful not to expose any part of your body. Then imagine the shells coming over and dropping near enough to make you nervous; imagine living for weeks and months in such a place, with bare subsistence, casualties frequent about you. You must do your part too, toward annoying the enemy; make him as miserable as you can, kill him if you can, or scare him into fits. Then imagine, if you can, when you would have any time for enjoyment or to be in fine spirits. Such was life in the trenches around Petersburg.[5]

In his history of the 55th North Carolina, Lieutenant Cooke provided a picture of what the trench line occupied by his regiment looked like.

> The part of the line occupied by our regiment was so near to that of the enemy that sharpshooting was kept up constantly between the lines with casualties of almostdaily occurrence. The enemy had a number of mortar guns planted just in rear of their lines, from which shells were discharged almost constantly night and day. As some measure of protection, the men and officers of the regiment dug holes in the side of the hill, upon which the line of our regiment was formed. The headquarters of the regiment was a hole six by nine feet square, thus made in the side of the hillwith an opening to the rear, and it was in this place that the writer, Adjutant of the regiment, received all orders from superior officers, received and made all reports and all regimental orders, and there the commanding officer and myself slept at night.[6]

Cooke also stated that it was "customary" for regiments to be relieved every 10 days and allowed to move to the rear and bath and wash their clothes.[7]

Another source of irritation and distress for Lee's men was the lack of food. Private Wilkerson informed his mother during the middle of July that he couldn't get enough to eat, even for fifty dollars. The young private was, however, able to purchase two small pies for two dollars, which was good for "about fore good mouthfuls." The lack of nutritious food lowered the overall health of the regiment. Wilkerson, himself sick at the time, complained "I haven't eat any vegatables this year, only a few green apples."[8]

Although some of Lee's men were receiving adequate food and supplies during the early months of the siege, several regiments in Heth's division were not. In a letter to his sister, Private Samuel P. Lockhart of the 27th North Carolina Regiment wrote, "we don't get anything to eat but bread and meat and coffee and peas." Lockhart's command may have been suffering from a lack of quality food but apparently, unlike the 55th, the 27th North Carolina at least got some vegetables.[9]

By August things had not changed much for the men in the 55th North Carolina. The regiment's troops received a ration of beef and cornmeal and then the following day the soldiers were given bacon and flour. Although alternating rations each day added some variety to the men's daily meals, Wilkerson declared "I could eate both days ration in one day easy a nought." The young private also described his average meal, writing that he cooked some flour for supper but only got a few peas for dinner. The rations may not have improved much, but at least Wilkerson could finally say that he was eating some vegetables.[10]

Concerns over the hardships brought about by the trenches and the lack of food were not the only distresses troubling the minds of the North Carolina troops that summer, especially those with loved ones living in the western portion of their home state. On June 13, 1864, Colonel George W. Kirk, a Federal cavalry officer, led about 300 men on a raid into western North Carolina. The force left Morristown, Tennessee, and planned to attack Morganton, North Carolina, which is located in Burke County, north of Cleveland County. By the morning of June 28, 1864, Kirk's troops had reached Camp Vance, a Confederate base used to train conscripts. The small force of Junior Reserves surrendered to Kirk's men, who then proceeded to burn the camp. Kirk's real objective was not to destroy this base, but to capture a train on the Western North Carolina Railroad and make a quick advance to Salisbury, North Carolina, to free Federal prisoners, and to possibly destroy an important railroad bridge over the Yadkin River, located north of Salisbury. Kirk and his men were opposed by home guards and prison guards, and had to retreat. He did, however, destroy a railroad depot and a few rail cars in Morganton. His raid netted 130 prisoners and a number of horses and mules.[11]

Lieutenant Hoyle, whose wife was among those living in western North Carolina, expressed his concerns for her safety, but also encouraged all to act with honor and remain committed to the cause.

> I have just heard that the yankees have been in Morganton, and at Camp Vance. I do not know whether it is true or not, but if the yankees get among you up there, you must all act the part of soldiers, and they will not find it convenient to stay with you long.[12]

The armies remained relatively quiet throughout July. Except for mortar exchanges and sharpshooters picking off anyone who was foolish enough to expose himself from behind the defenses, very little activity occurred. The constant threat of an attack always remained on the mind of every soldier, but no major advances were ordered. The period of relative peace ended however on July 27. Lee, realizing that Hancock's II Corps had crossed the James, believed the Federals were making an attempt to capture Richmond. In reality, Grant had hoped the move toward

First Lieutenant Charles M. Cooke, acting adjutant. First Lieutenant Cooke served as the regiment's adjutant from June 1864 until he was seriously wounded on March 30, 1865. Cooke recovered and wrote history of the 55th North Carolina. (Courtesy of the North Carolina Division of Archives and History, Raleigh, North Carolina.)

Richmond would force Lee to pull troops out of Petersburg and thus weaken the Confederate defenses before the mine his men had planted under the Rebel line was detonated. The Confederate commander quickly ordered Anderson to Chaffin's Bluff and sent Heth's division to support the First Corps.[13] Lieutenant Cooke described the incident in his history of the regiment.

> On the morning of 29 July, [actually the 27th] the Federal commander made a feint by advancing a part of his forces on the north side of James river, near Malvern Hill, towards Richmond. This was done in order to cover his real purpose of springing the mine near Petersburg, and to weaken opposition at that point by inducing us to withdraw our troops towards Richmond. The Fifty-fifth Regiment, with its brigade, was a part of the forces which were moved rapidly across the country, Crossing over the James river near Drewry's Bluff, to check the enemy's advance. We reached a point in front of the enemy not far from Malvern Hill, on the night of the 29th, and were placed in line to reinforce troops already there, but the enemy made no attempt to advance further.[14]

Grant's intentions were soon realized on the morning of July 30 when a tremendous explosion was heard for miles around. Near the center of the Confederate line, just above Baxter Road, the Federals had detonated a mine underneath the Confederate position. The explosion left a crater about thirty feet deep at the front of the Confederate line.[15]

The 55th, which just days before had been positioned to the right of where the explosion had occurred, were miles away near Drewry's Bluff, but even at that distance the regiment heard and felt the repercussions from the mine. Cooke stated, "we were awakened by the reverberation of a great sound which seemed to have been produced a long way off, and at the same time there was a trembling of the earth, such as that caused by an earthquake." The regiment received orders soon after the explosion occurred and hurriedly marched back toward Petersburg. After a hard march under the hot July sun, the 55th reached Petersburg during the evening of July 30.[16]

Although the mine had created a hole in Lee's line, the Federals were unable to capitalize on the momentary confusion. The Union troops ran into the crater but realized too late that it would be difficult to get back out. After somewhat reorganizing their line the Confederates made a vicious counterattack and were able to repel the Federal assault. The Rebels had stopped Grant's advance, but the fear created by the mine's explosion continued to linger for days. All along Lee's line Confederate soldiers informed their superiors that they could hear digging underneath their positions.[17] The psychological effects from the mine explosion also affected several members of the 55th North Carolina. Lieutenant Cooke described how the shock of the explosion had a detrimental effect on his regiment.

> The springing of the mine was a complete surprise to us, and both officers and men were for several weeks thereafter anxiously expecting a repetition of the act, and were nervous over it. At one time or another, every member of the regiment was sure that he heard the sound of the sappers and the miners digging away down in the ground beneath him. There was scarcely a night that some one of the regiment would not come out of his hole and crawl to the regimental headquarters and whisper the announcement that he could plainly hear the sound of the digging in the ground way below him.[18]

Cooke also stated that reassurances from regimental officers did not calm the soldiers and so the officers spent many nights investigating these false reports just to relax the men.[19]

As the summer months waned Confederate officers kept their men busy strengthening fortifications and making sure the soldiers kept their weapons in working condition.

In a letter written to his mother during the latter half of July, Private Wilkerson complained about the "unnecissary" duty he and his fellow soldiers were ordered to perform.

> We don't get time heare to do nothing for our selves. For we have enspection every day and we are purnish if our guns are found with any rust at all on them so we work hard for a good deal unnecissary work. I hope to live to see a day when all that will beover.[20]

The discomfort of trench life continued for the 55th North Carolina and most of Lee's troops as the summer of 1864 came to an end. As things settled down after the excitement of "The Crater," both armies resumed their daily mortar exchanges and their sharpshooters once again watched for any sign of life to snuff out. Wilkerson wrote "the shells is flying over my head now and bursting clost by us. We don't get much to eat." Not only were mortar shells keeping the men awake but also, according to Wilkerson, one third of the regiment had to perform picket duty every night and with the Federal pickets so nearby the men on duty couldn't sleep at all.[21]

Soldiers posted on the trench line were not the only ones in danger of being killed or wounded by Federal fire. With sporadic Union artillery shells exploding throughout the Confederate positions, finding a safe place to wait out the barrages was not an easy task. Even those hundreds of yards behind the front lines were at risk. Private William Craige of Company F was wounded while visiting the latrines. Lieutenant Hoyle explained his comrade's injuring to his wife, and expressed, possibly to alleviate her concerns, that the position being held by the 55th North Carolina was better than most.

> The yankees shell us occasionally, and Wm. Craige was wounded day before yesterday evening from a shell. He had gone out to the sinks (about 100 yards from the breast works) when a shell, thrown over, burst near him, and a ball from it struck him on the nose, tearing away that part of his nose nearest his forehead, passing diagonally just over the right eye. The eye was not injured, I don't consider the wound dangerous, but it will not doubt give him a good deal of pain. He is now sent to Richmond. We are still having very warm weather, and suffer a good deal from heat; however we have plenty of water of a fair quality, and we have no right to grumble at our position, as others on other parts of the line are seeing a great deal harder times. On some parts of the line a person can not raise his head above the works day nor night without being exposed to bullets.[22]

Day after day the Confederates remained in a constant state of readiness awaiting a Federal assault they were convinced was coming. Some of the men in the 55th were able to purchase extra food from locals desperate to make money. Wilkerson was able to buy a small plate of "greens," a dozen apples, and a half a loaf of bread for $4.50. This small sampling of food was probably very welcomed after weeks of insufficient rations. As the monotony of manning the Petersburg defenses began to sap the fighting men's spirits, a growing dissatisfaction with the lack of concern from Richmond officials was becoming more noticeable. The soldiers were tired of the poor quality and low quantity of food, claiming that their officers were unfairly allowed to take the best rations and clothing. The men were also angry that when they were lucky enough to receive new clothes and shoes, the items were always inadequately made. The lack of pay, food, and decent uniforms, and the fact that officers quickly grabbed the best of everything before the common soldiers infuriated the fighting men, but their belief that the Confederate government didn't care about their misfortune irritated them more than anything else.[23]

Early in August Lieutenant Colonel H. E. Peyton, the assistant adjutant and inspector general, inspected Davis's brigade, along with the rest of Heth's division. Peyton reported that the trench line recently occupied by Heth's troops had been in disorder before the major general's men were posted there, but added that he found "the arms and accouterments in very bad condition in all the regiments," except for the second and 11th Mississippi. The lieutenant colonel went on to describe the area in his official report.

> Guns and bayonets were lying loosely about the trenches and under the shelter-tents of the men, peelings fruit and rinds of melons were dropped promiscuously about the trenches, which, together with the accumulated dirt, indicated a neglect in the most necessary feature of cleanliness.[24]

Of the regiments in Davis's command the inspector singled out the 26th Mississippi as the worst offender. The 55th North Carolina was not specifically mentioned but obviously its area was in disorder as well. It should be noted that Peyton made a special inspection of Davis's brigade on September 5 and stated that there had been "a marked improvement in all respects" since his last visit.[25]

The 55th North Carolina remained in their position, south of the Crater, throughout the first few weeks of August. After Belo was wounded and removed from command on June 2 various officers commanded the regiment. Cooke stated that at one time or another captains Peter Mull, Robert W. Thomas, Walter A. Whitted, Benjamin F. Briggs, Nicholas W. Lillington, and John T. Peden led the 55th, and claimed that Whitted commanded more than any other officer did. In the *Official Records* Thomas is listed as being in command of the regiment on August 16, and probably led his men into battle at Davis's Farm, also known as the battle of Globe Tavern.[26]

In mid–August Grant, who had set up his headquarters at City Point, Virginia, 10 miles southeast of Petersburg, sent Hancock's corps, part of the Tenth Corps, and Gregg's division of cavalry north across the James. The Federal commander hoped a threat against Richmond would prevent Lee from reinforcing Early, who was trying to protect the vital Shenandoah Valley. Other obligations in the North forced Grant to suspend this operation prematurely.[27]

On August 18, Grant ordered Warren to advance and destroy as much of the Weldon Railroad as possible. Warren's column was on the move by 5:00 a.m. and marched to the Weldon Railroad near Globe Tavern. Upon being informed that Federal troops were nearing the Weldon Railroad, Beauregard, who had command in Petersburg while Lee was handling a possible Union attack on Richmond, authorized A. P. Hill to send five infantry brigades to push the Federals away from the rail line. Hill sent two infantry brigades under Heth's command and one battery under Thomas A. Brander to counter any Union attempt to hold the rail line. This railroad was extremely important to the Confederate army, which relied on the Weldon as its main supply line with the South.[28]

Sometime in the middle of the afternoon on August 18, the 55th North Carolina was ordered to form and be prepared to move out of the Petersburg line. August 18 happened to be a day when the regiment had been relieved and was in the rear resting and bathing. Also, about one-third of the brigade had been detached to strengthen fortifications. Private Wilkerson was among those who had been assigned to work on breastworks and was loading wood onto wagons when the order to fall in was given.[29]

Heth had ordered Davis's and Brigadier General Henry Walker's brigades to advance against Warren's troops that were tearing up the Weldon Railroad near Davis's Farm and were moving toward Petersburg. The 55th marched rapidly south toward Globe Tavern, which was about three miles below Petersburg. Upon arriving near Davis's Farm the regiment

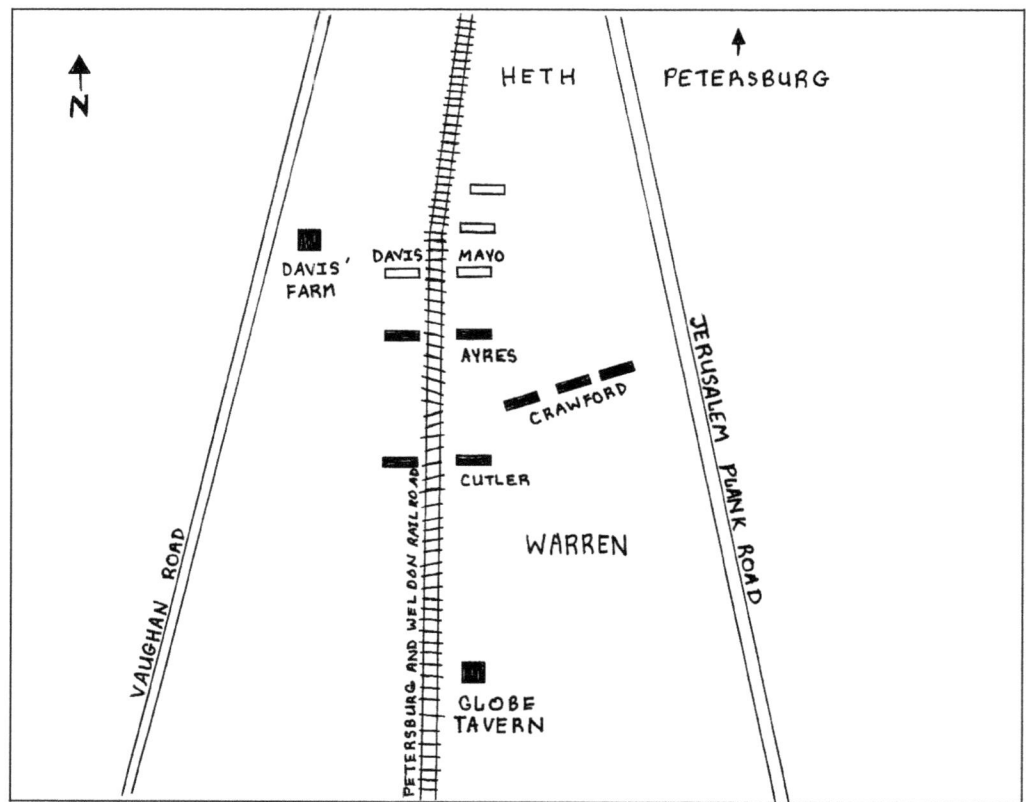

Heth's advance against Warren near Globe Tavern, August 18, 1864.

formed a line of battle and charged the Federals. Cooke stated the "charge was made with dash and spirit, at double-quick, for half a mile." The 55th was positioned in the center of Davis's command and had to advance through a cornfield, pushing Federal skirmishers back as they moved forward and continued through a sparse pine forest.[30]

Heth's troops formed into a line of battle with Davis's men on the west or right of the railroad and Walker's troops positioned on the left. The major general's soldiers slammed into Brigadier General Romeyn B. Ayres's division and were able to flank the Federal force. At first, Ayres's men were forced to retreat as Davis's and Walker's troops advanced rapidly toward their position.[31] After driving the Federals back in their initial assault the Confederates then advanced into a large forest, which was "very thick with small growth and under-brush." After pausing momentarily, Davis's troops continued forward, but the dense woods had made locating the Federals difficult and after being reinforced the Union troops were able to push back the Rebel attack. Cooke claimed that this counterattack occurred near dark and the Federals were able to pour a heavy fire into the Confederate line.[32]

Private Wilkerson, who participated in the battle near Davis's Farm, briefly described the fight in a letter to his family.

> We had orders to fall in and marched up their and form line of battle and thunder cloud come up and we got jest as wet as rats and skirmishes was put out and we had to charge the yankees. So we was fighting all the evening and in the night.[33]

Davis's command succeeded in pushing back two Federal lines but the additional troops and artillery forced the brigade to fall back and entrench. Joseph R. Davis described the day's events in a letter to his uncle Jefferson Davis.

> As you have seen in the papers we had an affair yesterday on the Weldon R.R. our line of battle was formed perpendicularly to the R R (two Brigades) H. H. Walker's on the left and mine on the right. I drove in the enemy's skirmishers and after engaging his line a few minutes ordered a charge and routed him along my entire front and drove him half a mile capturing over a hundred prisoners. The Brigade on my left having fallen back about two hundred yard, I halted and remained in position until ordered to withdraw about 9 p.m. We fought a greatly superior force — I lost at least 30 per cent of my brigade.[34]

Lieutenant Cooke stated in his history of the 55th North Carolina that the "losses of our regiment there were relatively greater than in any other battle in which it participated." The lieutenant claimed that of the 150 men who fought in the battle, over half were killed or wounded. Cooke declared that there was "scarcely an officer or man who did not bear either in his body or clothing the marks of the terrible conflict." Among those injured was Lieutenant Hoyle, who had been wounded in the right leg. Hoyle's leg had to be amputated and the young lieutenant who prayed every day that he would one day see his lovely wife again died in a Richmond hospital on or around September 1, 1864. Hoyle died "while gallantly leading his company" in battle. He had commanded at several bloody battles including Gettysburg. His presence would be sorely missed throughout the remaining eight months of the war.[35]

The following day the Confederates attacked the Federals again around 4:00 p.m. While Heth's troops assaulted the Union front, Mahone was ordered to strike the Union right. Mahone's troops swept down on Brigadier General Samuel Crawford's men, forcing the confused Federals to retreat. Heth's two brigades attacked the front and left and initially experienced success, breaking through the Union line around 4:30 p.m. Heth's troops engaged remnants of the 76th, 95th, and 147th New York Volunteers, the fourth Delaware Regiment, and the 56th and 157th Pennsylvania Volunteers. Davis's men, including the 55th North Carolina, pushed the Federals back, but

Private Rhodes Herndon Frazier, Company K. Private Frazier was wounded and captured at Gettysburg on July 3, 1863, and paroled on August 24, 1863. He returned to duty and was wounded in the right hand at Globe Tavern, Virginia, on August 18, 1864. Frazier's right hand was amputated and he was retired to the Invalid Corps on December 15, 1864. (Courtesy of the North Carolina Division of Archives and History, Raleigh, North Carolina).

once they reached the Union defenses they were repulsed with great loss.[36] Lieutenant Cooke provided a brief account of the regiment's actions on August 19, and explained that those working on the Petersburg defenses the day before had now rejoined the brigade.

> The next afternoon the men detailed the day before having come in, our regiment had nearly as many men in ranks as it had the day before, and Captain B.F. Briggs, of Company A, was in command. Our line was lengthened by fresh troops, and late in the afternoon another attempt was made to dislodge the enemy from his position, our regiment charging over the same ground as the day before, and it was repulsed at just about the same point, and with very nearly as great losses.[37]

After the Federals rallied they were able to force Mahone's troops to retreat and remained entrenched on the Weldon Railroad. During the fight Private James T. Jennings of Company K, 56th Pennsylvania Volunteers, captured the 55th North Carolina's colors, later receiving the Congressional Medal of Honor for his heroic deed.[38] This loss must have been demoralizing for the men in the 55th North Carolina. (The loss of the regimental colors must have been an experience the 55th wanted to forget; Cooke does not even men-

The 55th North Carolina battle flag. This flag was captured by Private James T. Jennings of the 56th Pennsylvania Volunteers near the Weldon Railroad on August 19, 1864. The flag now resides in the North Carolina Museum of History. (Courtesy of the North Carolina Museum of History, Raleigh, North Carolina.)

tion it in his history.) During the evening Hill ordered another assault, but the Rebels were again forced to fall back. It is not known if the 55th participated in this attack.[39] Private Wilkerson described the horrific cost of the battle in a letter to his family.

> Oh mother the men we have lost on the road and made nothing for the yankees is well fortified, most of our brigade is killed and wounded also our Regiment and company. Pete Phillips was killed thursday [August 18] and Stephen Sanford too and Jo Eritckes was missing surpose to be killed I saw cousin S. Sanford shot the ball went in his upperlip and went out back side of his head. Oh, I never sa search times in my life.[40]

On August 20 Hill hoped to launch another attack against Warren's V Corps. But heavy rains made an assault impracticable and the only action that occurred that day near the Weldon Railroad was between Confederate and Federal pickets.[41] Private Wilkerson was on picket duty during the day and barely escaped being captured.

> the yankees shooting at us all day and the Balls flying thick and fast but narry one hit me. I reckon I soht about one hundred times Saturday. [August 20] We was told to move our heads over the rail piles. Lieut Hadley sent Jim Eakes after cartridges one time and in the evening he sent me after some, and before I could get back the yankees charge our men and took the lines, and all the men got away, but some on the right. Oh aint I proud I was sent after cartridges for Lieutenant Hadley and Promfret Blackwell and Jim Eakes and all or our regt picket was taken prisonners but a few men. I would have been taken or killed out their.[42]

After moving to the rear Davis's troops were held in reserve. The following day Heth's other two brigades, Cooke's and Kirkland's, relieved Davis's brigade. Davis's men returned to their position along the Petersburg line and did not participate in the fighting that resumed near Globe Tavern on August 21.[43]

During the fighting near Globe Tavern between August 18 and 20 the Federals suffered 1,400 killed or wounded and had more than 2,500 men taken prisoner. The Confederate casualties are not known for sure; the losses in the 55th are thought to be 17 killed, 42 wounded, and seven captured. The fighting around Globe Tavern continued for several more days and even though Hill routed Hancock's corps at Ream's Station on August 24 the Federals still held the rail line.[44]

Sergeant John P. Cannady, Company K. Cannady served as a private with the 12th Regiment North Carolina Troops before transferring to the 55th in August 1862. He was promoted to sergeant in March 1863 and surrendered with his regiment at Appomattox Court House. He survived the war. (Courtesy of North Carolina Division of Archives and History, Raleigh, North Carolina.)

The battle around Globe Tavern had been devastating to the 55th. Once again Davis's men had been ordered to advance against an enemy that was well entrenched and supported by artillery, and the results were the same as they had been at Gettysburg. The engagement weakened the fighting spirit of Private Wilkerson, who expressed his feelings of hopelessness to his family by writing, "I am a fraid we will have to go up on the road in a few days a gain to charge the yankees for all of us to get killed."[45]

The soldiers of the 55th North Carolina had fought as well as could have been expected. Once again, like during the Battle of the Wilderness, several of the regiment's fighting men received the admiration of their country and were added to the Confederate Roll of Honor. Their names are listed below.

> Private Henderson H. Love, Company A
> Private George H. Champion, Company D (wounded)
> Private Willie Gurganus, Company E (Killed in action)
> Private George R. May, Company I (Died of wounds)[46]

The 55th North Carolina remained in its trench line around Petersburg throughout the rest of August and September. The regiment's low morale did not seem to have improved much since their engagement around Globe Tavern. Wilkerson wrote to his sister explaining to her that he was "as durty and lousey as a dog, we cant do no washing or not much." The young private informed his sister that he needed some soap and expressed his hope that the war would end soon, writing, "it is hope they will come to some conclusion for an honorable peace I am tired of this war."[47] While in the trenches Private David T. Toler of Company G wrote a five-stanza poem to his mother. The poem reflects the mood of many soldiers and how they felt about their loved ones at home. Below is a portion of his poem:

> Yes, dear mother, to the lovely place
> Of those around, thy homage pay,
> But wilt thou never kindly remember
> To think of him that's far away?
> Thy form, thine eye, thine angel smile,
> For many years I may not see,
> But wilt thou not sometimes the while,
> My mother dear, remember me?
> Remember me, I pray (but not
> In anger's gay and blooming hour,
> But when angel smile hath found its note,
> And sunshine smiles in every flower (
> But when falling leaf is dead,
> And withers sadly from the tree,
> And o'er the ruins of the year
> Cold autumn sweeps above the sea (
> My mother dear, remember me.
> Remember me — not I entreat
> In scenes of Festal week-day joy,
> For then it were not kindly of pleasure
> Thy thoughts thy pleasures should alloy,
> But on the sacred Sabbath day.
> And, dearest mother, on thy bended knee,
> When thou for those thou lov'st dost pray —
> My mother dear, then remember me.[48]

Food and want of proper clothing continued to be a problem for the Confederates in line around Petersburg. Wilkerson wrote his sister that his daily ration consisted of a pint of flour and "a little meat." The rainy weather and the everyday wear and tear had reduced most of the men in the 55th to rags. The men desperately needed pants and other clothing items. Trench life was wearing down the men, but at least they were, as Wilkerson claimed, no longer required to work all day on strengthening their fortifications.[49]

The 55th continued to lose men through desertions and sickness, and Federal mortar shells that were always "flying about" constantly harassed the soldiers The routine shots from snipers also kept the soldiers alert, but the boredom of manning the defensive line still dampened the men's spirits. September passed by in relative peace, but Grant was prepared to make another attempt at breaking the Petersburg stalemate.[50]

On September 28 Grant ordered Butler to assault the Richmond defenses north of the James River. Major General Edward O. C. Ord's XVIII Corps and Birney, in command of the X Corps, were to attack Lee's fortifications and move into the Confederate capital if possible. The following day the Federals struck Fort Harrison, which was part of the Richmond defenses. Birney's troops were able to capture several entrenched positions along the New Market line, but were unable to capture Fort Gilmer. While Butler's troops assaulted the Richmond line, Meade shifted troops around to keep the Rebels alert and prevent any reinforcements from being sent north of the James. Lee made a counterassault in an effort to regain his lost fortifications but was unsuccessful.[51]

The following day Meade ordered Warren's corps to attack the Confederate line south of Petersburg. The Federals first encountered a small detachment of cavalry and horse artillery entrenched on the Squirrel Level Road near Poplar Spring Church. Lee had ordered most of his infantry to fall back toward Petersburg to allow reinforcements to be sent north to assist the Richmond line, so several outer defense lines were lightly guarded. Hill, now temporarily in command of the Petersburg defenses, ordered Heth and Wilcox to counter the Federal strike. Once Hill's divisions arrived they quickly attacked Warren's troops and were able to repel the Federal advance.[52]

During the assault on Warren's troops Davis sent the 55th North Carolina several miles west to a reserve position where the Boydton Plank Road crossed Old Town Run. On October 1, Hill advanced his troops in an effort to retake the lost Confederate outer defenses. The Confederates made several attempts to break the Federals, but the Union line was too strong and Hill, not wanting to deplete his already thinned ranks, believed the task futile and stopped the attacks. The Rebels were able to capture several hundred Federals, but were unable to retake their outer lines.[53] Private Wilkerson described the regiment's actions in a letter to his father. The young private wrote, "it was and awful time Saturday charging the yankees in the rain through the woods and swamps and thickets." Wilkerson claimed that the Confederate assaults were confusing with "balls flying thick and fast in every direction."[54]

Although Davis's troops had been ordered to advance against well-fortified positions, the Confederate army could ill afford to lose more soldiers and Hill chose not to continue the attack. Hill's decision to cancel his assault after several unsuccessful charges kept the casualties in the 55th North Carolina low, so Cooke could claim that the regiment's losses during the engagement were "slight." The lieutenant general was able to prevent Grant from capturing the Boydton Road and the Southside Railroad, but the Federals were able to force Lee to extend his already thin lines.[55]

On October 2 the Federals advanced toward the Confederate lines again, but quickly retreated after being fired upon by entrenched Rebel troops. Davis's brigade remained in position at the southern end of the Petersburg line throughout the remaining weeks of October. The sporadic sniper and mortar fire continued but both armies remained behind their defenses. The men in the 55th North Carolina spent their days drilling and working on new breastworks. Some of the soldiers were lucky enough to receive food items from home, which gave them more than enough to eat. Private Wilkerson ate so much one day that he informed his parents "I eate untill I was in misery." Although food may have plentiful for at least some of the regiment many of the soldiers had no shoes and were suffering.[56]

On October 24 Grant instructed Meade to make an attempt to capture the Southside Railroad, south of Petersburg. Three days later the Federal operation began and approximately 43,000 Union troops advanced west toward Hill's flank. While the IX Corps kept Hill's troops busy, the II and V corps were to move around Hatcher's Run and capture the rail line. Meade's assault ended in complete failure. The troops in the IX Corps here quickly repulsed and Warren's V Corps got entangled and lost in the swampy terrain while trying to strike the Confederate right flank. Hancock's corps arrived at their objective point, but was forced to wait for Warren's men to appear. To counter the Federal advance Hill ordered Heth's and Wilcox's divisions to attack, supported by Major General Wade Hampton's cavalry.[57]

Heth, realizing that the Federals were attempting to turn his right flank, ordered Davis's brigade to advance and reinforce Hampton's cavalry that had already engaged Hancock's troops. Heth stated,"Gen'l Davis reached the Creek Road and Hatcher's Run in opportune time, checking the enemy's advance." Private Wilkerson reported that his regiment moved forward rapidly and that several times the Federals tried to halt Davis's advance, but were unsuccessful. Wilkerson also stated that Hampton's dismounted cavalry was able to hold the Federals in check until Davis's command could reinforce them.[58]

Upon reaching Hatcher's Run, Davis quickly ordered troops across the stream to counter the Federal advance across Burgess' Mill. Opposing the brigade across the creek was Brigadier General T. W. Egan's division of the II Corps, which now focused its attention on pushing Davis's unit back to the north bank of Hatcher's Run. Shortly after 1:00 p.m. Egan ordered the right wing of his command forward in an attempt to dislodge the Confederates on the south side of the creek. After a continuous fight the Federals were able to force Davis's troops back across Hatcher's Run.[59] Lieutenant Cooke, although possibly wrong on the time, described the fight near Burgess' Mill.

> In the battle of Hatcher's Run or Burgess' Mill, on 27 October, the right of our brigade rested on Hatcher's Run. One of the Mississippi Regiments was on the right, and our regiment was in the centre. About 4 o'clock in the afternoon, the enemy had broken through our lines on the south side of Hatcher's Run and the first we knew of it they had crossed the run and were firing into our rear. General Heth and General Davis, who were just in the rear of our regiment at the time, directed Colonel Stone, of the Second Mississippi, since Governor of the State of Mississippi, to wheel the three right regiments of the brigade perpendicular to our line, and to drive the enemy back across the run. The order was promptly executed, and the Fifty-fifth Regiment, being the third regiment from the right, was next to the angle, and was subjected, therefore, to enfilading fire from the main army of the enemy, and to a front fire from the flanking force.[60]

Cooke went on to report that his brigade succeeded in pushing the Union troops back across the run, but stated that the losses were "serious."

Private Wilkerson also recorded the activities of his regiment during the battle in a letter to his parents. The young soldier claimed that the Federals continued shooting at his unit throughout the entire rainy day and into the evening hours. Davis's troops were able to hold off Egan's division long enough for Mahone's men to strike the Federal right flank and rear. Mahone's assault experienced some initial success, but was beaten back with great loss. The Confederate forces suffered from Grant's attempt to take the Southside Railroad, but they were able to fend off the Union assaults and force the Federal commander to order his troops to fall back.[61]

Heth was extremely proud of his troops after the battle and commented on the performances of his divisions in his official report.

> My thanks are due to Brig. Gen'l MacRae [in command of Kirkland's brigade] and his gallant Brigade for the distinguished service they rendered — Cooke's brigade, and especially Davis's (the latter being more exposed) deserve to be specially mentioned for their coolness and soldierly manner which distinguished them on this day — Brigadesless resolute might have been shaken, receiving a fire, as they did, from the front, flank, and rear during the greater portion of this day.[62]

In his casualty report for the battle of Burgess' Mill, Davis claimed that the 55th suffered three men killed and 14 wounded, which is more than any of the other units in the brigade. After the fight Davis's men returned to their positions along the Petersburg line and would remain there until early in December. Although the Federals made no serious attempts to break the Confederate defenses where the 55th was posted, the men did not enjoy a peaceful month. The soldiers were still required to perform picket duty and at times engaged the Federals.[63]

The fighting men in the 55th North Carolina not only had to risk their lives on picket duty, but they also were drilling regularly twice a day and constantly ordered to work on the defenses. During the November, Robert W. Thomas probably commanded the regiment, as he was listed as being the officer in charge of the 55th during an inspection completed on November 30. After Belo was wounded and forced to leave the regiment the command structure continuously rotated between several officers. This constant change in the 55th's leadership probably lowered the overall discipline of the regiment.[64]

On November 8, 1864, the northern populace reelected Abraham Lincoln as their president. To the common soldier manning the trenches in Petersburg the news was interpreted as a sure sign that his misery would continue. Although many of the Confederate fighting men continued to support the war effort and were not depressed by Lincoln's reelection, they hoped and prayed that Grant would remain still at least until the spring of 1865. These men and all of the other Confederate troops entrenched around Petersburg quickly realized that the Federals were not prepared to rest for the winter.[65]

On December 7 the Federals began tearing up the Petersburg and Weldon Railroad near Belfield, Virginia, 40 miles south of Petersburg. Lee, believing the Federals were making an attempt to occupy Weldon, ordered Hill to support Hampton's cavalry, which had already been dispatched. The following day Heth's division marched toward Belfield, traveling south on the Boydton Plank Road. After spending the cold night near Dinwiddie Court House, the men suffering from the hail and freezing rain, they began marching at sunrise and reached an area about eight miles northwest of Belfield.[66]

The Federal force, consisting of parts of the V and II Corps and Gregg's cavalry corps, had begun destroying the rail line on December 8, and by the following day were retiring to the north because their supplies were running low. While they were moving north, Hampton's troopers made several assaults against their flanks. Hill's men, exhausted from their march, were not able to move quick enough to catch the Federals and only succeeded in capturing a few prisoners. Near Jarratt's Station, Heth's troops encountered Union cavalry and were ordered to engage.[67] Lieutenant Cooke provided a brief account of this engagement and why it was remembered in his history of the 55th North Carolina.

> We came upon the enemy near Jarratt's Station, and drove in his skirmish line. We formed in line of battle and charged through a piece of pine forest that was covered with sleet; the long icicles hung from every limb, and the trees were so weighted that many of the limbs touched the ground. It was fearfully cold and the men suffered terribly, for we were neither well shod, nor warmly clad. A few shots were fired into our column as we were marching through the forest, but when we emerged from it into an open field near the railroad, the enemy had fled. This movement was noted for the great suffering of the men on account of the severe weather.[68]

By December 15, after spending several nights sleeping in the snow and rain, the 55th North Carolina returned to the Petersburg trenches with the rest of Heth's troops. The men completed their winter quarters and braced themselves for another cold Virginia winter. If and when the men obtained food it wasn't very filling and the soldiers quickly became depressed and dispirited. Private Wilkerson stated, "We only eate twice a day now and not much at that. Some times 3 and Some times 4 bisquets."[69]

The soldiers and officers of the 55th North Carolina manning the trenches around Petersburg spent another Christmas away from their families. The misery continued into the new year and the regiment's morale remained low. Private Wilkerson wrote a letter to his mother during the last days of 1864 and characterized the sentiments of his regiment.

> We are a rune set of people and we are aldredy whipied. I am truly sorry for our men. You aught to heare the men talk it would make you shead tears. We dont get any mail now for several days back it has stop nor not much to eate for some time afew dry crackers and not a bit of meat and we dont get a cent of money they say the soldiers wont be paid off no more untill all of them reenlist for three year and all of the men talk of leaving numbers of them say thay entend to go home soon and some has aldredy gone.[70]

Wilkerson also concluded that the Confederate government was purposely keeping information from the soldiers. The men knew that the war effort was not going well; the young private believed Richmond officials were afraid to let the soldiers know the truth and wrote, "I dont believe thay want us to have any news."[71]

During the last few weeks of December, Major General George Stoneman led an assault against the salt works located in Saltville, Virginia, and succeeded in destroying the works. This news reached Private Wilkerson of the 55th before the end of the month and added to his already depressed demeanor. The young private lamented over the loss of the salt works and proceeded to inform his mother that he was beginning to lose hope, writing, "Dear mother if the lord dont be on our side, I dont know what will be come of us." With the loss of the salt works it would be even harder for the Confederate armies to transport food to their starving troops.[72]

Desertions continued to plague the Confederate armies throughout the winter of 1864–65. Religious revivalism continued much as it had the previous winter. About 60 chapels were built along the Petersburg line, but with the balance of war overwhelmingly shifting to the North and with inadequate amounts of food and clothing reaching the fighting men, revivals did little to stem the sinking morale.[73]

During the last weeks of January 1865 the 55th North Carolina Regiment was transferred to Brigadier General John R. Cooke's brigade. The regiment had served almost two years in Davis's brigade and had fought alongside Mississippians and Alabamians in some of the war's most horrific battles. The transfer did not remove the 55th from Heth's division of A. P. Hill's Third Corps. The regiment would spend the remaining months of the conflict fighting alongside the 15th, 27th, 46th, and 48th North Carolina regiments. The 55th now belonged to a North Carolina brigade.[74]

The regiment moved to the left of Cooke's position and worked on its new winter quarters during the first few days of February. The 55th would only be with its new brigade a few days before it was called upon to prove its worth. On February 5 Grant ordered the II Corps to capture the Boydton Plank Road. Heth's division was sent to repulse any Federal attempts to occupy the road. Shortly after 4:00 p.m. Cooke's brigade was ordered to advance toward the Federal position.[75] Wilkerson described his regiment's action in the attack.

> We was all ordered forward to charge the yankee works but not to much effect as we did not succeed in driving them from their fortifications after chargeing them severaldifferent times. We was fighting un till in the night. Oh mother it was awful times with us.[76]

Wilkerson claimed that he had shot 50 or 60 rounds at the Federals and had barely escaped serious injury or even death when a shell fragment ripped through his hat. He also

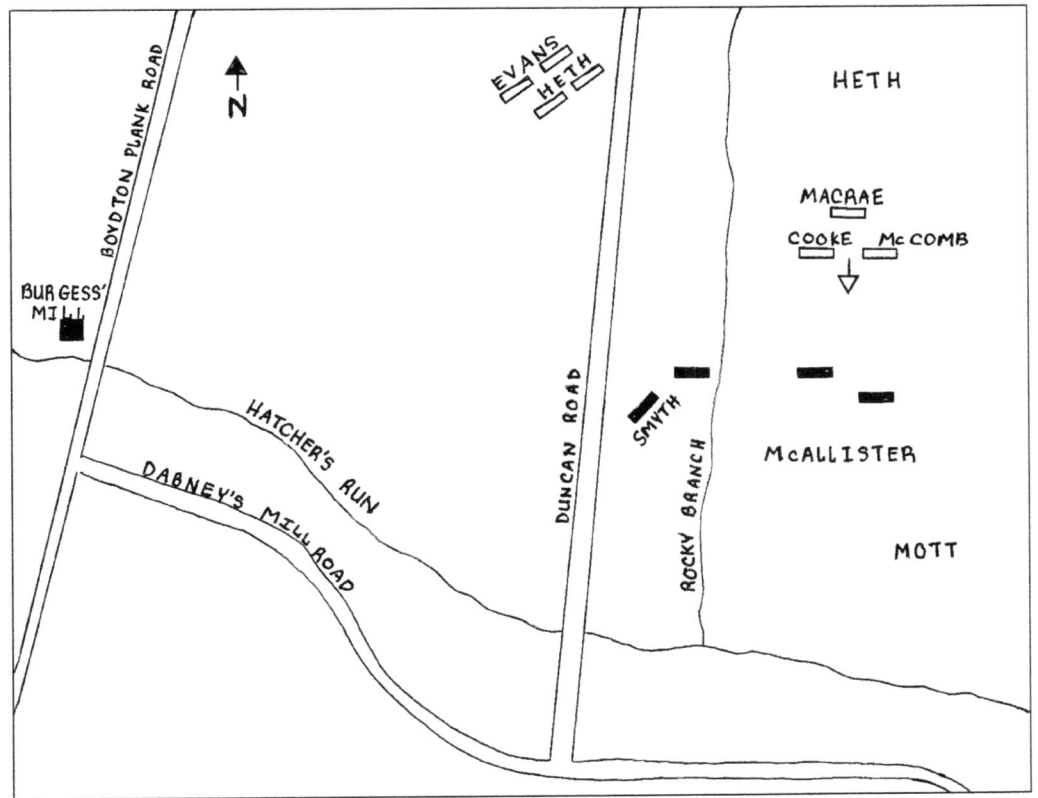

Heth's advance around 4:00pm on February 5, 1865

asserted that the multiple charges cost his regiment 25 men killed, wounded, or missing. The Federals continued to pour a murderous fire into the Confederate ranks. Cooke's troops took the brunt of the Union fire, causing many of the newer recruits and conscripts to throw down their arms and run in confusion to the rear. One of Cooke's infantrymen stated that even the presence of General Lee, who was at the rear of the attacking column, was unable to halt these green troops. Heth's assault had been repulsed.[77]

The following day the 55th North Carolina and the rest of Cooke's brigade were held in reserve. The men were ordered to stay in line and to be prepared to advance if the Federals made any offensive movements. The weather was bitterly cold and the troops were forced to remain in formation. Wilkerson wrote "we staided in the hail and rain all day and frizing, suffering greatly from cold. It seem like we would frize. The men's clothes froze on them that could not get any fire." The fighting in the area continued sporadically for the next several days, but the 55th was not involved. By February 7 the Federals had begun to fall back to their winter quarters, having suffered over 1,500 casualties compared to about 1,000 Confederate losses.[78]

By the middle of February, Wilkerson was nearly barefoot, but he finally had the opportunity to change his clothes, which he had not been able to do in weeks. With almost nothing on his feet and barely able to get enough to eat, Private Wilkerson continued to push himself to do his duty, but by the end of the month he had begun losing faith in the Southern cause. The weary soldier wrote, "I am getting clean out of heart. I have nearly los confidents in our men." The constant wave of deserters was really upsetting the dutiful young private and he lamented over what he felt was ruining the army.

It hurts my feelings to see our men are doing like runing a way and deserting every day and night. Our army are be coming wearker and wearker it looks very hard to have to stay heare all our lives, and under go what we do, and then to be Subjated by the yankees. Oh it is awful to think of.[79]

Throughout the remaining days of February and the greater part of March the majority of the 55th North Carolina remained behind fortifications along the southern end of the

Private John H. Williams, Company K. Private Williams resided in Granville County and worked as a farmer before enlisting in the service on May 6, 1862, at the age of 27. He was killed near Hatchr's Run, Virginia, on February 5, 1865. (Courtesy of the North Carolina Division of Archives and History, Raleigh, North Carolina.)

Petersburg line. In an effort to force Grant to shorten his lines, thus enabling the Confederates to send troops to assist General Joseph E. Johnston's army in North Carolina, Lee planned to attack the Federal line at Fort Stedman. Lee had hoped other options would be plausible, but the tired commander realized he had no realistic alternative.[80]

After secretly removing the obstructions in front of the Confederate line during the night of March 24–25 and advancing a small detachment of troops and axe men toward Fort Stedman, Major General John B. Gordon gave the order to attack at four o'clock on the morning of March 25. Gordon's men, however, were unable to capture the fortifications behind Stedman and when the Federals countered they were able to push the Confederates back to within sight of Hatcher's Run. Lee's desperate assault had failed, and now the Federals were in position to attack the right of the Petersburg line.[81]

During the night of March 24, Cooke's brigade was ordered to move toward Petersburg and take up position along the trenches near Hare's Hill. One of Cooke's men described the city as having "a gloomy, desolate, haunted appearance like some plauge had depopulated it and spread its deadly spell over it remains." Cooke's men had been sent to relieve troops being assembled for Gordon's assault. As the brigadier general's force slipped into their new line, they were shelled and had to endure constant mortar fire. Around 2:00 p.m. the following day the brigade was sent back to its original position, only to find that the Federals now occupied their picket line and had succeeded in capturing most of the unit's sick and wounded. Cooke quickly ordered his sharpshooters to push the Union troops back. Cooke's men were able to retake their picket line, but unable to recover any of their captured comrades.[82]

Grant began his offensive on March 29 by moving troops to the right of the Confederate line. The Southside Railroad, one of Lee's two "essential lines of communication" that were still operable, was the Federal commander's primary objective. On April 1 Sheridan's cavalry unit and most of the V Corps attacked Pickett's men and Fitz Lee's troopers at Five Forks. The Federals, who greatly outnumbered the Rebels, were able to push the Confederates back. Pickett's troops retreated in confusion and the entire mobile force Lee had organized to protect his right flank had been practically decimated.[83]

During the day of March 30, Cooke's men held out against several Union assaults. The 55th participated in these attacks and was in constant threat from Union mortar and sniper fire. During the time Brigadier General Cooke's men were fending off repeated Federal charges, Lieutenant Charles Cooke was seriously wounded. The courageous young adjutant recovered from his wounds and later wrote a history of the 55th North Carolina.[84]

On the morning of April 1 Cooke sent a detachment out to attack the Federal picket line in front of their position. These troops were able to capture part of the Union line, but were forced to fall back in the evening. That night the brigade was relieved by Davis's troops and ordered to take position in Fort Euliss, located near the southern bank of Hatcher's Run near Burgess' Mill.[85] The men understood that there was little hope of fending off the Federals. Colonel Samuel H. Walkup of the 48th North Carolina expressed his despair bluntly in a letter to his wife on April 1.

> You need not send my clothes, nor flour, nor anything else to me, my dearest, we will either be killed or captured or the road will be destroyed before this letter reaches you.... Be prepared for bad news from Lee's army. There is no reasonable prospect of good news.[86]

On April 2 Grant launched a tremendous attack against the Confederate lines around Petersburg. The Confederates were vastly outnumbered and were ill prepared to defend their entire line against a massive Union assault. South of the James River on a line approximately 20 miles long, Lee had only 16,000 troops and no reserves. Manning the Confederate line from the Appomattox River to Hatcher's Run were about 11,000 men, and on the remaining line from Hatcher's Run to Lieutenant's Run the Rebels numbered little more than 12,000. Grant's 100,000-plus army began their attack near dawn and succeeded in breaking the Confederate line. Wright's VI Corps carried the center and the IX Corps, under the command of Major General John Parke, broke through Lee's left. By the middle of the day the Confederate line was disintegrating and Lee was busy making plans to retreat west. Months of trench warfare were finally ending and the Confederates were on the run.[87]

The 55th North Carolina and the other regiments in Cooke's brigade were entrenched behind the protective defenses of Fort Euliss. However, their position was exposed on three sides to Federal fire. As Grant's men advanced against the Rebel lines, the soldiers in Fort Euliss were assaulted from three directions by infantry and artillery fire. Federal shells killed and wounded several of the brigade's troops during the morning, and the constant barrages left the men inside the works in constant peril. By early morning, the Confederate line left of the fort collapsed and Cooke's troops, now open to possible attacks from their rear, were forced to retreat.[88]

Major General Henry Heth described the Federal attack's effects on the Confederate defensive lines in his official report.

> On the morning of the 2nd the enemy succeeded breaking through our lines some three miles to my left and rapidly sweeping down the thin line guarding our breast works, he captured Davis' Miss. Brigade and a large portion of McCombs Tenn. Brigade. Cooke's Brigade numbering some 600 men vacated the redoubts and works on the west bank of Hatcher's Run and succeeded in making good his retreat.[89]

Cooke's troops retreated to Sutherland's Station, located on the Southside Railroad, and formed a line of battle in an attempt to slow the Federal momentum and to allow the Confederate supply trains time to escape. Earlier in the day A. P. Hill had been killed while he was inspecting his lines near the Boydton Plank Road. Heth, upon hearing of his commander's death, left Cooke in command at Sutherland Station and attempted to ride back to Petersburg to assume command of the Third Corps. Heth was unable to reach Petersburg and so attempted to return to his men, but the Federals had blocked his path. The determined general then swam his horse across the Appomattox River at Clarke's Mill, located several miles above Petersburg. Heth finally made it to Lee's headquarters and discovered, much to his astonishment, that the commanding general had decided to disband Hill's corps and place its three divisions under Longstreet. The army corps which the 55th North Carolina had fought with for nearly a year was no more, although the official transfer would not occur for several more days.[90]

Brigadier General John Cooke and his men stood their ground behind a low breastwork of fence rails. Cooke had about 3,000 men now under his command, and with the support of six field guns, he determined to stand and fight. Here Brigadier General Nelson A. Miles's division of the II Corps attacked the Confederates. The Rebels were able to hold off the Federal advance at first, until finally Union assaults on the Confederate left flank succeeded in rolling up most of the line. The scattered remnants of Heth's division were forced to fall back, and hundreds of soldiers from the several units were captured. The remaining men retreated, and the majority of them were able to rejoin Lee's main column now moving westward. As one historian of the Army of Northern Virginia stated in reference to those able to escape capture, "that any of them got away and succeeded in reaching Lee's line of march from Petersburg was due more to the character of the individual soldier than to the persistence of the old-time discipline of the Third Corps."[91]

Although most of the soldiers in the 55th North Carolina were able to escape Miles's Federals, 59 members of the regiment were taken prisoner or captured during the retreat. The remnants of Cooke's brigade now made an exhaustive attempt to reach Lee's main column. After marching until late in the evening, the weary unit rested until morning and then moved out toward Deep Creek. At Deep Creek the remaining members of the force engaged the Federals in a "sharp skirmish," but were able to continue their move to find the main Confederate line with the assistance of Rebel cavalry, who were able to hold off an attack from Brigadier General George Armstrong Custer's troopers. Finally, during the early hours of April 4, Cooke's ragtag unit joined up with Lee's main retreating force near the Appomattox River and Amelia Court House. Captain John A. Sloan of the 27th North Carolina described the meeting in his history of Company B, 27th North Carolina.[92]

> At one o'clock at night [April 4] we received marching orders. After three hours hard marching through fields, bog, and fen, we came upon the advance of the main army, which had just crossed the Appomattox on a pontoon bridge. We were delighted to meet our old comrades once more after three days' separation.[93]

Grant's attack on April 2, 1864, prompted a swift reaction from the Confederate government in Richmond. President Davis was on his way to Sunday services when Postmaster General John Reagan informed him that the Federals had broken Lee's lines around Petersburg. Davis went ahead to St. Paul's Episcopal Church, but a courier soon brought him word that Lee recommended Richmond be evacuated. The Confederate president excused himself from the service and walked to his office at the Custom's House. While waiting there for more news he was informed that Lee would need to retreat from his present position around Petersburg. Davis and Lee had discussed the need for the Army of Northern Virginia to retreat from the Petersburg defenses some time in the near future to prevent the total defeat of the fighting force, but the report that the commanding general was being forced to withdraw so unexpectedly stunned the president.[94]

Davis called his cabinet together along with the governor of Virginia and the mayor of Richmond and informed them of the situation. As the government officials gathered the Confederate archives and needed belongings, the president sent a telegraph message to General Lee asking if his army could hold back the Federals for a little while longer. Lee responded emphatically that he was unable to provide more time and that the capital should be evacuated as soon as possible. That night Davis and his cabinet boarded a train at the Richmond and Danville depot and at 11:00 p.m. began their journey to Danville, Virginia. The next day much of the former Confederate capital was in flames.[95]

Lee's battered and hungry army remained near Amelia Court House and waited for supplies to arrive. Lee had made preparations for rations to be at Amelia Court House, but they had not arrived. Lee sent out foraging parties and pleaded with local farmers and citizens to give anything they could to support his starving troops. On April 5, realizing that the Federals were moving toward his position, the Confederate commander began moving his army toward Farmville, west of his current position.[96]

By now A. P. Hill's former corps numbered a mere 8,000 men, and Heth's division had been reduced to the size of a single brigade. The remnants of the once proud Third Corps marched with Longstreet's troops toward Jetersville, southwest of Amelia Court House. Along the way the Confederates skirmished with small detachments of Federal infantry and cavalry. Lee had hoped to attack and defeat the Union forces at Jetersville, from which he had hoped to use the Richmond and Danville Railroad to move his troops into North Carolina, but soon realized there were too many to engage. Although Lee did not know it, the entire Union II Corps was now at Jetersville. Meade had begun preparing his forces for an all-out assault on Amelia Court House, which he intended to implement on the morning of April 6. Lee, however, had already planned his retreat. The Confederate commander realized if he wanted to reach Farmville, where supplies would be waiting, his army had to move swiftly. Farmville was a full 23 miles west of Jetersville and if the Federals arrived there first the Army of Northern Virginia would be powerless to hold off their enemy. As one Southern soldier wrote in his diary, the march to Farmville "is now a race for life or death."[97]

During the late hours of April 5 Longstreet began slowly moving his troops away from the nearby Federal force. The soldiers were ordered to pack cups and canteens away and refrain from talking to their comrades. His men marched north toward Amelia Springs and then turned west toward Deatonville. Although harassed throughout the march by Northern cavalry units the Confederates made their retreat without the main Union forces realizing their intentions. Lee's roundabout withdrawal may have confused the Federals, who did not attempt to block his move west.[98]

The following day, Ewell's and Anderson's troops were attacked by the Federals, under the command of Sheridan, near Sayler's Creek. The outnumbered Confederates were defeated and Ewell, Anderson, and several more Rebel generals were captured. The day's events prompted a highly excited General Lee to exclaim, "My God! Has the army been dissolved?" With Ewell's and Anderson's corps destroyed, Lee's army now consisted of Longstreet's and Gordon's battered corps. Lee continued moving his army into Farmville, where some of his troops received food for the first time since leaving Petersburg, and on the following day began marching toward Appomattox Station, where supplies were waiting for his weary soldiers.[99]

The remaining men of the 55th North Carolina marched along a crowded road covered deep in mud, but finally arrived at Farmville around dawn on April 7. The men hastily moved toward the railroad cars where boxes of rations were being passed out to the weary soldiers. Believing the bridges across the Appomattox River had been destroyed, and the water too rough to cross, Lee allowed his tired men a short rest. The hungry troops had only just begun to eat, some had not even received provisions yet, when news was received that the Federals were on their way to Farmville. Major General William Mahone's troops, left near the bridges, were unable to prevent Union troops under the command of Brigadier General Thomas Smyth from extinguishing the fire burning the High Bridge and succeeding in crossing to the northern side of the river. What remained of the Army of Northern Virginia was forced to retreat without being properly fed or rested.[100]

Lee ordered Longstreet to march his forces north toward Cumberland Church and then move west toward Lynchburg. The Federal V and VI Corps were closing in on Longstreet, and Union cavalry units harassed his men as they continued their retreat. The Confederate divisions were now disorganized and the morale of the men was rapidly declining, but they pushed on. Later that evening General Grant sent a message to Lee asking him to surrender.

The result of the last week must convince you of the hopelessness of further resistance on the part of the Army of Northern Virginia in this struggle. I feel that it is so, and regard it as my duty to shift from myself the responsibility of any further effusion of blood, by asking of you the surrender of that portion of the Confederate States army known as the Army of Northern Virginia.

U.S. Grant, Lieutenant-General[101]

Lee, however, wanted to know exactly what terms the Federal commander was willing to offer before he would discuss surrendering his army. After sending his response requesting the conditions of his possible surrender to Grant, Lee ordered Longstreet to continue his retreat west.[102]

The 55th North Carolina and the rest of Cooke's brigade had been posted with the rear guard and continued to skirmish with advancing Federals. By April 8, Lee's army had reached Appomattox Court House and halted. Cooke's troops were placed in a line of battle along the Richmond-Lynchburg Stage Road and were instructed to be ready to advance at any moment. According to one of his staff officers, Lee planned to march through Pittsylvania County toward Danville, Virginia, and hoped to open up communications with Johnston's army in North Carolina. But he would have to break away from Appomattox first.[103]

Grant did not receive Lee's reply asking what terms the Federal commander would propose until the morning of April 8. Although dissatisfied that the Confederate general refused to accept the surrender proposal, Grant retorted that the only condition he would insist upon was that all of the officers and soldiers under Lee's control be "disqualified for taking up arms against the Government of the United States until properly exchanged." Later that evening the Confederate commander received Grant's second message and responded with a letter stating that he did not believe "the emergency has risen to call for the surrender of this Army." He then went on to explain that he would be willing to meet with Grant to discuss peace terms, but not the surrender of the Army of Northern Virginia.[104]

After sending his correspondence through the lines to the Federal commander General Lee convened a council of war with his principal lieutenants, Longstreet, Gordon, and Fitz Lee. Lee informed his subordinates of the terms Grant had offered, but the officers present concluded that their only option was to try one more attempt to break away from the Federals and continue marching toward Danville. The attack would begin at 5:00 a.m.[105]

On April 9 Gordon's troops attempted to break out of Appomattox Court House, but were forced to fall back. The 55th North Carolina remained in the rear in reserve, waiting for the attack they were sure was coming. Gordon sent word to Lee that he could not hold unless heavily support by Longstreet. Lee, realizing that his army was outnumbered and surrounded, decided to offer his surrender to General Grant. Although some of Lee's officers suggested continuing the struggle by implementing a guerilla war, the honorable commander refused. Surrounded by an overwhelming force, starving and nearly out of supplies, the Army of Northern Virginia surrendered later that day. Captain W. A. Whitted commanded the 55th North Carolina at the time of the surrender at Appomattox Court House. Several days later, on April 12, 1865, 83 men who had fought bravely with the 55th North Carolina were paroled. For the soldiers serving in the Army of Northern Virginia the war was over, although some of the troops believed they would be paroled and fight again. After receiving their paroles the remaining few members of the 55th North Carolina began their last march home.[106]

Epilogue

After being paroled, the 83 soldiers from the 55th North Carolina began their long journey home. The tired and weary men marched together mostly by brigade, the men of the 55th traveled with Cooke's unit. After camping at several locations in Virginia, including Campbell Court House and Gorman Court House, the former Rebels continued south. After a journey that must have been accompanied by thoughts of what might have been, the soldiers were back in North Carolina. One by one, as individual soldiers neared their homes, the caravan of men became smaller until it was no more. Defeated and depressed, these once proud Confederate soldiers now had to endure the disheartening experience of living under Federal occupation.[1]

North Carolina's countryside, with a few exceptions, had escaped the horrors and destruction of the war. The conflict, however, did inflict serious wounds to the state's economy and many towns and communities lacked food and other basic necessities of life. Many soldiers found their former lives completely turned upside down; loved ones gone, homes and farms ravaged.[2] The loss of a large portion of an entire generation of young men hindered progress in some areas. Despite the negative impact of the war most Confederate veterans battled through the impoverishment and anxiety that greeted them after they finally made it home. Most of these former soldiers prospered and went on to rebuild the South.

It is unknown what became of every soldier who fought with the 55th North Carolina and survived the war, but there are records and other sources that provide some indication of what happened to a few. Several of the officers wrote memoirs or were the subjects of newspaper stories written about their lives. Many of the men devoted time to keeping the memory of the Confederacy alive and joined such organizations as the United Confederate Veterans.[3]

Throughout the war the men of the 55th continued to believe in one another and remained proud of their unit, and were thus able to perform so admirably when called upon. Letters written by members of the 55th indicate that the soldiers had a deep concern for the welfare of their comrades. When they went into battle the men in the regiment fought for each other. Even though the majority of the regiment's soldiers joined the struggle for Southern independence late, they fought with pride and determination and became an effective combat unit. Time after time the 55th found itself fighting a superior Federal force, but it rarely retreated. Only after the regiment began to disintegrate in the closing months of the war did the men begin to lose heart and fall back when challenged.

The regiment's cohesion was an important factor in motivating the soldiers to fight, but other aspects contributed to the unit's fighting spirit. National patriotism, and a sense of mission were also factors; however, the need to prove one's worth in combat prompted many of the men to continue the struggle.

As James M. McPherson asserts in *For Cause and Comrades: Why Men Fought in the Civil War*, most common soldiers were motivated by the courage and actions of their officers.[4] This is borne out by the audacity and bravery of the officers who served with the 55th North Carolina. In the heat of battle on July 1, 1863, John Connally had picked up the regiment's battle flag, knowing full well that he would become a prime target as a result, and rallied his men to charge forward. He was severely wounded in the process. On the same day, Belo had calmly directed his troops across a fence and into the Federal right flank. Time and time again company commanders like Captain Satterfield had risen to the challenge and pushed their men forward. Most of the officers who led by example had paid the ultimate price. But their men had honored their memory by fighting on.

The true spirit of the regiment, however, was found in the ranks of the common soldiers. Most of the privates whose letters told this history had not made it to Appomattox Court House. Joseph J. Hoyle, who had missed the simple pleasure of seeing his wife's face and being with her, never made it home. Also, privates George W. Pearsall and Gray and George Woodard never saw their families again. Nearly 200 men who served with the 55th died from disease, and Confederate and state records indicate that about 140 soldiers were reported killed in action, and about a dozen more were listed as missing in action.[5]

Although men who reluctantly joined the Confederate army filled the ranks of the regiment, the unit continued to prove its worth in battle and held firm to the Southern cause. Of the approximately 1,300 men who served with the regiment during the Civil War only about 70 were listed as deserting, and several of these soldiers returned to their command. Throughout the war more than 300 members of the unit were wounded in battle, some of them more than once, and over 300 men spent time in Federal prison camps.

As W. J. Cash wrote some 80 years after the Civil War, the blood and destruction of those four years did not destroy the Southern mind and will. Some of the Confederate soldiers never accepted the "new" South, and joined such terrorist groups as the Ku Klux Klan to reestablish white supremacy throughout the region. The war had transformed the people of the region into a much more cohesive group. The soldiers who had fought and bled with men from distant states were now molded together with them. They became more closely bonded as a society than they had been before 1861. The war made the South more homogeneous than it had been before the outbreak of hostilities.[6]

After the war the men who had served with the 55th spent the remaining years of their lives recounting the memories of companionship, of combat, and of death. Many went on to distinguish themselves as lawyers, politicians, and farmers. The majority of them simply picked up the pieces of their former lives and went about living as they had before the war, but the visions they carried of the bloodshed and carnage probably never left their thoughts.

The soldiers of the 55th along with those of every Confederate regiment became part of southern folklore. Judge Walter Clark, the editor of a series of histories written by former veterans about North Carolina's regiments during the Civil War, wrote the following tribute to the common soldier years after the war:

We had great generals but their fame rest upon incomparable soldiers who made them great. The greatest figure of that great time was the "Confederate soldier" of whom it can be said, not in eulogy but in simple truth, that as long as the breezes blow, while the grasses grow, while the rivers run his record will be summed up in eternal fame in this sentence: "He did his duty."[7]

The men who served with the 55th North Carolina may have shared a lifetime of experiences in two and a half years of horrific warfare. Historian Gerald Linderman asserts, "Every war begins as one war and becomes two, that watched by civilians and that fought by soldiers."[8] This conclusion can be applied to the written works completed that chronicle the events of the Civil War. The historians' views of the war are not always the same as those of the participants. Their stories have been chronicled by hundreds of historians and Civil War veterans, but the manner in which each soldier remembered the conflict and what he felt about it after 1865 will probably always remain unknown.

The 55th Regiment North Carolina Troops joined the fight for southern independence late. The unit missed the memorable battles of 1861 and 1862. However, though most of the soldiers had only been engaged in minor skirmishes before July 1863 they stood firm against some of the Federals' best troops at Gettysburg. From the Wilderness to Petersburg the command consistently held its line against repeated Federal attacks, but in the end the Union's superior manpower overwhelmed it. The regiment's ranks were not filled by men who had rushed to meet the Yankee "invaders" in 1861, but time after time from July 1863 until April 1865 the soldiers of the 55th fought with determination and courage in some of the Civil War's bloodiest battles.

Appendix A. The 10 Companies of the Regiment

Company	Name (if any)	County(ies)
Company A		Wilson, Wayne, and Nash
Company B		Wilkes
Company C	"Cleveland Grays"	Cleveland
Company D	"Cleveland Farmers"	Cleveland and Rutherford
Company E		Pitt, Martin, and Rutherford
Company F	"South Mountain Rangers"	Cleveland, Catawba, and Burke
Company G	"North Carolina Rebels"	Johnston, Wayne, and Duplin
Company H	"Alexander Boys"	Alexander, Onslow, and Iredell
Company I	"Franklin Farmers"	Franklin and Wake
Company K		Granville

The counties listed are only intended to represent where the majority of the men from each company lived before serving with the regiment. Also, in addition to the counties listed many of the officers came from Yadkin, Person, Forsyth, and Orange counties.

Appendix B.
Regimental Roster

Field and staff officers
(Some of the men listed in this section also appear in company rosters)

Colonel
John Kerr Connally (served as regimental colonel until being wounded at Gettysburg on July 1, 1863)

Lieutenant colonels
Alfred H. Belo (served as the regiment's assistant quartermaster, and as major until being promoted to lieutenant colonel on July 3, 1863; wounded at Gettysburg on July 1, 1863; returned to duty in January 1864, and was given command of the regiment; wounded in the left arm at Cold Harbor on June 2, 1864, and did not return to command of the 55th)
Abner S. Calloway (resigned on January 12, 1863)
Maurice T. Smith (killed at Gettysburg on July 1, 1863)

Major
James S. Whitehead (died on August 7, 1862, the cause of death not reported)

Adjutants
1st Lt. Charles M. Cooke (served as acting adjutant from June 1864 through April 9, 1865)
1st Lt. Charles R. Jones (served as acting adjutant for several months after July 1, 1863)
1st Lt. Henry T. Jordan (appointed adjutant on November 18, 1862, and served until being captured at Gettysburg on July 1, 1863; Remained at Johnson's Island until March 14, 1865)
1st Lt. William H. Young (Resigned on or about November 1, 1862.)

Assistant quartermasters
George Washington Blount (Appointed assistant quartermaster on May 20, 1862. Dismissed prior to November 1, 1862)

William P. Webb (appointed assistant quartermaster on April 30, 1863; relieved from duty and served as assistant quartermaster in the Forge Bureau in Georgia; had served as the 55th North Carolina's assistant commissary of substance from November 18, 1862, through April 30, 1863)

Chaplains

Issac G. Connalay (appointed on an unspecified date)
William B. Royall (served as chaplain from November 18, 1862, through July 24, 1863)

Surgeons

Benjamin T. Green (served as surgeon from November 18, 1862, until being captured at Gettysburg on or about July 5, 1863; returned to duty sometime after November 1863 and served until April 9, 1865)
James A. Smith (served as surgeon from May 19, 1862, through November 1, 1862)

Assistant surgeons

Isaac G. Cannady (served as assistant surgeon from May 20, 1862, through April 9, 1865)
W. T. Parker (date of appointment not reported; captured at Gettysburg on or about July 5, 1863; paroled in November 1863, but no further service record exists)

Hospital stewards

A. J. Stone (appointed hospital steward on an unspecified date and served until being transferred to the 48th North Carolina State Troops Regiment sometime between July and October 1864)
Peterson Thorp, Jr. (appointed hospital steward sometime between July and October 1864 and served until April 9, 1865)

Ensign

Marlin B. Galloway (appointed ensign on April 27, 1864, and served until being killed during the battle of the Wilderness on May 5, 1863)

Sergeants major

Jesse Allen Adams (served as acting sergeant major from May or June 1863 until being wounded and captured at Gettysburg on July 1, 1863; paroled in August 1863 and returned to duty; appointed sergeant major sometime between July and October 1864 and served until April 9, 1865)
William N. Holt (served as sergeant major from May or June 1862 through May 8, 1863, when he was promoted to third lieutenant, Company H)

Quartermaster sergeants

Alonzo H. Dunn (served as quartermaster sergeant until his death on July 12, 1862, the cause of death not reported)
Henry S. Furman (appointed quartermaster sergeant on October 7, 1862)

Commissary sergeant

William B. Royal (served as commissary sergeant from sometime after October 1863 until April 9, 1865)

Ordnance sergeant

J. W. C. Young (served as ordnance sergeant from November 19, 1862, until April 9, 1865)

Band

Henry C. Adcock; surrendered at Appomattox
Rufus M. Beam; surrendered at Appomattox
Francis N. Bernard; captured at Tabernacle Church, Virginia, April 3, 1865
John Paul Bernard; paroled on or around April 14, 1865
William H. Cleland; paroled at Houston, Texas, on or about August 4, 1865
Jacob C. Ellington; captured at Petersburg, Virginia, April 3, 1865
George Lewis Falls; surrendered at Appomattox
Eugene Geauffretean; captured at Tabernacle Church, Virginia, April 3, 1865
William H. Horne; surrendered at Appomattox
Charles E. Jacke; deserted on or about April 4, 1865
Jacob C. Pearson; surrendered at Appomattox
William H. Rowland; surrendered at Appomattox
William H. Shelly; captured near Sutherland's Station, Virginia, April 2, 1865
Burton P. Summerell; surrendered at Appomattox
Allen H. Taft; paroled on or around April 14, 1865
Henry C. Turnage; surrendered at Appomattox
Archibald A. Tyson; survived the war

COMPANIES

Company A

Officers

(Captains are listed in the order in which they served as commander; lieutenants are alphabetical)

Capt. William J. Bullock
Capt. Albert E. Upchurch
Capt. Benjamin F. Briggs
1st Lt. James H. Barnes

2nd Lt. Thomas R. Bass
1st Lt. George Washington Blount
3rd Lt. Peter M. Briggs
1st Lt. Thomas J. Hadley

Noncommissioned officers and privates

Pvt. Amos C. Adams
Pvt. Duncan L. F. Adams
Pvt. John W. Adams
Pvt. George W. Aquir
Pvt. Louis D. Aquir
Pvt. Isaac Aycock
Pvt. Jesse Aycock
Pvt. Richard H. Banks
Pvt. John T. Bardin
Pvt. Simon B. Bardin
Sgt. Augustus Barnes
Pvt. Caswell H. Barnes

Sgt. Enos Barnes
Cpl. John T. Barnes
Pvt. Larry Barnes
Pvt. Stephen Barnes
Pvt. William N. Barnes
Pvt. William W. Barnes
Pvt. Bennett Bass
Pvt. Bryant Bass
Pvt. Larry B. Bass
Pvt. Jesse R. Beaman
Pvt. James H. Bell
Pvt. William C. Best

Cpl. Henry W. Boswell
Pvt. Jethro Boswell
Pvt. Amos Boyett
Pvt. Enos B. Boyett
Pvt. Stephen Boyett
Pvt. Daniel Campbell
Pvt. Andrew J. Cook
Pvt. Jethro Cook
Pvt. James H. Daniel
Pvt. Henry C. Davis
Pvt. Henry R. Davis
Pvt. Jonathan B. Davis

1st Sgt. David Dew
Pvt. Benjamin Dickerson
Pvt. Leonard Dickinson
Pvt. Edwin Eatman
Pvt. Edwin G. Edmundson
Pvt. William P. Edwards
Pvt. Edwin G. Etheridge
Pvt. Granberry Etheridge
Pvt. James Etheridge
Pvt. Justice Etheridge
Pvt. Gabriel Farrell
Pvt. Granberry Farrell
Pvt. James W. Ferrell
Pvt. J. Findell
Pvt. Calvin Gardner
Pvt. James J. Grant
Sgt. John C. R. Hadley
Pvt. Thomas Hales
Cpl. Jethro Harrison
Sgt. John Hayles
Pvt. Nathan T. Hays
Pvt. William H. Holland
Pvt. William N. Holt
Sgt. John W. Hunt
Pvt. Columbus Jones
Sgt. Lewellyn Jones
Pvt. Reddick J. Jones
Pvt. H. Lamb
Pvt. Edwin Lamm
Pvt. Isham Lamm
Pvt. Jacob Lamm
Pvt. Tobias Lamm
Pvt. William Lamm
Pvt. George H. Lane
Pvt. Redman Lodge
Pvt. Henderson H. Love
Pvt. David Lucas
Pvt. Henry Lucas
Cpl. Joseph J. Marshbourn
Pvt. N. H. Mays
Pvt. James M. Mercer
Pvt. John J. Mercer
Pvt. Willie B. Mercer
Pvt. John W. Moore
Sgt. Francis M. Moye
James H. Narron (rank not listed)
Pvt. Ezekiel Newsom
Pvt. James M. Newsom
Pvt. William R. Newsom
Pvt. James J. Pate
Musician Jacob C. Pearson
Sgt. William H. Pearson
Pvt. Jesse H. Peel
Pvt. Matthew Peel
Pvt. Nathan Peele
Pvt. Wright E. Pender
Pvt. Augustus K. Perry
Pvt. Epenetus G. Pippin
Cpl. Robert M. Pittman
Pvt. Jackson Price
Pvt. James G. Proctor
Pvt. Calvin Raper
Pvt. Braswell Renfrow
Pvt. Burkett Renfrow
Pvt. Ruffin Rose
Pvt. Gordon Roundtree
John D. Ruffin (rank not listed)
Pvt. Blany Scott
Pvt. Elisha Scott
Cpl. Haywood Scott
Pvt. Henry Scott
Pvt. Richard Short
Pvt. John T. Simpson
Pvt. William Simpson
Pvt. Alexander Smith
Pvt. Jacob Stancill
Pvt. James H. Stancill
Pvt. Josiah Stancill
Pvt. A. J. Stone
Pvt. Jesse P. Sullivan
Pvt. R. Talton
Pvt. Woodard Thomas
Pvt. Josiah Thorn
Pvt. John M. Tilly
Pvt. John Tindall
Pvt. William B. Tindall
Pvt. J. Tomkins
Pvt. Barnes Tomlinson
Pvt. Eason T. Tomlinson
Pvt. Gary Tomlinson
Pvt. Jonathan Tomlinson
Pvt. Lewis D. W. Tomlinson
Pvt. Nathan Tomlinson
Pvt. Willie W. Tomlinson
Pvt. Sanders M. Trevathan
Cpl. Sion M. Upchurch
Pvt. Joseph Watson
Pvt. Noah Watson
Pvt. Willis Watson
Pvt. Berry Wester
Pvt. Eli Williamson
Pvt. Levi T. Williamson
Pvt. Willie S. Williamson
Pvt. Gary W. Woodard
Pvt. George W. Woodard
Pvt. Haywood Word
Pvt. Robert W. Yelverton

Company B

Officers

(Captains are listed in the order in which they served as commander; lieutenants are alphabetical)

Capt. Abner S. Calloway
Capt. Samuel J. Forester
Capt. George A. Gilreath
Capt. John T. Peden
Capt. Marcus C. Stevens
2nd Lt. Jesse T. Alexander
3rd Lt. George J. Bethel
3rd Lt. Leander Gilreath
2nd Lt. Hiram Greer

Noncommissioned officers and privates

Pvt. E. Anderson
Pvt. Jesse Anderson
Cpl. Martin Anderson
Pvt. William Anderson
Pvt. William Barker
Pvt. Alexander Becknal

Pvt. Leander Becknal
Cpl. Thomas S. Bell
Pvt. Calvin Benge
Pvt. Elisha Benge
Pvt. Henry Benge
Pvt. James Benge
Pvt. Meredith Benge
Pvt. Samuel Benge
Pvt. Daniel Billings
Pvt. William M. Billings
Pvt. John Bolin
Sgt. Thomas H. Branch
Pvt. B. R. Brown
Pvt. Finley Brown
Pvt. John S. Brown
Pvt. William O. Bryant
Pvt. Isaac Burchett
Pvt. John Carpenter
Pvt. John Carson
Pvt. John Chatham
Pvt. William Chatham
Pvt. Alexander Cheeks
Pvt. William A. Cockerham
Pvt. Oliver L. Couch
Pvt. W. Dickson
Pvt. Andrew W. Earp
Pvt. Hugh M. Eller
Pvt. James F. Eller
Jeff Forester (Capt. Forester's slave)
Pvt. William T. Foster
Pvt. Wiley Garriss
Sgt. Noah Gilreath
Sgt. Edmond J. Greer
Pvt. George A. Gregory
Pvt. James Gregory
Pvt. John Gregory
Pvt. Lewis M. Gregory
Pvt. Thomas G. Gregory
Pvt. Thomas Grutle
Pvt. Jefferson Hall
Pvt. William Hall
Pvt. George W. Hayes
Pvt. Henry Hayes
Cpl. William Hayes
1st Sgt. John A. Herbert
Sgt. Ervin Higgins
Pvt. W. Huander Higgins
Pvt. John Hinchey
Allen H. Hix (rank not listed)
Pvt. Enoch Holland
Pvt. Daniel H. Holloway
Pvt. James Hunt
Pvt. Gallenton W. Lee
Sgt. Elihu Lewis
Pvt. John Lewis
Pvt. Sanford Lewis
Pvt. William Love
Pvt. William O. McDonald
Pvt. John Maloney
Pvt. David Marlow
Pvt. Elbert Marlow
Pvt. James M. Marlow
Pvt. Martin Marlow
Pvt. Melvin Marlow
Sgt. James A. Marrow
Pvt. John McNeill
Pvt. John A. Milam
Pvt. Alfred Minton
Pvt. Hugh Minton
Pvt. Winburn Minton
Pvt. Moses Money
Pvt. Alexander Moore
Pvt. James M. Moore
Pvt. Martin Moore
Pvt. Riley L. Moore
Pvt. Robert Moore
Pvt. William Moore
Cpl. Bartlett Mullis
Pvt. William Myers
Pvt. William Owens
Pvt. James B. Pearson
Sgt. Thomas S. Pearson
Pvt. William A. Pearson
Pvt. John W. Phillips
Pvt. Jordan Phillips
Pvt. William R. Presnall
Pvt. J. Franklin Privett
Pvt. J. M. Privett
Pvt. Lewis Privett
Cpl. Mathew Privett
Sgt. Asa Rash
Pvt. Henry Rash
Pvt. Israel Rash
Pvt. Lewis Rash
Pvt. Benjamin Rhodes
Pvt. Jesse Riddle
Sgt. John Robinson
Pvt. Edward Rose
Pvt. William Rose
Pvt. Leonidas St. John
Pvt. David Sanders
Cpl. James A. Sharp
Pvt. Even Shoemaker
Pvt. Jacob Shumate
Sgt. Thomas S. Shumate
Pvt. Richard Sidon
Pvt. Solomon Sloop
Pvt. James Smith
Pvt. James A. Smith
Pvt. Alexander Speaks
Pvt. Sidney Summerlin
Pvt. William Tedder
Pvt. James P. Turner
Pvt. John E. Turner
Pvt. R. L. D. Walker
Sgt. Larkin Walsh
Pvt. Samuel Wiley
Cpl. David Williams
Pvt. William Wright
Pvt. Robert Yates

Company C

Officers

(Captains are listed in the order in which they served as commander; lieutenants are alphabetical)

Capt. Dickson Falls
Capt. Edward D. Dixon
Capt. Charles R. Jones
Capt. Peter M. Briggs
1st Lt. George J. Bethel
2nd Lt. Philip R. Elam
3rd Lt. Thomas D. Falls
3rd Lt. William Quinn

Noncommissioned officers and privates

Pvt. George Barrett
Pvt. Perry Barrett
1st Sgt. Aaron R. Beam
Pvt. Joshua C. Beam
Pvt. M. Rufus Beam
Pvt. James H. Biggerstaff
Pvt. Jesse Blythe
Sgt. John D. Boggs
Pvt. Thomas Branton
Pvt. F. H. Bridges
Pvt. James W. Brown
Sgt. William L. Brown
Pvt. Samuel A. Bryant
Pvt. William P. Bryant
Pvt. Lawson H. Camp
Pvt. David G. Carpenter
Pvt. George P. Carpenter
Pvt. Jacob Carpenter
Pvt. Peter Carpenter
Pvt. Peter Z. Carpenter
Pvt. Robert C. Carpenter
Pvt. John B. Carroll
Pvt. C. Sylvester Cobb
Pvt. Martin Cornwell
Pvt. J. D. Costner
Pvt. John M. Costner
Pvt. John Crotts
Pvt. Joseph Crotts
Pvt. George F. Crowder
Cpl. James C. Crowder
Pvt. John P. Crowder
Pvt. Joseph P. Crowder
Pvt. George P. Davis
Pvt. A. Crowel Digh
Pvt. James R. Eaker
Pvt. David W. Elliott
Pvt. Jonas Elmore
Cpl. John W. Eskridge
Pvt. Richard C. Eskridge
Pvt. A. N. Falls
Pvt. George L. Falls
Pvt. C. F. Felmot
Pvt. Aaron L. Froneberger
Pvt. Ely Furgeson
Sgt. Albert G. Gant
Pvt. A. B. Gardner
Pvt. William Gillis
Pvt. John T. Gladden
Pvt. W. H. H. Glasgow
Pvt. Simeon C. Gold
Pvt. Drury W. Goodson
Pvt. David T. Griffin
Pvt. Farington Griffin
Pvt. A. E. Grigg
Pvt. George W. Harden
Pvt. Doctor F. Harmon
Pvt. Peter A. Hastings
Pvt. Jeremiah Heavener
Pvt. Eusibius S. Hendrick
Pvt. J. D. Herner
Pvt. Levi C. Huffstetler
Pvt. J. M. Jones
Pvt. Martin Jones
Pvt. Joseph J. Kistler
Pvt. Jacob C. Lackey
Pvt. Thomas O. Lackey
Pvt. J. L. Lattimer
Pvt. Christopher Lewis
Cpl. Edward F. M. Lewis
Pvt. William Lindsey
Cpl. Newton J. Long
Pvt. Thomas Long
Pvt. J. Z. Lowrance
Pvt. Marcus D. Lowrance
Pvt. James P. Martin
Pvt. Reuben H. Martin
Pvt. Thomas W. Martin
Cpl. Lewis McDonald
Pvt. Thomas Mitchum
Pvt. Abraham Mooney, Jr.
Pvt. Abraham Mooney, Sr.
Pvt. Jacob C. Mooney
Pvt. Peter C. Mooney
Pvt. Simpson T. Moore
Pvt. Adam Morrison
Pvt. Jeremiah Morrison
Pvt. Archibald Moss
Pvt. James Moss
Pvt. Marion J. Neal
Pvt. J. F. Nowlin
Pvt. Isaac R. Oates
Pvt. James H. Oates
Sgt. Samuel W. Oates
Pvt. William W. Patterson
Pvt. John H. Peeler
Pvt. Samuel L. Putnam
Pvt. John T. Ramsour
Pvt. Thomas Randall
Pvt. James P. Roach
Pvt. Newton Roach
Pvt. Daniel Sellers
John L. Shade (rank not listed)
Pvt. Henry Shitle
Pvt. Monroe M. Simmons
Pvt. James Smith
Pvt. Marcus C. Smith
Pvt. James W. Spangler
Cpl. George W. Sparrow
Pvt. Thomas A. Sparrow
Pvt. Crawford Spurlin
Pvt. Alfred H. Sweezy
Pvt. Samuel W. Torance
Pvt. George A. Turner
Pvt. William R. Vandyke
Cpl. Franklin T. Warlick
Pvt. Thomas Watson
Pvt. Abram Weaver
Pvt. Brison W. Weaver
Pvt. William Weaver
Pvt. Calvin Whistenant
Pvt. Joseph Whistenant
Pvt. Burrel M. White
Pvt. Henry White
Pvt. Hugh White
Pvt. James L. White
Pvt. Michael White
Cpl. Alexander Williams
Pvt. Doctor F. Williams
Pvt. William E. Williams
Pvt. Thomas P. Willis
Pvt. Moses A. Wilson
Pvt. Phillip D. Wilson
Pvt. S. Wilson
Pvt. Anderson Womack
Cpl. John P. Womack
Pvt. William W. Womack

Company D

Officers

Capt. Silas D. Randall
3rd Lt. Joseph B. Cabaniss
1st Lt. Albert Green
3rd Lt. Edmond J. Lovelace
2nd Lt. James H. Randall
1st Lt. William H. Townes

Noncommissioned officers and privates

Pvt. Jacob E. Aderholt
Pvt. James E. Arnold
Pvt. Richard H. L. Barnett
Pvt. Samuel M. Bass
Pvt. Peter Bean
Pvt. John W. Beason
Pvt. Thomas Beheler
Pvt. Jasper N. Blackwell
Sgt. Burwell W. Blanton
Pvt. Charles B. Blanton
Pvt. Drury A. Blanton
Pvt. Hart S. Blanton
Pvt. David Bostic
Pvt. George W. Bowen
Pvt. Samuel C. Bowen
1st Sgt. B. H. Bridgers
Pvt. Andrew H. Bridges
Pvt. Isaac J. Bridges
Pvt. William F. Bryson
Pvt. Athel M. Cabaniss
Sgt. Marcus L. Carroll
Pvt. George H. Champion
Pvt. Richard C. Champion
Cpl. David Dellinger
Pvt. John H. Dellinger
Pvt. William A. Dickey
Pvt. Laurance G. Duncan
Pvt. M. L. Earls
Pvt. Barnett W. Eskridge
Pvt. Oliver N. Eskridge
Pvt. William J. Gibson
Cpl. Benjamin Green
Pvt. David H. Green
Pvt. Drury A. Green
Pvt. Elijah Green
Pvt. John Green
Pvt. John P. Green
Pvt. Jonas Green
Cpl. Joseph Green
Pvt. Reuben H. Green
Sgt. Thomas Green
Pvt. Thomas Green, Jr.
Pvt. Thomas Green, Sr.
Pvt. W. M. Green
Pvt. Willis W. Green
Pvt. Zachariah O. Green
Pvt. Aaron B. Hamrick
Pvt. Abram Hamrick
Pvt. Andy M. Hamrick
Cpl. Charles J. Hamrick
Pvt. David Hamrick
Pvt. David Hamrick, Jr.
Pvt. Elijah Hamrick
Pvt. Elijah Hamrick, Jr.
Pvt. Gabriel Hamrick
Pvt. Henry G. Hamrick
Pvt. Isaac Hamrick
Pvt. James Hamrick
Pvt. Nero W. Hamrick
Pvt. Oliver A. Hamrick
Sgt. Reuben Hamrick
Pvt. Thomas Hamrick
Pvt. William R. Hamrick
Pvt. Jefferson T. Harrel
Pvt. Hosea H. Harrill
Pvt. Robert E. Harrill
Pvt. William M. Harrill
Pvt. John F. Harris
Pvt. William H. Hayes
Pvt. William D. Hendrick
G. W. Hendricks (rank not listed)
Pvt. James H. Jenkins
Pvt. Jerome L. Lankford
Pvt. Walter Y. Lankford
Pvt. Urias Ledbetter
Pvt. William Ledbetter
Pvt. Samuel Ledford
Pvt. John W. Lienberger
Pvt. James W. Lovelace
Cpl. Nathan C. Lovelace
Pvt. Thomas Lovelace
Pvt. William G. Lovelace
Pvt. William W. Lovelace
Pvt. Willis G. Lovelace
Pvt. Bryson L. McDaniel
Pvt. Willis A. McKinney
Z. M. McKinney (rank not listed)
Pvt. Berry H. McSwain
Pvt. Doctor T. J. M. McSwain
Pvt. Elijah McSwain
Pvt. George W. McSwain
Pvt. J. F. McSwain
Pvt. Oliver McSwain
Pvt. Joe R. B. Magners
Pvt. Abraham M. Martin
Pvt. John Millins
Pvt. George W. Mooney
Pvt. James C. Moore
Pvt. William Moten
Pvt. D. D. Neal
Pvt. Edwin Padgett
Pvt. James M. Pinson
Pvt. Abel Postin
Pvt. Daniel Postin
Pvt. Isaac Price
Pvt. William C. Pruett
Pvt. Wylies S. Pruett
Pvt. William S. Pryor
Pvt. Edward C. Quinn
George W. Quinn (rank not listed)
Pvt. G. W. Randall
Pvt. J. A. Randall
Pvt. John A. Randall
Pvt. Miller H. Randall
Pvt. Romulus M. S. Randall
Pvt. Edward R. Rippy
Pvt. James Rippy
Pvt. Iredell E. Rollins
J. A. Rome (rank not listed)
Pvt. Adolphus D. Runyan
Pvt. Jacob Runyan
Cpl. James M. Runyan
Pvt. Almarine D. Scruggs

Pvt. John Sealy
Pvt. John M. Shitle
Pvt. Charles C. N. Smith
Sgt. David H. Smith
Sgt. Lewis L. Smith
Pvt. Adam P. Spake
Pvt. James Toomey
Pvt. Hasiel Turner

Pvt. J. N. Turner
Cpl. Mastin Turner
Pvt. John Weaver
Pvt. Lewis Weaver
Pvt. Starling Weaver
Pvt. James J. Webb
Pvt. E. H. Wesson
Pvt. James H. White

Pvt. Jerome White
Pvt. Elliott C. Wood
Pvt. James D. Wood
Pvt. William M. Wright
Pvt. John Wylie
Pvt. Lee Wylie
Pvt. Edward W. Yarboro

Company E

Officers

(Captains are listed in the order in which they served as commander; lieutenants are alphabetical)

Capt. James S. Whitehead
Capt. Henry W. Brown

Capt. Howell G. Whitehead
1st Lt. James A. Hanrahan

3rd Lt. Godfrey E. Taft
2nd Lt. William S. Wilson

Noncommissioned officers and privates

Pvt. Jesse H. Adams
Pvt. Lewis A. Adams
Pvt. Prince W. Arnold
Pvt. Timothy Baker
Pvt. Henry A. Barnhill
Pvt. Francis N. Bernard
Pvt. John P. Bernard
Pvt. Isaiah S. Boyd
Pvt. Samuel Boyd
Pvt. Joseph Braddy
Cpl. Elihu Briley
Pvt. John S. W. Brown
Pvt. James E. Bullock
Pvt. James J. Bullock
Pvt. William R. Bullock
Pvt. William S. Bullock
Pvt. Caleb Cannon
Pvt. John W. Cannon
Pvt. Alfred B. Carney
Sgt. James H. Cason
Pvt. McGilbra L. Cherry
Pvt. John Chesnut
Pvt. John B. Congleton
Pvt. John S. Corbit
Pvt. Allen Crawford
Cpl. William B. Daniel
Pvt. Skelton Dennis
Pvt. James W. Dixon
Pvt. Joseph G. Dixon
Pvt. William B. Dixon
Pvt. Abe Dudley
Pvt. John Q. Dudley

Pvt. William L. Dudley
Pvt. J. J. Edwards
Pvt. James Edwards
Pvt. James E. Edwards
Pvt. William S. Edwards
Pvt. Jacob C. Ellington
C. Etheridge (rank not listed)
Pvt. Edmund Evans
Pvt. James H. Evans
1st Sgt. James B. Everett
Pvt. James L. Everett
Pvt. Simon D. Everett
Sgt. William H. Everett
Pvt. Mansel Flake
Cpl. James L. Fleming
Pvt. Kenneth H. Fleming
Pvt. William B. Fleming
Pvt. Wyatt A. Forbes
Sgt. Marlin B. Galloway
Pvt. William C. Gardner
Pvt. Adam Gaskins
Pvt. John A. Gaskins
Pvt. William H. Gurganus
Pvt. Willie Gurganus
Cpl. Joseph J. Haddock
Pvt. William Haddock
Pvt. Henry Hampton
Pvt. Cornelius Hardy
Pvt. Matthias Harris
Sgt. John F. Hellen
Pvt. James R. Hoord
Cpl. William H. Horne

Pvt. James M. Horton
Sgt. Charles E. Jacke
Pvt. George Jackson
Pvt. Richard H. Johnson
Pvt. William F. Johnson
Pvt. Benjamin A. Jones
Pvt. Henry B. Manning
Pvt. Jesse B. Manning
Pvt. James A. May
Pvt. John A. May
Pvt. John Mills, Jr.
Pvt. John Mills, Sr.
Pvt. Robert H. Mills
Pvt. William Page
Pvt. Willie A. Pitt
Pvt. James A. Pollard
Pvt. Joseph T. Pollard
Pvt. Richard E. Pollard
Pvt. Charles A. Randolph
Pvt. Willis R. Richard
Cpl. Robert V. Ricks
Pvt. Franklin Rodgers
Pvt. William H. Shelly
Pvt. Alexander J. Smith
Pvt. Cicero M. Smith
Pvt. John H. Smith
Pvt. R. W. Smith
Pvt. John R. Stocks
Pvt. Burton P. Summerell
Pvt. Allen H. Taft
Pvt. William B. Taylor
Pvt. Benjamin Teel

Pvt. Druery W. Teel
Pvt. James Teel
Pvt. Benjamin F. Tucker
Pvt. Joshua L. Tucker
Pvt. Henry C. Turnage
Pvt. Alfred A. Tyson
Pvt. Lemuel V. Tyson
Pvt. Seth Tyson
Pvt. Drew Vincent
Pvt. Willie R. Whichard
Pvt. Calvin A. White
Pvt. Lawrence A. White
Pvt. McGilbra White
Pvt. Benjamin N. Whitehurst
Sgt. J. A. Whitley
Cpl. John W. Wilson
Sgt. Jesse H. Woolard
Pvt. John P. Woolard
Pvt. Oscar Wooten
Pvt. John Worthington

Company F

Officers

(Captains are listed in the order in which they served as commander; lieutenants are alphabetical)

Capt. Peter M. Mull
Capt. Godfrey E. Taft
2nd Lt. Henry Cline
1st Lt. Joseph J. Hoyle
1st Lt. William H. Hull
2nd Lt. Peter P. Mull
3rd Lt. Eli Newton
1st Lt. Archibald H. A. Williams

Noncommissioned officers and privates

Pvt. William P. Bigham
Pvt. Jacob A. Bivens
Pvt. Peter M. Bivens
Pvt. Daniel W. Boyles
Pvt. William M. Boyles
Pvt. Williamson F. Brackett
Pvt. Zachariah Brackett
Pvt. Sidney Bradshaw
Pvt. David A. Brendle
Pvt. Wesley M. Brendle
Brittain (first name and rank not listed)
Pvt. Aaron Buff
Pvt. Christopher Buff
Pvt. David Buff, Jr.
Pvt. David Buff, Sr.
Pvt. James Buff
Pvt. Peter Buff
Pvt. Philip Buff
Pvt. David A. Bumgarner
Pvt. William P. Bumgarner
Pvt. Massenburg Burton
William Burton (rank not listed)
Pvt. Adam Canipe
Pvt. Albert Canipe
Pvt. Daniel E. Canipe
Pvt. David Canipe
Pvt. John A. Canipe
Pvt. Joseph Canipe
Pvt. Maxwell Canipe
Pvt. Noah J. Canipe
Pvt. John Carpenter
Pvt. William R. Chapman
1st Sgt. John Cline
Pvt. Aaron Cook, Jr.
Pvt. Aaron Cook, Sr.
Pvt. Harrison Cook
Pvt. Jesse Cook
Pvt. Noah W. Cook
Pvt. William Cook
Pvt. William Craig
Pvt. John S. Crow
Pvt. John R. Dickson
Pvt. William Downs
Pvt. John F. Elmore
Pvt. William Elmore
Pvt. William M. Freeman
Pvt. Jacob A. Gales
Pvt. Joseph C. Gantt
Pvt. James C. Goodson
Pvt. Miles Goodson
Sgt. Ephraim Gross
Pvt. Robert J. Hicks
Pvt. William H. Hicks
Pvt. Eli Hoyle
Pvt. Henry Hoyle
Pvt. Joel Hoyle
Pvt. Joseph Hoyle
Pvt. Levi Hoyle
Pvt. Robert D. Hoyle
Pvt. Solomon Hoyle
Pvt. Hiram Hudson
Pvt. John D. Hudson
Pvt. Thomas Huffman
Pvt. Benjamin Hull
Sgt. Albert P. Ivester
Pvt. Allen R. Johnson
Pvt. Andrew J. Johnson
Pvt. James M. Keever
Cpl. Julius A. Kennedy
Pvt. Peter Lail
Pvt. John Ledford
Pvt. William Ledford
Pvt. David Logan
Pvt. H. Loman
Pvt. Robert A. McCall
Pvt. Andrew McClurd
Pvt. Wade McClurd
Pvt. Jonathan McNeely
Pvt. Samuel McNeilly
Pvt. Zachariah D. McNeilly
Pvt. Leander M. Martin
Pvt. Ezra Mull
Pvt. John M. Mull
Pvt. Alfred Newton
Pvt. Eli Newton
Pvt. George A. Newton
Pvt. Henry Norman
Pvt. Robert H. Norman
Pvt. Alfred G. Peeler
Pvt. Lafayette Pope
Pvt. Joseph Prewit
Peter Prewitt (rank not listed)
Pvt. James T. Price

Pvt. Caleb Randall
Pvt. William S. Seagle
Pvt. Anderson Self
Sgt. Isaac R. Self
Pvt. Jacob R. Self
Pvt. Robert Self
Pvt. Rufus Self
Pvt. William J. Self
Pvt. Daniel F. Shuford
Pvt. Henry P. Shuford
Pvt. Peter M. Shuford
Pvt. John Smith
Pvt. James P. Stamey
Pvt. John Swink
Pvt. William N. Swink

Pvt. Robert Swofford
Pvt. Aaron Tallent
Pvt. Jesse E. Tallent
Pvt. David W. Turner
Pvt. James Turner
Pvt. James P. Walker
Sgt. Andrew Warlick
Pvt. David P. Warlick
Pvt. Noah B. Warlick
Pvt. George White
Cpl. Peter R. White
Cpl. Stephen J. White
Pvt. Andrew P. Williams
Sgt. Westly A. Williams
Pvt. William T. Williams

Pvt. Henry J. Willis
Pvt. Jacob B. Willis
Pvt. James Willis
1st Sgt. James R. Willis
Pvt. John Y. Willis
Pvt. Robert H. Willis
Pvt. Samuel O. Willis
Pvt. Solomon Willis
Pvt. Thomas Willis
Pvt. Levi Wise
Pvt. Major Wortman
Pvt. William S. Wortman
Pvt. Silas M. Wright
Pvt. Samuel Young

Company G

Officers

(Captains are listed in the order in which they served as commander; lieutenants are alphabetical)

Capt. Jesse P. Williams
Capt. Walter A. Whitted
Capt. William R. M. Chandler

3rd Lt. Alexander T. Grady
1st Lt. Charles R. Jones
2nd Lt. Mordecai Lee

1st Lt. Marcus C. Stevens
2nd Lt. Charles Williams

Noncommissioned officers and privates

Pvt. Jesse A. Adams
Pvt. Howard Anderson
Pvt. Charles H. Benson
Cpl. James H. Best
Pvt. Fountain M. Bizzell
Pvt. William A. Blackman
W. Bollins (rank not listed)
Pvt. John W. Brock
Cpl. Lemuel G. Budd
Pvt. William Budd
Pvt. John Carroway
Pvt. John R. Chance
Pvt. Nathan D. Chance
Pvt. John Cole
Pvt. Thomas Cole
Pvt. Ephraim Cotton
Pvt. Calvin Dail
Pvt. Lemuel L. Dail
Pvt. William H. Darden
Pvt. John C. Faircloth
Pvt. Stephen W. Faircloth
Pvt. William Faircloth
Pvt. William Fields
Pvt. Murdoch W. Finlayson

Pvt. Carlo Fraucissa
Pvt. Jesse B. Garris
Pvt. John T. Garris
Musician Eugene Geauffretean
Pvt. Hazy G. Goodson
Pvt. Joshua Goodson
Pvt. Peter Gording
Pvt. Frederick Grady
Pvt. Joseph Grant
Pvt. D. E. Grantham
Sgt. Marshall P. Grantham
Pvt. William E. Grantham
Pvt. William F. Grantham
Pvt. John Greene
Pvt. Stephen Hardison
Pvt. James Hardy
Pvt. Augustus Holloman
Pvt. William A. Holloman
Pvt. William N. Holt
Pvt. Daniel T. Hood
Pvt. John Hood
Pvt. Abner Ingram
Cpl. Bryant Ingram

Pvt. John B. Ingram
Lewis Keathly (rank not listed)
Pvt. Richard W. Kelly
Cpl. Barnabas King
Pvt. James Lane
Pvt. John Q. Lane
Pvt. Julius A. Lee
Pvt. Lovett Lee
Cpl. Walter A. Lee
Cpl. Young N. Lee
Pvt. J. W. Leviner
Pvt. James Lewis
Pvt. John Lewis
Pvt. William Lewis
Pvt. Gibson Lilley
Pvt. Isaac L. Martin
Sgt. Waitman G. Martin
Pvt. Josiah McClenny
Pvt. Stephen W. Morris
Pvt. John Murphy
Pvt. Junius Outlaw
Pvt. G. S. Patterson
1st Sgt. John R. Peacock

Pvt. George W. Pearsall
Pvt. Luke Pearsall
Pvt. John W. Powell
David H. Price (rank not listed)
Pvt. Eden Price
Pvt. George M. D. Price
Pvt. Henry W. Price
Pvt. Jesse B. Price
Pvt. Joseph Price
Pvt. Levan B. Price
Pvt. William D. Price
Pvt. Timothy Reaves
Pvt. James Reeves
Pvt. Atlas J. K. Rhodes
Pvt. James H. Rhodes
Pvt. Joseph E. Rhodes
1st Sgt. Elezar Rich
Cpl. Pinkney Rich
Pvt. Ryal W. Roberts
Pvt. William H. Rowland
Pvt. Henry Sasser
Pvt. James Smith
Sgt. John R. Smith
Pvt. William H. Stevens
Pvt. Isaac Strickland
Pvt. James M. Strickland
Pvt. James W. Strickland
Pvt. Jesse B. Strickland
Pvt. John D. Strickland
Pvt. Monroe Strickland
Pvt. Adam Sullivan
Sgt. Adam J. Summerlin
Pvt. John Summerlin
Pvt. John Taylor
Pvt. David J. Thompson
Pvt. Josiah Thompson
L. G. Thompson (rank not listed)
Pvt. David T. Toler
Pvt. Elisha Uzzell
Pvt. John H. Whitfield
Pvt. Jordan Williams
Pvt. Major Williams
Pvt. John A. Woodall
Pvt. Thomas Woodall

Company H

Officers

(Captains are listed in the order in which they served as commander; lieutenants are alphabetical)

Capt. Vandever Teague
Capt. Andrew J. Pollock
Capt. E. Hayne Davis
Capt. Edward F. Satterfield
Capt. Nicholas W. Lillington
2nd Lt. Benjamin J. Blount
1st Lt. Lewis Davis
2nd Lt. William W. Davis
3rd Lt. William N. Holt
1st Lt. James A. Marrow
1st Lt. John R. Pearson
3rd Lt. William W. Smith

Noncommissioned officers and privates

Sgt. John J. Austin
Cpl. Abraham T. Autaway
Pvt. John Baker
Pvt. Michael M. Baker
Pvt. William Barlow
Pvt. William H. Basden
Sgt. Michael Bebber
Sgt. Henry A. Belo
Pvt. Joseph Benfield
Pvt. Benjamin E. Bentley
Pvt. William F. Bentley
Pvt. Daniel Boan
Pvt. Abraham A. Bolick
Pvt. Alexander A. Bolick, Sr.
Pvt. Richard Cearley
Pvt. William R. Childers
Pvt. Calvin D. Costin
Pvt. Russell J. Costin
Pvt. John Davidson
Pvt. Solomon Dison
Pvt. Edward Dundoud
Pvt. William Ekard
Pvt. Enoch F. Ellis
1st Sgt. John Ellis
Pvt. Albert A. Gaultney
Cpl. John W. Grey
Pvt. Lewis Gurganus
Pvt. David S. Harrington
Pvt. Joseph Hayes
Pvt. John Hogan
Cpl. William A. Hollar
Pvt. Thomas Isenhower
Pvt. James G. James
Pvt. John G. James
Pvt. Jesse J. Jarman
Pvt. Alfred Jolly
Pvt. Amos Jones
Pvt. John B. Kerley
Nelson Kerley (rank not listed)
Pvt. Wilson Kerley
Cpl. Daniel N. Kever
Pvt. J. J. Lockamy
Pvt. Noah Logan
Cpl. William H. Manning
Pvt. Alexander C. Matheson
Pvt. Eli Matheson
Pvt. Thomas L. Maultby
Pvt. John D. McCurry
Pvt. William McDaniel
Pvt. Andrew W. McGee
Pvt. Patrick McLain
Pvt. Jerre S. Meadows
Pvt. John H. Meadows
Pvt. Washington Merritt
Pvt. Davidson Miller
Pvt. John F. Milstead
Pvt. Philetus Moore
Pvt. John Mullis
Pvt. Leroy M. Mullis
Sgt. William L. Mullis
Pvt. John Murphy
Pvt. Martin Murphy
Pvt. Henry C. Otrich
Pvt. McLane Padgett
Pvt. Samuel Padgett

Cpl. Alexander Palmer
Pvt. William J. Parleir
Pvt. J. Patchett
Pvt. Thomas J. Payne
Pvt. Benjamin Pearce
Pvt. Peter Phillips
Pvt. John W. Phipps
Pvt. Lawson Pressley
Pvt. Isaac Pressnell
Pvt. Leander C. Price
Pvt. James S. Rawls
Pvt. Michael Rawls
Sgt. Jesse Reavis

Pvt. Columbus D. Rector
Pvt. William Russell
Pvt. P. T. Sessoms
Pvt. Curtis Simpson
Pvt. Thomas Simpson, Jr.
Pvt. John W. Sloop
Pvt. John Smith
Pvt. Robert F. Smith
Pvt. Thomas A. Smith
Pvt. James J. Starnes
Pvt. Benjamin F. Sweet
G. W. Sweet (rank not listed)
Pvt. Henry Swinson

Sgt. Jesse W. Swinson
Pvt. John Swinson
Pvt. Joshua L. Taylor
Pvt. J. B. Thompson
Pvt. Wright W. Waller
Pvt. Micajah B. Willeford
Pvt. J. D. Williams
Pvt. Joseph H. Williams
Pvt. John W. Williford
Pvt. Asa Z. Winsett
Pvt. Riley Winsett

Company I

Officers

(Captains are listed in the order in which they served as commander; lieutenants are alphabetical)

Capt. Wilson H. Williams
Capt. Peter M. Briggs
1st Lt. Thomas H. Conyers

3rd Lt. Albert B. Cooke
1st Lt. Charles M. Cooke
1st Lt. Elbert B. Salmons

3rd Lt. Burton H. Winston

Noncommissioned officers and privates

Pvt. Sidney S. Abernathy
Pvt. Atlas J. Allen
Pvt. Wesley Allison
Pvt. Calvin F. Bailey
Pvt. Lemuel D. Ball
Pvt. J. B. Barefoot
Pvt. Woodley Barkan
Sgt. Shemuel C. Blackley
Pvt. Wesley P. Blanks
Pvt. Clinton Bond
Pvt. James H. Bond
Pvt. William J. Bond
Pvt. James J. Bowman
1st Sgt. Thomas W. Bragg
Sgt. Thomas H. Branch
Pvt. Samuel R. Braswell
Pvt. Joseph J. Bridges
Pvt. Gillis Brooks
Pvt. Sabret H. Card
Pvt. Benjamin Catlett
Cpl. Burgess G. Catlett
Pvt. George W. Catlett
Pvt. Sylvester C. Catlett
Pvt. William H. Cleland
Pvt. Henry H. Cooke
Pvt. George Cooley

Pvt. Allen Davis
Pvt. Redin Davis
Cpl. Alfred T. Dent
Cpl. Leonidas W. Dent
Pvt. William Dulin
Pvt. Allen R. Dunn
Pvt. Alonzo H. Dunn
Pvt. John H. Ellington
Pvt. James Elmore
Pvt. L. E. Estis
Pvt. George Evans
Pvt. Alsey Felce
Thomas Flynn (rank not listed)
Pvt. William L. Fort
Pvt. Henry S. Fuller
Pvt. William T. Fuller
Pvt. Henry S. Furman
Pvt. Albert Gay
Pvt. E. N. Gay
Pvt. Lemon Gay
Pvt. Sidney Gay
Pvt. James M. Green
Pvt. John Green
Pvt. William J. Green
Pvt. William R. Gren

Pvt. Howell Griffin
Sgt. Jesse P. Griffin
Pvt. Richard N. Griffin
Pvt. William H. Haley
Pvt. Thomas Hall
Pvt. W. T. Halsey
Pvt. William Harp
Sgt. James T. Harris
Pvt. John Harris
Pvt. William C. Harris
Pvt. Henry F. Holden
Pvt. William T. Holmes
William Hoof (rank not listed)
Pvt. Samuel R. Horne
Pvt. Jonas Hudson
Pvt. James W. Inscoe
Pvt. Minton Jones
Pvt. George Kearney
Pvt. Thomas E. Lee
Pvt. Richard Levister
Pvt. Sanford W. Lowry
Pvt. Benjamin G. Mason
Pvt. George R. May
Pvt. Nathan May
Pvt. Josiah J. Medlin

Pvt. William G. Medlin
1st Sgt. James A. Minga
Pvt. Robert Minga
Pvt. Victor Minga
Cpl. William H. Moore
Pvt. Thomas Neal
Pvt. James B. Nelson
Pvt. Berry Pearce
Pvt. Levi E. Pearce
Pvt. Minton L. Perry
Pvt. Sydney A. Perry
Silas Pettiford (Sgt. Blackley's slave)
Pvt. L. Poole
Pvt. A. V. Reeder
Pvt. Crawford W. Sandling
Pvt. Henry K. Sandling
Pvt. Edwin Scanlin
Pvt. Miles Scarborough
Sgt. Alphonso S. Sherrod
1st Sgt. William B. Smith
1st Sgt. Thomas H. Speed
Pvt. D. T. Stone
Pvt. Silas M. Stone
Pvt. William L. Synom
Pvt. Joseph W. Tucker
Pvt. John W. Walker
Pvt. Thomas Welch
Pvt. Hinton W. Wiggins
Pvt. Perry Wiggins
Pvt. Sidney Wiggins
Pvt. E. B. Williams
Pvt. Green Williams
Pvt. Josiah C. Williams
Sgt. George Winston
Pvt. Peyton D. Winston
Pvt. Rufus H. Winston
Pvt. William A. Winston
Cpl. J. W. C. Young

Company K

Officers

(Captains are listed in the order in which they served as commander; lieutenants are alphabetical)

Capt. Maurice T. Smith
Capt. Robert W. Thomas
2nd Lt. William R. M. Chandler
1st Lt. Benjamin D. Howard
3rd Lt. Reuben McD. Royster
3rd Lt. Solomon T. Satterwhite
2nd Lt. William H. B. Satterwhite
1st Lt. Wilkins Stovall
2nd Lt. William H. Webb, Jr.

Noncommissioned officers and privates

Pvt. Alexander Adcock
Pvt. Henry C. Adcock
Pvt. James W. Adcock
Pvt. William H. Adcock
Pvt. Joseph H. Allen
Pvt. Pomphret Blackwell
Pvt. William M. Blackwell
Pvt. Chesley Bowling
Pvt. John H. Boyd
Pvt. John H. Boyd
Pvt. James G. Brown
Sgt. John P. Cannady
Pvt. Edward E. Chalkley
Cpl. James H. Chandler
Pvt. John Cliborne
Pvt. Joseph H. Critcher
Pvt. George W. Currin
Pvt. Hampton Currin
Pvt. James C. Currin
Pvt. James D. Currin
Sgt. Jeremiah H. Currin
Pvt. John W. Currin
Pvt. Lotan G. W. Currin
Pvt. Marcus G. Currin
Pvt. Thomas H. Currin
Pvt. G. S. Daniel
Pvt. John W. Daniel
Pvt. Louis C. Daniel
Pvt. Richard A. Daniel
Pvt. Thomas B. Daniel
Pvt. Zachariah G. Daniel
Jessie Dean (rank not listed)
Pvt. John H. Dean
Pvt. Lorenzo D. Dean
Pvt. John Dunn
Pvt. Albert Eakes
Pvt. James K. Eakes
Pvt. Robert S. Eakes
Pvt. William S. Eakes
Pvt. John P. Elixson
Pvt. Robert B. Elixson
Pvt. John W. Fleming
Pvt. Augustus D. Frazier
Pvt. Elijah C. Frazier
Pvt. Rhodes H. Frazier
Pvt. Steven Frazier
Pvt. Samuel A. Gooch
Pvt. William H. Green
Pvt. Alex Greenway
Pvt. Robert G. Harris
Pvt. George R. Hayes
Pvt. Christopher C. Heggie
Pvt. Marion H. Hester
Pvt. James S. Hobgood
Pvt. Samuel C. Hobgood
Pvt. Amos Howard
Pvt. Joseph Howard
Pvt. Joseph T. Howard
Sgt. Samuel L. Howard
Pvt. William H. Howard
Pvt. Edward H. Jones
Pvt. R. B. Jones
Pvt. James C. Knott
Pvt. John Knott
Pvt. Robert W. Knott
Pvt. Thomas Knott
Pvt. William W. Knott
Pvt. William B. Land
Pvt. John T. Murray
Pvt. M. V. B. Murray
Pvt. Robert S. Norwood
Cpl. John D. O'Bryant
Pvt. Samuel H. O'Bryant
Pvt. Drury M. Patterson
Pvt. Peter Phillips

Pvt. William H. Phillips
Pvt. Stephen R. Puckett
Pvt. William A. Puckett
Pvt. S. Rees
Pvt. Nathaniel Riley
Pvt. Nathaniel Riley
Pvt. George W. Royster
Pvt. Robert D. Royster
Pvt. William E. Royster
Cpl. Richard H. Russell
Pvt. Robert F. Sandford
Pvt. Stephen H. Sanford
Cpl. Thomas H. Sanford
Pvt. Charles Satterwhite
Pvt. James H. Shanks
Pvt. Samuel L. Slaughter

Cpl. Charles L. Stovall
Pvt. John T. Stovall
Cpl. Joseph L. Thomas
Pvt. Maurice S. Thomas
Pvt. Washington H. Thomas
Pvt. Benjamin P. Thorp
Pvt. Peterson Thorp, Jr.
Pvt. William Vaughn
Pvt. Bennett Veazey
Cpl. William H. Veazey
Pvt. Carey W. Walker
Pvt. James N. Waller
Sgt. William P. Webb
Pvt. Alex S. West
Pvt. George S. West
Pvt. William O. West

Pvt. James K. Wilkerson
John P. Wilkerson (rank not listed)
Pvt. Joseph F. Wilkerson
Pvt. Peter Wilkerson
Pvt. Richard Wilkerson
Pvt. Robert D. Wilkerson
Shurp Wilkerson (rank not listed)
Cpl. William H. Wilkerson
Pvt. David A. Williams
Pvt. John H. Williams
Pvt. D. T. Wood
Pvt. John D. Yancey
Pvt. Brantley M. York

Records indicate that the following men served with the 55th North Carolina, but the companies in which they served are not reported:

George W. James (rank not listed)
Pvt. Albert Lackey
Pvt. William D. Shores
Pvt. Wiley Smith

Appendix C.
Officers and Enlisted Men Who Died from Disease While Serving with the Regiment

Field and staff officers

Maj. James S. Whitehead, August 1862
Capt. Albert E. Upchurch, Co. A, 1863 (POW)*
2nd Lt. Benjamin J. Blount, Co. H, 1863 (POW)

1st Lt. Elbert B. Salmons, Co. I, 1862.
2nd Lt. William H. Webb, Co. K, 1863 (POW)

NONCOMMISSIONED OFFICERS AND PRIVATES
(ARRANGED BY COMPANY)

Company A

Pvt. Duncan L. F. Adams, 1863
Pvt. George W. Arquir, 1863
Pvt. Isaac Aycock, 1864
Pvt. John T. Bardin, 1862
Pvt. Jesse R. Beaman, 1863 (POW)
Pvt. William C. Best, 1865 (POW)
Pvt. Jethro Boswell, 1863 (POW)
Pvt. Stephen Boyett, 1865 (POW)
Pvt. Henry R. Davis, 1863 (POW)
Pvt. Gabriel Farrell, 1864
Pvt. Granberry W. Ferrell, 1863
Pvt. James W. Ferrell, 1863 (POW)

Pvt. Redman Lodge, 1862
Pvt. David Lucas, 1863
Pvt. John J. Mercer, 1863 (POW)
Pvt. James J. Pate, 1862
Sgt. William H. Pearson, 1865 (POW)
Pvt. Calvin Raper, 1864 (POW)
Pvt. Jesse P. Sullivan, 1863 (POW)
Pvt. Lewis D. Tomlinson, 1863
Pvt. Willie W. Tomlinson, 1863
Pvt. Joseph Watson, 1863 (POW)
Pvt. Berry Wester, 1862
Pvt. George W. Woodard, 1864

*(POW) indicates that the soldier died while in a Union prison camp.

Officers and Enlisted Men Who Died from Disease While Serving with the Regiment

Company B

Cpl. Martin Anderson, 1862
Pvt. Calvin Benge, 1863
Pvt. Andrew W. Earp, 1863 (POW)
Sgt. Edmond J. Greer, 1864 (POW)
Pvt. John A. Milan, 1864

Pvt. Robert Moore, 1862
Pvt. James B. Pearson, 1863 (POW)
Pvt. John W. Phillips, 1862
Pvt. R. L. D. Walker, 1862
Cpl. David Williams, 1863

Company C

Pvt. Joshua C. Beam, 1864 (POW)
Sgt. John D. Boggs, 1865 (POW)
Pvt. Peter Z. Carpenter, 1865 (POW)
Pvt. John B. Carroll, 1863 (POW)
Pvt. J. D. Costner, 1863 (POW)
Pvt. John M. Costner, 1862
Pvt. John Crotts, 1863
Pvt. Joseph Crotts, 1863 (POW)
Pvt. John P. Crowder, 1864 (POW)
Pvt. Crowel A. Digh, 1863 (POW)
Pvt. Jonas Elmore, 1865 (POW)
Pvt. Ely Furgeson, 1863
Pvt. Drury W. Goodson, 1864

Pvt. David T. Griffin, 1864 (POW)
Pvt. Doctor F. Harmon, 1863 (POW)
Pvt. Eusibius S. Hendrick, 1863 (POW)
Pvt. Marcus D. Lowrance, 1862
Pvt. Peter C. Mooney, 1862
Pvt. J. F. Nowlin, 1863 (POW)
Pvt. John T. Ramsour, 1863
Cpl. George W. Sparrow, 1863
Pvt. Thomas A. Sparrow, 1864
Pvt. William R. Vandyke, 1864 (POW)
Pvt. Calvin Whistenant, 1864
Cpl. Alexander Williams, 1862
Pvt. Moses A. Wilson, 1865

Company D

Pvt. Richard C. Champion, 1863 (POW)
Pvt. M. L. Earls, 1864
Pvt. Barnett W. Eskridge, 1863
Pvt. Jonas Green, 1863
Cpl. Joseph Green, 1864
Pvt. Thomas Green, Sr., 1865 (POW)
Pvt. Willis W. Green, 1863

Pvt. Elijah Hamrick, Jr., 1863
Pvt. Jerome L. Lankford, 1863 (POW)
Pvt. Urias Ledbetter, 1864
Pvt. James W. Lovelace, 1863 (POW)
Pvt. William G. Lovelace, 1864 (POW)
Pvt. James C. Moore, 1862
Pvt. John Wylie, 1863

Company E

Pvt. Isaiah S. Boyd, 1863
Pvt. William S. Edwards, 1863 (POW)
Cpl. James L. Fleming, 1863 (POW)
Pvt. William C. Gardner, 1865 (POW)
Pvt. Richard H. Johnson, 1863
Pvt. James A. May, 1862

Pvt. John A. May, 1862
Pvt. Willie A. Pitt, 1862
Pvt. Drew Vincent, 1863
Cpl. John W. Wilson, 1865 (POW)
Pvt. Oscar Wooten, 1863 (POW)

Company F

Pvt. Daniel W. Boyles, 1863
Pvt. Zachariah Bracket, 1864
Pvt. Aaron Buff, 1864
Pvt. Adam Canipe, 1862
Pvt. Albert Canipe, 1862
Pvt. John F. Elmore, 1862
Sgt. Ephraim Gross, 1862
Pvt. Levi Hoyle, 1862
Pvt. Robert D. Hoyle, 1862
Pvt. Hiram Hudson, 1864
Pvt. Andrew J. Johnson, 1863
Pvt. Robert A. McCall, 1862
Pvt. Zachariah D. McNeilly, 1864
Pvt. John M. Mull, 1865 (POW)
Pvt. George A. Newton, 1863
Pvt. Lafayette Pope, 1862
Pvt. James Price, 1862
Pvt. Caleb Randall, 1862
Pvt. William S. Seagle, 1863 (POW)
Pvt. Robert Self, 1865 (POW)
Pvt. John Swink, 1863 (POW)
Pvt. William N. Swink, 1863 (POW)
Pvt. David W. Turner, 1863 (POW)
Pvt. James Turner, 1863
Pvt. David P. Warlick, 1862
Pvt. James Willis, 1863
Pvt. John Y. Willis, 1862
Pvt. Samuel O. Willis, 1865 (POW)
Pvt. Major Wortman, 1862

Company G

Cpl. Lemuel G. Budd, 1863 (POW)
Pvt. Joshua Goodson, 1863
Pvt. Joseph Grant, 1863
Pvt. Abner Ingram, 1863 (POW)
Cpl. Bryant Ingram, 1863 (POW)
Cpl. Young N. Lee, 1865 (POW)
Pvt. Isaac L. Martin, 1862
Pvt. James Reeves, 1863 (POW)
Pvt. Ryal W. Roberts, 1863
Pvt. Henry Sasser, 1863
Pvt. James Smith, 1863 (POW)
Sgt. John R. Smith, 1862
Pvt. William H. Stevens, 1863
Pvt. James W. Strickland, 1864 (POW)

Company H

Sgt. John J. Austin, 1863 (POW)
Pvt. Calvin D. Costin, 1862
Pvt. William Ekard, 1863
Pvt. Enoch F. Ellis, 1862
Pvt. John H. Meadows, 1862
Pvt. Benjamin Pearce, 1863 (POW)
Pvt. Lawson Pressley, 1865 (POW)
Pvt. James S. Rawls, 1863
Pvt. Columbus D. Rector, 1863 (POW)
Pvt. P. T. Sessoms, 1864 (POW)
Pvt. Benjamin F. Sweet, 1863 (POW)
Pvt. J. B. Thompson, 1862
Pvt. Wright W. Waller, 1864
Pvt. Riley Winsett, 1863

Company I

Pvt. Wesley P. Blanks, 1862
Pvt. James Bowman, 1863 (POW)
Pvt. William Card, 1863 (POW)
Pvt. Benjamin Catlett, 1863 (POW)
Pvt. George Evans, 1863 (POW)
Pvt. E. N. Gay, 1863
Pvt. Lemon Gay, 1863 (POW)
Pvt. William H. Haley, 1863 (POW)
Pvt. John Harris, 1865 (POW)
Pvt. William T. Holmes, 1863
Pvt. James W. Inscoe, 1863 (POW)
Pvt. Josiah J. Medlin, 1862

1st Sgt. James A. Minga, 1863 (POW)
Pvt. Levy E. Pearce, 1863 (POW)
Pvt. L. Miles Scarborough, 1864 (POW)

Pvt. Sidney Wiggins, 1862
Pvt. Peyton Winston, 1865 (POW)
Pvt. Rufus H. Winston, 1864 (POW)

Company K

Pvt. Alexander Adcock, 1862
Pvt. William H. Adcock, 1864
Pvt. Chesley Bowling, 1863 (POW)
Pvt. John H. Boyd, 1863 (POW)
Pvt. John Cliborne, 1864
Pvt. Robert B. Elixson, 1864 (POW)
Pvt. Steven Frazier, 1863
Pvt. R. B. Jones, 1864 (POW)

Pvt. M. V. B. Murray, 1863
Pvt. Robert D. Royster, 1863
Pvt. James H. Shanks, 1862
Cpl. Charles L. Stovall, 1863
Pvt. Bennett Veazey, 1863
Pvt. Joseph F. Wilkerson, 1863
Pvt. Brantley M. York, 1863

This list is not intended to establish that the above listed soldiers were the only members of the 55th North Carolina to die from disease during the Civil War. There are many individual records that do not explain the cause of death, and so it can be assumed that at least a portion of those soldiers died from diseases as well.

Appendix D.
Officers and Enlisted Men Who Were Killed in Action or Reported Missing in Action While Serving with the Regiment

Field and staff officers

Lt. Col. Maurice T. Smith, Gettysburg
Ens. Marlin B. Galloway, Wilderness
Capt. George A. Gilreath, Co. A, Gettysburg
1st Lt. William Hunt Townes, Co. D, Globe Tavern
2nd Lt. William S. Wilson, Co. E, Gettysburg (Missing in action and presumed dead)
1st Lt. Joseph J. Hoyle, Co. F, Globe Tavern
2nd Lt. Mordecai Lee, Co. G, Gettysburg
Capt. Edward Fletcher Satterfield, Co. H, Gettysburg

NONCOMMISSIONED OFFICERS AND PRIVATES
(ARRANGED BY COMPANY)

Company A

Pvt. Larry Barnes, Gettysburg
Pvt. James H. Bell, Wilderness
Pvt. Amos Boyett, Wilderness
Pvt. Justice Etheridge, Wilderness
Pvt. William H. Holland, Peebles' Farm
Pvt. Reddick J. Jones, Petersburg

Cpl. Joseph J. Marshbourn, Gettysburg
Pvt. Gordon Roundtree, Gettysburg
Cpl. Haywood Scott, Wilderness
Pvt. Henry Scott, Gettysburg
Pvt. Barnes Tomlinson, Wilderness
Pvt. Gary Wilson Woodard, Gettysburg

Company B

Pvt. Jesse Anderson, Globe Tavern
Pvt. Meredith Benge, Wilderness
Pvt. William O. Bryant, Gettysburg
Pvt. Thomas Grutle, Gettysburg
Sgt. Elihu Lewis, Wilderness
Pvt. John Lewis, Wilderness
Pvt. David Marlow, Gettysburg
Pvt. John McNeil, Gettysburg
Pvt. Winburn Minton, Wilderness
Pvt. William A. Pearson, Gettysburg
Cpl. Mathew Privett, Wilderness
Pvt. Leonidas St. John, Falling Waters
Pvt. James Smith, Gettysburg (MIA)
Pvt. John E. Turner, Wilderness
Sgt. Larkin Walsh, Suffolk

Company C

Pvt. A. N. Falls, Gettysburg
Pvt. John T. Gladden, Gettysburg
Pvt. Simeon C. Gold, Gettysburg
Pvt. A. E. Grigg, Appomattox
Pvt. William W. Patterson, Burgess' Mill
Pvt. Thomas Randall, Wilderness
Pvt. James P. Roach, Washington, NC
Pvt. Marcus C. Smith, Gettysburg
Pvt. Thomas Watson, Gettysburg
Pvt. Abram Weaver, Wilderness (MIA)
Pvt. Brison W. Weaver, Washington, NC
Pvt. Burrel M. White, Gettysburg (MIA)
Pvt. Henry White, Gettysburg
Pvt. James L. White, Gettysburg
Cpl. John P. Womack, Gettysburg

Company D

Pvt. Jacob E. Aderholt, Globe Tavern
Sgt. Burwell W. Blanton, Wilderness
Pvt. William J. Gibson, Wilderness
Pvt. David H. Green, Gettysburg
Pvt. Drury A. Green, Gettysburg
Pvt. Aaron B. Hamrick, Globe Tavern
Pvt. David Hamrick, Jr., Gettysburg
Pvt. Elijah Hamrick, Wilderness
Pvt. Nero W. Hamrick, Spotsylvania
Pvt. Oliver A. Hamrick, Gettysburg
Pvt. William Ledbetter, Gettysburg
Pvt. Samuel Ledford, Gettysburg
Pvt. Willis A. McKinney, Falling Waters
Pvt. Doctor T. J. M. McSwain, Gettysburg
Cpl. James M. Runyan, Gettysburg

Company E

Pvt. Henry A. Barnhill, Talley's Mill (MIA)
Pvt. Joseph Braddy, Burgess' Mill
Pvt. Alfred B. Carney, Petersburg
Sgt. James H. Cason, Globe Tavern
Pvt. John Q. Dudley, Wilderness
Pvt. James E. Edwards, Globe Tavern
Pvt. James L. Everett, Gettysburg
Pvt. Simon D. Everett, Gettysburg
Pvt. William B. Fleming, Talley's Mill
Pvt. Wyatt A. Forbes, Gettysburg
Pvt. John A Gaskins, Wilderness
Pvt. Willie Gurganus, Globe Tavern

Pvt. Henry B. Manning, Wilderness
Pvt. William B. Taylor, Gettysburg

Pvt. James Teel, Gettysburg
Pvt. John P. Woolard, Washington, NC

Company F

Pvt. William M. Boyles, Gettysburg
Pvt. Williamson F. Brackett, Gettysburg
Pvt. Jesse Cook, Talley's Mill
Pvt John D. Hudson, Petersburg
Pvt. Benjamin Hull, Spotsylvania
Pvt. David Logan, Wilderness
Pvt. Andrew McClurd, Wilderness
Pvt. Samuel McNeily, Gettysburg
Pvt. Ezra Mull, Petersburg

Pvt. William J. Self, Gettysburg
Pvt. Robert Swofford, Gettysburg (MIA)
Pvt. George White, Wilderness
Pvt. Andrew P. Williams, Cold Harbor
Pvt. William T. Williams, Wilderness
Pvt. Thomas Willis, Gettysburg
Pvt. Levi Wise, Falling Waters
Pvt. Samuel Young, Washington, NC

Company G

Pvt. Charles H. Benson, Gettysburg
Pvt. John C. Faircloth, Gettysburg
Pvt. William Faircloth, Gettysburg
Pvt. Jesse B. Garris, Wilderness
Pvt. William F. Grantham, Globe Tavern
Pvt. Stephen Hardison, Suffolk
Pvt. John Lewis, Washington, NC

Sgt. Waitman G. Martin, Wilderness
Pvt. Josiah McClenny, Gettysburg
Pvt. George W. Pearsall, Cold Harbor
Pvt. John W. Powell, Globe Tavern
Pvt. W. Henry Price, Gettysburg
Pvt. John Summerlin, Gettysburg
Pvt. John Taylor, Gettysburg

Company H

Sgt. Henry A. Belo, Wilderness
Pvt. Joseph Hayes, Wilderness
Pvt. Eli Matheson, Gettysburg
Pvt. Jerre S. Meadows, Gettysburg

Pvt. Washington Merritt, Falling Waters
Pvt. Henry C. Otrich, Gettysburg
Cpl. Alexander Palmer, Wilderness
Pvt. John Swinson, Wilderness

Company I

Pvt. Alsey Felce, Gettysburg
Pvt. Thomas Hall, Washington, NC
Pvt. William C. Harris, Gettysburg
Pvt. Benjamin G. Mason, Burgess' Mill

Pvt. George R. May, Globe Tavern
Pvt. Crawford W. Sandling, Globe Tavern
Pvt. Joseph W. Tucker, Globe Tavern
Pvt. Green Williams, Gettysburg (MIA)

Company K

Pvt. Joseph H. Critcher, Globe Tavern (MIA)
Pvt. George W. Currin, Gettysburg
Pvt. Hampton Currin, Gettysburg

Pvt. James D. Currin, Gettysburg
Pvt. Thomas H. Currin, Gettysburg
Pvt. John W. Daniel, Gettysburg (MIA)

Pvt. Alex Greenway, Gettysburg
Pvt. William H. Howard, Gettysburg
Pvt. James C. Knott, Gettysburg
Pvt. William W. Knott, Wilderness
Pvt. William B. Lamb, Gettysburg
Cpl. John D. O'Bryant, Gettysburg (MIA)
Pvt. Samuel H. O'Bryant, Gettysburg (MIA)
Pvt. Peter Phillips, Globe Tavern
Pvt. William H. Phillips, Globe Tavern
Pvt. William A. Puckett, Gettysburg
Cpl. Richard H. Russell, Petersburg
Pvt. Stephen H. Sanford, Globe Tavern
Pvt. John T. Stovall, Spotsylvania
Pvt. William Vaughn, Gettysburg
Cpl. William H. Veazey, Cold Harbor
Pvt. Richard Wilkerson, Gettysburg
Pvt. Shurp Wilkerson, Cold Harbor
Pvt. John H. Williams, Petersburg

Chapter Notes

Introduction

1. John G. Barrett, *The Civil War in North Carolina* (Chapel Hill: The University of North Carolina Press, 1963), 9–10; John C. Insoe and Gordon B. McKinney, *The Heart of Confederate Appalachia: Western North Carolina in the Civil War* (Chapel Hill and London: The University of North Carolina Press, 2000), 56–57, 62–63.

2. Insoe and McKinney, *The Heart of Confederate Appalachia*, 46–47; Barrett, *The Civil War in North Carolina*, 30.

3. William S. Powell, *North Carolina Through Four Centuries* (Chapel Hill: University of North Carolina Press, 1989), 356, 389; Ella Lonn, *Desertion During the Civil War* (New York and London: Century, 1928), 231. Of the over 23,000 deserters around 8,000 returned to service. Of the 40,275 soldiers from North Carolina who died during the war 19,673 were killed in battle and 20,602 died from disease. For a list of those killed in action while serving with the 55th see Appendix D; for a list of those who died of disease while serving with the 55th see Appendix C.

4. Barrett, *The Civil War in North Carolina,* 20–21, 28–29; Hugh Talmage Lefler and Albert R. Newsome, *North Carolina: The History of a Southern State* (Chapel Hill: University of North Carolina Press, 1973), 429–430. Among these soldiers North Carolina also provided the following list of officers—25 lieutenant colonels, 36 colonels, 27 majors, and nine generals.

5. T.H. Pearce, *They Fought: The Story of Franklin County Men in the Years 1861–1865* (Adams, 1969), 45; Emory M. Thomas, *The Confederate Nation: 1861–1865* (New York: Harper & Row, 1979), 152–53.

6. 1860 Federal Census; Guion Griffis Johnson, *Ante-Bellum North Carolina: A Social History* (Chapel Hill: University of North Carolina Press, 1937), 53, 482.

7. Louis H. Manarin and W.T. Jordan, Jr., eds., *North Carolina Troops, 1861–1865: A Roster*, 14 vols. (Raleigh, NC: Division of Archives and History, 1966–99), 13: 430–532; Compiled Military Service Records for North Carolina (Microfilm version, M270, Reels 514–518) North Carolina Department of Archives and History, Raleigh. Over 700 of the men who served with the 55th were farmers or farm laborers.

8. James M. McPherson, *For Cause and Comrades: Why Men Fought in the Civil War* (New York and Oxford: Oxford University Press, 1997), 101. For those soldiers writing of patriotic themes see: James K. Wilkerson to his sister, February 14, 1865, Wilkerson Papers, Perkins Library Manuscripts Department, Duke University, Durham, North Carolina; Joseph J Hoyle to "Mr. Editor," December 22, 1862, *Spirit of the Age*, January 5, 1863, and January 24, 1863, *Spirit of the Age*, January 26, 1863, and Joseph J. Hoyle to Mrs. Wise, July 17, 1863, Peter Mull Collection, North Carolina Department of Archives and History, Raleigh. It should be noted that McPherson does not attempt to imply that his study is definitive, but should be understood to only represent the views and beliefs of a small sampling of Civil War soldiers.

9. George W. Pearsall to his wife Sarah, June 2, 1864, George W. Pearsall Papers, North Carolina Division of Archives and History, Raleigh. Also see James K. Wilkerson to his father, October 13, 1862, Wilkerson Papers.

10. Gary W. Gallagher, ed., *Three Days at Gettysburg: Essays on Confederate and Union Leadership* (Kent, Ohio and London: The Kent State University Press, 1999), 79.

Chapter 1

1. David J. Eicher, *The Longest Night: A Military History of the Civil War* (New York: Simon & Schuster, 2001), 66.

2. Pearce, *They Fought*, 49; Manarin and Jordan, *North Carolina Troops*, 13:349; Charles M. Cooke, "Fifty-fifth Regiment," in *Histories of the Several Regiments and Battalions from North Carolina in the Great War, 1861–1865*, Walter Clark, ed. 5 vols. (Goldsboro, NC: Nash Brothers, 1901), 3:287–88. To see company names and what counties were represented by the 10 companies see Appendix B.

3. 1860 Federal Census; Compiled Military Service Records, M270, Reels 514–18; Also see Manarin and Jordan. *North Carolina Troops* 13: 430–532.

4. "Obituary of Lt. Sidney Smith Abernethy," *Confederate Veteran*, 7 (1899), 301; Joseph J. Hoyle to his wife Sarah, May 23, 1862, Joseph J. Hoyle Papers, Perkins Library Manuscripts Department, Duke University, Durham, North Carolina (hereafter referred to as Hoyle Papers); According to Confederate service records Sidney Smith Albernathy also served as a private in Company I of this regiment before being elected second lieutenant

of Company D, 30th North Carolina on September 27, 1862.

5. Manarin and Jordan, *North Carolina Troops*, 13:430; Robert K. Krick, *Lee's Colonels: A Biographical Register of the Field Officers of the Army of Northern Virginia* (Dayton, Ohio: Morningside Bookshop, 1979), 86; Stuart Wright, ed., *Memoirs of Alfred Horatio Belo: Reminiscences of a North Carolina Volunteer* (Gaithersburg, Maryland: Olde Soldier, n.d), 12, n43.

6. Wright, *Belo*, 12–13; Krick, *Lee's Colonels*, 44–45.

7. James S. Whitehead Diary, Division of Archives and History, Raleigh, North Carolina; Manarin and Jordan, *North Carolina Troops*, 430, 476.

8. Krick, *Lee's Colonels*, 70, 327; Manarin and Jordan, *North Carolina Troops*, 430; Cooke, "Fifty-fifth Regiment," 288.

9. Joseph J. Hoyle to his wife, May 17, 1862, Hoyle Papers.

10. James K. Wilkerson to his parents, June 3, 1862, James K. Wilkerson Papers, Perkins Library Manuscripts Department, Duke University, Durham, North Carolina (hereafter referred to as Wilkerson Papers); J.J. Hoyle to "Mr. Editor," June 11, 1862, *Spirit of the Age* (Raleigh), June 16, 1862.

11. Joseph J. Hoyle to his wife, May 23, 1862, Hoyle Papers; J.J. Hoyle to "Mr. Editor," June 11, 1862, *Spirit of the Age*, June 16, 1862; Compiled Military Service Records, M270, Reels 514–18.

12. Bell Irvin Wiley, *The Life of Johnny Reb: The Common Soldier of the Confederacy* (Baton Rouge: Louisiana State University Press, 1992), 244–45

13. Compiled Military Service Records, M270, Reel 517.

14. James K. Wilkerson to his parents, June 12, 1862, Wilkerson Papers.

15. Joseph J. Hoyle to his wife, May 30, 1862, Hoyle Papers.

16. Joseph J. Hoyle to his wife, May 30, 1862, and June 4, 1862, Hoyle Papers; James K. Wilkerson to his father, June 3, 1862, Wilkerson Papers.

17. James K. Wilkerson to his parents, June 28, 1862, Wilkerson Papers; Eicher, *The Longest Night*, 410–11.

18. James K. Wilkerson to his parents, June 28, 1862, Wilkerson Papers.

19. J.J. Hoyle to "Mr. Editor," July 24, 1862, *Spirit of the Age*, July 28, 1862.

20. Ezra Mull to "Dear Editor," July 24, 1862, *Spirit of the Age*, July 28, 1862.

21. James K. Wilkerson to his parents, July 9, 1862, Wilkerson Papers.

22. J.J. Hoyle to "Mr. Editor," July 24, 1862, *Spirit of the Age*, July 28, 1862.

23. Joseph J. Hoyle to his wife Sarah, July 27, and August 1, 1862, Hoyle Papers.

24. Joseph J. Hoyle to his wife Sarah, August 1, 1862, Hoyle Papers.

25. Joseph J. Hoyle to his wife Sarah, August 1, 1862, Hoyle Papers. To understand what soldiers who never participated in a battle felt about combat and how they reacted to their first experience under fire see Bell Wiley, *The Life of Johnny Reb*, 28–35.

26. John G. Barrett, *North Carolina as a Civil War Battleground, 1861–1865* (Raleigh: North Carolina Department of Cultural Resources, 1980), 15, 17.

27. James M. McPherson, *Battle Cry of Freedom: The Civil War Era* (New York: Oxford University Press, 1988), 370.

28. Barrett, *North Carolina as a Civil War Battleground*, 17; Barrett, *The Civil War in North Carolina*, 35–36.

29. Barrett, *The Civil War in North Carolina*, 66–69; James M. McPherson, *Ordeal by Fire: The Civil War and Reconstruction* (New York: University of Oxford Press, 1992), 180–81.

30. Barrett. *North Carolina as a Civil War Battlefield*, 43–44.

31. U.S. War Department, *The War of the Rebellion: A Compilation of the Official Records of the Union and Confederate Armies*, 127 vols., index, and atlas (Washington, D.C.: Government Printing Office, 1880–1901) Series 1, 9:410–13 (hereafter referred to as OR (Army), with all citations referring to series 1).

32. OR (Army), 9:414.

33. Cooke, "Fifty-fifth Regiment," 289.

34. OR (Army), 9:414–15.

35. Pearce, *They Fought*, 93; William B. Royall to "Bro. Hufham," August 11, 1862, *Biblical Recorder* (Raleigh), August 20, 1862.

36. William B. Royall to "Bro. Hufham," August 11, 1862, *Biblical Recorder*, August 20, 1862; Manarin and Jordan, eds., *North Carolina Troops*, 13:490.

37. Joseph J. Hoyle to his wife Sarah, August 14, 31, 1862, Hoyle Papers. For a list of soldiers who died from disease while serving with the 55th North Carolina see Appendix C.

38. John Kerr Connally to E. White, August 20, 1862, T.L. Clingman Papers, Southern Historical Papers, University of North Carolina, Chapel Hill; Insoe and McKinney, *The Heart of Confederate Appalachia*, 126–27. Throughout the war Wilkes County and several other western North Carolina counties remained hotbeds for Confederate deserters.

39. Joseph J. Hoyle to his wife Sarah, September 1, 1862, Hoyle Papers.

40. OR (Army), 9:452, 456.

41. OR (Army), 9:463, 478.

42. The number of soldiers from the 55th NC Regiment that were sick during this period was gathered from the Compiled Military Services Records (North Carolina), M270, Reels 514–518, and Manarin and Jordan, *North Carolina Troops*, 13:430–532.

43. Barrett, *The Civil War in North Carolina*, 133.

44. Barrett, *The Civil War in North Carolina*, 133–34.

45. J.J. Hoyle to "Mr. Editor," September 10, 1862, *Spirit of the Age*, September 15, 1862; Cooke. "Fifty-fifth Regiment," 289.

46. J.J. Hoyle to "Mr. Editor," September 10, 1862, *Spirit of the Age*, September 15, 1862; Cooke, "Fifty-fifth Regiment," 289–90.

47. Barrett, *The Civil War in North Carolina*, 134; J.J. Hoyle to "Mr. Editor," September 10, 1862, *Spirit of the Age*, September 15, 1862; Pearce, *They Fought*, 94.

48. J.J. Hoyle to "Mr. Editor," September 10, 1862, *Spirit of the Age*, September 15, 1862; OR (Army), 18:7–9.

49. OR (Army), 18:6–7; J.J. Hoyle to "Mr. Editor," September 10, 1862, *Spirit of the Age*, September 15, 1862; Cooke. "Fifty-fifth Regiment," 290.

50. U.S. War Department, *Official Records of the Union and Confederate Navies in the War of the Rebellion* (Washington D.C: Government Printing Office) 31 vol. 1894–1914, Series 1, 8:6–8; hereafter cited as OR (Navy), with all citations referring to series 1.

51. OR (Army), 18:6–10; Cooke. "Fifty-fifth Regiment," 290; OR (Navy), 8:6–8.

52. J. J. Hoyle to "Mr. Editor," September 10, 1862, *Spirit of the Age*, September 15, 1862.

53. J.J. Hoyle to "Mr. Editor," September 10, 1862, *Spirit of the Age*, September 15, 1862; OR (Army), 18:6–8.

54. This figure does not include the casualties from the *Picket*, which were 20 men killed and six wounded.

55. *OR* (Army), 18:6–7, 10.
56. J.J. Hoyle to "Mr. Editor," September 10, 1862, *Spirit of the Age*, September 15, 1862; James K. Wilkerson to his parents, September 10, 1862, Wilkerson Papers.
57. Cooke, "Fifty-fifth Regiment," 290.
58. James K. Wilkerson to his parents, September 10, 1862, and September 24, 1862, Wilkerson Papers.
59. J.J Hoyle to "Mr. Editor," September 28, 1862, *Spirit of the Age*, October 6; 1862, James K. Wilkerson to his mother, September 28, 1862, Wilkerson Papers.
60. J.J. Hoyle to "Mr. Editor," September 28, 1862, *Spirit of the Age*, October 6, 1862.
61. J. J. Hoyle to "Mr. Editor," September 28, 1862, *Spirit of the Age*, October 6, 1862.
62. J.J. Hoyle to "Mr. Editor," September 28, 1862, *Spirit of the Age*, October 6, 1862.
63. James K. Wilkerson to his parents, October 6, 1862, Wilkerson Papers.
64. James K. Wilkerson to his parents, October 6, 1862, Wilkerson Papers.

Chapter 2

1. James K. Wilkerson to his father, October 13, 1862, Wilkerson Papers; Joseph J. Hoyle to his wife Sarah, October 8, 1862, Hoyle Papers.
2. Cooke, "Fifty-fifth Regiment," 290; James K. Wilkerson to his father, October 31, 1862, Wilkerson Papers.
3. James K. Wilkerson to his father, October 31, 1862, Wilkerson Papers.
4. Joseph J. Hoyle to his wife Sarah, October 8, 1862, Hoyle Papers
5. Joseph J. Hoyle to his wife Sarah, November 7, 1862, Hoyle Papers.
6. James K. Wilkerson to his family, November 24, 1862, Wilkerson Papers; Manarin and Jordan, *North Carolina Troops*, 13:354–355; Wright, *Belo*, 13.
7. Joseph J. Hoyle to his wife Sarah, November 9, 1862, Hoyle Papers. The Federals did move numerous forces into southeastern Virginia during this time, and with Major General John Peck's arrival at Suffolk on September 22, 1862, the concerns that the Union would move on the valuable rail lines that helped sustain Lee's army increased.
8. James K. Wilkerson to hisparents, October 6, 1862, and to his mother, November 1, 1862, Wilkerson Papers.
9. James K. Wilkerson to his parents, December 16, 1862, Wilkerson Papers.
10. J.J. Hoyle to "Mr. Editor," December 22, 1862, *Spirit of the Age*, January 5, 1863.
11. Ibid.
12. Information on illnesses was gathered from the Compiled Military Service Records (North Carolina), M270, Reel 514–18, and Manarin and Jordan, *North Carolina Troops*, 430–532; Wiley, *The Life of Johnny Reb*, 56–57.
13. Joseph J. Hoyle to his wife Sarah, November 21, 1862, Hoyle Papers.
14. J.J. Hoyle to "Mr. Editor," December 22, 1862, *Spirit of the Age*, January 5, 1863.
15. Robert F. Smith to B.M. Smith, January 26, 1863, Patterson-Cavin Family Papers, Perkins Library Manuscripts Department, Duke University, Durham, North Carolina (hereafter referred to as Patterson-Cavin Papers).
16. *North Carolina Standard* (Raleigh), December 16, 1862.
17. Ibid.

18. Ella Lonn, *Desertion During the Civil War* (New York: Century, 1928), 5–7.
19. James K. Wilkerson to his father, December 16, 1862, Wilkerson Papers. The names of deserters were obtained from Manarin and Jordan, *North Carolina Troops*, 13:430–532.
20. Manarin and Jordan, *North Carolina Troops*, 13:433, 444, 453, 485, 497.
21. Ibid, 436–37.
22. Compiled Military Service Records, M270, Reel 514; James K. Wilkerson to his father, December 16, 1862, Wilkerson Papers.
23. James K. Wilkerson to his parents, January 16, 1863, Wilkerson Papers.
24. James K. Wilkerson to his father, February 8, 1863; J.J. Hoyle to "Mr. Editor," February 2, 1863, *Spirit of the Age*, February 9, 1863.
25. James K. Wilkerson to his father, February 8, 1863, Wilkerson Papers.
26. J.J. Hoyle to "Mr. Editor," February 2, 1863, *Spirit of the Age*, February 9, 1863.
27. Gray W. Woodard to his father, March 6, 1863, Hugh Buckner Johnston Collection, PC 206, Division of Archives and History, Raleigh, North Carolina. (hereafter referred to as Johnston Collection); J.J. Hoyle to "Mr. Editor," March 2, 1863, *Spirit of the Age*, March 9, 1863.
28. Manarin and Jordan, *North Carolina Troops*, 13:355.
29. *OR* (Army) 18:910; Cooke, "Fifty-fifth Regiment," 290–91.
30. Jon L. Wakelyn, *Biographical Dictionary of the Confederacy* (Westport, Connecticut: Greenwood, 1977), 163.
31. George Falls Diary, Civil War Roster Project, Document No. 909, North Carolina Division of Archives and History, Raleigh; James K. Wilkerson to his father, March 30, 1863, Wilkerson Papers; Joseph J. Hoyle to his wife Sarah, March 6, 1863, Hoyle Papers.
32. Gary W. Woodard to his father, March 6, 1863, Johnston Collection; James K. Wilkerson to his mother, March 31, 1863, Wilkerson Papers.
33. Moxley Sorrel, *Recollections of a Confederate Staff Officer*, ed. Bell Irvin Wiley (Wilmington, NC: Broadfoot, 1987), 144–45.
34. Wiley, *The Life of Johnny Reb*, 91; *OR* (Army), 25,2:687–88.
35. Wiley, *The Life of Johnny Reb*, 97. It is interesting to note that the men in the 55th North Carolina were also receiving a more plentiful daily ration than Lee's men stationed near Fredericksburg. This fact supports the contention that the southern rail system had drastically deteriorated by the end of 1862. Troops in North Carolina and southern Virginia were in closer proximity to supplies and thus able to receive larger rations.
36. J.G. Randall, *The Civil War and Reconstruction* (Boston: DC, Heath, 1937), 314–15.
37. Wright, *Belo*, 14n. The force sent to Suffolk would ultimately be reinforced to 29,000.
38. Steven A. Cormier, *The Siege of Suffolk: The Forgotten Campaign, April 11–May 4, 1863* (Lynchburg, VA: H.E. Howard, 1989), 5–6.
39. Cormier, *The Siege of Suffolk*, 6–7.
40. Douglas Southall Freeman, *Lee's Lieutenants: A Study in Command*, 3 vols. (New York: Charles Scribner's Sons, 1946), 2:468.
41. Jeffrey D. Wert, *General James Longstreet: The Confederacy's Most Controversial Soldier, A Biography* (New York: Simon & Schuster, 1993), 227–29.
42. Wert, *General James Longstreet*, 232–233; Cormier, *The Siege of Suffolk*, 16–18.
43. Cormier, *The Siege of Suffolk*, 300–301; James K.

Wilkerson to his father, March 30, 1863, Wilkerson Papers.

44. Samuel G. French, *Two Wars: An Autobiography of Gen. Samuel G. French* (Nashville, TN: Confederate Veteran, 1901), 160.

45. "Simple Story of a Soldier — V, VI," *Confederate Veteran*, 21 (1913), 22.

46. J. G. C. to "Bro Hufham," *Biblical Recorder*, March 25, 1863.

47. Peter Mull Pay, Clothing, and Description Day Book: 55th Regt., Co. F, Peter Mull Collection.

48. Ibid.

49. Wert, *General James Longstreet*, 234–35.

50. OR (Army), 18: 338, 326; Cormier, *The Siege of Suffolk*, 128, 358; French, *Autobiography*, 160.

51. OR (Army), 18: 327; I.G.C. to "Bro. Hufham," April 22, 1863, *Biblical Recorder*, May 6, 1863.

52. OR (Army), 18: 338, 997, 998; Cormier, *The Siege of Suffolk*, 145–46.

53. OR (Navy), 8:716–17, 734; Cormier, *The Siege of Suffolk*, 108, 136–40.

54. Cormier, *The Siege of Suffolk*, 146; OR (Army), 18:1001.

55. OR (Army), 18:332, 338.

56. OR (Army), 18:338.

57. Freeman, *Lee's Lieutenants*, 2:485–486; OR (Army), 18: 304.

58. OR (Army), 18:338.

59. OR (Army), 18:338–39.

60. OR (Army), 18:339.

61. OR (Army), 18:339; Cormier, *The Siege of Suffolk*, 152–53.

62. I.G.C. to "Bro. Hufham," April 22, 1863, *Biblical Recorder*, May 6, 1863.

63. J.J Hoyle to "Mr. Editor," April 27, 1863, *Spirit of the Age*, May 4, 1863; Joseph J. Hoyle to his wife Sarah, May 15, 1863, Hoyle Papers.

64. I.G.C. to "Bro. Hufham," April 22, 1863, *Biblical Recorder*, May 6, 1863.

65. OR (Army), 18: 338–340.

66. I.G.C. to "Bro. Hufham," April 22, 1863, *Biblical Recorder*, May 6, 1863. (At times his letters are signed, most likely in error, as J. G. C.)

67. OR (Army), 18:326-27, 325.

68. Weymouth T. Jordan Jr., "North Carolinians ... Must Bear the Blame: Calumny, an Affaire d'Honneur, and Expiation for the Fifty-fifth Regiment North Carolina Troops at the Siege of Suffolk, April-May 1863," *North Carolina Historical Review* (July 1994), 311.

69. French, *Autobiography*, 161; OR (Army), 18:326.

70. Jordan., "North Carolinians... Must Bear the Blame," 319–20.

71. OR (Army), 18:326–27.

72. Cormier *The Siege of Suffolk*, 156.

73. Cormier *The Siege of Suffolk*, 154–55.

74. OR (Army), 18:338.

75. OR (Army), 18:337.

76. Cormier, *The Siege of Suffolk*, 147.

77. For a summary of Connally's culpability and an explanation of how the 55th North Carolina could have effectively repulsed the Federal assault see Cormier, *The Siege of Suffolk*, 156–58.

78. Bertram Wyatt Brown, *Southern Honor: Ethics & Behavior in the Old South* (New York: Oxford University Press, 1982), 351, 360.

79. William C. Oates, *The War between the Union and the Confederacy and Its Lost Opportunities* (New York and Washington: Neale Publishing Co., 1905) 176–78.

80. Freeman, *Lee's Lieutenants*, 2:487–88.

81. Cooke, "Fifty-fifth Regiment," 292. Devout Christians could decline to participate in a duel without being perceived as cowards or without incurring public censure. See Bertram Wyatt-Brown, *Southern Honor*, 354.

82. Stuart Thurman Wright, *Historical Sketch of Person County* (Danville, VA: Womack, 1974), 107–08; Wright, *Belo*, 17.

83. Steven Stubbs, *Duty • Honor • Valor* (Philadelphia, MS: Dancing Rabbit, 2000), 373–74.

84. Oates, *The War between the Union and the Confederacy*, 177; Wright, *Historical Sketch of Person County*, 108.

85. For the North Carolina version see Cooke, "Fifty-fifth Regiment," 292, and Wright, *Belo*, 17. For the Alabama version see Oates, *The War between the Union and the Confederacy*, 177-78.

86. Cormier, *The Siege of Suffolk*, 163–164; Freeman, *Lee's Lieutenants*, 2:489–90.

87. Wright, *Historical Sketch of Person County*, 108; Wright, *Belo*, 17.

88. I.G.C. to "Bro. Hufham," April 22, 1863, *Biblical Recorder*, May 6, 1863.

89. George Fall's Diary; J.J. Hoyle to "Mr. Editor," April 27, 1863, *Spirit of the Age*, May 4, 1863.

90. OR (Army), 18:1015; Manarin and Jordan, *North Carolina Troops*, 13:368.

91. R.F. Smith to his wife and brother, April 22, 1863, Patterson-Cavin Papers.

92. J.G.C. to "Bro. Hufham," May 2, 1863, *Biblical Recorder*, May 13, 1863; R. F. Smith to his wife, April 22, 1863, Patterson-Cavin Papers.

93. James K. Wilkerson to his mother, May 10, 1863, Wilkerson Papers.

94. Stubbs, *Duty • Honor • Valor*, 376; OR. (Army), 18:299; Cormier, *The Siege of Suffolk*, 246.

95. J.G.C. to "Bro. Hufham," May 2, 1863, *Biblical Recorder*, May 13, 1863; Cormier, *The Siege of Suffolk*, 246–47.

96. Phillip Corell, ed., *History of the Naval Brigade: 99th N.Y. Volunteers, Union Coast Guard, 1861–1865* (New York: Regimental Veteran Associate., 1905), 15.

97. Cooke, "Fifty-fifth Regiment," 293; Cormier, *The Siege of Suffolk*, 247.

98. James K. Wilkerson to his father, May 10, 1863, Wilkerson Papers.

99. Wright, *Belo*, 18.

100. Cooke, "Fifty-fifth Regiment," 294.

101. James K. Wilkerson to his father, May 10, 1863, Wilkerson Papers.

102. J.G.C. to "Bro. Hufman," May 2, 1863, *Biblical Recorder*, May 13, 1863.

103. Cormier, *The Siege of Suffolk*, 252, 308–10.

104. Ibid.

105. OR (Army), 18:1038; Manarin and Jordan, *North Carolina Troops*, 13:370; Cormier, *The Siege of Suffolk*, 252.

106. Manarin and Jordan, *North Carolina Troops*, 13:370–71; Cormier, *The Siege of Suffolk*, 285.

107. Manarin and Jordan, *North Carolina Troops*, 13:370–71; Cormier, *The Siege of Suffolk*, 252.

108. Cormier, *The Suffolk Campaign*, 290–91.

109. David J. Eicher, *The Longest Night: A Military History of the Civil War* (New York: Simon & Schuster, 2001), 453; Sorrell, *Recollections of a Confederate Staff Officer*, 145–46.

110. J.G.C. to "Bro Hufham," May 2, 1863, *Biblical Recorder*, May 13, 1863.

111. J.G.C. to "Bro. Hufham," May 2, 1863, *Biblical Recorder*, May 13, 1863.

112. Manarin and Jordan, *North Carolina Troops*, 13:489, 495, 473.

Chapter 3

1. Stubbs, *Duty • Honor • Valor*, 378.
2. Stubbs, *Duty • Honor • Valor*, 379; James K. Wilkerson to his father, May 10, 1863, Wilkerson Papers; J.J. Hoyle to "Mr. Editor," May 15, 1863, *Spirit of the Age*, May 25, 1863; I.G.C. to "Bro Hufman," May, 1863, *Biblical Recorder*, June 3, 1863.
3. James K. Wilkerson to his parents, May 31, 1863, Wilkerson Papers; Manarin and Jordan, *North Carolina Troops*, 13:371.
4. Michael A. Palmer, *Lee Moves North: Robert E. Lee on the Offensive* (New York: John Wiley, 1998), 46–50.
5. Palmer, *Lee Moves North*, 51.
6. Douglas Southall Freeman, *R.E. Lee: A Biography*, 4 vols. (New York: Charles Scribner's Sons, 1935), 3:18–19.
7. Stubbs, *Duty • Honor • Valor*, 382-83; William Woods Hassler, *A. P. Hill: Lee's Forgotten General* (Richmond, VA: Garrett & Massie, 1957), 142–43.
8. Wakelyn, *Biographical Dictionary of the Confederacy*, 228. For a more in-depth study of A. P. Hill see James I. Robertson Jr., *General A. P. Hill: Confederate Warrior* (New York: Random House, 1987).
9. Freeman, *R.E. Lee*, 3:11–12; Hassler, *A. P. Hill*, 144–145.
10. Henry Heth, *The Memoirs of Henry Heth*, ed. James L. Morrison Jr. (Westport, CT: Greenwood Press, 1974), 172n; Wakelyn, *Biographical Dictionary of the Confederacy*, 227–228.
11. J. G. C. to "Bro Hufman," May, 1863, *Biblical Recorder*, June 3, 1863.
12. Joseph J. Hoyle to his wife Sarah, June 5, 1863, Hoyle Papers; Stubbs, *Duty • Honor • Valor*, 383.
13. Stubbs, *Duty • Honor • Valor*, 383-84; Joseph J. Hoyle to his wife Sarah, June 5, 1863, Hoyle Papers; James K. Wilkerson to his parents, June 10, 1863, Wilkerson Papers.
14. James K. Wilkerson to his parents, June 10, 1863, Wilkerson Papers.
15. Freeman, *R.E. Lee*, 27.
16. James K. Wilkerson to his parents, June 10, 1863, Wilkerson Papers; Robertson, *General A.P. Hill*, 199.
17. Robertson, *General A.P. Hill*, 198; Cooke, "Fifty-fifth Regiment," 295.
18. T. Harry Williams, *Lincoln and His Generals* (New York: Vintage, 1952), 252.
19. Edwin B. Coddington, *The Gettysburg Campaign: A Study in Command* (Dayton, OH: Morningside, 1979), 73; Howell G. Whitehead Diary (typescript), June 15, 1863, Civil War Roster Project, Document No. 0696, North Carolina Division of Archives and History, Raleigh (hereafter referred to as H.G. Whitehead Diary).
20. R.F. Smith to his wife, June 12, 1863, Patterson-Cavin Papers. Private Smith may have taken matters into his own hands. In December the weary private was court-martialed and sentenced to three years hard labor. The reason for his court-martial was not reported but may have been for desertion. See Manarin and Jordan, *North Carolina Troops*, 13:512.
21. J.J. Hoyle to "Mr. Editor," June 15, 1863, *Spirit of the Age*, June 29, 1863.
22. Charles Marshall, *Lee's Aide-De-Camp*. ed. Frederick Maurice (Lincoln and London: University of Nebraska Press, 2000), 195-96; Robertson, *General A.P. Hill*, 200.
23. George Falls Diary; Stubbs, *Duty • Honor • Valor*, 397; Marshall, *Aide-De-Camp*, 196.
24. Joseph J. Hoyle to his wife, Sarah, June 17, 1863, Hoyle Papers; Lieutenant General Richard S. Ewell's forces captured Winchester, Virginia, on June 15, 1863, and captured about 4,000 Federal troops, not the 12,000 claimed by Lieutenant Hoyle.
25. Joseph J. Hoyle to his wife Sarah, June 17, 1863, Hoyle Papers.
26. H.G. Whitehead Diary, June 16, 1863.
27. Edward D. Dixon Recollections (typescript), 1-2, Southern Historical Collection, Wilson Library, University of North Carolina, Chapel Hill.
28. LeGrand James Wilson, *The Confederate Soldier* (Memphis, TN: Memphis State University Press, 1973) 110–11.
29. Joseph J. Hoyle to his wife Sarah, June 17, 1863, Hoyle Papers.
30. Wilson, *The Confederate Soldier*, 112.
31. Whitehead Diary, June 17, 18, 22, 1863.
32. Wilson, *The Confederate Soldier*, 112; Stubbs, *Duty • Honor • Valor*, 399–400.
33. Stubbs, *Duty • Honor • Valor*, 400–401; H.G. Whitehead Diary, June 24, 1863; Joseph J. Hoyle to his wife Sarah, June 25, 1862, Hoyle Papers. While on the march Joseph Hoyle had little time to write his wife, he therefore sent her chronological day-by-day accounts in several letters. These letters contained multiple dates. To avoid confusion, references made to these day-by-day accounts will be dated using the dates Hoyle referred to in the letter.
34. Wilson, *The Confederate Soldier*, 113.
35. H.G. Whitehead Diary, June 27, 1863; Joseph J. Hoyle to his wife Sarah, June 1862, Hoyle Papers.
36. Joseph J. Hoyle to his wife Sarah, June 24, 1863, Hoyle Papers.
37. Ibid, June 25, 1863.
38. Wilson, *The Confederate Soldier*, 113.
39. Joseph J. Hoyle to his wife Sarah, June 29, 1863, Hoyle Papers; George Falls Diary; H.G. Whitehead Diary, June 30, 1863.
40. Clifford Dowdey, *Death of a Nation: The Confederate Army at Gettysburg* (New York: Barnes and Noble, 1998), 6–7.
41. Palmer, *Lee Moves North*, 69–71; Dowdy, *Death of a Nation*, 7.
42. Coddington, *The Gettysburg Campaign*, 121–22.
43. Williams, *Lincoln and His Generals*, 258–59.
44. Coddington, *The Gettysburg Campaign*, 154.
45. Samuel Hankins, "Simple Story of a Soldier," *Confederate Veteran*, 21 (1929), 114.
46. Hankins, "Simple Story of a Soldier," 114–15.
47. Wilson, *The Confederate Soldier*, 115.
48. Clyde N. Wilson, *Carolina Cavalier: The Life and Mind of James Johnston Pettigrew* (Athens and London: University of Georgia Press, 1990), 191–92; Dowdey, *Death of a Nation*, 77–78; Coddington, *The Gettysburg Campaign*, 232.
49. Palmer, *Lee Moves North*, 79; Robertson, *General A.P. Hill*, 205–06.
50. Warren W. Hassler. Jr., *Crisis at the Crossroads: The First Day at Gettysburg* (University, AL: University of Alabama Press, 1970), 29; Hassler, *A. P. Hill*, 153.
51. Terrence J. Winschel, "Part 1, Heavy was Their Loss: Joe Davis's Brigade at Gettysburg," No. 2 (January 1990) *The Gettysburg Magazine*, 8; John W. Busey and David G. Martin, *Regimental Strengths and Losses at Gettysburg* (Highstown, NJ: Longstreet House, 1986), 175; D. Scott Hartwig, "Guts and Good Leadership: The Action at the Railroad Cut, July 1, 1863," No. 1 (July 1989), *The Gettysburg Magazine*, 9.
52. Newel Cheney, "The Opening of the Battle on the Chambersburg Road," *Battles and Leaders of the Civil War*, ed. Robert Underwood Johnson and Clarence Clough Buel, 4 vols. (New York: Castle, 1956), 3:274n–275n; Hassler, *Crisis at the Crossroads*, 31.

53. Winschel, "Part 1, Heavy Was Their Loss," 8; Coddington, *The Gettysburg Campaign*, 266.
54. Hassler, *Crisis at the Crossroads*, 32; Winschel, "Part 1, Heavy was Their Loss," 8.
55. Wright, *Belo*, 20; Winschel, "Part 1, Heavy Was Their Loss," 10; S.A. Ashe, "The First Day at Gettysburg," *Confederate Veteran*, 38 (1930), 379.
56. A.H. Belo, "The Battle of Gettysburg," *Confederate Veteran*, 8 (1900), 165; Wright, *Belo*, 20; Winschel, "Part 1, Heavy Was Their Loss," 10.
57. Harry W. Pfanz, *Gettysburg — The First Day* (Chapel Hill & London: University of North Carolina Press, 2001), 63–64.
58. Ibid., 64.
59. Hassler, *Crisis at the Crossroads*, 42; Glenn Tucker, *Lee and Longstreet at Gettysburg* (Indianapolis: Bobbs-Merrill, 1968), 214.
60. R.L. Murray, *First on the Field: Cortland's 76th and Oswego's 147th New York State Volunteer Regiments at Gettysburg* (New York: Benedum Books, 1998), 17–18; William F. Fox, *New York at Gettysburg*, 3 vols (Albany: J.B. Lyon, 1902), 2:616.
61. *OR* (Army), 27, 1:285.
62. Hassler, *Crisis at the Crossroads*, 43–44.
63. Hartwig, "Guts and Good Leadership," 9.
64. Winschel, "Part 1, Heavy Was Their Loss." 10; Wright, *Belo*, 20.
65. Moore, *First on the Field*, 19; *OR* (Army), 27, 1:285.
66. H.G. Whitehead Diary, July 1, 1863; Clement A. Evans, ed., *Confederate Military History*, 11 vols. (Atlanta: Confederate Publishing, 1899), 4: 174–175; Gary W. Gallagher, ed, *Three Days at Gettysburg*, 82.
67. Wright, *Belo*, 20.
68. Hartwig, "Guts and Good Leadership," 9; Fox, *New York at Gettysburg*, 2:616.
69. Winschel, "Part 1, Heavy Was Their Loss," 10-11.
70. Fox, *New York at Gettysburg*, 3:992.
71. Hassler, *Crisis at the Crossroads*, 46–47; Moore, *First on the Field*, 27–30.
72. *OR* (Army), 27, 2:649.
73. Joseph Allan Frank and George A. Reaves, *"Seeing the Elephant" Raw Recruits at the Battle of Shiloh* (New York: Greenwood, 1989), 118.
74. Hartwig, "Guts and Good Leadership," 11.
75. Hartwig, "Guts and Good Leadership," 11; Wright, *Belo*, 21.
76. David L. and Audrey J. Ladd, ed., *The Bachelder Papers: Gettysburg in Their Own Words*, 3 vols. (Dayton, OH: Morningside, 1994) 1:323–324; Rufus R. Dawes, *Service with the Sixth Wisconsin Volunteers*, ed. by Alan T. Nolan (Madison: State Historical Society of Wisconsin, 1962), 167; W. B. Murphy to Dr. F. A. Dearborn, June 29, 1900, (typescript) Edward S. Bragg Papers, Wisconsin Historical Society, Madison.
77. Dawes, *Service with the Sixth Wisconsin Volunteers*, 167.
78. Cooke, "Fifty-fifth Regiment," 297–298; Belo, "The Battle of Gettysburg," *Confederate Veteran*, 165.
79. *OR* (Army), 27, 2:649. It is interesting to note that Rufus Dawes and Major Edward Pye, commander of the 95th New York, had practically the same conversation as Belo and Blair, and came to the conclusion that they had no choice but to attack into the railroad cut. For an explanation of Dawes and Pye's conversation see Lance J. Herdegen and W. J. K. Beaudot, *In the Bloody Railroad Cut at Gettysburg* (Dayton, OH: Morningside, 1990), 185–87.
80. Wright, *Belo*, 21; Hartwig, "Guts and Good Leadership," 13.
81. H.G. Whitehead Diary, July 1, 1863.
82. Dawes, *Service with the Sixth Wisconsin Volunteers*, 168.
83. H.G. Whitehead Diary, July 1, 1863.
84. Wright, *Belo*, 21.
85. Hartwig, "Guts and Good Leadership," 14; Edwin W. Beitzell, *Point Lookout Camp for Confederates* (Maryland: published by the author, 1972), 191.
86. Herdegen and Beaudot, *In the Bloody Railroad Cut at Gettysburg*, 206.
87. *OR* (Army) 27, 1:276; Cooke, "Fifty-fifth Regiment," 298.
88. Joseph J. Hoyle to his wife Sarah, July 1, 1863, Hoyle Papers.
89. Coddington, *The Gettysburg Campaign*, 280; Freeman, *Lee's Lieutenants*, 3:81.
90. Joseph J. Hoyle to his wife Sarah, July 1, 1863, Hoyle Papers.
91. *OR* (Army), 27, 2:638.
92. Freeman, *R.E. Lee*, 3:69–70.
93. Ibid.
94. Morrison, *The Memoirs of Henry Heth*, 175.
95. Freeman, *Lee's Lieutenants*, 3:87–88.
96. Winschel, "Part 1, Heavy Was Their Loss," 13.
97. Hassler, *Crisis at the Crossroads*, 119-121; *OR* (Army), 27, 2:669.
98. *OR* (Army), 27, 2:649; Coddington, *The Gettysburg Campaign*, 294.
99. Joseph J. Hoyle to his wife Sarah, July 1, 1863, Hoyle Papers.
100. Wright, *Belo*, 21; Cooke, "Fifty-fifth Regiment," 299; Letter of Jeremiah Morrison, Military Collection 71, Folder 34, North Carolina State Archives, Raleigh.
101. *OR* (Army), 27, 2:649, 637–38.
102. Joseph J. Hoyle to his wife Sarah, July 1, 1863, Hoyle Papers.
103. *OR* (Army), 27, 2:648–650.
104. Wilson, *The Confederate Soldier*, 118–19.
105. H.G. Whitehead Diary, July 1, 1863.
106. Gallagher, *Three Days at Gettysburg*, 84.
107. Ibid., 80.
108. *OR* (Army), 27, 1:638.
109. H.G. Whitehead Diary, July 1, 1863; Joseph J. Hoyle to his wife Sarah, July 1, 1863, Hoyle Papers.
110. Cooke. "Fifty-fifth Regiment," 299. Henry Heth had been wounded during the afternoon engagement on July 1 and was still unable to command his troops on July 3, 1863.
111. Stubbs, *Duty • Honor • Valor*, 416-17.
112. Joseph J. Hoyle to his wife Sarah, July 2, 1863, Hoyle Papers.
113. Freeman, *R.E. Lee*, 3:103–105; Dowdey, *Death of a Nation*, 245-46; Stephen W. Sears, *Gettysburg* (Boston and New York: Houghton Mifflin, 2003), 345–349.
114. Sears, *Gettysburg*, 349–350.
115. *OR* (Army), 27, 2:320; Carol Reardon, *Pickett's Charge in History & in Memory* (Chapel Hill and London: University of North Carolina Press, 1997), 4–5.
116. Gary W. Gallagher, ed., *Fighting for the Confederacy: The Personal Recollections of General Edward Porter Alexander* (Chapel Hill and London: University of North Carolina Press, 1989), 245–46.
117. Coddington, *The Gettysburg Campaign*, 493; Gallagher, *Fighting for the Confederacy*, 257.
118. Frank A. Haskell, *The Battle of Gettysburg* (Madison, WI: Wisconsin History Commission, 1908), 100.
119. Coddington, *The Gettysburg Campaign*, 493–94.
120. H.G. Whitehead Diary, July 3, 1863.
121. Wilson, *The Confederate Soldier*, 120.
122. *OR* (Army), 27, 2:650; Maude Morrow Brown, *The University Greys: Company A, Eleventh Mississippi*

Regiment, Army of Northern Virginia (Richmond: Garrett and Massie, 1940), 38.
123. H.G. Whitehead Diary, July 3, 1863.
124. Glenn Tucker, *High Tide at Gettysburg: The Campaign in Pennsylvania* (Indianapolis and New York: Bobbs-Merrill 1958), 354; Coddington, *The Gettysburg Campaign*, 498–99.
125. Gallagher, *Fighting for the Confederacy*, 258–59.
126. Dowdey, *Death of a Nation*, 296–299; Coddington, *The Gettysburg Campaign*, 500–501.
127. Stubbs, *Duty • Honor • Valor*, 419; Morrison, ed. *The Memoirs of Henry Heth*, 176-77.
128. Wilson, *The Most Promising Young Man of the South*, 67.
129. Haskell, *The Battle of Gettysburg*, 112–13.
130. Fox, *New York at Gettysburg*, 1:77.
131. Tucker, *High Tide at Gettysburg*, 368.
132. Cooke, "Fifty-fifth Regiment," 299.
133. H.G. Whitehead Diary, July 3, 1863.
134. Stubbs, *Duty • Honor • Valor*, 425; Tucker, *High Tide at Gettysburg*, 368.
135. OR (Army), 27, 2:651.
136. Stubbs, *Duty • Honor • Valor*, 426; OR (Army), 27, 2:651.
137. Coddington, *The Gettysburg Campaign*, 506.
138. OR (Army), 27, 1:462.
139. Stubbs, *Duty • Honor • Valor*, 420.
140. R.L. Moore, *The Redemption of the "Harper's Ferry Cowards": The Story of the 111th and 126th New York State Volunteer Regiments at Gettysburg* (Wolcott, NY, published by the author, 1994), 131.
141. OR (Army), 27, 1:454.
142. Joseph J. Hoyle to his wife Sarah, July 3, 1863, Hoyle Papers.
143. Moore, *The Redemption of the "Harper's Ferry Cowards,"* 135, 139.
144. OR (Army), 27, 2:651.
145. S.A. Ashe, "The Pettigrew-Pickett Charge," in Clark's *Regiments*, vol. 5, 145–46.
146. John Keegan, *The Face of Battle* (New York: Viking, 1976), 309. In his influential study of the nature of battle, Keegan asserts that it is the soldier's "right to flight" that makes combat bearable for most fighting men, which adds an interesting view of those who, after crossing a field of about a mile in length on July 3, 1863, realized their only chance to fight another day was to retreat.
147. Earl J. Hess, *Pickett's Charge — The Last Attack at Gettysburg* (Chapel Hill & London: University of North Carolina Press, 2001), 206, 252; Brown, *The University Greys*, 44–45.
148. Cooke, "Fifty-fifth Regiment," 299. Falls and Whitley were promoted on July 3 for their courage during battle.
149. J.A. Whitley letter, *The Galveston Daily News*, June 21, 1896.
150. Stuart, *Historical Sketch of Person County*, 111. It is argued that Captain Satterfield was killed by infantry fire and not artillery. This argument is based on the belief that there was no artillery located near the Bryan Barn; however, Osborn's battery was located near the 8th Ohio and would have been in range to fire on the charging Confederates. See John R. Satterfield, "Farthest at Gettysburg: The Story of a Confederate Captain," No. 26 (January 2002), *The Gettysburg Magazine*, 104.
151. Stuart, *Historical Sketch of Person County*, 111–12.
152. Moore, *The Redemption of the "Harper's Ferry Cowards,"* 141; T.D. Falls Recollection, *The Galveston Daily News*, June 21, 1896.
153. Stubbs, *Duty • Honor • Valor*, 431.
154. OR (Army), 27, 2:650-651.

155. OR (Army), 27, 2:333. In their study of the casualties sustained by individual regiments during the battle of Gettysburg, John W. Busey and David G. Martin asserted that the 55th had 55 soldiers killed, 143 wounded, and 22 missing — making the total 220. See Busey and Martin, *Regimental Strengths and Losses at Gettysburg* (Hightstown, NJ: Longstreet House, 1986), 290.
156. R.W. Thomas to the *Weekly State Journal*, (Raleigh, NC), August 12, 1863.
157. Cooke, "Fifty-fifth Regiment," 302.
158. Joseph J. Hoyle to his wife Sarah, July 9, 1863, Hoyle Papers.
159. Cooke, "Fifty-fifth Regiment," 302; Lieut. C. H. casualty report, the *Weekly State Journal*, August 5, 1863. Although Connally never commanded the 55th again he would return to active duty in late 1864 as the commanding officer of a brigade of Junior and Senior reserves in North Carolina. Connally commanded these troops during the Wilmington campaign of 1864–1865. It is interesting to note that among the senior reservist Connally commanded was William Pettigrew, brother of James Johnston Pettigrew. For an in-depth study of the Wilmington campaign and Connally's participation in it, see Chris E. Fonvielle Jr., *The Wilmington Campaign: Last Rays of Departing Hope* (Campbell, CA: Savas, 1997).
160. Manarin and Jordan, *North Carolina Troops*, 13:434.
161. Lieut. C. H. casualty report to the *Weekly State Journal*, August 5, 1863.
162. Those officers who were captured — Albert E. Upchurch; Company A Edward D. Dixon, Company C; Silas Dixon Randall, Company D; H. G. Whitehead, Company E; and Wilson High Williams, Company I; 1st Lieutenant George J. Bethell, Company C; 2nd Lieutenants Philip R. Elam, Company C; James H. Randall, Company D; Peter P. Mull, Company F; Benjamin J. Blount, Company H; William H. Webb, Company K; 3rd Lieutenants Thomas D. Falls, Joseph B. Cabaniss, Company D; William N. Holt, Company H; Burton H. Winston, Company I; and Reuben McDonald Royster, Company K were Confined first at Fort Delaware, Delaware and transported to Johnson's Island, Ohio. Secretary of War Edwin Stanton decreed that after June 1862 all Confederate officers were to be kept at Johnson's Island. The 13 barracks (12 for POW's and one hospital) were not built for long-term use, lacked a sturdy foundation, and were cheaply constructed. Each block or barracks contained 1 wood-burning stove, which proved insufficient in warming the men during the cold Ohio winters. As the war continued the prison, made to hold 1,000 prisoners, became overcrowded and rat infested. Needless to say the quality of life at Johnson's Island was extremely low. Although conditions were bad only two of the 55th North Carolina officers captured at Gettysburg, Albert E. UpChurch of Company A and Benjamin J. Blount of Company H, died in prison. For a summary study of Johnson's Island prison see Lonnie R. Speer, *Portals to Hell: Military Prisons of the Civil War* (Mechanicsburg, PA: Stackpole Books, 1997). To gain an understanding of how prison life affected members of the 55th see Howell G. Whitehead's Diary, North Carolina State Archives, and Edward D. Dixon Recollections at the University of North Carolina at Chapel Hill.
163. See S.A. Ashe, "The Pettigrew-Pickett Charge," in Clark's *Regiments*, Vol. 5.
164. Hess, *Pickett's Charge*, 359–61; William C. Gardner to Miss Liddy, September 16, 1863, Roach Family Papers, Joyner Library Manuscript Department, East Carolina University, Greenville, North Carolina.
165. Reardon, *Pickett's Charge in History & Memory*, 84–107; Hassler, *A. P. Hill*, 165.

166. Reardon, *Pickett's Charge in History & Memory*, 131–32, For a full understanding of North Carolina's claims see the published work *Five Points in the Record of North Carolina in the Great War of 1861–5*. (Goldsboro, N.C.: Nash Brothers, 1904). This work was compiled by several former Confederate soldiers from North Carolina as a response to Virginia judge George L. Christian's statements questioning the accuracy of North Carolina's assertion that its soldiers were "First at Bethel, Farthest at Gettysburg, Farthest at Chickamauga, and Last at Appomattox."
167. *Bachelder Papers*, 1:1002, 523.
168. *Bachelder Papers*, 2:1800.
169. Cooke, "Fifty-fifth Regiment," 299.
170. Joseph J. Hoyle to his wife Sarah, July 9, 1863, Hoyle Papers.
171. Palmer, *Lee Moves North*, 87.
172. Joseph J. Hoyle to his wife Sarah, July 4, 1863, Hoyle Papers.
173. Gerald A. Patterson, *Debris of Battle: The Wounded of Gettysburg* (Mechanicsburg, PA: Stackpole 1997), 16.
174. Marshall, *Lee's Aide-De-Camp*, 243; Craig L. Symonds, *Gettysburg: A Battlefield Atlas* (Baltimore: Nautical & Aviation Publishing Company of America, 1992), 83.
175. Wilson, *The Confederate Soldier*, 125–26.
176. H.G. Whitehead Diary, July 5, 1863; OR (Army), 27, 2:214, 280.
177. Stuart, *Belo*, 22.
178. Ibid. Major Belo spent several weeks at an officers hospital located in the old Baptist Female Seminary in Richmond. When he was well enough to travel his father took him home. Belo arrived in Salem, North Carolina, on August 7, 1863. After sufficiently recovering he returned to his regiment in January 1864.
179. Joseph J. Hoyle to his wife Sarah, July 5–8, 1863, Hoyle Papers.
180. Gary W. Gallagher, ed., *The Third Day at Gettysburg and Beyond* (Chapel Hill & London: University of North Carolina Press, 1994), 164, 170.
181. Douglas Southall Freeman, ed., *Lee's Dispatches: Unpublished Letters of General Robert E. Lee, C.S.A. to Jefferson Davis and the War Department of the Confederate States of America, 1862–65* (New York: G.P. Putnam's Sons, 1957); 103–4, Joseph J. Hoyle to his wife Sarah, July 10, 11, 1863, Hoyle Papers.
182. Joseph J. Hoyle to his wife Sarah, July 12, 1863, Hoyle Papers; Gallagher, *The Third Day at Gettysburg and Beyond*, 171–72.
183. Coddington, *The Gettysburg Campaign*, 569–70; Freeman, *Lee's Dispatches*. 105–6.
184. Morrison, *The Memoirs of Henry Heth*, 178; Joseph J. Hoyle to his wife Sarah, July 13, 1863, Hoyle Papers.
185. Stubbs, *Duty • Honor • Valor*, 444–45.
186. Morrison, *The Memoirs of Henry Heth*, 179.
187. OR (Army), 27, 1: 990.
188. Joseph J. Hoyle to his wife Sarah, July 14, 1863, Hoyle Papers.
189. Coddington, *The Gettysburg Campaign*, 571.
190. Ibid., 571–72.
191. OR (Army), 27, 2:337.
192. Manarin and Jordan, *North Carolina Troops*, 13:387.
193. OR (Army), 27, 1:929, 27, 2:609.
194. H.G. Conner, "Thomas Jefferson Hadley Obituary," *Confederate Veteran*, 25 (1933), 470; Manarin and Jordan, *North Carolina Troops*, 13:523.
195. Joseph R. Davis to Jefferson Davis, September 2, 1863, Museum of the Confederacy Library, Richmond, Virginia (hereafter cited as Davis Papers).
196. Joseph J. Hoyle to his wife Sarah, July 15, 1863, Hoyle Papers.
197. Joseph J. Hoyle to his wife Sarah, July 21, 1863, Hoyle Papers; James K. Wilkerson to his mother, July 28, 1863, Wilkerson Papers; Stubbs, *Duty • Honor • Valor*, 456–57.
198. James K. Wilkerson to his mother, July 28, 1863, Wilkerson Papers; Manarin and Jordan, *North Carolina Troops*, 13:523–524. The light of Company K is evident in the remaining nine companies as well. As mentioned in footnote 151, the loss of company commanders was staggering; however, the losses in lower-ranking officers made filling the vacant positions even more difficult. Company A, as mentioned above, lost Lieutenant. Thomas J. Hadley for several months, and in Company B Lieutenant John T. Peden was wounded in the head on July 1, 1863, but would return to duty as a captain. In Company C Lieutenant George J. Bethel was captured on July 1, 1863, and spent the remaining days of the war at Johnson's Island, Lieutenant Philip Ramseur Elam was wounded and captured on July 3, 1863, but returned for duty after being paroled on April 30, 1864, Lieutenant Thomas D. Falls, one of the three men from the 55th to make it to the stone wall, was wounded and captured on July 3, 1863, and imprisoned at Johnson's Island for the remainder of the war. In Company D. Lieutenant Joseph B. Cabaniss was captured on July 1, 1863, was sent to Johnson's Island and was paroled on March 20, 1864, Lieutenant James Harvey Randall was wounded and captured on July 5, 1863, and spent the rest of the war in Johnson's Island prison. In Company E Lieutenant James A. Hanrahan was wounded and captured on July 14, 1863, and spent the war at Johnson's Island prison. In Company F Lieutenant Peter P. Mull was wounded and captured on July 3, 1863, and was sent to Johnson's Island for the rest of the war, Lieutenant Archibald Williams was wounded on July 3, 1863, but remained on duty. In Company G the only officer wounded was Captain Walter A. Whitted, who returned for duty. In Company H. Lieutenant Benjamin J. Blount was captured on July 1, 1863, and was imprisoned in Johnson's Island prison where he died on December 15, 1863, of "erysipelas & dyptheria," Lt. William N. Holt was wounded and captured on July 3, 1863, and was paroled on September 25, 1863. In Company I Lieutenant Burton H. Winston was wounded on July 1 and was captured on July 5, 1863. Winston spent the remaining war days in prison at Johnson's Island. In Company K Lieutenant Reuben Royster was wounded and captured on July 1, 1863, and spent the war at Johnson's Island, Lieutenant Stovall, mentioned above, was wounded and captured on July 14, 1863, and was also sent to Johnson's Island, Lt. William H. Webb, Jr., was wounded and captured on July 3, 1863. Webb died in a hospital in Chester, Pennsylvania, on September 21, 1863, of "pyaemia." All of the information on wounded and captured officers was obtained from Manarin and Jordan's *North Carolina Troops*, 13:430–532. Information regarding George Bethel was also obtained from his mother's diary, Mary Jeffreys Bethell Diary, Southern Historical Collection, University of North Carolina, Chapel Hill.
199. Joseph J. Hoyle to his wife Sarah, July 20, 1863, Hoyle Papers; Manarin and Jordan, eds., *North Carolina Troops*. 13:485–86.
200. James K. Wilkerson to his mother, July 28 and 31, 1863, Wilkerson Papers.
201. Ibid.
202. Ibid., July 28, 1863.

Chapter 4

1. Lonn, *Desertion During the Civil War,* 18, 32, 231.
2. James K. Wilkerson to his father, August 11, 1863, Wilkerson Papers; Joseph J. Hoyle to his wife Sarah, July 25, 1863, Hoyle Papers. Manarin and Jordan's work indicates that only seven members of the 55th were reported as absent without leave or as deserters during this time. See. Manarin and Jordan, *North Carolina Troops,* 13:388.
3. Stubbs, *Duty • Honor • Valor,* 456.
4. Robertson, *General A.P. Hill,* 230–232. It should be noted that Hill's numbers also increased because wounded soldiers and officers were returning from the hospitals, and new recruits and conscripts helped fill the ranks. Douglas Southall Freeman asserted in his work *Lee's Lieutenants: A Study of Command,* vol. 3, 218–19, that Davis's proclamation did not have a great effect on bringing deserters back to the army.
5. E.H. Jones to his father, August 24, 1863, Henry Jones Papers, Perkins Library Manuscript Department, Duke University, Durham, North Carolina.
6. James K. Wilkerson to his father, August 11, 1863, Wilkerson Papers.
7. Bell Irvin Wiley, *The Life of Billy Yank: The Common Soldier of the Union* (Baton Rouge and London: Louisiana State University Press, 1952), 358, the version used for this work was the 1992 printing.
8. Joseph Allan Frank, *With Ballot and Bayonet: The Political Socialization of American Civil War Soldiers* (Athens, GA, and London: The University of Georgia Press, 1998), vii–viii.
9. Frank, *With Ballot and Bayonet,* 97.
10. Ibid. 97–98.
11. "Convention of N.C. Troops," *Spirit of the Age,* August 24, 1863.
12. Ibid.
13. Ibid.
14. Ibid.
15. *OR* (Army), 29, 2:624; Stubbs, *Duty • Honor • Valor,* 457.
16. Robertson, *General A.P. Hill,* 231.
17. *OR* (Army), 29, 2:681, 811.
18. Robertson. *General A.P. Hill,* 230–31; Joseph J. Hoyle to his wife Sarah, September 28, 1863, Hoyle Papers.
19. Robertson, *General A.P. Hill,* 232.
20. William C. Gardner to Miss Liddy, September 16, 1863, Roach Family Papers.
21. Joseph J. Hoyle to his wife Sarah, September 17, 1863, Hoyle Papers.
22. Freeman, *Lee's Lieutenants,* 3: 221–23.
23. Joseph J. Hoyle to his wife Sarah, September 17, 1863, Hoyle Papers.
24. Joseph J. Hoyle to his wife Sarah, September 28, 1863, Hoyle Papers.
25. McPherson, *Ordeal by Fire,* 334–336; Freeman, *Lee's Lieutenants,* 3:231.
26. For a general understanding of the opposing views historians have on why Lee chose to switch to the offensive in the fall of 1863 see Michael A. Palmer, *Lee Moves North: Robert E. Lee on the Offensive,* 96–97.
27. Robertson, *General A.P. Hill,* 233; Stubbs, *Duty • Honor • Valor,* 469–470; Palmer, *Lee Moves North,* 105.
28. Stubbs, *Duty • Honor • Valor,* 471; Robertson, *A.P. Hill,* 233–34.
29. Palmer, *Lee Moves North,* 107–108.
30. *OR* (Army), 29, 1:430; Freeman, *Lee's Lieutenants,* 3:240–41.
31. Freeman, *Lee's Lieutenants,* 3:241–42; *OR* (Army), 29, 1:430.
32. *OR* (Army), 29, 1:430; Stubbs, *Duty • Honor • Valor,* 472.
33. Palmer, *Lee Moves North,* 111–12.
34. Freeman, *Lee's Lieutenants,* 3:245–246; Palmer, *Lee Moves North,* 112–13.
35. Cooke, "Fifty-fifth Regiment," 303; Manarin and Jordan, *North Carolina Troops,* 13:389.
36. George W. Pearsall to his wife Sarah, October 15, 1863, George W. Pearsall letters, PC 832, Division of Archives and History, Raleigh, North Carolina (hereafter referred to as Pearsall Letters).
37. Joseph J. Hoyle to his wife Sarah, October, 1863, Hoyle Papers
38. Morrison, *The Memoirs of Henry Heth,* 180.
39. Stubbs, *Duty • Honor • Valor,* 476; Joseph J. Hoyle to his wife Sarah, October 27, 1863, Hoyle Papers.
40. Stubbs, *Duty • Honor • Valor,* 476; Joseph J. Hoyle to his wife Sarah, November 10, 1863, Hoyle Papers.
41. Joseph J. Hoyle to his wife Sarah, November 10, 1863, Hoyle Papers.
42. Stubbs, *Duty • Honor • Valor,* 477–79; Cooke, "Fifty-fifth Regiment," 303; George W. Woodard to his sister, December 6, 1863, Johnston Collection.
43. Stubbs, *Duty • Honor • Valor,* 477–79; Cooke, "Fifty-fifth Regiment," 303; George W. Woodard to his sister, December 6, 1863, Johnston Collection; Joseph J. Hoyle to his wife Sarah, December 4, 1863, Hoyle Papers.
44. Joseph J. Hoyle to his wife Sarah, December 4, 1863, Hoyle Papers.
45. George W. Woodard to his sister, December 6, 1863, Johnston Collection; George Falls Diary.
46. George W. Woodard to John B. Woodard, December 25, 1863, Johnston Collection.
47. Robertson, *General A.P. Hill,* 245; George W. Woodard to John B. Woodard, December 25, 1863, Johnston Collection. Although Private Woodard's comments may have reflected conditions in the 55th camp, several members of the 42nd Mississippi were able to obtain some old-fashioned eggnog, and applejack and had a merry Christmas together. Wilson, *The Confederate Soldier,* 161–63.
48. George W. Woodard to his brother, December 27, 1863, Johnston Collection; Brown, *The University Greys,* 51.
49. *OR* (Army), 29, 2:866–68.
50. Ibid.
51. William W. Hassler, ed., *One of Lee's Best Men: The Civil War Letters of General William Dorsey Pender* (Chapel Hill & London: University of North Carolina Press, 1956), 244.
52. Compiled Services Records (North Carolina), M270–514.
53. Stuart, *Belo,* 23; Cooke. "Fifty-fifth Regiment," 302. The injury Belo sustained while commanding the 55th on July 1 almost proved fatal. By the time the wounded major had reached Winchester, Virginia, Confederate surgeons felt the only chance of saving his life was to amputate his leg. Belo recovered, and was able to keep his leg.
54. Wilson, *The Confederate Soldier,* 149–50.
55. Stubbs, *Duty • Honor • Valor,* 483–84.
56. Stubbs, *Duty • Honor • Valor,* 484; Wilson, *The Confederate Soldier,* 165.
57. William M. Dame, *From Rapidan to Richmond and the Spotsylvania Campaign* (Baltimore, MD.: Green-Lucas, 1920), 59; Stuart, *Belo,* 24.
58. Stuart, *Belo,* 24.
59. George W. Pearsall to his wife, February 15, 1863, Pearsall Letters.
60. George W. Woodard to his brother, January 23, 1864, to his brother John B. Woodard, January 29, 1864,

to his sister, February 11, 1864, Report of Soldier's Death, April 1, 1864, Johnston Collection.

61. Receipt for Deceased Soldier's Effects, July 13, 1864, Johnston Collection.

62. Joseph J. Hoyle to his wife Sarah, February 22, 1864, Hoyle Papers.

63. Brown, *The University Greys*, 51.

64. Joseph J. Hoyle to his wife Sarah, February 29, 1864, Hoyle Papers. The three men being sentenced to hard labor were mentioned by last name and belonged to Company F. Bracket (most likely Zachariah Bracket, who deserted on April 19, 1863) and Hoyle (probably Joseph Hoyle, not related, deserted on June 21, 1863) were sentenced to one year hard labor and the loss of one year's pay; however, both men were ordered to stay with the 55th. Chapman (probably William Riley Chapman, who deserted on July 11, 1863) was sentenced to four years hard labor "with ball and chain."

65. Joseph J. Hoyle to his wife Sarah, January 30, 1864, Hoyle Papers.

66. Stuart, *Belo*, 23; Freeman, *Lee's Lieutenants*, 3:334. For a better understanding of what has become known as "Dahlgren's Raid" see William A. Tidwell, *Come Retribution: The Confederate Secret Service and the Assassination of Lincoln* (University Press of Mississippi, 1988, Barnes and Noble edition, 1997), 241–51,

67. Stuart, *Belo*, 23.

68. Cooke, "Fifty-fifth Regiment," 303.

69. For understanding of the arguments for and against the belief that religion was a dominant factor in combat motivation see Samuel J. Watson, "Religion and Combat Motivation in the Confederate Armies," *The Journal of Military History* 58 (January 1994), 29–55. For an how religion affected the common soldier during the Civil War see Steven E. Woodworth, *While God Is Marching On: The Religious World of Civil War Soldiers* (Lawrence: University Press of Kansas, 2001).

70. Joseph J. Hoyle to his wife Sarah, May 30, 1862, Hoyle Papers.

71. Stubbs, *Duty • Honor • Valor*, 483; Brown, *The University Greys*, 51.

72. Wiley, *The Life of Johnny Reb*, 180–182; Watson, "Religion and Combat Motivation in the Confederate Armies," 51–52; Woodworth, *While God Is Marching On*, 230.

73. J. Henry Smith to "Dear Brother:", March 7, 1864, *North Carolina Presbyterian* (Fayetteville), March 16, 1864.

74. Joseph J. Hoyle to his wife Sarah, March 20, 1864, Hoyle Papers.

75. Ibid., February 22, 1864.

76. Woodworth, *While God Is Marching On*, 234–36.

77. J. Henry Smith to "Dear Brother," March 7, 1864, *North Carolina Presbyterian*, March 16, 1864; Wilson, *The Confederate Soldier*, 145–46.

78. Wilson, *The Confederate Soldier*, 147–48.

79. Joseph J. Hoyle to his wife Sarah, February 22, 1864, Hoyle Papers.

80. Stuart, *Belo*, 23.

81. Randall M. Miller, Harry S. Stout, and Charles Reagan Wilson, eds., *Religion and the American Civil War* (New York: Oxford University Press, 1998), 307–08.

82. Reid Mitchell asserts in his essay *Christian Soldiers? Perfecting the Confederacy* that J. William Jones and William W. Bennett, among others, attempt to portray Southern soldiers as more Christian and therefore more in line with God. See Miller, Stout, and Wilson, *Religion and the American Civil War*, 297–308.

83. Joseph J. Hoyle to his wife Sarah, May 17, 1862, Hoyle Papers.

84. Ezra Mull to "Dear Editor," July 24, 1862, *Spirit of the Age*, July 28, 1862; William Royall to "Bro Hufham," August 11, 1862, *Biblical Recorder*, August 20, 1862.

85. Joseph J. Hoyle to his wife Sarah, September 12, 1862, July 3, 1863, Hoyle Papers.

86. George W. Pearsall to his wife, October 15, 1863, Pearsall Letters.

Chapter 5

1. Brooks D. Simpson, *Ulysses S. Grant: Triumph over Adversity, 1822–1865* (Boston and New York: Houghton Mifflin, 2000), 257, 263–64.

2. Mary Drake McFeely and William S. McFeely, eds., *Ulysses S. Grant: Memoirs and Selected Letters* (New York: Library of America, 1990), 477–78.

3. McPherson, *Battle Cry of Freedom*, 722.

4. Ibid.; Simpson, *Ulysses S. Grant*, 268–270.

5. Joseph J. Hoyle to his wife, March 7, 1864, Hoyle Papers; Freeman, ed. *Lee's Dispatches*, 153.

6. Joseph J. Hoyle to his wife Sarah, April 17, 1864, Hoyle Papers.

7. Dame, *From the Rapidan to Richmond and the Spotsylvania Campaign,* 62; Joseph J. Hoyle to his wife Sarah, April 17, 1864, Hoyle Papers.

8. Joseph J. Hoyle to his wife Sarah, April 17, 1864, Hoyle Papers; James K. Wilkerson to his parents, April 28, 1864, Wilkerson Papers.

9. James K. Wilkerson to his parents, April 28, 1864, Wilkerson Papers.

10. Joseph J. Hoyle to his wife Sarah, April 20, 1864, Hoyle Papers; James K. Wilkerson to his parents, April 28, 1864, Wilkerson Papers; OR (Army), 32, 3:672. President Davis had requested that these two units, which were at that time under the command of Lieutenant General Leonidas Polk, and serving in the West, be sent to his nephew's brigade. Colonel A. E. Reynolds commanded the 26th Mississippi and Lieutenant Colonel G. H. Forney commanded the first Confederate Battalion, which was made up of men from Alabama.

11. Joseph J. Hoyle to his wife Sarah, April 20, 1864, Hoyle Papers.

12. Ibid., April 17, 1864.

13. Ibid., April 24, 1864.

14. Ibid., May 1, 1864.

15. Robertson, *General A.P. Hill*, 251; Freeman, *Lee's Lieutenants*, 3:342–45; Simpson, *Ulysses S. Grant*, 287–88.

16. Gordon C Rhea, *The Battle of the Wilderness: May 5–6, 1864* (Baton Rouge and London: Louisiana State University Press, 1994), 60, 63.

17. Rhea, *The Battle of the Wilderness*, 25–27.

18. Simpson, *Ulysses S. Grant*, 288–290; Rhea, *The Battle of the Wilderness*, 55.

19. McFeely and McFeely, *Ulysses S. Grant: Memoirs and Selected Letters,* 516–18.

20. Noah Andre Trudeau, " A Frightful and Frightening Place," *Civil War Times Illustrated* (May 1999), 44–45.

21. Gary W. Gallagher, ed., *The Wilderness Campaign* (Chapel Hill & London: University of North Carolina Press, 1997), 143–45.

22. Rhea, *The Battle of the Wilderness*, 22–24, 79; Robertson, *General A.P. Hill*, 251.

23. Rhea, *The Battle of the Wilderness*, 80.

24. Freeman, *Lee's Lieutenants*, 3:346–48; Trudeau, "A Frightful and Frightening Place," 45.

25. Stubbs, *Duty • Honor • Valor*, 510–511; Robertson, *General AP. Hill*, 251–52; Rhea, *The Battle of the Wilderness*, 85.

26. Trudeau, "A Frightful and Frightening Place," 46–47; Stubbs, *Duty • Honor • Valor*, 512.

27. Stubbs, *Duty • Honor • Valor*, 513–14; Thomas Buford, Thomas H. Chilton, and Ben Price Jr., *The Lamar Rifles: A History of Company G, Eleventh Mississippi Regiment, C.S.A* (Roanoke, VA: Stone, 1902), 60; Morrison, *The Memoirs of Henry Heth*. 182.
28. John Michael Priest, *Nowhere to Run: The Wilderness, May 4th & 5th, 1864* (Shippensburg, PA: White Mane, 1995), 147–48; Cooke, "Fifty-fifth Regiment," 304.
29. Cooke, "Fifty-fifth Regiment," 304.
30. "Maj. A. M. O'Neal to his wife," *Confederate Veteran*, 18 (1910), 87; In his study of the Wilderness, John Michael Priest asserts that O'Neal was a captain serving with the 42nd Mississippi, however, the 42nd's rosters do not list any officer or soldier named O'Neal, or O'Neil, which is how Priest has it spelled in his work. Priest, *Nowhere to Run*, 147–148.
31. Rhea, *The Battle of the Wilderness*, 200–1; Robert Hunt Rhodes, ed., *All for the Union: The Civil War Diary and Letters of Elisha Hunt Rhodes* (New York: Orion Books, 1991), 143–44.
32. Stubbs, *Duty • Honor • Valor*, 516; Cooke, "Fifty-fifth Regiment," 304.
33. Freeman, *Lee's Lieutenants*, 3:352–53; Rhea, *The Battle of the Wilderness*, 204–6.
34. Rhea, *The Battle of the Wilderness*, 223–29; Cooke, "Fifty-fifth Regiment," 304.
35. Cooke, "Fifty-fifth Regiment," 304; Buford, Chilton, and Price, *Lamar Rifles*, 60; George W. Pearsall to his wife, May 7, 1864, May 11, 1864, Pearsall Letters.
36. Cooke, "Fifty-fifth Regiment," 304–5; Brown, *The University Greys*, 53; Rhea, *The Battle of the Wilderness*, 229.
37. Cooke, "Fifty-fifth Regiment," 305.
38. Rhea, *The Battle of the Wilderness*, 229.
39. Joseph J. Hoyle to his wife Sarah, May 7, 1864, Hoyle Papers; George W. Pearsall to his wife, May 7, 1864, Pearsall Letters; Cooke, "Fifty-fifth Regiment," 305; Stuart, *Belo*, 24–25. The losses suffered by the Federals in front of the 55th's line were also heavy. Cooke stated that 157 Union soldiers lay dead before their line.
40. Rhea, *The Battle of the Wilderness*, 241–42.
41. Freeman, *Lee's Lieutenants*, 3:353.
42. Rhodes, *All for the Union*, 144.
43. Noah Andre Trudeau, *Bloody Roads South: The Wilderness to Cold Harbor, May–June 1864* (Boston: Little, Brown and Company, 1989), 76–77; Morrison, *The Memoirs of Henry Heth*, 183–84.
44. Rhea, *The Battle of the Wilderness*, 272–73; Trudeau, *Bloody Roads South*, 77–78.
45. Priest, *Nowhere to Run*, 225.
46. Simpson, *Ulysses S. Grant*, 296–97.
47. Freeman, *Lee's Lieutenants*, 3:355; McPherson, *Ordeal by Fire*, 416; *OR* (Army), 36, 1:321, 677.
48. Cooke, "Fifty-fifth Regiment," 305; Buford, Chilton, and Price, *The Lamar Rifles*, 61; Stubbs, *Duty • Honor • Valor*, 520–21.
49. Stuart, *Belo*, 25; Stubbs, *Duty • Honor • Valor*, 520; Joseph J. Hoyle to his wife Sarah, May 7, 1864, Hoyle Papers; John Michael Priest, *Victory Without Triumph: The Wilderness, May 6th & 7th 1864*, (Shippensburg, PA: White Mane, 1996), 36.
50. *OR* (Army), 36, 1:1055; Buford, Chilton, and Price, *The Lamar Rifles*, 61.
51. George W. Pearsall to his wife, May 11, 1864, Pearsall Letters.
52. Priest, *Victory Without Triumph*, 139.
53. C.S. Venable, "The Campaign from the Wilderness to Petersburg," *Southern Historical Society Papers* 14 (1886), 526.
54. Rhea, *The Battle of the Wilderness*, 370, 374–75.
55. Ibid., 389–90, 392–96.
56. Stubbs, *Duty • Honor • Valor*, 532-34; Rhea, *The Battle of the Wilderness*, 398–401.
57. McFeely and McFeely, *Ulysses S. Grant: Memoirs and Letters*, 534; Thomas Livermore, *Numbers and Losses in the Civil War in America, 1861-1865* (Boston: Houghton Mifflin, 1901), 110–11.
58. Rhea, *The Battle of the Wilderness*, 440; McPherson, *Ordeal by Fire*, 416.
59. Henry Heth, Official Report, May 6, 1864, Henry Heth Papers, Museum of the Confederacy Library, Richmond, Virginia; Manarin and Jordan, *North Carolina Troops*, 13:401.
60. *OR* (Army), 11, 2:992.
61. Ibid.
62. *OR* (Army), 36, 1:1100. The spelling of William Fleming was changed to correlate with Confederate records, as well as Andrew Mcgee's middle initial. Records indicate Charles Stovall of Company K died in July 1863, which would make his addition to the Roll of Honor for the Wilderness impossible.
63. McFeely and McFeely, *Ulysses S. Grant: Memoirs and Letters*, 536–40; J. Tracy Power, *Lee's Miserables: Life in the Army of Northern Virginia from the Wilderness to Appomattox* (Chapel Hill and London: University of North Carolina Press, 1998), 24–25.
64. Gordon C. Rhea, *The Battles for Spotsylvania Court House and the Road to Yellow Tavern, May 7–12, 1864* (Baton Rouge and London: Louisiana State University Press, 1997), 10–11, 25.
65. McPherson, *Ordeal by Fire*, 418; Rhea, *The Battles for Spotsylvania Court House*, 58–59.
66. Robertson, *General A.P. Hill*, 268; William D. Matter, *If It Takes All Summer: The Battle of Spotsylvania* (Chapel Hill & London: University of North Carolina Press, 1988), 75.
67. Buford, Chilton, and Price, *The Lamar Rifles*, 63; Robertson, *General A.P. Hill*, 268–69; Stubbs, *Duty • Honor • Valor*, 544–45.
68. Stubbs, *Duty • Honor • Valor*, 545–46; Trudeau, *Bloody Roads South*, 144–47; Matter, *If It Takes All Summer*, 102.
69. Cooke, "Fifty-fifth Regiment," 305; Stuart, *Belo*, 25–26.
70. Rhea, *The Battles for Spotsylvania Court House*, 123.
71. Ibid.
72. Stubbs, *Duty • Honor • Valor*, 546; Rhea, *The Battles for Spotsylvania Court House*, 125–26; Trudeau, *Bloody Roads South*, 148–49; Matter, *If It Takes All Summer*, 144–45.
73. Buford, Chilton, and Price, *The Lamar Rifles*, 62–63; Freeman, *Lee's Lieutenants*, 3:392; Rhea, *The Battles for Spotsylvania Court House*, 126–27.
74. Rhea, *The Battles for Spotsylvania Court House*, 136–37.
75. Cooke, "Fifty-fifth Regiment," 305; Rhea, *The Battles for Spotsylvania Court House*, 136.
76. Stuart, *Belo*, 26.
77. Jubal Anderson Early, *Autobiographical Sketch and Narrative of the War Between the States* (Philadelphia: J.B Lippincott, 1912), 354.
78. George W. Pearsall to his wife Sarah, May 11, 1864, Pearsall Letters; Joseph J. Hoyle to his wife, May 11, 1864, Hoyle Papers.
79. Francis A. Walker, *History of the Second Army Corps in the Army of the Potomac* (New York: Scribner, 1891), 454–55.
80. Cooke, "Fifty-fifth Regiment," 305–06.
81. Walker, *History of the Second Army Corps in the Army of the Potomac*, 451.
82. *OR* (Army), 36, 1:332–33.

83. Rhea, *The Battles for Spotsylvania Court House*, 144–149, 177–81; Stubbs, *Duty • Honor • Valor*, 550; Matter, *If It Takes All Summer*, 158.
84. Rhea, *The Battles for Spotsylvania Court House*, 208–11; Power, *Lee's Miserables*, 57.
85. Stubbs, *Duty • Honor • Valor*, 550–51; Joseph J. Hoyle to his wife Sarah, May 11, 1864, Hoyle Papers; Rhodes, *All for the Union*, 150.
86. George W. Pearsall to his wife, May 11, 1864, Pearsall Letters.
87. Freeman, *Lee's Lieutenants*, 3:398.
88. Robertson, *General A.P. Hill*, 269–70.
89. Stubbs, *Duty • Honor • Valor*, 551–52.
90. Simpson, *Ulysses S. Grant*, 310–11; Rhea, *The Battles for Spotsylvania Court House*, 257–59.
91. Freeman, *Lee's Lieutenants*, 3:407; Stubbs, *Duty • Honor • Valor*, 552–53; Matter, *If It Takes All Summer*, 208–10.
92. Rhea, *The Battles for Spotsylvania Court House*, 294; Matter, *If It Takes All Summer*, 233.
93. Stubbs, *Duty • Honor • Valor*, 554; Rhea, *The Battles for Spotsylvania Court House*, 296–98.
94. Freeman, *Lee's Lieutenants*, 3:408–9; Matter, *If It takes All Summer*, 259–60.
95. Cooke, "Fifty-fifth Regiment," 306; George W. Pearsall to his wife, May 15, 1864, Pearsall Letters; Joseph J. Hoyle to his wife Sarah, May 19, 1864, Hoyle Papers; Morrison, *The Memoirs of Henry Heth*, 187–189; Buford, Chilton, and Price, *The Lamar Rifles*, 65.
96. Gordon C. Rhea, *To the North Anna River: Grant and Lee, May 13–25, 1864* (Baton Rouge: Louisiana State University Press, 2000), 22, 24–25.
97. Rhea, *To the North Anna River*, 66–67, 93–94.
98. Simpson, *Ulysses S. Grant*, 313–14; Stubbs, *Duty • Honor • Valor*, 561–562; Rhea, *To the North Anna River*, 140–41.
99. George W. Pearsall to his wife Sarah, May 18, 1864, Pearsall Letters; Joseph J. Hoyle to his wife, May 19, 1864, Hoyle Papers.
100. Rhea, *To the North Anna River*, 167, 185; Joseph J. Hoyle to his wife Sarah, May 20, 1864, Hoyle Papers.
101. Stubbs, *Duty • Honor • Valor*, 562; Rhea, *To the North Anna River*, 212, 216–17.
102. Stubbs, *Duty • Honor • Valor*, 562–63; George W. Pearsall to his wife, May 23, 1864, Pearsall Letters; Joseph J. Hoyle to his wife Sarah, May 25, 1864, Hoyle Papers.
103. Joseph J. Hoyle to his wife Sarah, May 25, 1864, Hoyle Papers.
104. Rhea, *To the North Anna River*, 326, 367; George W. Pearsall to his wife, May 29, 1864, Pearsall Letters.
105. Joseph J. Hoyle to his wife Sarah, May 29, 1864, Hoyle Papers.
106. Charles R. Jones, "Historical Sketch of the 55th North Carolina," *Our Living and Our Dead*, April 22, 1874; George W. Pearsall to his mother, May 30, 1864, and to his wife May 29, 1864, Pearsall Letters.
107. Stubbs, *Duty • Honor • Valor*, 566–67; George W. Pearsall to his wife, May 29, 1864, Pearsall Letters; Ernest B. Furgurson, *Not War But Murder: Cold Harbor 1864* (New York: Alfred A. Knopf, 2000), 53–54.
108. Freeman, *Lee's Lieutenants*, 3:501–3.
109. Ibid., 3:502; Gallagher, *Fighting for the Confederacy*, 397.
110. Furgurson, *Not War But Murder*, 64, 77–78.
111. Trudeau, *Bloody Roads South*, 262–63; Furgurson, *Not War But Murder*, 81–82.
112. Freeman, *Lee's Lieutenants*, 3:506; Stubbs, *Duty • Honor • Valor*, 568–69.
113. Trudeau, *Bloody Roads South*, 268–70; Freeman, *Lee's Lieutenants*, 3:507–8.
114. Charles R. Jones, "Historical Sketch of the 55th North Carolina," *Our Living and Our Dead*, April 22, 1874; Manarin and Jordan, *North Carolina Troops*, 13:406.
115. Simpson, *Ulysses S. Grant*, 322–24.
116. Stubbs, *Duty • Honor • Valor*, 570–71.
117. Morrison, *The Memoirs of Henry Heth*, 188–89; Cooke, "Fifty-fifth Regiment," 306; Gordon C. Rhea, *Cold Harbor: Grant and Lee, May 26–June 3 1864* (Baton Rouge: Louisiana State University Press, 2002), 301.
118. Heth's Report, December 7, 1864, Heth Papers.
119. Joseph J. Hoyle to his wife Sarah, June 4, 1864, Hoyle Papers.
120. James K. Wilkerson to his mother, June 5, 1864, Wilkerson Papers.
121. Wright, *Belo*, 27
122. Cooke, "Fifty-fifth Regiment," 306.
123. Wright, *Belo*, 27. Colonel Belo would never serve with the 55th again; however, his service to his country did not end at Cold Harbor. After recovering he later tried to continue the struggle for Southern independence by traveling west to join General Kirby Smith's army, which was west of the Mississippi River. Before he arrived, however, Smith's forces had also surrendered.
124. George W. Pearsall to his wife, June 2, 1864, Pearsall Letters.
125. John W. Powell to Sarah Pearsall, June 5, 1864, Pearsall Letters. Several revealing facts about soldiering in the Army of Northern Virginia can be understood by reading Powell's letter to Sarah Pearsall. First, George's personal belongings shed light on what some soldiers carried with them. Private Pearsall had one pocketknife, a pocketbook with several steel pens, several letters from home, and one almanac. Powell informed Sarah that they knew where George was buried if she wanted to move his body. However, at the time the letter was sent the Federals were holding the ground in which the young private had been buried. Another sad commentary expressed by this letter is that it appears Sarah had to pay for the postage because Powell had no postage stamps.
126. Stubbs, *Duty • Honor • Valor*, 573–74; Simpson, *Ulysses S. Grant*, 325–26.
127. Joseph J. Hoyle to his wife Sarah, June 4, 1864, Hoyle Papers.
128. Joseph J. Hoyle to his wife Sarah, June 4, 1864, Hoyle Papers; James K. Wilkerson to his mother, June 5, 1864, Wilkerson Papers.
129. Simpson, *Ulysses S. Grant*, 328–29; Wilson, *The Confederate Soldier*, 179.
130. Noah Andre Trudeau, *The Last Citadel: Petersburg, Virginia, June 1864–April 1865* (Boston: Little, Brown, 1991), 14–19; David C. Love, *The Prairie Guards: A History of Their Organization, Their Heroism, Their Battles and Their Triumphs* (Starkville, MS: n.p., 1890), 17.
131. James K. Wilkerson to his sister, June 16, 1864, Wilkerson Papers.
132. Trudeau, *The Last Citadel*, 22–24; Simpson, *Ulysses. S. Grant*, 336–38.
133. Stubbs, *Duty • Honor • Valor*, 582; Joseph J. Hoyle to his wife Sarah, June 24, 1864, Hoyle Papers.
134. Joseph J. Hoyle to his wife Sarah, June 21, 1864, and June 24, 1864, Hoyle Papers; James K. Wilkerson to his mother, July 17, 1864, Wilkerson Papers.

Chapter 6

1. Joseph J. Hoyle to his wife Sarah, July 11, 1864, Hoyle Papers.
2. Ibid., July 5, 1864.
3. Freeman, *R.E. Lee*, 3:463.

4. Wiley, *The Life of Johnny Reb*, 79; Freeman, *R.E. Lee*, 3:463–64.
5. Brown, *The University Greys*, 55–56.
6. Cooke, "Fifty-fifth Regiment," 307.
7. Ibid., 309.
8. James K. Wilkerson to his mother, July 17, 1864, Wilkerson Papers.
9. Samuel P. Lockhart to his sister, July 18, 1864, Hugh Conway Browning Papers, Perkins Library Manuscript Department, Duke University, Durham, North Carolina.
10. James K. Wilkerson to his mother, August 8, 1864, Wilkerson Papers.
11. Barrett, *The Civil War in North Carolina*, 233–35.
12. Joseph J. Hoyle to his wife Sarah, July 5, 1864, Hoyle Papers.
13. Freeman, *R.E. Lee*, 3:465; McFeely and McFeely, *Ulysses S. Grant*, 608.
14. Cooke, "Fifty-fifth Regiment," 307–8.
15. OR (Army), 40, 1:557, 787.
16. Cooke, "Fifty-fifth Regiment," 308.
17. Power, *Lee's Miserables*, 179–80.
18. Cooke "Fifty-fifth Regiment," 308–09.
19. Ibid., 309.
20. James K. Wilkerson to his mother, July 20, 1864, Wilkerson Papers.
21. Power, *Lee's Miserables*, 180; James K. Wilkerson to his mother, August 8, 1864, Wilkerson Papers.
22. Joseph J. Hoyle to his wife Sarah, August 8, 1864, Hoyle Papers.
23. James K. Wilkerson to his family, August 23, 1864, Wilkerson Papers; Power, *Lee's Miserables*, 180–81.
24. OR (Army), 42, 2:1273.
25. Ibid., 1278.
26. Ibid., 1218.
27. McFeely and McFeely, *Ulysses S. Grant*, 618–19. During this time Sherman requested reinforcements to assist his campaign in the West and possible riots and insurrections over the draft in the North forced Washington to inform Grant that he may be asked to send troops north to suppress any violent eruptions.
28. McFeely and McFeely, *Ulysses S. Grant*, 619; Freeman, *Lee's Lieutenants*, 3:588–89; OR (Army), 42, 1:858; Trudeau, *The Last Citadel*, 161.
29. Cooke, "Fifty-fifth Regiment," 309; James K. Wilkerson to his family, August 23, 1864, Wilkerson Papers.
30. Stubbs, *Duty • Honor • Valor*, 591; Cooke, "Fifty-fifth Regiment," 309.
31. Stubbs, *Duty • Honor • Valor*, 591; OR 42, 1: 471–72.
32. Cooke; "Fifty-fifth Regiment," 309–10; OR (Army), 42, 1:471–72.
33. James K. Wilkerson to his family, August 23, 1864, Wilkerson Papers.
34. Joseph R. Davis to Jefferson Davis, August 19, 1864, Davis Papers.
35. Cooke, "Fifty-fifth Regiment," 310; Manarin and Jordan, *North Carolina Troops*, 13:485.
36. Orlando B. Wilcox, "Actions on the Weldon Railroad," *Battles and Leaders of the Civil War*, 4:568–69; OR (Army), 42, 1:483–84.
37. Cooke, "Fifty-fifth Regiment," 310.
38. OR (Army), 42, 1:489, 849.
39. Robertson, *General A.P. Hill*, 297.
40. James K. Wilkerson to his family, August 23, 1864, Wilkerson Papers.
41. Robertson, *General A.P. Hill*, 297; Trudeau, *The Last Citadel*, 169.
42. James K. Wilkerson to his family, August 23, 1864, Wilkerson Papers. Lt. Thomas J. Hadley and Private Pomphret Blackwell were both captured on August 20, 1864.
43. Trudeau, *The Last Citadel*, 171; Cooke, "Fifty-fifth Regiment," 310; Stubbs, *Duty • Honor •Valor*, 593–94.
44. Stubbs, *Duty • Honor • Valor*, 592–94; Manarin and Jordan, *North Carolina Troops*, 13:413.
45. James K. Wilkerson to his family, August 23, 1864, Wilkerson Papers. For an understanding of why the Confederate army chose to implement disastrous frontal assaults throughout the war see Grady McWhiney and Perry D. Jamieson, *Attack and Die: Civil War Military Tactics and the Southern Heritage* (University, AL: University of Alabama Press, 1982).
46. According to Manarin and Jordan either Private Abraham Anderson Bolick or Private Alexander A. Bolick Sr. was named on the Roll of Honor for gallantry at Globe Tavern. Manarin and Jordan, *North Carolina Troops*, 13:507.
47. James K. Wilkerson to his sister Sarah, August 29, 1864, Wilkerson Papers.
48. David T. Toler poem, David T. Toler Collection, North Carolina Department of Archives and History, Raleigh.
49. Power, *Lee's Miserables*, 181; James K. Wilkerson to his sister Sarah, August 29, 1864, and to his mother, August 30, 1864, Wilkerson Papers.
50. James K. Wilkerson to his sister Sarah, August 29, 1864, Wilkerson Papers; OR (Army), 42, 3:177, 181. Early in October several members from Davis's brigade, including one soldier from the 55th, slipped out of their trenches and fled to the Union line. Both reported to be conscripts.
51. McFeely and McFeely, *Ulysses S. Grant*, 625–27; Robertson, *General A.P. Hill*, 303–4.
52. Trudeau, *The Last Citadel*, 212–14; Power, *Lee's Miserables*, 206.
53. Manarin and Jordan, *North Carolina Troops*, 13:415; Robertson, *General A.P. Hill*, 304; OR (Army), 42, 1:852; Richard J. Sommers, *Richmond Redeemed: The Siege at Petersburg* (Garden City, NY: Doubleday, 1981), 393–95.
54. James K. Wilkerson to his father, October, 5, 1864, Wilkerson Papers.
55. Cooke, "Fifty-fifth Regiment," 310; Robertson, *A.P. Hill*, 304–5.
56. Morrison, *The Memoirs of Henry Heth*, 192; James K. Wilkerson to his mother, October 22, 1864, to his parents, October 21, 1864, and to his mother, October 5, 1864, Wilkerson Papers.
57. McFeely and McFeely, *Ulysses S. Grant*, 630; Robertson, *General A.P. Hill*, 306–7.
58. Heth's Report, February 1, 1865, Heth Papers; *A.P. Hill*, 306–7; James K. Wilkerson to his parents, October 30, 1864, Wilkerson Papers.
59. Heth's Report, February 1, 1865, Heth Papers; OR (Army), 42, 1:297.
60. Cooke, "Fifty-fifth Regiment," 310–11.
61. James K. Wilkerson to his parents, October 30, 1864, Wilkerson Papers; OR (Army), 42, 1:297–98; McFeely and McFeely, *Ulysses. S. Grant*, 630.
62. Heth's Report, February 1, 1865, Heth Papers.
63. Davis, Casualty Report, November 1, 1864, Davis Papers; Love, *The Prairie Guards*, 17; James K. Wilkerson to his parents, November 14, 1864, Wilkerson Papers.
64. James K. Wilkerson to his parents, November 14, 1864, Wilkerson Papers; OR (Army), 42, 3:1240.
65. Power, *Lee's Miserables*, 217–19.
66. Freeman, *R.E. Lee*, 521; Heth's Report, February 1, 1865, Heth Papers; Robertson, *General A.P. Hill*, 308.
67. Walker, *History of the Second Army Corps in the Army of the Potomac*, 642; Freeman, *R.E. Lee*, 521; Heth's Report, February 1, 1865, Heth Papers.
68. Cooke, "Fifty-fifth Regiment," 311.

69. James K. Wilkerson to his mother, December 15, 1864, and to his sisters, December 21, 1864, Wilkerson Papers; Power, *Lee's Miserables*, 220, 229.
70. James K. Wilkerson to his mother, December 29, 1864, Wilkerson Papers.
71. Ibid.
72. OR (Army), 36, 1:42–43; James K. Wilkerson to his mother, December 29, 1864, Wilkerson Papers.
73. Power, *Lee's Miserables*, 235–37; Wiley, *The Life of Johnny Reb*, 182.
74. OR (Army), 46, 2:1173; Cooke, "Fifty-fifth Regiment," 311; Samuel H. Walkup Diary, 1865, Samuel H. Walkup Journal, Perkins Library Manuscripts Department, Duke University, Durham, North Carolina (hereafter referred to as Walkup Journal).
75. George Falls Diary; Robertson, *General A.P. Hill*, 311; Trudeau, *The Last Citadel*, 315.
76. James K. Wilkerson to his mother, February 9, 1865, Wilkerson Papers.
77. Ibid.; Trudeau, *The Last Citadel*, 316–17; John A. Sloan, *Reminiscences of the Guilford Grays, Co. B, 27th N.C. Regiment* (Washington, DC: R.O. Polkinhorn, 1883), 110.
78. James K. Wilkerson to his mother, February 9, 1865, Wilkerson Papers; Trudeau, *The Last Citadel*, 322.
79. James K. Wilkerson to his sister Sarah, February 14, 1865, Wilkerson Papers.
80. George Falls Diary; Freeman, *R.E. Lee*, 4:8–12. Part of the 55th North Carolina was dispatched to North Carolina at the end of February to arrest deserters and return them to their commands. This detachment commanded by Lieutenant Colonel A.C. McAllister of the 46th North Carolina, and known as the Cooke-Lane Detachment, included at least one company from the 55th, Company K, Private Wilkerson's unit. See Manarin and Jordan, *North Carolina Troops*, 13:421.
81. Freeman, *R.E. Lee*, 4:17–19; Liz Carson Reed, "Battle in Desperation," *Civil War Times Illustrated*, 34 (April 1995), 80–81.
82. Sloan, *The Guilford Grays*, 111; Samuel H. Walkup Diary, 1865, Walkup Journal.
83. McPherson, *Ordeal by Fire*, 479, 481; OR (Army), 46, 1:1263–1264, 1300; 46, 3:1288; Freeman, *R.E. Lee*, 4:39–40.
84. Sloan, *The Guilford Grays*, 111; Cooke, "Fifty-fifth Regiment," 312.
85. Sloan, *The Guilford Grays*, 111–112; Cooke, "Fifty-fifth Regiment," 312; James A. Graham, "Cooke's Brigade," in Walter Clark's *Histories of the Several Regiments and Battalions from North Carolina in the Great War*, 5 vols. (Goldsboro, NC: Nash Brothers, 1901), 5:509.
86. Samuel H. Walkup to his wife, March 30, 1865, April 1, 1865, Samuel H. Walkup Papers, Southern Historical Collection, University of North Carolina, Chapel Hill.
87. Freeman, *R.E. Lee*, 4:43–44; Simpson, *Ulysses S. Grant*, 424–25.
88. Sloan, *The Guilford Grays*, 112; Graham, "Cooke's Brigade," 5:509.
89. Heth's Report, April 4, 1865, Heth Papers.
90. William Marvel, *Lee's Last Retreat: The Flight to Appomattox* (Chapel Hill & London: University of North Carolina Press, 2002), 16–19. For a more detailed description of the Death of A. P. Hill see Freeman, *Lee's Lieutenant's*, 3, 676–79, and Robertson, *General A. P. Hill*, 316–18.
91. Marvel, *Lee's Last Retreat*, 19; Sloan, *The Guilford Grays*, 112; OR (Army), 46, 1:711–12; Freeman, *Lee's Lieutenants*, 3:688.
92. Manarin and Jordan, *North Carolina Troops*, 13:424; Graham, "Cooke's Brigade," 509; Sloan, *The Guilford Grays*, 112–13; Marvel, *Lee's Last Retreat*, 30. Several of those captured died in Federal prisons while waiting to be paroled.
93. Sloan, *The Guilford Grays*, 113.
94. William J. Cooper Jr., *Jefferson Davis, American* (New York: Vintage Books, 2001), 561–62; William C. Davis, *An Honorable Defeat: The Last Days of the Confederate Government* (New York: Harcourt, 2001), 56–58.
95. Cooper, *Jefferson Davis*, 562–63; Davis, *An Honorable Defeat*, 64–65; Freeman, *Lee's Lieutenants*, 3:685–86. Secretary of War John C. Breckinridge, a former vice president of the United States and a presidential candidate in the 1860 election remained behind to direct the rest of the evacuation. The fire that consumed much of Richmond was begun by the Confederates while trying to burn tobacco stores and ammunition depots.
96. Power, *Lee's Miserables*, 275–76; Marvel, *Lee's Last Retreat*, 50–55.
97. Marvel, *Lee's Last Retreat*, 61–63; Freeman, *Lee's Lieutenants*, 3:692–94.
98. Marvel, *Lee's Last Retreat*, 63–66; Eicher, *The Longest Night*, 815.
99. Emory M. Thomas, *Robert E. Lee: A Biography* (New York: W W Norton, 1995), 357–58; Simpson, *Ulysses S. Grant*, 427–28; Gallagher, *Fighting for the Confederacy*, 522–23; Marshall, *Lee's Aide-De-Camp*, 254.
100. Marvel, *Lee's Last Retreat*, 122–124; Thomas, *Robert E. Lee*, 359.
101. McFeely and McFeely, *Ulysses S. Grant: Memoirs and Selected Letters*, 727.
102. McFeely and McFeely, *Ulysses S. Grant: Memoirs and Selected Letters*, 727; Thomas, *Robert E. Lee*, 359–60; Marvel, *Lee's Last Retreat*, 133.
103. Sloan, *The Guilford Grays*, 114–15; Marshall, *Lee's Aide-De-Camp*, 258.
104. McFeely and McFeely, *Ulysses S. Grant: Memoirs and Selected Letters*, 727; Thomas, *Robert E. Lee*, 361.
105. Freeman, *Lee's lieutenants*, 3:724–25; Thomas, *Robert E. Lee*, 360–61.
106. Gallagher *Fighting for the Confederacy*, 530–31; Freeman, *R.E. Lee*, 122–25; Cooke, "Fifty-fifth Regiment," 312; R. A. Brock, ed., *Appomattox Roster: A List of the Paroles of the Army of Northern Virginia Issued at Appomattox Court House on April 9, 1865* (New York: Antiquarian Press, 1962), 282–84.

Epilogue

1. George Falls Diary; Power, *Lee's Miserables*, 319–20.
2. Johnson J. Hayes, *The Land of Wilkes* (Wilkesboro, NC: Wilkes County Historical Society, 1962), 172.
3. "Colonel J.K. Connally joins his Comrades of Gettysburg," *The Asheville Citizen*, February 2, 1904; "Col. John K. Connally Passes to his Reward," *Asheville Gazette*, February 1, 1904.
4. McPherson, *For Cause and Comrades*, 53–54.
5. Compiled Military Service Records (North Carolina), M270, Reels 514–18. Another 70 men who served with the regiment also died during the war, but the causes of their deaths were not reported. Also, before the war ended dozens of soldiers resigned, were discharged for being "unfit" for military service, and several joined Union regiments.
6. W. J. Cash, *The Mind of the South* (New York: Vintage Books edition, 1991), 103–4.
7. Hayes, *The Land of Wilkes*, 154.
8. Gerald Linderman, *Embattled Courage: The Experience of Combat in the American Civil War* (New York: Free Press, 1987), 1.

Bibliography

Manuscripts and Documents

CHAPEL HILL, NC
  WILSON LIBRARY, UNIVERSITY OF NORTH CAROLINA

Mary Jeffreys Bethell Diary
T.L. Clingman Papers
Edward D. Dixon Papers
Satterfield and Merritt Family Papers
Samuel H. Walkup Papers

DURHAM, NC
  PERKINS LIBRARY, DUKE UNIVERSITY

Hugh Conway Browning Papers
Joseph J. Hoyle Papers
Henry W. Jones Papers
Peter M. Mull Papers
Patterson-Cavin Family Papers
Samuel H. Walkup Journal
James King Wilkerson Papers.

GETTYSBURG, PA
  GETTYSBURG NATIONAL MILITARY PARK LIBRARY

55th Regiment File
July 1, 1863: Action at the Railroad Cut File

GREENVILLE, NC
  JOYNER LIBRARY, EAST CAROLINA UNIVERSITY

Roach Family Papers

MADISON, WI
  WISCONSIN HISTORICAL SOCIETY

Edward S. Bragg Papers

RALEIGH, NC
  NORTH CAROLINA STATE ARCHIVES, DIVISION OF ARCHIVES AND HISTORY

1850 Federal Census
1860 Federal Census
Hugh Buckner Johnston Collection
Peter M. Mull Papers
George W. Pearsall Letters
David T. Toler Papers
Howell G. Whitehead Diary (typescript)
Military Collection (Civil War)
Military Service Records (Microfilm M270)

RICHMOND, VA
  MUSEUM OF THE CONFEDERACY LIBRARY

Henry Heth Papers
Joseph R. Davis Papers

Printed Sources

Atlas to Accompany the Official Records of the Union and Confederate Armies. Washington, DC: Government Printing Office, 1891–95.

Brown, Maud Morrow. *The University Greys: Company A Eleventh Mississippi Regiment, Army of Northern Virginia, 1861–1865*. Richmond, VA: Garrett and Massie, 1940.

Buford, Thomas P., Thomas H. Chilton, and Ben Price, Jr. *Lamar Rifles: A History of Company G, Eleventh Mississippi Regiment, C.S.A.* Roanoke, VA: Stone, 1902[?].

Clark, Walter, ed. *Histories of the Several Regiments and Battalions from North Carolina in the Great War 1861–1865*. 5 vols. Raleigh, NC: Nash Brothers, 1901.

Corell, Phillip, ed. *History of the Naval Brigade: 99th N.Y. Volunteers, Union Coast Guard, 1861–1865*. New York: Regimental Veteran, 1905.

Dame, William M. *From the Rapidan to Richmond and the Spottsylvania Campaign*. Baltimore, MD: Green-Lucas, 1920.

Dawes, Rufus R. *Service with the Sixth Wisconsin Volunteers*. Madison: The State Historical Society of Wisconsin for Wisconsin Civil War Centennial Commission, 1962.

Early, Jubal Anderson. *Autobiographical Sketch and Narrative of the War Between the States*. Philadelphia: J.B. Lippincott, 1912.

Evans, Clement A., ed. *Confederate Military History*. 12 vols. Atlanta, GA: Confederate Publishing, 1899.

Five Points in the Record of North Carolina in the Great War of 1861–5. Goldsboro, NC: Nash Brothers, 1904.

Fox, William F. *New York at Gettysburg*. 3 vols. Albany: J.B. Lyon, 1902.

Freeman, Douglas Southall, ed. *Lee's Dispatches: Unpublished Letters of General Robert E. Lee, C.S.A. to Jefferson Davis and the War Department of The Confederate States of America, 1862–65*. New York: G.P. Putnam's Sons, 1957.

French, Samuel G. *Two Wars: An Autobiography of Gen. Samuel G. French, An Officer in the Armies of the United States and the Confederate States, A Graduate from the U. S. Military Academy West Point, 1843*. Nashville, TN: Confederate Veteran, 1901.

Gallagher, Gary W., ed. *Fighting for the Confederacy: The Personal Recollections of General Edward Porter Alexander*. Chapel Hill and London: University of North Carolina Press, 1989.

Haskell, Frank Aretas. *The Battle of Gettysburg*. Madison: Wisconsin History Commission, 1908.

Hassler, William W., ed. *One of Lee's Best Men: The Civil War Letters of General William Dorsey Pender*. Chapel Hill and London: University of North Carolina Press, 1965.

Johnson, Robert U., and Clarence C. Buel, eds. *Battles and Leaders of the Civil War*. 4 vols. New York: Thomas Yoseloff, 1956.

Ladd, David L., and Audrey J. Ladd, eds. *The Bachelder Papers: Gettysburg in Their Own Words*. 3 vols. Dayton, OH: Morningside House, 1994.

Livermore, Thomas L. *Numbers and Losses in the Civil War in America: 1861–1865*. Boston: Houghton Mifflin, 1901.

Love, David C. *The Prairie Guards: A History of Their Organization, Their Heroism, Their Battles and Their Triumphs*. Starkville, MS: n.p., 1890.

Marshall, Charles. *Lee's Aide-de-Camp: Being the Papers of Colonel Charles Marshall Sometime Aide-de-Camp, Military Secretary, and Assistant Adjutant General on the Staff of Robert E. Lee, 1862–1865*. Edited by Frederick Maurice. Lincoln and London: University of Nebraska Press, 2000.

McFeely, Mary Drake, and William S. McFeely, eds. *Ulysses S. Grant: Memoirs and Selected Letters*. New York: The Library of America, 1990.

Morrison, James L., Jr., ed. *The Memoirs of Henry Heth*. Westport, CT, and London: Greenwood, 1974.

Oates, William C. *The War Between the Union and the Confederacy*. New York and Washington: Neale Publishing, 1905.

Rhodes, Robert Hunt, ed. *All for the Union: The Civil War Diary and Letters of Elisha Hunt Rhodes*. New York: Orion, 1985.

Rush, Richard, et al., eds. *Official Records of the Union and Confederate Navies*. 31 vols. Washington, DC: General Printing Office, 1894–1927.

Scott, R.N. et al., eds. *The War of the Rebellion: A Compilation of the Official Records of the Union and Confederate Armies*. 128 vols. Washington, DC: Government Printing Office, 1880–1901.

Sloan, John A. *Reminiscences of the Guilford Grays, Co. B, 27th N.C. Regiment*. Washington, DC: R.O Polkinhorn, 1883.

Sorrell, Moxley. *Recollections of a Confederate Staff Officer*. Edited by Bell Irvin Wiley. Wilmington, NC: Broadfoot Publishing, 1987.

Walker, Francis A. *History of the Second Army Corps in the Army of the Potomac.* New York: Charles Scribner's Sons, 1886.
Wilson, LeGrand James. *The Confederate Soldier.* Memphis, TN: Memphis State University Press, 1973.
Wright, Stuart, ed. *Memoirs of Alfred Horatio Belo: Reminiscences of a North Carolina Volunteer.* Gaithersburg, MD: Olde Soldier, n.d.

Secondary Sources

Barrett, John G. *The Civil War in North Carolina.* Chapel Hill: University of North Carolina Press, 1963.
_____. *North Carolina as a Civil War Battlefield, 1861–1865.* Raleigh: North Carolina Department of Cultural Resources, 1980.
Beitzell, Edwin W. *Point Lookout Camp for Confederates.* Maryland: Edwin W. Beitzell, 1972.
Brock, R. A. *Appomattox Roster: A List of the Paroles of the Army of Northern Virginia.* New York: Antiquarian, 1962.
Busey, John W., and David G. Martin. *Regimental Strengths and Losses at Gettysburg.* Hightstown, NJ: Longstreet House, 1986.
Coddington, Edwin B. *The Gettysburg Campaign: A Study in Command.* Dayton, OH: Morningside, 1979.
Cooper, William J., Jr. *Jefferson Davis, American.* New York: Vintage, 2001.
Cormier, Steven A. *The Siege of Suffolk: The Forgotten Campaign, April 11–May 4, 1863.* Lynchburg, VA: H. E. Howard, 1989.
Davis, William C. *An Honorable Defeat: The Last Days of the Confederate Government.* New York: Harcourt, 2001.
Dowdey, Clifford. *Death of a Nation: The Confederate Army at Gettysburg.* New York: Barnes and Noble, 1998.
Eicher, David J. *The Longest Night: A Military History of the Civil War.* New York: Simon & Schuster, 2001.
Fonvielle, Chris E., Jr. *The Wilmington Campaign: Last Rays of Departing Hope.* Campbell, CA: Savas, 1997.
Frank, Joseph Allan. *With Ballot and Bayonet: The Political Socialization of American Civil War Soldiers.* Athens & London: University of Georgia Press, 1998.
_____, and George A. Reaves. *"Seeing the Elephant": Raw Recruits at the Battle of Shiloh.* New York: Greenwood, 1989.
Freeman, Douglas Southall. *Lee's Lieutenants: A Study in Command.* 3 vols. New York: Charles Scribner's Sons, 1944.
_____, *R.E. Lee: A Biography.* 4 vols. New York and London: Charles Scribner's Sons, 1934–35.
Furgurson, Ernest B. *Not War But Murder: Cold Harbor 1864.* New York: Alfred A. Knopf, 2000.
Gallagher, Gary W., ed. *The Third Day at Gettysburg and Beyond.* Chapel Hill: University of North Carolina Press, 1994.
_____, ed. *Three Days at Gettysburg: Essays on Confederate and Union Leadership.* Kent, OH, and London: Kent State University Press, 1999.
Griffith, Paddy. *Battle Tactics of the Civil War.* New Haven and London: Yale University Press, 1987.
Hassler, Warren W., Jr. *Crisis at the Crossroads: The First Day at Gettysburg.* Montgomery: University of Alabama Press, 1970.
Hassler, William W. *A. P. Hill: Lee's Forgotten General.* Richmond, VA: Garrett & Massie, 1957.
Hayes, Johnson J. *The Land of Wilkes.* Charlotte, NC: Heritage, 1962.
Herdegen, Lance J., and William J. K. Beaudot. *In the Bloody Railroad Cut at Gettysburg.* Dayton, OH: Morningside, 1990.
Hess, Earl J. *Pickett's Charge— The Last Attack at Gettysburg.* Chapel Hill & London: University of North Carolina Press, 2001.
Inscoe, John C., and Gordon B. McKinney. *The Heart of Confederate Appalachia: Western North Carolina in the Civil War.* Chapel Hill and London: University of North Carolina Press, 2000.
Johnson, Guion Griffis. *Ante-Bellum North Carolina: A Social History.* Chapel Hill: University of North Carolina Press, 1937.
Keegan, John. *The Face of Battle.* New York: Viking, 1976.
King, Henry T. *Sketches of Pitt County, 1704–1910.* Greenville, NC: Era, 1976.
Krick, Robert K. *Lee's Colonels: A Biographical Register of the Field Officers of the Army of Northern Virginia.* Dayton, OH: Morningside Bookshop, 1979.
Linderman, Gerald F. *Embattled Courage; The Experience of Combat in the American Civil War.* New York: The Free Press, 1987.
Lonn, Ella. *Desertion During the Civil War.* New York and London: Century, 1928.

Manarin, Louis H., and W. T. Jordan, Jr., eds. *North Carolina Troops 1861–1865: A Roster.* 14 vols. Raleigh: North Carolina Division of Archives and History, 1966–99.

Martin, David G. *Gettysburg July 1.* Conshohocken, PA: Combined Books, 1995.

Marvel, William. *Lee's Last Retreat: The Flight to Appomattox.* Chapel Hill & London: University of North Carolina Press, 2002.

Matter, William D. *If It Takes All Summer: The Battle of Spotsylvania.* Chapel Hill and London: University of North Carolina Press, 1988.

McPherson, James M. *Battle Cry of Freedom: The Civil War Era.* New York and Oxford: Oxford University Press, 1988.

_____. *Ordeal by Fire: The Civil War and Reconstruction.* New York: McGraw-Hill, 1992.

_____. *For Cause and Comrades: Why Men Fought in the Civil War.* New York and Oxford: Oxford University Press, 1997.

McWhiney, Grady, and Perry D. Jamieson. *Attack and Die: Civil War Military Tactics and the Southern Heritage.* Tuscaloosa: University of Alabama Press, 1982.

Miller, Randall M., Harry S. Stout, and Charles Reagan Wilson, eds. *Religion and the American Civil War.* New York and Oxford: Oxford University Press, 1998.

Mitchell, Reid. *Civil War Soldiers.* New York: Viking, 1988.

Murray, R.L. *First on the Field: Cortland's 76th and Oswego's 147th New York State Volunteer Regiments at Gettysburg.* Wolcott, NY: Benedum, 1998.

_____. *The Redemption of the "Harper's Ferry Cowards": The Story of the 111th and 126th New York State Volunteer Regiments at Gettysburg.* Wolcott, NY: 1994.

Nolan, Alan T. *The Iron Brigade: A Military History.* Bloomington: Indiana University Press, 1994.

Palmer, Michael A. *Lee Moves North: Robert E. Lee on the Offensive.* New York: John Wiley & Sons, 1998.

Patterson, Gerard A. *Debris of Battle: The Wounded of Gettysburg.* Mechanicsburg, PA: Stackpole, 1997.

Pearce, T.H. *They Fought: The Story of Franklin County Men in the Years 1861–1865.* Adams, 1969.

Pfanz, Harry W. *Gettysburg— The First Day.* Chapel Hill & London: University of North Carolina Press, 2001.

Power, J. Tracy. *Lee's Miserables: Life in the Army of Northern Virginia from the Wilderness to Appomattox.* Chapel Hill and London: University of North Carolina Press, 1998.

Priest, John Michael. *Nowhere to Run: The Wilderness, May 4th & 5th, 1864.* Shippensburg, PA: White Mane, 1995.

_____. *Victory Without Triumph: The Wilderness, May 6th & 7th, 1864.* Shippensburg, PA: White Mane, 1996.

Randall, J. G. *The Civil War and Reconstruction.* Boston: D. C. Heath, 1937.

Reardon, Carol. *Pickett's Charge in History and Memory.* Chapel Hill and London: University of North Carolina Press, 1997.

Rhea, Gordon C. *The Battle of the Wilderness: May 5–6, 1864.* Baton Rouge: Louisiana State University Press, 1994.

_____. *The Battles for Spotsylvania Court House and the Road to Yellow Tavern: May 7–12, 1864.* Baton Rouge and London: Louisiana State University Press, 1997.

_____. *To the North Anna River: Grant and Lee, May 13–25, 1864.* Baton Rouge: Louisiana State University Press, 2000.

_____. *Cold Harbor: Grant and Lee, May 26— June 3 1864.* Baton Rouge: Louisiana State University Press, 2002.

Robertson, James I., Jr. *General A. P. Hill: The Story of a Confederate Warrior.* New York: Random House, 1987.

_____. *Stonewall Jackson: The Man, the Soldier, the Legend.* New York: Simon & Schuster Macmillan, 1997.

Sears, Stephen W. *Gettysburg.* Boston and New York: Houghton Mifflin, 2003.

Simpson, Brooks D. *Ulysses S. Grant: Triumph over Adversity, 1822–1865.* Boston and New York: Houghton Mifflin, 2000.

Sommers, Richard J. *Richmond Redeemed: The Siege at Petersburg.* New York: Doubleday, 1981.

Speer, Lonnie R. *Portals to Hell: Military Prisons of the Civil War.* Mechanicsburg, PA: Stackpole, 1997.

Stubbs, Steven H. *Duty • Honor • Valor: The Story of the Eleventh Mississippi Infantry Regiment.* Philadelphia, MS: Dancing Rabbit, 2000.

Sutherland, Daniel E. *Seasons of War: The Ordeal of a Confederate Community, 1861–1865.* New York: Free Press, 1995.

Symonds, Craig L. *Gettysburg: A Battlefield Atlas.* Baltimore: Nautical & Aviation Publishing Company of America, 1992.

Thomas, Emory M. *The Confederate Nation: 1861–1865.* New York: Harper & Row, 1979.

_____. *Robert E. Lee: A Biography.* New York: W. W. Norton, 1995.

Tidwell, William A. *Come Retribution: The Confederate Secret Service and the Assassination of Lincoln*. New York: Barnes and Noble, 1997.
Trudeau, Noah Andre. *Bloody Roads South: The Wilderness to Cold Harbor, May–June, 1864*. Boston: Little, Brown, 1989.
____. *The Last Citadel: Petersburg, Virginia, June 1864–April 1865*. Boston: Little, Brown, 1991.
Tucker, Glenn. *High Tide at Gettysburg: The Campaign in Pennsylvania*. New York: Bobbs-Merrill, 1958.
____. *Lee and Longstreet at Gettysburg*. Indianapolis: Bobbs-Merrill, 1968.
Wakelyn, Jon L. *Biographical Dictionary of the Confederacy*. Westport, CT: Greenwood, 1977.
Wert, Jeffry D. *General James Longstreet: The Confederacy's Most Controversial Soldier, A Biography*. New York: Simon & Schuster, 1993.
____. *Gettysburg: Day Three*. New York: Simon & Schuster, 2001.
Wiley, Bell Irvin. *The Life of Johnny Reb: The Common Soldier of the Confederacy*. Baton Rouge and London: Louisiana State University Press, 1943.
____. *The Life of Billy Yank: The Common Soldier of the Union*. Baton Rouge and London: Louisiana State University Press, 1952.
____. *The Plain People of the Confederacy*. Gloucester, MA: Peter Smith, 1971.
Williams, T. Harry. *Lincoln and His Generals*. New York: Vintage, 1952.
Wilson, Clyde N. *The Most Promising Young Man of the South: James Johnston Pettigrew and His Men at Gettysburg*. Abilene, TX: McWhiney Foundation Press, 1998.
Woodworth, Steven E. *While God Is Marching On: The Religious World of Civil War Soldiers*. Lawrence: University Press of Kansas, 2001.
Wright, Stuart T. *Historical Sketch of Person County*. Danville, VA: Womack, 1974.

Newspapers

The Asheville Citizen (Asheville, NC)
Asheville Gazette (Asheville, NC)
Biblical Recorder (Raleigh, NC)
Galveston Daily News (Galveston, TX)
Raleigh Register (Raleigh, NC)
Spirit of the Age (Raleigh, NC)
Standard (Raleigh, NC)
Weekly State Journal (Raleigh, NC)

Articles and Periodicals

Ashe, S.A. "The First Day at Gettysburg." *Confederate Veteran* 38 (1930): 378–81.
Belo, Alfred H. "The Battle of Gettysburg." *Confederate Veteran* 8 (1900): 165–67.
Hankins, Samuel. "Simple Story of a Soldier — V, VI." *Confederate Veteran* 21 (1913): 21–22.
Hankins, Samuel. "Simple Story of a Soldier — VII, VIII." *Confederate Veteran* 21 (1913): 113–115.
Hartwig, D. Scott. "Guts and Good Leadership; The Action at the Railroad Cut, July 1, 1863." *Gettysburg Magazine* 1 (1989): 5–14.
Jordan, Weymouth T., Jr. "North Carolinians...Must Bear the Blame: Calumny," an Affaire d'Honneur, and Expiation for the Fifty-fifth Regiment North Carolina Troops at the Siege of Suffolk, April–May 1863." *North Carolina Historical Review* 71 (July 1994): 306–30.
Jones, Charles R. "Historical Sketch of the 55th North Carolina." *Our Living and Our Dead*, April 22, 1874.
O'Neal, A. M. "Maj. A. M. O'Neal to his Wife." *Confederate Veteran* 18 (1910): 87–88.
Reed, Liz Carson. "Battle in Desperation." *Civil War Times Illustrated* 34 (April 1995): 32–38, 80–81.
Satterfield, John R. "Farthest at Gettysburg: The Story of a Confederate Captain." *Gettysburg Magazine* 26 (January 2002): 94–113.
Trudeau, Noah Andre. "A Frightful and Frightening Place." *Civil War Times Illustrated* 38 (May 1999): 42–55.
Venable, Charles S. "The Campaign from the Wilderness to Petersburg." *Southern Historical Society Papers* 14 (1886): 522–42.
Watson, Samuel J. "Religion and Combat Motivation in the Confederate Armies." *The Journal of Military History* 58 (January 1994): 29–55.
Winschel, Terrence J. "Part I: Heavy Was Their Loss: Joe Davis's Brigade at Gettysburg." *Gettysburg Magazine* 2 (January 1990): 5–14.
____. "Part II: Heavy Was Their Loss: Joe Davis's Brigade at Gettysburg." *Gettysburg Magazine* 3 (July 1990): 77–85.
"Sidney Smith Abernethy," *Confederate Veteran*. 7 (1899): 301.

Index

Abernethy, Sydney Smith 6
Alabama units: 1st Confederate Battalion 22, 92, 96, 97, 100, 101, 102; infantry (13th) 66; (48th) 27, 33
Albemarle Sound, NC 10, 11
Alexander, Edward Porter 58, 59
Amelia Court House, VA 139, 140
Amelia Springs, VA 140
Amissville, VA 80
Anderson, Richard H. 80, 104, 105, 111, 114, 118, 140
Anderson's division 80, 81, 96
Antietam, battle of 59
Appomattox Court House, VA viii, 3, 4, 5, 22, 141
Appomattox Station, VA 140
Archer, James J. 46, 53, 65
Archer's brigade 41, 46, 48, 56, 57, 60, 65, 66, 70
Armstrong, Samuel C. 70
Army of the Potomac 23, 24, 37, 40, 46, 52, 57, 78, 83, 107, 112, 114, 118, 120
Ashe, S. A. 63, 69
Atlanta, GA 91
Ayres, Romeyn B. 126

Bachelder, John B. 70
Banks, Nathaniel 91
Barlow, Francis C. 98, 105, 107
Bass, Bryant 5, 21
Batts, William 83
Beaufort, NC 11
Beauregard, Pierre G.T. 24, 119, 125
Belfield, VA 133
Belo, Alfred H. 7, 25, 27, 29, 30, 31, 32, 33, 34, 35, 36, 48, 50, 51, 52, 53, 54, 55, 56, 63, 68, 72, 84, 85, 87, 89, 98, 99, 101, 106, 116, 125, 133, 143
Belo, Henry 99
Benge, Samuel 103
Berryville, VA 44
Biblical Recorder 34, 36, 38, 41, 90

Big Bethal, VA 1
Birney, David G. 98, 105, 131
Blackwell, Promfret 129
Blair, John 51
The Bloody Angle (Spotsylvania) 109–110
Boggs, Francis 32
Boggs, John D. 103
Bogue Sound, NC 10
Boozeman, David L. 27
Bragg, Braxton 24, 79, 82
Brander, Thomas A. 125
Brandy Station, VA 82; battle 45
Briggs, Benjamin F. 125, 128
Briscoe, James C. 105
Bristoe Station, battle of 80–82, 90, 93
Brockenbrough, John M. 65
Brockenbrough's brigade 41, 60, 62, 65
Brown, John 44
Buford, John 46, 47, 74
Buford, T.P. 121
Buford's brigade 47, 48, 49, 52, 74
Bull Run, battle of 3, 4, 7
Bullock, William J. 21
Bunker Hill, VA 74
Burgess' Mill, battle of 132–133
Burke County, NC 122
Burnside, Ambrose E. 3, 11, 12, 23, 83, 95, 101, 102, 109, 110, 111
Butler, Benjamin F. 11, 91, 131

Calloway, Abner S. 7–8
Camp Butler, VA 23
Camp Campbell, NC 10
Camp French, VA 17, 21
Camp Green, VA 22
Camp Hoke, VA 37
Camp Holmes, NC 22
Camp Mangum, NC 5, 6, 8, 9, 75
Camp Vance, NC 122
Campbell Court House, VA 142
Canipi, John A. 115
Cannady, Isaac G. 30
Carlisle, PA 45

Cash, W.J. 143
Cashtown, PA 45, 46, 56, 57, 71
Chamberlain, Joshua L. 58
Chambers, Christopher 33
Chambersburg, PA 45
Champion, George H. 130
Chancellorsville, VA 83; battle of viii, 3, 37, 40, 43, 44, 58, 83
Chandler, William 75
Charlestown, WV 44
Chattanooga, battle of 83
Chickamauga, battle of 79, 83
City Point, VA 125
Clark, Henry T. 7, 12
Clark, Walter viii, 143
Cleveland County, NC 5, 122
Cold Harbor, VA 114, 117, 118; battle of 7, 114–118
Colston, Raleigh E. 22
Colston's brigade 22
Confederate government 2, 8, 21, 22, 23, 77, 79, 103, 120, 134, 139
Connally, John Kerr 6, 7, 13, 15, 20, 21, 25, 26, 27, 28, 30, 32, 33, 34, 35, 36, 38, 49, 50, 51, 54, 56, 68, 71, 84, 143
Connecticut units: infantry (8th) 27
Conscription Act 2, 77, 78
Cook, John E. 49, 50
Cook, Noah W. 38
Cooke, Charles M. viii, 35, 36, 87, 98, 99, 107, 115, 116, 121, 123, 125, 126, 127, 128, 131, 132, 134, 137
Cooke, John R. 81, 138
Cooke's brigade 3, 81, 117, 129, 133, 135, 136, 137, 138, 139, 142
Cooper, Samuel 37, 103
Core Sound, NC 10
Craige, William 124
Crawford, Samuel 127
Crittenden, Thomas L. 110
Crittenden's brigade 110
Culpeper Court House, VA 18, 75, 78, 80, 82, 94
Cunningham, George A. 29, 32

Cushings, William B. 27
Cussons, John 33, 34
Custer, George A. 139
Cutler, Lysander 48
Cutler's brigade 49–52

Dahlgren Raid 87–88
Dame, William Meade 85
Danville, VA 139, 141
Davis, Henry C. 21
Davis, Isaac 22
Davis, Jefferson 22, 40, 74, 76, 77, 92, 94, 113, 127, 139
Davis, Joseph R. 22, 37, 39, 41, 46, 47, 48, 50, 51, 53, 55, 56, 57, 58, 59, 62, 65, 70, 73, 74, 84, 86, 94, 110, 115, 127, 131, 132, 133
Davis's brigade 3, 22, 24, 34, 37, 41, 43, 44, 45, 73, 74, 77, 81, 82, 85, 86, 88, 89, 92, 93, 94, 96, 98, 99, 100, 101, 102, 104, 106, 110, 111, 112, 114, 115, 119, 124, 125, 126, 127, 129, 130, 131, 132, 135, 137; at Gettysburg 46–50, 53–60, 62, 63, 65, 66, 71
Dawes, Rufus R. 51, 52, 53
Deatonville, VA 140
Delaware units: infantry (1st) 62; (4th) 127
Dinwiddie Court House, VA 133
Dixon, Edward D. 43

Eakes, Jim 129
Early, Jubal A. 45, 104, 106, 114, 115, 125
Egan, T.W. 132, 133
Ellis, John W. 1
Eritckes, Jo 129
Ewell, Richard S. 40, 54, 80, 95, 96, 99, 104, 111
Ewell's corps 41, 43, 45, 53, 54, 56, 58, 96, 108, 111, 114, 140

Falling Waters, battle of 73–75, 94
Falls, T.D. 63, 65, 69, 70
Farmville, VA 139
Fayetteville, PA 45
Feeney, William A. 56
Field, Charles W. 107
Five Forks, battle of 137
Fleming, William B. 103
Forester, Samuel J. 21
Forsyth County, NC 7
Fort Caswell, NC 19, 20
Fort Clark, NC 7, 11
Fort Delaware, DE 53
Fort Euliss, VA 137, 138
Fort Gilmer, VA 131
Fort Harrison, VA 131
Fort Hatteras, NC 7, 11
Fort Monroe, VA 23
Fort Ocracoke, NC 11
Fort Oregon, NC 11
Fort Stedman, VA 137
Fort Sumter, SC 1, 24
Foster, John G. 11, 15
Foster, William T. 20
Franklin, VA 37, 39
Fredericksburg, VA 19, 41, 42, 82, 96, 108, 112; battle of 3, 19, 23, 59

French, Samuel G. 14, 17, 21, 22, 25, 26, 27, 29, 30, 31, 34, 37
French, William H. 72
French's division 37
Front Royal, VA 44
Fry, Birkett D. 65, 66, 70
Funkstown, MD 44

Gaines's Mill, VA 117
Galloway, Marlin 50
Galveston Daily News 63
Gardner, William C. 69
Getty, George W. 97, 98
Gettysburg, PA 46, 47, 48, 49, 53, 54, 55, 56, 71, 75, 77, 80, 89, 94, 96, 130, 144; battle of vii, 3, 9, 40, 47–71, 75, 76, 84
Gibbon, John 98
Gilreath, George A. 61, 67, 68
Globe Tavern, VA 125, 129, 130; battle of 125–130
Goldsboro, NC 11, 15
Goldsborough, L.M. 11
Gordon, John B. 108, 109, 137, 140, 141
Gordonsville, VA 87, 95
Gorman Court House, VA 142
Grady, Alexander T. 21
Grant, Ulysses S. 90, 91, 93, 94, 95, 96, 100, 102, 103, 104, 105, 107, 108, 109, 110, 111, 112, 113, 114, 115, 117, 118, 119, 120, 122, 123, 125, 131, 132, 133, 135, 137, 138, 139, 140, 141
Grantham, Marshall P. 103
Granville County, NC 8
Greencastle, PA 72
Greenville, NC 13
Greenwich, VA 80
Gregg, David M. 94
Gregg's division 95, 125, 133
Grimes, Bryan 77
Grover, Andrew J. 49
Gurganus, Willie 130

Hadley, Thomas J. 74, 77, 129
Hagerstown, MD 45, 46, 66, 72, 73
Hall, James 51
Halleck, Henry 45
Hampton, Wade 80
Hampton Roads, VA 26
Hampton's division 80, 105, 132, 133, 134
Hancock, Winfield S. 95, 98, 100, 101, 102, 105, 107, 108, 110, 111, 115, 122, 125, 129, 132
Hanover Junction, VA 41, 104, 112
Harpers Ferry, VA 44, 45
Harrisburg, PA 45
Haskell, Frank A. 60
Hatcher's Run, battle of 135–136
Hatteras Inlet, NC 7, 11
Hays, Alexander 62
Heth, Henry 40, 46, 47, 48, 53, 54, 55, 57, 60, 65, 71, 73, 74, 78, 80, 81, 82, 96, 97, 98, 100, 107, 108, 114, 115, 129, 131, 132, 133, 136, 138
Heth's division 46, 47, 48, 49, 58, 59, 60, 63, 69, 70, 71, 73, 78, 80,

81, 82, 96, 99, 101, 104, 105, 106, 107, 112, 118, 121, 123, 124, 125, 126, 127, 133, 134, 135, 138, 139
Hicks, William 115
Hill, Ambrose P. 40, 41, 42, 46, 54, 57, 71, 78, 80, 81, 82, 89, 95, 96, 99, 100, 104, 118, 125, 128, 129, 131, 133, 138, 139
Hill's corps 41, 43, 45, 54, 59, 76, 78, 80, 81, 82, 89, 96, 99, 100, 104, 108, 110, 112, 131, 132, 134, 135, 138, 139
Hinchey, John 20
Hodges, Alpheus 47
Hoke, Robert F. 7, 114
Hoke's division 114
Holden, William W. 77, 78
Holmes, Theophilus H. 12
Hood, John B. 26, 30, 31, 32
Hood's division 24, 27, 31, 32
Hooker, Joseph 23, 35, 37, 38, 42, 43, 45, 46
Hoyle, Joseph J. 8, 9, 10, 12, 13, 14, 15, 17, 18, 19, 21, 22, 28, 30, 34, 39, 42, 43, 44, 45, 53, 54, 58, 63, 67, 70, 71, 72, 73, 74, 75, 76, 79, 81, 82, 83, 86, 87, 88, 89, 92, 93, 99, 101, 107, 108, 110, 111, 112, 113, 115, 117, 119, 120, 122, 124, 127, 143
Hoyle, Sarah 9, 18, 43, 79, 86, 87, 89
Hoyle, Solomon 12
Hugo, Victor 41
Hull, William H. 10
Humphreys, Andrew A. 94

Illinois units: cavalry (8th) 47
Imboden, John 71, 72
Iron Brigade 56, 57
Ivor Station, VA 22, 37, 39, 41

Jackson, Thomas J. "Stonewall" 7, 37, 40, 89, 105
Jackson's corps 88, 89
Jenkins, Micah 31, 37, 101
Jennings, James T. viii, 128
Jetersville, VA 140
Johnson, Edward 108
Johnson, P.J. 18
Johnson's Island, OH 74
Johnston, Joseph E. 91, 137, 141
Jones, Charles R. 77
Jones, E. H. 76
Jordan, Henry T. 19, 30, 64, 68

Keitt, Lawrence M. 114
Kershaw, Joseph 114
Kershaw's division 114
Kilpatrick, Hugh J. 74, 87
Kinston, NC 9, 10, 11, 12, 13, 15, 16
Kirk, George W. 122
Kirkland, William W. 81
Kirkland's brigade 81, 129, 133
Knob Creek, NC 19
Ku Klux Klan 143

Lacy, B. Tucker 89
La Grange, NC 13
Lane, James H. 109

Law, Evander McIvor 27, 28, 29, 30, 31, 32, 33
Lee, Fitzhugh 80, 93, 114, 137, 141
Lee, Robert E. 12, 13, 16, 18, 23, 24, 36, 37, 38, 40, 41, 42, 43, 45, 76, 78, 79, 80, 82, 84, 85, 86, 89, 92, 94, 95, 96, 99, 100, 102, 104, 105, 108, 109, 110, 111, 113, 114, 117, 118, 119, 120, 122, 123, 131, 136, 137, 139, 140, 141; at Gettysburg 46, 53, 54, 57, 58, 59, 69, 70, 71, 72, 73
Lillington, Nicholas W. 125
Lincoln, Abraham 1, 23, 42, 45, 91, 133
Livermore, Thomas 102
Lockhart, Samuel P. 121
London, England 92
Longstreet, James 18, 23, 24, 25, 26, 27, 30, 31, 32, 34, 35, 36, 37, 38, 40, 58, 59, 69, 70, 79, 93, 95, 96, 99, 100, 101, 102, 104, 138, 140, 141
Longstreet's corps 24, 43, 45, 54, 58, 60, 71, 96, 101, 140
Love, Henderson H. 130
Lynchburg, VA 140

MacRae, William 133
Mahone, William 127, 140
Mahone's division 101, 105, 107, 127, 133, 140
Maine units: artillery (2nd) 48, 49, 51; infantry (17th) 105; (20th) 58
Manassas, VA 80, 81; second battle of 59, 80
Marlicks, Andrew 115
Marshall, James K. 60, 65, 66
Martin, James G. 14
Martin, S. Taylor 32
Martinsburg, VA 74
Massachusetts units: infantry (7th) 97; (10th) 97; (37th) 97
May, George R. 130
Mayo, R.M. 62
Mayo's brigade 62, 110
McClellan, George B. 11, 12, 23
McComb's brigade 138
McGee, Andrew W. 103
McGowan, Samuel F. 98
McGowan's brigade 98
Meade, George G. 46, 58, 71, 72, 73, 75, 78, 79, 80, 86, 91, 94, 96, 103, 109, 131, 132, 140
Mexican War 40–41
Michigan units: cavalry (6th) 74
Miles, Nelson A. 138, 139
Miller, H.R. 56
Mississippi units: infantry (2nd) 22, 48, 49, 50, 51, 53, 56, 57, 62, 63, 72, 96, 132; (10th) 22; (11th) 22, 33, 35, 47, 56, 57, 62, 63, 72, 96, 101, 105, 119, 121, 125; (26th) 22, 92, 125; (42nd) 22, 43, 48, 49, 50, 51, 56, 62, 63, 96, 100
Mitchell, S.P. 37
Mobile, AL 91
Morganton, NC 122
Morrison, Jeremiah 54

Morristown, TN 122
Moseley, Hillary 56
Mott, Gershom 98
Mull, Ezra 10
Mull, Peter M. 5, 13, 15, 35, 68, 75, 79, 125
Mull, Peter P. 75
Murphy, William P. 51

New Baltimore, VA 80
New Bern, NC 11, 15, 16
New Jersey units: infantry (12th) 62
New Verdiersville, VA 96
New York units: cavalry (1st) 72; (6th) 48; (9th) 47, 48; infantry (76th) 48, 49, 50, 127; (84th) 51, 53; (89th) 27; (95th) 51, 53, 127; (99th) 35; (111th) 62; (117th) 39; (125th) 62, 70; (126th) 63; (147th) 48, 49, 50, 127
Newport News, VA 23, 24
Nicoll, Sylvester D. 14
Nixon, Richard 35
Norfolk, VA 23, 26
North Carolina Presbyterian 88
North Carolina *Standard* 19, 20, 77
North Carolina units: artillery (1st) 13; (10th) 13; infantry (1st) 17, 84; (3rd) 84; (4th) 77; (8th) 13; (10th) 7; (11th) 2; (13th) 83; (15th) 135; (17th) 13; (21st) 6, 7; (26th) 49; (27th) 121, 135, 139; (30th) 6; (33rd) 84; (46th) 135; (48th) 135, 137; (55th) camp life and supplies 6, 8, 9, 17, 18, 21, 34, 39–40, 42, 76, 77, 83–85, 88–90, 92, 93, 121–122, 124, 130, 134; desertion 3, 12, 20, 76, 86–87, 131; duel between officers 32–34; officer corps 6–8, 21, 25, 54–55, 56, 68–69, 75, 116, 117, 125; organization of 2–3, 5–8; sickness, disease, and casualties 8, 10, 12, 14–15, 19, 20, 36, 38, 50, 53, 54, 55, 63, 66–67, 72, 74, 86, 92, 99, 102, 110, 116, 124, 127, 129, 131, 133, 143
Northrop, Lucius B. 23

Oak Island, NC 19
Ohio units: infantry (8th) 62
O'Neil, Alfred M. 97
Orange Court House, VA 78, 80, 82, 83, 86, 87, 89, 91, 93
Ord, Edward O.C. 131
Osborn, Thomas W. 62

Pamlico Sound, NC 10, 11
Parke, John 138
Pearce, Berry 103
Pearsall, George W. 3, 81, 86, 90, 98, 99, 101, 107, 108, 110, 111, 112, 113, 116, 117, 143
Peck, John J. 26, 35, 39
Peden, John T. 125
Pegram, W.J. 48, 65
Pender, Dorsey 60, 84
Pender's division 54, 59, 60, 73

Pennsylvania units: infantry (56th) viii, 48, 49, 50, 127, 128; (149th) 54; (157th) 127
Petersburg, VA 16, 17, 18, 19, 21, 23, 24, 31, 41, 91, 118, 119, 120, 121, 123, 124, 125, 128, 129, 131, 132, 133, 134, 136, 137, 138, 139, 140, 144
Pettigrew, James J. 3, 46, 58, 60, 65, 66, 69, 70, 71, 74
Pettigrew's brigade 41, 46, 60, 65, 66
Peyton, Henry E. 124
Phillips, Pete 129
Pickett, George E. 24, 32, 58, 59, 60, 69, 70
Pickett-Pettigrew Charge vii, 3, 60–66, 69, 70, 71, 108
Pickett's division 24, 31, 32, 37, 40, 59–65, 70, 137
Pierce, J.V. 50
Pitt County, NC 5, 7
Pittsylvania County, VA 141
Pleasonton, Alfred 45
Plymouth, NC 14
Poague, William T. 81, 100
Point Lookout, MD 53
Pool, Stephen D. 13
Portsmouth, VA 26
Potter, Edward E. 14, 15
Potter, Robert B. 115
Powell, John W. 117

Quinn, William 21

Raleigh, NC 2, 5, 7, 8, 9, 12, 15
Randal, Miller H. 103
Randall, G.W. 38
Raper, Calvin 53
Rapidan Station, VA 82
Rappahannock Station, VA 82
Reagan, John 40, 139
Ream's Station, VA 129
Renfrow, Braswell 20
Reynolds, John 48, 49
Reynolds, Reuben O. 72
Rhode Island units: infantry (2nd) 97
Rhodes, Elisha Hunt 97
Richardsville, VA 94
Richmond, VA 2, 10, 11, 12, 17, 23, 24, 37, 41, 68, 77, 78, 84, 89, 91, 94, 99, 104, 107, 111, 112, 113, 114, 117, 122, 123, 124, 125, 127, 131, 134, 139
Richmond Daily Dispatch 78
Roanoke Island, NC 11
Roberts, A.K. 56
Robertson, Jerome B. 30
Rodes, Robert 115
Rodes' division 53, 54, 109, 115
Royall, William B. 11, 12
Ruffin, John D. 9

Salisbury, NC 122
Saltville, VA 134
Sanford, Stephen 129
Satterfield, E. Fletcher 33, 63, 64, 65, 68, 69, 70, 143
Satterfield, Sue E. 65

Sawyer, Franklin 62
Sayler's Creek, battle of 140
Scales, Alfred M. 98
Scales's brigade 54, 98
Scott, Haywood 103
Second U.S. Artillery 48
Seddon, James A. 23, 24, 84
Sedgwick, John 94, 104
Selma, AL 91
Seven Days' battles 3
Sharpsburg, MD 45
Shepherdstown, WV 44, 45
Sheridan, Philip H. 114, 137
Sherman, William T. 91
Sherrill, Roderick M. 17
Shumaker, L.M. 26, 29, 32
Sigel, Franz 91
Sloan, John A. 139
Smith, J. Henry 88
Smith, Maurice T. 8, 13, 16, 25, 27, 28, 29, 30, 33, 36, 50, 55, 56, 68
Smith, R.F. 34, 36, 42
Smith, William F. 114, 115
Smoot, David L. 26
Smyth, Thomas 140
Sorrel, G. Moxley 34, 38, 101
Sperryville, VA 44, 80
Spirit of the Age 8, 10, 14, 15, 19, 28
Spotsylvania, battles of 105–112
Spotsylvania Court House, VA 96, 103, 104, 105, 108, 110, 111, 112
Steuart, George H. 84
Stevens, Marcus C. 67
Stone, John M. 50, 51, 56, 72, 96, 97, 98, 100, 101, 102, 132
Stoneman, George 134
Stovall, Charles L. 103
Stovall, Wilkins 74, 75
Stribling, Robert M. 26
Stringham, Silas 11
Stuart, J.E.B. 45, 53, 80, 107
Stuart's corps 80
Suffolk, VA 9, 23, 24, 25, 26, 28, 31, 34, 35, 36, 37, 38, 39
Sullivan, Jesse P. 53
Sutherland's Station, VA 138

Tallen, Jesse 87
Talley's Mill, battle of 104–107
Terrell, Leigh R. 27, 29, 30, 33
Terry, Alfred 35
Thomas, E.L. 98, 99
Thomas, Robert W. 67, 75, 84, 125, 133
Thorpe, Benjamin 49
Toler, David T. 130
Townes, W.H. 33
Trenton NC 15, 16
Trimble, Isaac R. 60, 63
Tucker, R.S. 13, 14

United Confederate Veterans 142
United States Naval Academy 6
Upchurch, Albert E. 68
Upton, Emory 107

Vance, Zebulon B. 77, 78, 84
Venable, Charles 101
Vicksburg, MS 40, 83
Virginia units: infantry (47th) 62

Wadsworth, James 50
Walker, Francis A. 107
Walker, Henry H. 81, 125, 126, 127
Walker's brigade 81, 126
Walkup, Samuel H. 137
Ward, Benjamin F. 33
Ward, J. Hobart 107
Ward, Robert 100
Warren, Gouverneur K. 81, 94, 96, 105, 110, 112, 114, 125, 129, 131, 132
Warrenton, VA 80
Washington D.C. 45
Washington, N.C.: battle of 13–15, 68, 90
Waterloo, VA 80
Waynesboro, PA 72
Webb, William H., Jr. 75
Webb, William P. 64
Weber, Peter A. 74
Weekly State Journal 67
Weisiger, David 109, 110

Weld, Stephen M., Jr. 111
West Chester, PA 53
West Point Military Academy 40
Whitehead, Howell G. 5, 43, 44, 50, 52, 57, 59, 61, 72
Whitehead, James S. 7
Whitley, J.A. 63, 64, 69, 70
Whitted, Walter A. 67, 125, 141
Wilcox, Cadmus M. 80, 98, 99, 100, 101, 112, 131
Wilcox's division 112, 132, 133, 135
Wilderness, battle of 3, 96–103, 107, 110, 130, 144
Wilkerson, James K. 9, 10, 15, 16, 17, 18, 20, 22, 34, 35, 36, 39, 41, 42, 75, 76, 77, 92, 115, 117, 118, 121, 122, 124, 125, 126, 129, 130, 131, 132, 134, 136
Wilkes County, NC 12
Willcox, Orlando B. 110
Williams, Andrew 117
Williams, Archibald 75
Williams, J.D. 65
Williams, Jesse P. 21
Williams, Westly A. 38, 103
Williams, William H. 26
Williams, Wilson 13
Williamsburg, PA 72
Wilmington, NC 24
Wilson, James H. 94
Wilson, LeGrand James 43, 44, 45, 56, 57, 59, 72, 84, 85, 89
Winchester, VA 74
Wisconsin units: infantry (6th) 51, 52, 57
Witherspoon, Thomas D. 89
Woodward, George G. 83, 86, 143
Wright, Horatio G. 105, 107, 109, 110, 111, 114, 115, 138
Wyse Fork, NC 15, 16

Yadkin County, NC 6
Yellow Tavern 107
Yorktown, VA 23

www.ingramcontent.com/pod-product-compliance
Ingram Content Group UK Ltd.
Pitfield, Milton Keynes, MK11 3LW, UK
UKHW050524150426
5217IPUK00026B/1790